Occupied America

The Chicano's Struggle Toward Liberation

Rodolfo Acuña

California State University at Northridge

Canfield Press **San Francisco**

A Department of Harper & Row, Publishers, Inc.

New York • Evanston • London

In previous printings of this book, I neglected to recognize the works of Francisca Reyes Esparza and Carlos Larralde, relatives of Juan Cortina, who have collected documents relating to his political activities. Statements found on pages 40, 46, 47, 48, 49, 50, and 114 are based primarily on their research, now contained in the library of Larralde.

Cover and interior book illustrations reprinted by permission of Dover Publications, Inc., from Jorge Encisco, *Design Motifs of Ancient Mexico.* Copyright © 1947 by Jorge Encisco; copyright © 1953 by Dover Publications, Inc.

Cover and interior book design by Gracia A. Alkema

International Standard Book Number: 0—06—380350—X (paperback edition)
0—06—380351—7 (clothbound edition)
Library of Congress Catalogue Card Number: 72–86850

77 78 79 80 15 14 13 12 11

Preface

Occupied America has evolved from my belief that the history of Chicanos in the United States must be reexamined. My framework has been the Chicano's struggle for liberation, for being a Chicano myself, I have experienced the inequities of this supposedly democratic society; I have seen that people of Mexican extraction in the United States are, in a very real sense, captives of the system that renders them second-class citizens. As a historian, I wanted to know what has happened in the last 124 years that has kept Chicanos at the short end of the proverbial stick. Traditional explanations of racism, nativism, and economic exploitation provided only a partial answer, in my opinion. Other groups have been the victims of such forces, but—with the obvious exceptions of the Indians and the Blacks—they have managed to achieve a degree of acceptance and self-determination far greater than that of Chicanos.

As my research progressed, I became convinced that the experience of Chicanos in the United States parallels that of other Third World peoples who have suffered under the colonialism of technologically superior nations. Thus, the thesis of this monograph is that Chicanos in the United States are a colonized people. The conquest of the Mexicans, the occupation of their land, and the continued oppression they have faced documents this thesis. The story that emerges is of a group of people who collectively have been losers in a society that loves only winners.

This text, obviously, will find many applications in Chicano studies courses, especially those emphasizing Chicano history, and in general courses in U.S. history, Southwest history, and state histories of California, Texas, Arizona, and New Mexico. But the material encompassed in this book does not limit itself to any one discipline. Although the focus is primarily historical, educators, sociologists, political scientists—as well as Mr. Everyman—will find much that is pertinent to their particular fields or interests. Thus, this book can also be used in sections of U.S. government or political science, ethnic minority studies in sociology, and history of education courses.

I have divided the material into two parts. The first concentrates primarily on the nineteenth century and the U.S. conquest of the Southwest, with separate chapters devoted to the four major states of the area. The second part centers around the experiences of Chicanos in the twentieth century, beginning with attempts to restrict Mexican immigration and continuing to the 1970s and the growth of the movement. The general introduction and the part introductions provide a more detailed view of the chapters that follow. Since the extensive notes at the end of each chapter can serve as a bibliography for further reading, the book can be adapted to classes that run a quarter, semester, or even longer.

Not everyone, I know, will accept the perspective that emerges in this work. Even as I was researching and writing, I constantly had to fight the resentment I felt—a resentment generated by the tale of cruel and brutal exploitation that I saw unfolding. But my hope is that even those who disagree with me will consider the "other side" and perhaps increase their own awareness that this country's ideals of justice and equality are still not reality. There are over seven million Chicanos in the United States today, and they cannot be ignored.

At this point, I would like to acknowledge the many people who helped to sensitize me. It would be impossible to list all of them by name in the confines of this preface. My involvement in the establishment of the Chicano Studies Department at San Fernando Valley State College (now California State University at Northridge) has been invaluable. The common struggle with students, community, and faculty to survive has personalized my perspective. The clerical assistance of Avie Hernández, Marta Arce, and others considerably facilitated the writing. The review of Carlos Cortez, a professor at the University of California, Riverside, and his constructive criticisms of my first draft helped direct the work. I am especially indebted to my production editor, Gracia Alkema, who was tough and who many times angered me, but she continually forced me to define my terms and clarify concepts. Lastly, but above all, I acknowledge my family—my parents, my two sons, and especially my wife. I have neglected them in writing this monograph. I hope that through an understanding of the colonization of the Chicano I can become more human with them as well as others.

Rodolfo Acuña

Northridge, California
September, 1972

Contents

Introduction   *1*

Part One   **Conquest and Colonization: An Overview**   6

Chapter One   *Legacy of Hate: The Conquest of the Southwest*   9

The Clash of Two Cultures — The Texas Revolt — The
Mexican-American War — The Rationale for Conquest — The Myth
of a Nonviolent Nation — The Treaty of Guadalupe Hidalgo —
Conclusion

Chapter Two   *Remember the Alamo: The Colonization of Texas*   34

The Apologists — The Texas Robber Barons — The Revolt of Chino
Cortina — The People's Revolt — Conclusion

Chapter Three   *Freedom in a Cage: The Expansion into New
                   Mexico*   55

The Myth of the Bloodless Conquest — The Land Grab in New
Mexico — The Americanization of the Catholic Church — The Great
Land Robbers — The Lincoln County War — The Resistance —
Conclusion

Chapter Four   *Sonora Invaded: The Occupation of Arizona*   80

The Drive on Sonora — From Peonage to Poverty — Violence and
Polarization — Competition Among the Oppressed — The Paradox of
Mexican Immigration — Unionism Comes to the Southwest —
Conclusion

Chapter Five   *California Lost: America for Anglo-Americans*   101

The Occupation of California — The Mexicans' Economic
Subjugation — Violence in Occupied California — Currents of
Resistance — Conclusion

Part Two   *A Radical View of the 20th Century Chicano*   *120*

Chapter Six   *Greasers Go Home*   *123*

Background to the Mexican's Importation — The Importation of the
Mexican — Mexican Migration Patterns — Public Opinion Toward
Mexican Immigration — Debate on the 1924 Act — Box Bill — The
1928 Hearings — The 1930 Hearings — The Restrictionist Victory —
Institutional Neglect and Abandonment —Anglo-American Labor —
Anglo-American Public Education — Religion's Role in
Americanization — Conclusion

Chapter Seven   *The Road to Delano*   *153*

A Voice of Dissent — The Cantaloupe Strike — The Berry Strike of
1933 — The San Antonio Pecan Shellers' Strike — The Struggle
Continues — The Di Giorgio Strike at Arvin, California — The
Beginning of the Crusade — Conclusion

Chapter Eight   *An Era of Repression*   *187*

Early Organizations — The Deportation of the Chicano — The Case
of Jésus Pallares — The 1930s — World War II — Los Angeles:
Confrontation of the Early 1940s — The Sleepy Lagoon Case — The
So-Called Pachuco Riots — Toward the 1960s — The Breaking of a
Movement — Reactions of the 1950s — Conclusion

Chapter Nine   *Goodbye America, I*   *222*

The Catalysts — The Brown Berets — José Ángel Gutíerrez — Reies
López Tijerina — Corky Gonzales: Barrio Leader — Conclusion

Chapter Ten   *Goodbye America, II*   *246*

The Political Realities — The California Story — The Texas Story —
The Story of the Catholic Church — The Chicano National
Moratorium — September 16, 1970 — January 9, 1971 — January 31,
1971 — Subversion and the Provocateurs — Justice in the Southwest
— Attitude of Law Enforcement Agents — Trial by One's Peers —
Conclusion

Index   *279*

Introduction

History can either oppress or liberate a people. Generalizations and stereotypes about the Mexican have been circulated in the United States for over 124 years. Adjectives such as "treacherous," "lazy," "adulterous," and terms such as "meskin," or "greaser," have become synonymous with "Mexican" in the minds of many Anglo-Americans. Little has been done to expose the false premises on which such cultural and racial slurs have been based. Incomplete or biased analyses by historians have perpetuated factual errors and created myths. The Anglo-American public has believed and encouraged the historian's and social commentator's portrayal of the Mexican as "the enemy." The tragedy is that the myths have degraded the Mexican people—not only in the eyes of those who feel superior, but also in their own eyes.

Many of these myths have their foundation in the nineteenth century, when Anglo-Americans began infiltrating into the Mexican territory of Texas. They were nurtured by the accounts these Anglos gave of their Mexican neighbors, by the clash between Anglos and Mexicans in the Texas revolt of 1836, and by the Mexican-American War that erupted in 1846. Anglo-American historians glorified and justified the deeds of the "heroic" men who "won the West"—at the expense of the Mexicans, who were fighting to preserve their homeland. The Mexican became the outsider, and his subordinate status in the United States after 1848 was explained as the inevitable result of a clash between dynamic, industrious Anglo-Americans and apathetic, culturally deprived Mexicans.

These are myths that must be challenged—not only for the sake of historical accuracy, but for another, and even more crucial, reason. Mexicans—*Chicanos*—in the United States today are an oppressed people. They are citizens, but their citizenship is second-class at best. They are exploited and manipulated by those with more power. And, sadly, many believe that the only way to get along in Anglo-America is to become "Americanized" themselves. Awareness of their history—of their contributions and struggles, of the fact that they were not the "treacherous enemy" that Anglo-American histories have said they were—can restore pride and a sense of heritage to a people who have been oppressed for so long. In short, awareness can help them to liberate themselves.

It would be impossible in the space of one volume to refute the assumptions and historical inaccuracies of 124 years of Southwest history. This text, then, is not an attempt at a definitive history of the Chicano and his struggle toward liberation. Rather, I have attempted to underscore my thesis that Chicanos are a colonized people in the United States through the use of both public records and secondary sources. The result, I hope, is a clear alternative to traditional explanations offered by historians. But even more, I hope that the story of occupied America, and its thematic approach to Anglo imperialism, will spur Third World historians to take on the monumental task of primary research that still needs to be done in relation to the Southwest and the Chicano. Then, and perhaps much more effectively than I have done, they can challenge the conclusions of other historians.

Before focusing on my thesis of the colonization of the Chicano, I would like to clarify several points. *First,* the title of this monograph might appear to be a misnomer. Many readers will argue that *Occupied Mexico* would have been more appropriate since the monograph is about the occupation of an area formerly belonging to Mexico. While this argument is valid, I feel that *Occupied America* is more precise, for "America" is the identification that Europeans gave to two continents. When the name was later appropriated by thirteen colonies, the designation "America" was deemed the exclusive province of the new nation, and United States citizens considered themselves the "Americans." Chicanos, as well as other peoples, however, refute this exclusivity and correctly maintain that all inhabitants—on both north and south continents—are Americans and that the whole hemisphere is indeed America. Thus, I hold that Anglo control of Mexico's northwest territory is an occupation of a part of the American hemisphere.

Although some readers might consider it a trivial matter, I feel compelled to distinguish between United States Americans and other Americans. Thus, in referring to people of the United States, I have used the term Anglo-American, or simply Anglo (derived from Anglo-Saxon), to underline the distinction. Similarly, I refer to U.S. settlers in Texas as Anglo-*Tejanos* (Anglo-Texans), in contrast to the native Texan population, which was Indian and Mexican.

Second, some U.S. citizens of Mexican extraction might object to the identification of "Chicano" in the title, for many call themselves simply *Mexicanos* or Mexicans. Moreover, a minority refer to themselves as Spanish-Americans or Latin Americans. Recently, the label Mexican-American has become popular, following the hyphenization tradition of other ethnic groups. Anglo-Americans have promoted the use of this label, and for a time it seemed as if it would be universally accepted. But within the last four years, activists have begun to question this identification. At first, some just dropped the hyphen and symbolically broke with the Americanization tradition. Others sought to identify themselves with a name of their own choice. They selected the term Chicano, which had often been used to designate lower-class Mexicans. Even though it had negative connotations for the middle class, activists considered that it was a symbol of resistance as well as a demand for self-determination. Such self-identification is, I believe, a necessary step in the process of awareness by which Chicanos can liberate themselves collectively.

In this work, I often use the terms Mexican and Chicano interchangeably. Mexican is used more in the first part of the book in recognition of the fact that nineteenth-century Mexicans were a conquered people. In the second part, which deals with the twentieth century and the changing situation in the

United States, Chicano is used to distinguish Mexicans living north of the border from those residing in Mexico.

Central to the thesis of this monograph is my contention that the conquest of the Southwest created a colonial situation in the traditional sense—with the Mexican land and population being controlled by an imperialistic United States. Further, I contend that this colonization—with variations—is still with us today. Thus, I refer to the colony, initially, in the traditional definition of the term, and later (taking into account the variations) as an internal colony.

From the Chicano perspective, it is obvious that these two types of colonies are a reality. In discussions with non-Chicano friends, however, I have encountered considerable resistance. In fact, even colleagues sympathetic to the Chicano cause vehemently deny that Chicanos are—or have been—colonized. They admit the exploitation and discrimination, but they add that this has been the experience of most "Americans"—especially European and Asian immigrants and Black Americans. While I agree that exploitation and racism have victimized most out-groups in the United States, this does not preclude the reality of the colonial relationship between the Anglo-American privileged and the Chicano.

I feel that the parallels between the Chicanos' experience in the United States and the colonization of other Third World peoples are too similar to dismiss. Attendant to the definition of colonization are the following conditions:

1. The land of one people is invaded by people from another country, who later use military force to gain and maintain control.

2. The original inhabitants become subjects of the conquerors involuntarily.

3. The conquered have an alien culture and government imposed upon them.

4. The conquered become the victims of racism and cultural genocide and are relegated to a submerged status.

5. The conquered are rendered politically and economically powerless.

6. The conquerors feel they have a "mission" in occupying the area in question and believe that they have undeniable privileges by virtue of their conquest.

These points also apply to the relationship between Chicanos and Anglos in Mexico's northwest territory.

In the traditional historian's viewpoint, however, there are two differences that impede universal acceptance of the reality of Anglo-American colonialism in this area.

1. Geographically the land taken from Mexico bordered the United States rather than being an area distant from the "mother country."

Too many historians have accepted—subconsciously, if not conveniently—the myth that the area was always intended to be an integral part of the United States. Instead of conceptualizing the conquered territory as northern Mexico, they perceive it in terms of the "American" Southwest. Further, the stereotype of the colonialist pictures him wearing Wellington boots and carrying a swagger stick, and that stereotype is usually associated with overseas situations—certainly not in territory contiguous to an "expanding" country.

2. Historians also believe that the Southwest was won in fair and just warfare, as opposed to unjust imperialism.

The rationale has been that the land came to the United States as the result of competition, and in winning the game, the country was generous in paying for its prize. In the case of Texas, they believe Mexico attacked the "freedom-loving" Anglo-Americans. It is difficult for citizens of the United States to accept the fact that their nation has been and is imperialistic. Imperialism, to them, is an affliction of other countries.

While I acknowledge the geographical proximity of the area—and the fact that this is a modification of the strict definition of colonialism—I refute the conclusion that the Texan and Mexican-American wars were just or that Mexico provoked them. Further, I illustrate in this monograph that the conditions attendant to colonialism, listed above, accompanied the U.S. take-over of the Southwest. For these reasons, I maintain that colonialism in the traditional sense did exist in the Southwest, and that the conquerors dominated and exploited the conquered.

The colonization still exists today, but as I mentioned before, there are variations. Anglo-Americans still exploit and manipulate Mexicans and still relegate them to a submerged caste. Mexicans are still denied political and economic determination and are still the victims of racial stereotypes and racial slurs promulgated by those who feel they are superior. Thus, I contend that Mexicans in the United States are still a colonized people, but now the colonization is *internal*—it is occurring *within* the country rather than being imposed by an external power. The territories of the Southwest are states within the United States, and theoretically permanent residents of Mexican extraction are U.S. citizens. Yet the rights of citizenship are too often circumvented or denied outright.

In reality, there is little difference between the Chicano's status in the *traditional colony* of the nineteenth century and in the *internal colony* of the twentieth century. The relationship between Anglos and Chicanos remains the same—that of master-servant. The principal difference is that Mexicans in the traditional colony were indigenous to the conquered land. Now, while some are descendants of Mexicans living in the area before the conquest, large numbers are technically descendants of immigrants. After 1910, in fact, almost one-eighth of Mexico's population migrated to the United States, largely as a result of the push-and-pull of economic necessity. Southwest agribusinessmen "imported" Mexican workers to fill the need for cheap labor, and this influx signaled the beginning of even greater Anglo manipulation of Mexican settlements or *colonias.*

The original *colonias* expanded in size with the increased immigration and new settlements sprang up. They became nations within a nation, in effect, for psychologically, socially, and culturally they remained Mexican. But the *colonias* had little or no control over their political, economic, or educational destinies. In almost every case, they remained separate and unequal to Anglo-American communities. The elected representatives within the *colonias* were usually Anglo-Americans or Mexicans under their control, and they established a bureaucracy to control the political life of the Mexican settlements—for the benefit of the Anglo privileged.

Further, Anglos controlled the educational system—they administered the schools and taught in the classrooms, and designed the curriculum not to meet the needs of Chicano students but to Americanize them. The police patrolling the *colonia* lived, for the most part, outside the area. Their main purpose was to protect Anglo property. Anglos owned the business and industry in the *colonias,* and capital that could have been used to improve the economic situation within the *colonias* was taken into Anglo-American sectors, in much the same way that capital is drained from underdeveloped countries by foreign economic imperialists. In addition, the *colonias* became employment centers for industrialists, who were assured of a ready supply of cheap labor.

This pattern is one that emerged in most Chicano communities, and one that contradicts the belief in Anglo-American equality. In sum, even though the 1960 census documented that 85 percent of Chicanos are native-born U.S. citizens, most Anglo-Americans still considered them Mexicans and outsiders.

In discussing the traditional and internal colonization of the Chicano, it is not my intention to rekindle hatreds, nor to condemn all Anglo-Americans collectively for the ignominies that the Mexican in the United States has suffered. Rather, my purpose is to bring about an awareness—among both Anglo-Americans and Chicanos—of the forces that control and manipulate seven million people in this country and keep them colonized. If Chicanos can become aware of *why* they are oppressed and *how* the exploitation is perpetuated, they can work more effectively toward ending their colonization.

I realize that the initial stages of such awareness might result in intolerance among some Chicanos. However, I caution the reader that this work does not create a rationale for brown power just because it condemns the injustices of Anglo power. Extended visits in Mexico have taught me that Chicano power is no better than any other power. Those who seek power are deprived of their humanity to the point that they themselves become the oppressors. Paulo Freire has written:

> The great humanistic and historical task of the oppressed [is]: to liberate themselves and their oppressors as well. The oppressors, who oppress, exploit, and rape by virtue of their power, cannot find in this power the strength to liberate either the oppressed or themselves. Only the power that springs from the weakness of the oppressed will be sufficiently strong to free you.[1]

It is my hope that *Occupied America* can help us perceive the social, political, and economic contradictions of the power that has enabled Anglo-American colonizers to dominate Chicanos—and that has too often made Chicanos accept and, in some instances, support the domination. Awareness will help us take action against the forces that oppress not only Chicanos but the oppressor himself.

---

[1]Paulo Freire, *Pedagogy of the Oppressed* (New York: Herder and Herder, 1972), p. 28.

Part One

Conquest and Colonization:
An Overview

*T*his part presents a historical overview of the U.S. Southwest that differs considerably from most Anglo-American histories. We contradict traditional assumptions about the events leading up to the Mexican-American War and what happened when the United States emerged from that war in possession of Mexico's northwest territory. There has been a disinclination among Anglo-American historians to view the war with Mexico as an outright act of imperialism, or to consider the U.S. occupation of the territory as parallel to colonial situations in other parts of the world. Yet this section attempts to demonstrate the reality of the conquest and colonization, which has resulted in the oppression of Mexicans in the United States.

The physical conquest of Mexico's northwest began when Anglo-American settlers infiltrated Texas in the 1820s and then forcibly seized the area in 1836. The Mexicans living in the captured land became a colonized people who were dominated by the Anglo-American conquerors. Although the U.S. government did not directly participate in the conquest and colonization, Anglo-Texans never ceased to be Anglo-Americans who remained loyal to the United States. Furthermore, the Texas experience set the stage for the insidious U.S. invasion, brutal conquest, and occupation of the rest of Mexico's northwest.

This part also attempts to demonstrate that the Mexican-American War was not only an unjust war, but that it was just as brutal as the repression perpetuated by other colonial regimes. The Anglo-Texans' treatment of the Mexican was violent and often inhuman. The Anglo-American invasion of Mexico was as vicious as that of Hitler's invasion of Poland and other central European nations, or, for that matter, U.S. involvement in Vietnam. Chapter 1 gives a historical overview of the Texas revolt and the Mexican-American War, as well as the legacy of hate left by the conflicts. We have used mostly Anglo-American sources to show that information on the atrocities of the war is readily available, even though Anglo historians have largely ignored the violence.

Racism, we maintain, is at the heart of colonialism. It facilitated, as well as promoted, the social domination of the Mexican. There is ample evidence that Anglo-Americans arriving in the Southwest believed that they were racially superior to the swarthy Mexicans, whom they considered a mongrel race of Indian halfbreeds. The *gringo's* traditional antipathy toward the Indian was transferred to the Mexican. In turn, these racist attitudes were carried over to the colonization and were used to subjugate the native population.

Attendant to the Anglo-Americans' racism was their claim of cultural superiority. Many conquerors hated the Mexican's Catholic faith, and further considered the Mexican to be lazy, apathetic, superstitious, and otherwise morally deficient. This ethnocentrism must be emphasized, since it ignited and sustained the assault on Mexican values, language, and way of life. Moreover, it underlay the exploitation and subjugation of the conquered.

Chapters 2 through 5 expose the methods of colonization in the Southwest. After the conquest, a colonial administration was established that advanced the designs of the Anglo-Americans, enabling them to deny the Mexican any semblance of political or economic power. Through physical violence and control of government bureaucracy at local, state, and federal levels, the *gringo* robbed the Mexican of his land and submerged his culture. Although there were some differences, the conquest and colonization followed a similar pattern in Texas, New Mexico, Arizona, and California: the Mexican was manipulated, controlled, and rendered powerless.

From the beginning of the occupation, the Mexican did attempt to organize against his oppressors. In the chapters that follow, we document numerous instances of Mexican resistance. We also refute myths of Mexican docility after the conquest, for the Mexican fought to retain his culture and language even during periods of intense repression. He was not always successful, and many times his efforts were rewarded by even greater measures of suppression. Nonetheless, a study of his reactions to the Anglo colonization supports what many Chicano scholars have claimed: that the movement did not begin in the 1960s but that it has been an ongoing struggle toward liberation.

Chapter One

Legacy of Hate:
The Conquest of the Southwest

The tragedy of the Mexican cession is that most Anglo-Americans have failed to recognize that the United States committed an act of violence against the Mexican people when it took Mexico's northwestern territory. The violence was not limited to the taking of the land; Mexico's territory was invaded, her people murdered, her land raped, and her possessions plundered. The memory of this destruction generated a distrust and dislike that is still vivid in the minds of many Mexicans, for the violence of the United States left deep scars. And for Chicanos—the Mexicans remaining within the boundaries of the new United States territories—the aggression was even more insidious, for the outcome of the Texas and Mexican-American wars made them a conquered people. The Anglo-Americans were the conquerors, and they evinced all of the arrogance of military victors.

The conquerors imposed upon the vanquished their version of what had happened in the wars. They created myths about the invasions and events that

9

triggered them, especially in relation to the Texas War of 1836. Anglo-Americans in Texas were portrayed as freedom-loving settlers forced to rebel against the tyranny of Mexico. The most popular of the myths was that of the Alamo, which, in effect, became a justification to keep Mexicans in their place. According to Anglo-Americans, the Alamo was a symbolic confrontation between good and evil; the treacherous Mexicans succeeded in taking the fort only because they outnumbered the patriots and "fought dirty." This myth, with its ringing plea to "Remember the Alamo!" colored Anglo attitudes toward Mexicans, for it served to stereotype the Mexican eternally as the enemy and the Texas patriots as the stalwarts of freedom and democracy.

Such myths, as well as the Anglo-Americans' biased versions of Mexican American history, helped to justify the inferior status to which the Chicano has been relegated—that of a conquered people. After the conquest, the original inhabitants found themselves continually denigrated by the Anglo-American victors. The fundamental issue that the wars were imperialistic and unjust was forgotten, and historians clothed the Anglo invasions of Mexican territory with the mantle of legitimacy. In the process, the violence and the aggression have been forgotten, and thus the myth that the United States is a peace-loving nation dedicated to democracy is perpetuated.[1]

The Clash of Two Cultures

An integral part of the Anglo rationalizations for the conquest has been a tendency either to ignore or distort the events that led up to the initial clash in 1836. To Anglo-Americans, the Texas War was the result of a tyrannical or, at best, an incompetent Mexican government that was antithetical to the ideals of democracy and justice. Even today, such relatively unbiased sources as Cecil Robinson play down the expansionistic, land-hungry characteristics of the Texas settlers, and they write glowingly of the democratic civilization they represented:

> The Americans who came into Texas ... brought with them a deeply rooted democratic tradition. Herein lay the basis of another conflict, which was essentially cultural in its nature. The American colonist and the native Mexican soon discovered that the same words could have vastly different meanings, depending on the traditions and conditional attitudes of those who spoke them. *Democracy, justice,* and *Christianity,* thought at first to be ideals held in common, became rallying cries of a revolution because of the different interpretations put upon them by the American colonists and their Mexican rulers in Texas.[2]

The Anglo-American settlement in Texas began as early as 1819 when the United States acquired Florida from Spain. The Transcontinental Treaty with Spain drew the boundary of the United States in such a way that it excluded Texas. By the time the treaty was ratified in February 1821, Texas was part of Coahuila, a state in the independent Republic of Mexico. Meanwhile, Anglo-Americans made forays into Texas similar to those they had made into

correrías 10

Florida. In 1819, James Long led an abortive invasion of the province with the aim of creating the "Republic of Texas." Long, like many Anglos, believed that Texas belonged to the United States and that "Congress had no right or power to sell, exchange, or relinquish an 'American possession.'"[3]

For a time Anglo filibustering* activity in Texas was dormant, and Mexican authorities offered free land to groups of settlers. Moses Austin was given permission to establish a settlement in Texas, and although he died shortly afterwards, his son, Stephen, carried out his plan. In December 1821, Stephen founded the settlement of San Felipe de Austin. Soon Anglos were settling in Texas in great numbers; by 1830 there were about 20,000 settlers, along with about 2000 slaves.

Although settlers were supposed to abide by the conditions established by the Mexican government—that all immigrants must be Catholics and that they must take an oath of allegiance to Mexico—Anglo-Americans circumvented these laws. Moreover, they became resentful when Mexico tried to enforce the rules they had promised to obey. Mexico became increasingly alarmed at the continuing flood of immigrants, most of whom retained their Protestant religion.[4]

It was soon apparent that the Anglo-Texans had no intention of obeying Mexican law, for they believed that Mexico was incapable of putting into effect any form of democracy. Many settlers, among them Hayden Edwards, considered Mexicans to be the intruders of the Texas territory; these Anglos encroached upon lands belonging to native Mexicans. In Edwards' case, his grant conflicted with claims of Mexicans, Indians, as well as Anglo-American settlers. When he arbitrarily attempted to evict settlers from the land before a decision could be reached, Mexican authorities nullified his settlement contract and ordered him out of the territory. He and his followers seized the town of Nacogdoches, and on December 21, 1826, they proclaimed that they had established the Republic of Fredonia. Mexican officials, who were supported by some settlers (such as Stephen Austin), suffocated the Edwards revolt; however, the Anglo-American attitude was a portent of what was to follow. Many U.S. newspapers played up the rebellion as "200 Men Against a Nation!" and described Edwards and his followers as "apostles of democracy crushed by an alien civilization."[5]

It was at this time that U.S. President John Quincy Adams offered to buy Texas from Mexico for the sum of $1 million. Mexican authorities, however, were convinced that the United States had aided and abetted the Fredonia war, and they refused. Mexico tried to consolidate its control over Texas, but the number of Anglo-American settlers and the vastness of the territory made it an almost impossible task.[6]

Anglo-Americans in Texas were already creating a privileged caste, which depended in great part on the economic advantage given to them by their

---

*The term *filibustering* means to carry out insurrectionist or revolutionary activity in a foreign country.

slaves. When, like most progressive nations, Mexico abolished slavery on September 15, 1829, by order of President Vicente Guerrero, Texans evaded the law by "freeing" their slaves and then signing them to lifelong contracts as indentured servants.[7] Despite this circumvention of the law, Anglos saw abolition as an invasion of their personal liberties. The tension, already rife, was compounded when Mexico decreed in 1830 that further Anglo-American immigration to Texas was to be cut off.[8] Anglos were outraged at the restrictions. Ill feelings between Mexicans and Anglos were aggravated further during the presidency of Andrew Jackson. Like Adams, Jackson attempted to negotiate with Mexico for the purchase of Texas, but he was willing to pay as much as $5 million. Mexico, already xenophobic as a result of the huge numbers of Anglo settlers, their economic dominance of the region, and their refusal to submit to Mexican laws, resisted the diplomatic pressure and moved more soldiers into the state of Coahuila, of which Texas was a part. Even before the Mexican reinforcements crossed into Texas, polarization between Mexicans and Anglo-Texans was pronounced, and the Anglos viewed the move as a Mexican invasion.

Anglo historians have repeatedly interpreted the events following this action as examples of the oppressive and arbitrary nature of the Mexican government, as contrasted to the democratic-oriented aims of the Texas settlers. When Texans defied the collection of customs and were incensed over Mexican attempts to end smuggling, United States citizens were sympathetic. It was obvious that the "war party" that rioted at Anáhuac in December 1831 had popular support. One of the leaders of the war party, Sam Houston, "was a known protégé of Andrew Jackson, now president of the United States. . . . Houston's motivation was to bring Texas eventually into the United States."[9]

In various ways the Anglos, who had been granted permission by the Mexican government to settle in Texas, worked to undermine the authority of their host. Anglo-Americans became more unwilling to display even a façade of respect for Mexican laws, and in the summer of 1832, a group of them attacked a Mexican garrison and were routed. In that same year, Colonel Juan Almonte made a goodwill tour of Texas and submitted a secret report on conditions in that province. The report recommended many concessions to the *Tejanos,* but it also urged that "the province be well stocked with Mexican troops."[10] The Texas historian Fehrenbach criticized the Mexican actions: "It was virtually impossible for even a Mexican of goodwill to comprehend the fact that Anglo-Americans were capable of regulating themselves."[11] He continued:

> For this reason, the moves now made by the colonists were misunderstood by both Mexican liberals and conservatives alike. On their own initiative, the settlers of the *ayuntamiento* (city council) of San Felipe called a convention to meet on October 1, 1832. Sixteen Anglo-Texas districts responded.[12]

At this convention the Anglos drafted resolutions directed to the Mexican government and to the state of Coahuila. In essence, they called for more autonomy for Texas. Fehrenbach, like other U.S. historians, erroneously painted the picture of an oppressive Mexican government that was unsympathetic to the "colonist's just demands":

> Each of those resolutions was emphatically preceded by professions of loyalty to the *Mexican Confederation and the Constitution.* These were wholly sincere. But what the Texans were asking for was cultural pluralism, under Mexican sovereignty, and pluralism was not only foreign to the Hispanic nature but, in the light of the phobia against the United States that suffused most Mexicans, impossible to be weighed on merits. In fact, the very assemblies, so peaceful and so natural to the English-speaking experience and tradition, were entirely extra-legal under Mexican law. In Mexico, no initiative, except riot and insurrection, ever began with the people. Both liberals and conservatives, in office, ruled by decree. In this light, every Mexican official in Texas and in Mexico could only view the convention as some sort of enormous plot, aimed at the foundations of the nation.[13]

Fehrenbach and other Anglo-American historians failed to realize the existence of cultural pluralism in Mexico, where even Anglo-Americans were allowed to retain their culture. In truth, it was the Anglo who considered cultural pluralism alien to his nature. The events that followed bore out the Mexican's concern over the increasing Anglo-American independence in Texas.

A second convention was held in January 1833. Fehrenbach alleges that the Anglo-Americans acted in the traditional Anglo-American manner by drafting a constitution and presenting it to the central government, but he charges that the Mexicans looked upon it as a *pronunciamento*—a call to arms. He further states that Mexican historians viewed it as "a well-conceived plot to separate Texas from Mexico," which he admits "cannot entirely be denied," since prominent Anglo-Americans, among them Sam Houston, agitated for independence.[14] The delegates appointed Austin to submit the grievances and resolutions to Mexico City.

Austin left for Mexico City to press the demands of the Anglo-Americans in Texas. His priorities were to get the Mexican authorities to lift their restrictions on Anglo-American immigration and to grant Texas separate statehood. The slave issue also burned in his mind. Austin was anything but conciliatory, writing to a friend from Mexico City, "If our application is refused . . . I shall be in favor of organizing *without it.* I see no other way of saving the country from total anarchy and ruin. I am totally done with conciliatory measures and, for the future, shall be uncompromising as to Texas."[15]

On October 2, 1833, he wrote a letter to the *ayuntamiento* at San Antonio encouraging it to declare Texas a separate state. He later excused his action, explaining that he had done so "in a moment of irritation and impatience"; nevertheless, his actions were not those of a moderate. The contents of the note fell into the hands of the Mexican authorities, who had begun to question Austin's good faith. Subsequently, they imprisoned him, and much of what Austin had accomplished in the way of compromise was undone. Contributing to the general distrust were the actions of U.S. Minister to Mexico Anthony Butler, whose crude attempts to bribe Mexican officials to sell Texas infuriated Mexicans. He offered one official $200,000 to play ball.[16] Matters grew worse when, in May 1834, Antonio López de Santa Anna seized the presidency.

López de Santa Anna is an enigma in Mexican history. From his rise to power at Tampico in 1829 to his fall in 1855, he remained a disruptive influence in Mexican politics. During this period there was a struggle for control of the country between the conservatives, who represented the landed interests of the nation (along with the church and military), and the liberals, who wanted Mexico to become a modern state, controlled by the merchants of the nation. Santa Anna manipulated both factions, switching from one party to another in order to seize power. He greatly added to the disunity of the times, weakening Mexico and making it easy prey to the ambitions of the United States. Moreover, Santa Anna's perfidy has given United States historians a scapegoat in assigning responsibility for the wars. Many historians point out that there were secessionist movements in several of the Mexican states as the result of Santa Anna's abolition of federalism; however, these same historians fail to point out that the United States went through a similar phase in its quest to forge a nation.

Whatever Santa Anna's role, the Texas revolt had already been planned, with men such as William Barret Travis, F. M. Johnson, and Sam Houston active in agitating for separation from Mexico. For that matter, the majority of Anglo-Americans were unwilling to submit to the Mexican government.

The war party in Texas was strong. In the autumn of 1834, Henry Smith published a pamphlet entitled *Security for Texas.* He advocated open defiance of the Mexican authority. The political situation became more polarized, and Mexican troops assembled in Coahuila. Intrigue dominated the Texas scene. Not only were there many individuals advocating independence, but Anglo land companies had agents, both in Washington, D.C., and in Texas, lobbying for a change. Prominent among these companies was the Galveston Bay and Texas Land Company of New York, which was in collusion with Anthony Butler, the U.S. Minister to Mexico.[17]

On July 13, 1835, a general amnesty released Austin from prison. While on his way to Texas, he wrote a letter from New Orleans to a cousin expressing the view that Texas should be Americanized even though it was still a state of Mexico, and indicating that it should one day come under the American flag. In this letter he called for a massive immigration of Anglo-Americans, "*each man with his rifle,*" whom he hoped would come "passports or no passports, *anyhow.*" He continued: "For fourteen years I have had a hard time of it, but nothing shall daunt my courage or abate my ... object ... to *Americanize* Texas."[18]

Fehrenbach defended Austin's letter and admonished Mexican historians for their condemnation of the Texas leader:

> The call for a massive and illegal entry of armed Americans was not so much a plot to join Texas to the United States as it was Austin seeking, from the most

logical source, all the help he could get—just as Israelis, beset by Arabs, called upon Jewry all over the world. Neither Texas in the 19th century, nor Israel more than a century later, had any doubt of their right to defend themselves. What was at stake was more than mere boundaries.[19]

The Texas Revolt

It would be simplistic to blame Austin and all the Anglo-Texan settlers for the conflict. Austin was, indeed, better than most; he belonged to the peace party, which at first opposed a confrontation with the Mexicans. Ultimately, however, this faction joined the "hawks." Eugene C. Barker, a Texas historian, states that the immediate cause of the war was "the overthrow of the nominal republic and the substitution of centralized oligarchy," which allegedly would have placed the Texans more strictly under the control of Mexico.[20] Barker, however, admits that "Earnest patriots like Benjamin Lundy, William Ellery Channing, and John Quincy Adams saw in the Texas revolution a disgraceful affair promoted by sordid slaveholders and land speculators. Even to the critical ear of the modern historian their arguments sound plausible."[21] However, he denies that the slave issue had anything to do with the revolt and says that the land question retarded rather than accelerated the hostilities.

Barker draws a parallel between the Texas revolt and the American Revolution, stating: "In each, the general cause of revolt was the same—a sudden effort to extend imperial authority at the expense of local privilege."[22] In fact, in both instances the central governments were attempting to enforce existing laws that conflicted with the illegal activities of some very articulate men. Barker further attempts to justify the Anglo-Texans' actions by observing: "At the close of summer in 1835 the Texans saw themselves in danger of becoming the alien subjects of a people to whom they deliberately believed themselves morally, intellectually, and politically superior. The racial feeling, indeed, underlay and colored Texan-Mexican relations from the establishment of the first Anglo-American colony in 1821."[23] Therefore, the conflict, according to Barker, was inevitable and, consequently, justified.

It is difficult to pin the Texan apologists down. They admit that racism played a leading role in the causes for revolt; that smugglers were upset with Mexico's enforcement of her import laws; that Texans were upset about emancipation laws; and that an increasing number of the new arrivals from the United States actively agitated for independence. But despite these admissions, historians like Barker refuse to assign guilt to their countrymen. Instead, Barker writes: "Had there been no atmosphere of racial distrust enveloping the relations of Mexico and the colonists, a crisis might not have followed. Mexico might not have thought it necessary to insist so drastically on unequivocal submission, or the colonists might not have believed so firmly that submission would endanger their liberty."[24] Barker is simply justifying Anglo-American racism and, in the process, is spreading around the guilt by speculating about what might have been.

15

In any case, the antipathies of the Texans escalated into a full-scale rebellion. Austin gave the call to arms on September 19, 1835, stating, "War is our only recourse. There is no other remedy."[25] It was symbolically significant that he changed his name back from Estévan to Stephen.[26]

Too many historians have portrayed Mexico's attempt to suffocate the insurrection as an invasion and the Texas victory that followed as a victory of a small band of patriots against the "Huns" from the south. Dr. Félix D. Almaraz, a member of the history department of the University of Texas at Austin, underscores this, writing: "All too often, Texan specialists have interpreted the war as the defeat of a culturally inferior people by a culturally superior class of Anglo frontiersmen. . . ."[27]

In reality, the Anglo-Americans enjoyed very real advantages. As mentioned, they had a sizeable population; they were "defending" terrain with which they were familiar; and although most of the 5000-or-so Mexicans living in the territory did not join them, the Anglos themselves were united. In contrast, the Mexican nation was divided, and the centers of power were thousands of miles away from Texas. From the interior of Mexico, Santa Anna led an army of about 6000 conscripts, many of whom had been forced into the army and were then marched hundreds of miles over hot, arid desert land. In addition, many were Mayan and did not speak Spanish. In February 1836, the majority arrived in San Antonio, Texas, sick and ill-prepared to fight. Although the Mexican army outnumbered the Anglo contingent, the latter were much better armed and enjoyed the position of being the defenders. (Until World War I, this was a decided advantage during wartime.) Santa Anna, on the other hand, had overextended his supply lines and was many miles from his base of power.

The 187 men who were defending San Antonio refused to surrender to Santa Anna's forces and took refuge in a former mission, the Alamo. In the ten days of fighting that followed, the Texans inflicted heavy casualties on the Mexican forces, but eventually the Mexicans' sheer superiority in numbers won out. Much has been written about Mexican cruelty in relation to the Alamo affair and about the heroics of the doomed men. The result, as mentioned early in this chapter, was the creation of the Alamo myth. Within the broad framework of what actually happened—187 Texans barricading themselves in the Alamo in defiance of Santa Anna's force and the eventual triumph of the Mexicans—there has been much distortion. Walter Lord, in an article entitled "Myths and Realities of the Alamo," sets much of the record straight.[28] Since the myth has provided Anglo-Americans with a major justification for their historical and psychological subjugation of the Chicano, the story of the Alamo demands a brief retelling.

Texas mythology portrays the Alamo heroes as freedom-loving defenders of their homes; they were supposedly all good Texans. Actually, two-thirds of the defenders were recent arrivals from the United States, and only a half dozen had been in Texas for more than six years.[29] Moreover, the character of the defenders is questionable. A work that is admittedly biased, but that nevertheless casts considerable light on the Alamo and its defenders, is Rafael Trujillo Herrera's *Olvídate de El Alamo.*[30] Trujillo advances the thesis that the United States was an aggressor nation and that it should rename itself the United States of Anglo-America. The use of "America" to him symbolizes the ambitions of Anglo-Americans to conquer the whole of the Western Hemisphere. According to Trujillo, the men in the Alamo were adventurers and not virtuous idealists as they frequently are portrayed by Texas historians. Trujillo reveals that William Barret Travis was a murderer; he killed a man who had made advances to his wife. Rather than confess, Travis allowed a slave to be tried and convicted for his crime, and he fled to Texas, abandoning his wife and two children. James Bowie was an infamous brawler who had made a fortune running slaves and had wandered into Texas searching for lost mines and more money. And then there was the fading Davey Crockett, a legend in his own time, who fought for the sake of fighting. Many others in the Alamo were men who had come to Texas for riches and glory; a minority were men who had responded to Austin's call to arms. These defenders were not the sort of men who could be classified as peaceful settlers fighting for their homes.

The folklore of the Alamo goes beyond the legendary names of the defenders. According to Walter Lord, it is riddled with dramatic half-truths that have been accepted as history.[31] The defenders at the Alamo are portrayed as selfless heroes who sacrificed their lives to buy more time for their comrades-in-arms. As the story is told, William Barret Travis told his men that they were doomed; he drew a line in the sand with his sword, saying that all who crossed it would elect to remain and fight to the last. Supposedly all the men there valiantly stepped across the line, with a man in a cot begging to be carried across it. This hopelessness and bravery of the defenders has been dramaticized in many Hollywood movies.

The facts are that the Alamo had little strategic value, the men fully expected help, and the Alamo was the best fortified fort west of the Mississippi. While the defenders only numbered about 180, they had twenty-one cannons to the Mexican's eight or ten. The Anglo-Americans were expert marksmen and had rifles with a range of 200 yards; in contrast, the Mexicans were poorly equipped, inadequately trained, and were armed with smooth-bore muskets with a range of only 70 yards. In addition, the walls of the Alamo were thick, concealing the defenders, while the latter had clear shots. In short, ill-prepared, ill-equipped, and ill-fed Mexicans attacked well-armed and professional soldiers.* Lastly, from all reliable sources, it is doubtful whether Travis ever drew a line in the sand. The San Antonio survivors, females and noncombatants, did not tell the story until many years later, when the tale had become well circulated and the myth was a legend. In addition, there was a man who escaped, Louis Rose.[32]

Probably the most widely circulated story was that of the alleged heroism

---

*Santa Anna had not committed all of his soldiers to the Alamo. The majority were assigned to other commands.

and last stand of the aging Davey Crockett who, when the end came, fell "fighting like a tiger," killing Mexicans with his bare hands. This is a myth; seven of the defenders surrendered, and Crockett was among them. They were executed.[33]

The importance of these myths about the Alamo is that they falsely build up the valor of the Anglo-Texans at the expense of the Mexicans, who have been portrayed as treacherous, ruthless killers. This stereotyping conditioned Anglo attitudes about the Mexicans, and it served as a rationalization for later aggression against Mexico and the Anglo's mistreatment of Chicanos. It is also significant that the Spanish-surnamed "defenders" within the Alamo conspicuously have been omitted from the roll call of Texas heroes.

As stated previously, the Alamo had no strategic military value. It represented a battle where two fools engaged in a useless conflict. Travis's stand delayed Santa Anna's timetable by only four days, as the Mexicans took San Antonio on March 6, 1836. At first, the stand at the Alamo did not even have propaganda value. Afterwards, Houston's army dwindled, with many volunteers rushing home to help their families flee from the advancing Mexican army. Moreover, most Anglo-Texans were not proud of the Alamo and realized they had been badly beaten.[34] It did, nevertheless, eventually result in massive aid from the United States in the form of volunteers, arms, and money. The cry of "Remember the Alamo" became a call to arms for Anglo-Americans in both Texas and the United States.[35]

After the Alamo and the defeat of another garrison at Goliad, southeast of San Antonio, Santa Anna was in full control. He ran Sam Houston out of the territory northwest of the San Jacinto River and then camped an army of about 1100 men near San Jacinto. There, he skirmished with Houston on April 20, 1836, but did not follow up his advantage. Predicting that Houston would attack on April 22, Santa Anna and his men settled down and rested for the anticipated battle. The Texans, however, attacked during the *siesta* hour on April 21. Santa Anna had made an incredible blunder. He knew that Houston had an army of 1000, yet he was lax in his precautionary defenses. The surprise attack caught him totally off guard. Shouts of "Remember the Alamo! Remember Goliad!" filled the air.

Many historians have dwelt upon the violence and cruelty of the Mexicans in Texas, especially in relation to the victory at Goliad. It is true that Santa Anna gave no quarter in his encounters with the Texans, but the issue of Anglo-American violence usually has been evaded. The battle at San Jacinto was literally a slaughter of the Mexican forces. Few prisoners were taken. Instead, those who surrendered "were clubbed and stabbed, some on their knees. The slaughter ... became methodical: the Texan riflemen knelt and poured a steady fire into the packed, jostling ranks. ..."[36] They shot the "Meskins" down as they fled. The final count showed 630 Mexicans dead versus 2 Texans.

The battle of San Jacinto generated considerable pride among Anglo-Americans in Texas and the United States. However, the widow Peggy

McCormick, on whose property the battle was fought, was more candid about the feelings of her race toward Mexicans. She "objected strenuously that the hundreds of unburied Mexicans ruined the value of her property." She called Houston shortly after the battle and requested that he remove "them stinking Mexicans." Houston replied: "Madam, your land will be famed in history as the classic spot upon which the glorious victory of San Jacinto was gained!" The lady replied: "To the devil with your glorious victory! . . . Take off your stinking Mexicans."[37]

Houston's successful surprise attack ended the war. He captured Santa Anna, who had no choice but to sign the territory away. In October, Houston was elected president of the Republic of Texas.

The Texas victory prepared the way for the Mexican-American War. It whipped up emotions against Mexicans and fed the growing nationalism of the young Anglo-American nation. It is true that the United States had not officially taken sides, but men, money, and supplies had poured in to aid fellow Anglo-Americans. Of course, not all Anglo-Americans approved of the war, but as it proceeded many sided with the Anglos in Texas. An awareness of the struggle of fellow Anglo-Americans increased. The battle of the Alamo swung many of the fence sitters behind the Anglo-*Tejanos*. The deaths of Bowie, Crockett, and Travis seemed to justify whatever happened to the Mexicans, much the same as the death of Custer would later seem to justify the slaughter of the red man. More important was the hatred generated by the war. The Mexican was pictured as cruel, treacherous, tyrannical, and as an enemy who could not be trusted. These stereotypes lingered long after the war and can still be detected in Anglo attitudes toward the Chicano. The Texas War left a legacy of hate and determined the status of the Mexicans left behind as that of a conquered people.

The Mexican-American War

The war with Mexico typifies the expansionistic fervor of the United States during the nineteenth century. Inexorably, it seemed, the nation moved its boundaries westward, often by provoking its neighbors into war. In the mid-1840s, Mexico was the target. Anglo-Americans could not resist expansion into territory that seemed so lucrative—in this case, the unused land of the Mexican-held Southwest.

Although the United States was not a nation of overwhelming size or wealth, it was a dangerous country with which to share a border; it was arrogant in foreign affairs, partially because its citizens believed in their inherent cultural and racial superiority. Mexico, on the other hand, was considered to be a nation with a future greater than of the United States. However, it was plagued with financial problems, internal ethnic conflicts, and poor leadership. The general anarchy within the nation conspired against its cohesive development.[38]

The Texas War, which Harriet Martineau called "the most high-handed theft of modern times," was only the prelude. Carl Degler, in *Out of Our Past,* has summed up the realities:

> [It] had not ended in a clear-cut victory for the Texans because Mexico refused to acknowledge the independence of the newly declared Republic even though the Mexican government was powerless to exercise control over its erstwhile subjects. This, however, did not prevent the Texans from negotiating annexation to the United States. In 1845, as inclusion of Texas in the United States came closer to reality, Mexico agreed to full recognition of the Republic of Texas on the condition that annexation to the United States would not take place. In the light of history, Mexico had good reason to fear that annexation was merely a prelude to further encroachments upon Mexican territory. Neither the United States nor the Texans, however, permitted the Mexican concern to impede annexation. When Texas was incorporated into the American Union, the stage was set for war between the United States and Mexico.[39]

By 1844, the pull of "Manifest Destiny" in relation to Texas took precedence over any considerations of Mexico's legal right to the Southwest. James K. Polk, who strongly advocated the annexation of Texas and expansionism in general, won the presidency by only a small margin, but his election was interpreted as a mandate for national expansion. Outgoing President Tyler decided to act and called upon Congress to annex Texas by joint resolution; the measure was passed a few days before the inauguration of Polk, who accepted the arrangement. In December 1845, Texas became a state.

Mexico promptly broke off diplomatic relations with the United States, and Polk ordered General Zachary Taylor into Texas to protect the border. The location of the border, however, was dubious. Texas contended it was at the Rio Grande, but based on historical precedent, Mexico claimed it was 150 miles further north, at the Nueces River.[40] Taylor took his forces across the Nueces into the disputed territory, but refrained for a time from proceeding to the Rio Grande.

Meanwhile, in November 1845, Polk sent John Slidell on a secret mission to Mexico to negotiate for the disputed area. The presence of Anglo-American troops between the Nueces and the Rio Grande and the annexation of Texas seemed to make an absurdity of negotiations, and the Mexicans refused to see Polk's minister. Moreover, Slidell insisted on being received on terms offered by the United States, which was full acceptance of his credentials instead of the ad hoc status offered by Mexican authorities.[41] Slidell returned to Washington in March 1846, convinced that Mexico would have to be "chastised" before it would negotiate. By March 28, Taylor had advanced to the Rio Grande with an army 4000 strong.

Polk, incensed at Mexico's refusal to meet with Slidell on his terms and at General Mairano Paredes' reaffirmation of his country's claims to all of Texas, had already decided to fight. When Mexican forces crossed the Rio Grande and attacked Taylor's contingent, a move that Polk undoubtedly expected, the president had his excuse. He prepared his war message, and on

May 13, 1846, Congress declared war and authorized the recruitment and supplying of 50,000 troops.

As Polk saw it, "Mexico has . . . shed American blood upon the American soil."[42] In other words, the United States was justified in its actions; the country was provoked into war.

Years later, Ulysses S. Grant said that he believed Polk wanted and planned for war to be provoked, and that the annexation of Texas was, in fact, an act of aggression. He added: "I had a horror of the Mexican War . . . only I had not moral courage enough to resign . . . . I considered my supreme duty was to my flag."[43]

From the beginning, the outcome of the war was never in doubt. The poorly equipped and poorly led Mexican army stood little chance against the thrust of expansion-minded Anglos. But even before war had been declared, Anglo-Americans, and Polk in particular, were sure of success. Polk's plan for the war consisted of three stages: (1) Mexicans would be cleared out of Texas; (2) Anglos would occupy California and New Mexico; and (3) U.S. forces would march to Mexico City to force the beaten government to make peace on Polk's terms. And that was the way the campaign basically went. In the end, at a relatively small cost in men and money, the war netted the United States huge territorial gains: all of the Pacific coast from below San Diego to the Forty-ninth Parallel, and the whole area between the coast and the Continental Divide.

The Rationale for Conquest

Glenn W. Price, author of *Origins of the War with Mexico: The Polk-Stockton Intrigue,* stated: "Americans have found it rather more difficult than other peoples to deal rationally with their wars. We have thought of ourselves as unique, and of this society as specially planned and created to avoid the errors of all other nations."[44]

Many Anglo-American historians still attempt to ignore the Mexican-American War by simply stating that it was a "bad war," which took place during the United States' era of Manifest Destiny. This is as dangerous as German historians dismissing World War II by saying that it occurred during Germany's era of *lebensraum.* In fact, the very discussion of Manifest Destiny has distracted historians from the central issue of planned Anglo-American aggression.

Historians write that Manifest Destiny had its roots in Puritan ideas, which continue to influence Anglo-American thought to this day. The doctrine of Manifest Destiny was based in concept on that of predestination, which was part of the Calvinist doctrine: God destined you to go either to heaven or to hell. This belief in predestination was based in great measure on the doctrine of the "chosen people," of the Old Testament. The Puritans believed they were the chosen people of the New World. This belief carried over to the Anglo-American conviction that God had made them custodians of democracy and that they had a mission to spread its principles. As the young nation expanded west, survived its infancy in spite of the War of 1812, and enjoyed both commercial and industrial success, its sense of destiny heightened. The Monroe Doctrine of the 1820s told the world that the Americas were no longer open for colonialization or conquest; however, it did not say anything about that limitation applying to the United States. Many citizens were beginning to believe that God had destined them to own and occupy all of the land from ocean to ocean and pole to pole. This mission was to spread the principles of democracy and Christianity to the unfortunates of the hemisphere. In the 1830s and 1840s, Mexico became the victim of this early-day Anglo-American version of *lebensraum.*

Further obscuring the issue of planned Anglo-American aggression is what Professor Price exposes as the rhetoric of peace, which the United States has traditionally used to justify its aggressions. The Mexican-American War is a study in the use of this rhetoric.

Consider, for example, Polk's war message of May 11, 1846, in which he gave his reasons for going to war:

> The strong desire to establish peace with Mexico on liberal and honorable terms, and the readiness of this Government to regulate and adjust our boundary and other causes of difference with that power on such fair and equitable principles as would lead to permanent relations of the most friendly nature, induced me in September last to seek reopening of diplomatic relations between the two countries.[45]

He went on to state that the United States had made every effort not to inflame Mexicans, but that the Mexican government had refused to receive an Anglo-American minister. Polk then reviewed the events leading to the war and concluded: "As war exists, and, notwithstanding all our efforts to avoid it, exists by the act of Mexico herself, we are called upon every consideration of duty and patriotism to vindicate with decision the honor, the rights, and the interests of our country."[46]

This rhetoric—that it was the duty of the United States to go to war to maintain the peace and uphold its honor—is reminiscent of most U.S. involvements. The need to justify the United States' actions is evident in histories that offer different theories as to why the United States stole Mexico's territory. In 1920 Justin F. Smith received a Pulitzer prize in Anglo-American history for a work that blamed the war on Mexico. What is amazing is that Smith allegedly examined more than 100,000 manuscripts, 120,000 books and pamphlets, and 200 or more periodicals to come to this conclusion. It is fair to speculate that he was rewarded for relieving the Anglo-American conscience. This two-volume "study," entitled *The War with Mexico,* used analyses such as the following to support its thesis:

> At the beginning of her independent existence, our people felt earnestly and enthusiastically anxious to maintain cordial relations with our sister republic,

and many crossed the line of absurd sentimentality in the cause. Friction was inevitable, however. The Americans were direct, positive, brusque, angular and pushing; and they would not understand their neighbors on the south. The Mexicans were equally unable to fathom our goodwill, sincerity, patriotism, resoluteness and courage; and certain features of their character and national condition made it far from easy to get on with them.[47]

This attitude of righteousness on the part of government officials and historians toward their aggressions spills over to the relationships between the majority society and minority groups. Anglo-Americans believe that the war was advantageous to the Southwest and to the Mexicans who remained or later migrated there. They now had the benefits of democracy and were liberated from their tyrannical past. In other words, Mexicans should be grateful to the Anglo-Americans. If Mexicans and the Anglo-Americans clash, the rationale runs, naturally it is because the Mexican cannot understand or appreciate the merits of a free society, which must be defended against the ingrates. Therefore, domestic war, or repression, is justified by the same kind of rhetoric that justifies international aggression.

Fortunately, revisionist historians challenged the propagandists. Ramón Eduardo Ruíz has swept away the smoke screen created by many of his predecessors. In *The Mexican War: Was It Manifest Destiny?* he writes:

No war waged by the United States has won more striking victories than the Mexican War of 1846–1848. After an unbroken string of military triumphs from Buena Vista to Chapultepec and the operation of their first foreign capital, Americans added the sprawling territories of New Mexico and California to their domain. The United States had also fulfilled its Manifest Destiny, that belief of American expansionists that Providence had willed them a moral mission to occupy all adjacent lands. No American can deny that war had proved profitable.[48]

Ruíz further points out that there is little interest in the United States in what has been labeled the Mexican War, reinforcing the tendency of Anglo-Americans to forget unpleasant memories. Ruíz contrasts the bland Anglo-American reaction to the war with that of the Mexican: "The war is one of the tragedies of history. Unlike the Americans who have relegated the conflict to the past, Mexicans have not forgotten. Mexico emerged from the war bereft of half of its territory, a beaten, discouraged, and divided people."[49] Ruíz's work reviews the different theories behind the war, demonstrating the attempts of scholars to justify the war.

Recent works by other authors indict the United States for having "manufactured the war." Price's bold revisionist monograph, mentioned earlier, clearly shows Mexico as the victim of a conspiracy to force it into war in order to steal its territory. The work centers around the activities of Commodore Robert F. Stockton, who went to Texas before it was annexed to the United States, and who encouraged republican leaders of that state to attack Mexico in order to draw the latter into a war. Stockton assured them that the United States would back Texas when it was invaded; in turn, California and the Southwest would be annexed to the United States. In this scheme Stockton, a very wealthy man, used his own money, and he received the active encouragement of President James Polk, a man who rhetorically spoke of peace.

The Myth of a Nonviolent Nation

Most works on the Mexican-American War have dwelt on the causes and results of the war, sometimes dealing with war strategy. It is necessary, however, to go beyond this point, since the war has left very real scars, and since Anglo-American actions in Mexico are remembered as vividly as some Southerners remember Sherman's march to the sea. Surely the Mexicans' attitude toward Anglo-Americans has been influenced by the war just as the United States' easy victory conditioned Anglo-American behavior toward Mexicans. Fortunately, many Anglo-Americans condemned this aggression and flatly accused their fellows of being insolent, land hungry, and of having manufactured the war. Abiel Abbott Livermore in *The War with Mexico Reviewed** accused his country, writing:

> Again, the pride of race has swollen to still greater insolence the pride of country, always quite active enough for the due observance of the claims of universal brotherhood. The Anglo-Saxons have been apparently persuaded to think themselves the chosen people, anointed race of the Lord, commissioned to drive out the heathen, and plant their religion and institutions in every Canaan they could subjugate.[50]

Livermore's work, published in 1850, was awarded the American Peace Society prize for "the best Review of the Mexican War and the principles of Christianity, and an enlightened statesmanship." As the cause of the war, he wrote: "Our treatment both of the red man and the black man has habituated us to feel our power and forget right."[51] He further observed: "The passion for land, also, is a leading characteristic of the American people. . . . The god Terminus is an unknown deity in America. Like the hunger of the pauper boy of fiction, the cry had been, 'more, more, give us more.' "[52]

Through Livermore, a perspective unfolds that is not included in most books on the war. Otis A. Singletary's *The Mexican War,* like others of this mold, merely narrates the battles and their outcomes. Livermore builds an excellent case upon which to convict the United States of war crimes if the standards set by the Nuremburg trials after World War II had been followed: he describes an active policy of conquest and plunder.

---

*Some historians question the validity of Livermore's work because he was an abolitionist who allegedly set out to prove that the war was a slaveholders' crusade. However, history is the process of selection, and I find Livermore's book enlightening and in many ways more honest than the works of Justin Smith, who tailors the facts to fit his conclusions.

There is ample evidence that the United States provoked the war. We have already quoted General Grant's impressions. The war itself was even more insidious. Zachary Taylor's artillery leveled the Mexican city of Matamoros, killing hundreds of innocent civilians with *la bomba* (the bomb). Many Mexicans jumped into the Rio Grande, relieved of their pain by a watery grave.[53] The occupation that followed was even more terrorizing. Taylor's regular army was allegedly kept in control, but the volunteers presented another matter.

> The regulars regarded the volunteers, of whom about two thousand had reached Matamoros by the end of May, with impatience and contempt. . . . They robbed Mexicans of their cattle and corn, stole their fences for firewood, got drunk, and killed several inoffensive inhabitants of the town in the streets.[54]

There were numerous eyewitnesses to these incidents. For example, on July 25, 1846, Grant wrote to Julia Dent:

> Since we have been in Matamoros a great many murders have been committed, and what is strange there seemes [sic] to be very week [sic] means made use of to prevent frequent repetitions. Some of the volunteers and about all the Texans seem to think it perfectly right to impose on the people of a conquered City to any extent, and even to murder them where the act can be covered by dark. And how much they seem to enjoy acts of violence too! I would not pretend to guess the number of murders that have been committed upon the persons of poor Mexicans and our soldiers, since we have been here, but the number would startle you.[55]

Meanwhile, correspondents reported acts of useless and wanton destruction.[56]

Taylor knew about the atrocities, but as Grant observed, little was done to restrain the men. In a letter to his superiors, Taylor admitted that "There is scarcely a form of crime that has not been reported to me as committed by them."[57] Taylor requested that they send no further troops from the state of Texas to him. These marauding acts were not limited to Taylor's men. The cannons from U.S. naval ships destroyed much of the civilian sector of Vera Cruz, leveling a hospital, churches, and homes. The bomb did not discriminate as to age or sex. Anglo-American troops repeated their performance in almost every city they invaded; first it was put to the test of fire and then plundered. The *gringo* volunteers had little respect for anything, desecrating churches and abusing priests and nuns.

During these campaigns, military executions were common. Captured soldiers and civilians were executed, usually hanged, for cooperating with the guerillas. An interesting sidelight is that many Irish immigrants, as well as some other Anglos, deserted to the Mexican side, forming the San Patricio Corps. They went over to the Mexicans "due to the inborn distaste of the masses for war, to bad treatment, and to poor subsistence."[58] Many of the Irish were also Catholics, and they resented the treatment of Catholic priests and

25

nuns by the invading Protestants. It is estimated that as many as 260 Anglo-Americans fought with the Mexicans at Churubusco in 1847. "Some eighty appear to have been captured. . . . A number were found not guilty of deserting and were released. About fifteen, who had deserted before the declaration of war, were merely branded with a "D," and fifty of those taken at Churubusco were executed."[59] Others received two hundred lashes and were forced to dig graves for their executed comrades.[60]

We do not have to go to Mexican sources to chronicle the reign of terror spread by the Yankee troops. Memoirs, diaries, and news articles written by Anglo-Americans document it. Here, we shall concentrate on Samuel E. Chamberlain's *My Confessions.* He was only 17 when he enlisted in the army to fight the "greasers." Most of his "confessions" deal with the invasion of Mexico and the atrocities of the Anglos, especially the Texas Rangers. The author creates a mood, reflecting the racism of the invaders. At the Mexican city of Parras, he wrote: "We found the patrol had been guilty of many outrages. . . . They had ridden into the church of San José during Mass, the place crowded with kneeling women and children, and with oaths and ribald jest had arrested soldiers who had permission to be present."[61]

On another occasion, he described a massacre by volunteers, mostly from Yell's Cavalry, at a cave:

> On reaching the place we found a "greaser" shot and *scalped,* but still breathing; the poor fellow held in his hands a Rosary and a medal of the "Virgin of Guadalupe," only his feeble motions kept the fierce harpies from falling on him while yet alive. A Sabre thrust was given him in mercy, and on we went at a run. Soon shouts and curses, cries of women and children reached our ears, coming apparently from a cave at the end of the ravine. Climbing over rocks we reached the entrance, and as soon as we could see in the comparative darkness a horrid sight was before us. The cave was full of our volunteers yelling like fiends, while on the rocky floor lay over twenty Mexicans, dead and dying in pools of blood. Women and children were clinging to the knees of the murderers shrieking for mercy.[62]

Chamberlain continued:

> Most of the butchered Mexicans had been scalped; only three men were found unharmed. A rough crucifix was fastened to a rock, and some irreverent wretch had crowned the image with a bloody scalp. A sickening smell filled the place. The surviving women and children sent up loud screams on seeing us, thinking we had returned to finish the work!

Chamberlain concluded: "No one was punished for this outrage."[63]

Near Satillo, Chamberlain reported the actions of Texas Rangers. His descriptions are graphic. A drunken Anglo "entered the church and tore down a large wooden figure of our Saviour, and making his lariat fast around its neck, he mounted his horse and galloped up and down the *plazuela,* dragging the image behind him. The venerable white-haired Priest, in attempting to rescue it, was thrown down and trampled under the feet of the Ranger's horse."[64] The Mexicans were enraged and attacked the Texan; meanwhile, the Rangers had returned: "As they charged into the square, they saw their miserable comrade hanging to the cross, his skin hanging in strips, surrounded by crowds of Mexicans. With yells of horror, the Rangers charged on the mass with Bowie Knife and revolver, sparing neither age or sex in their terrible fury."[65]

Chamberlain is explicit in his contempt for the Rangers: "General Taylor not only collected the money [from the Mexican people]* assessed by force of arms, but he let loose on the country packs of human bloodhounds called Texas Rangers."[66] He goes on to describe the Rangers' brutality at the Rancho de San Francisco on the Camargo road near Agua Fria:

> The place was surrounded, the doors forced in, and all the males capable of bearing arms were dragged out, tied to a post and shot! . . . Thirty-six Mexicans were shot at this place, a half hour given for the horrified survivors, women and children, to remove their little household goods, then the torch was applied to the houses, and by the light of the conflagration the ferocious *Tejanos* rode off to fresh scenes of blood.[67]

These wanton acts of cruelty, witnessed by one man, are augmented by the reports of other chroniclers, adding to the evidence that the United States, through the deeds of its soldiers, left a legacy of hate in Mexico.

The omission of war atrocities in Anglo-American histories has led too many Anglo-Americans to view the conflict as a glamorous war, where Mexicans were beaten in a fair fight and were lucky to have lost only their land. This indifference on the part of Anglos has rubbed salt in the Mexicans' wounds and has kept alive old hatreds. It has perpetuated the reality for Chicanos that they are a conquered people: the Mexicans and the Indians are the only peoples in the United States who were forced to become part of that country after the occupation of their lands by Anglo-American troops.

The Treaty of Guadalupe Hidalgo

By late August 1847, the war was almost at an end, with General Winfield Scott defeating Santa Anna in a hard-fought battle at Churubusco. It placed the Anglo-Americans at the gates of Mexico City. Santa Anna made overtures for an armistice, and for two weeks negotiations were conducted. However, Santa Anna reorganized his defenses during this period, and, in turn, the Anglo-Americans renewed their relentless attacks. On September 13, 1847, Scott drove into the city. Although the Mexicans fought valiantly for their capital, the battle left 4000 of their men dead with another 3000 taken prisoner. On September 13, before the occupation of Mexico began, the *Niños Heroes*

---

*According to Chamberlain, Taylor collected over $1 million from the inhabitants of Nuevo Veon and Tamaulipas.

(the Boy Heros) fought off the conquerors and leapt to their deaths rather than surrender. These teenage cadets were Francisco Márquez, Agustín Melgar, Juan Escutia, Fernando Montes Oca, Vicente Suárez, and Juan de la Barrera. They became "a symbol and image of this unrighteous war.[68]

Although the Mexicans were beaten, fighting continued. The presidency devolved to the presiding justice of the Supreme Court, Manuel de la Peña y Peña. He knew that Mexico had lost and that it was his duty to salvage as much as possible. Pressure mounted, for the United States was in control of much of present-day Mexico.

Nicholas Trist, sent to Mexico to act as peace commissioner, had been unable to start negotiations until January 1848. Trist arrived in Vera Cruz on May 6, 1847, where he had a "vigorous but temporary tiff with Scott." Negotiations were conducted through the British legation, but were delayed by Trist's illness. This delay compromised a speedy settlement, and after the fall of Mexico City, Secretary of State James Buchanan wanted to revise Trist's instructions. He ordered Trist to break off negotiations and come home.[69] Polk apparently had begun to consider demanding more territory from Mexico and paying less for it. Trist, however, with the support of Winfield Scott, decided to ignore Polk's order, and he proceeded to negotiate on the original terms. Mexico, badly beaten, her government in a state of turmoil, had no choice but to agree to the Anglo-American's proposals.

On February 2, 1848, the Mexicans agreed to the Treaty of Guadalupe Hidalgo, in which Mexico accepted the Rio Grande as the Texas border and ceded the Southwest (which incorporates the present-day states of Arizona, California, New Mexico, Utah, Nevada, and parts of Colorado) to the United States in return for $15 million.

Polk was furious about the treaty; he considered Trist "contemptibly base" for having ignored his orders. Yet he had no choice but to submit the treaty to the Senate. With the exception of article X, the Senate ratified the treaty on March 10, 1848, by a vote of 28 to 14. To insist on more territory would have meant more fighting, and both Polk and the Senate realized that the war was already beginning to be unpopular in many sections. The treaty was sent to the Mexican Congress for its ratification; although the Congress had difficulty forming a quorum, the agreement was ratified on May 19 by a 52 to 35 vote.[70] Hostilities between the two nations were now officially ended. Trist, however, was branded as a "scoundrel," because Polk was disappointed in the settlement. There was considerable support and fervor in the United States for the acquisition of all Mexico.[71]

Contrary to popular belief, Mexico did not abandon its citizens who lived within the bounds of the new U.S. territory. The Mexican negotiators were concerned about the Mexicans left behind, and they expressed great reservations about these people being forced to "merge or blend" into Anglo-American culture. They protested the exclusion of provisions that protected the Mexican citizens' rights, land titles, and religion.[72] They wanted to know the Mexican's status, and they wanted to protect his rights by treaty.

The provisions that specifically refer to the Mexican and his rights are found in articles VIII and IX and the omitted article X. Taken in the context of the reluctance of Mexican officials to abandon their people to a nation that had virtually no respect for Mexicans, it is easier to understand why Chicanos are so angry about violations to their cultural identity.

Under the Treaty of Guadalupe Hidalgo, the Mexican left behind had one year to choose whether to return to the interior of Mexico or to remain in "occupied Mexico." About 2000 elected to leave; however, most remained in what they considered *their* territory. This situation was very similar to that of other conquered people, for the legality of the forced seizure is still an issue.

Article IX of the treaty guaranteed Mexicans "the enjoyment of all the rights of citizens of the United States according to the principles of the Constitution; and in the meantime shall be maintained and protected in the free enjoyment of their liberty and property, and secured in the free exercise of their religion without restriction."[73] This article and the United States' adherence to it have long been debated by scholars. Most sources admit that the Anglo-Americans have respected the Chicano's religion; on the other hand, Chicanos and well-known scholars contend that the rights of cultural integrity and rights of citizenship have been constantly violated. Lynn I. Perrigo in *The American Southwest* summarizes the guarantees of articles VIII and IX, writing: "In other words, besides the right and duties of American citizenship, they [the Mexicans] would have some special privileges derived from their previous customs in language, law, and religion."[74]

In spite of these guarantees, Chicanos have been subjected to cultural genocide, as well as to violations of their rights. *A Documentary History of the Mexican Americans,* published in 1971, states:

> As the only minority, apart from the Indians, ever acquired by conquest, the Mexican Americans have been subjected to economic, social, and political discrimination, as well as a great deal of violence at the hands of their Anglo conquerors. During the period from 1865 to 1920, there were more lynchings of Mexican Americans in the Southwest. But the worst violence has been the unrelenting discrimination against the cultural heritage—the language and customs—of the Mexican Americans, coupled with the economic exploitation of the entire group. Property rights were guaranteed, but not protected, by either the federal or state governments. Equal protection under law has consistently been a mockery in the Mexican-American communities.[75]

Just as controversial is the explicit protection of property. Although most analyses do not consider the omitted article X, this article had comprehensive guarantees protecting "all prior and pending titles to property of every description."[76] When this provision was deleted by the U.S. Senate, Mexican officials protested. Anglo-American emissaries reassured them by drafting a Statement of Protocol on May 26, 1848, which read:

> The American government by suppressing the Xth article of the Treaty of Guadalupe Hidalgo did not in any way intend to annul the grants of lands made

by Mexico in the ceded territories. These grants ... preserve the legal value which they may possess, and the grantees may cause their legitimate (titles) to be acknowledged before the American tribunals.

Conformable to the law of the United States, legitimate titles to every description of property, personal and real, existing in the ceded territories, are those which were legitimate titles under the Mexican law of California and New Mexico up to the 13th of May, 1846, and in Texas up to the 2nd of March, 1836.[77]

It is doubtful, considering the Mexican opposition to the treaty, whether the Mexican Congress would have ratified the treaty without this clarification. The vote was close. The Statement of Protocol was reinforced by articles VIII and XI, which guaranteed Mexicans rights of property and protection under the law. In addition, court decisions have generally interpreted the treaty as protecting land titles and water rights. Nevertheless, the fact remains that property was seized and individual rights were violated—largely through political manipulation.

It is one thing to make a treaty and another to live up to it. The United States has had a singularly poor record in complying with its treaty obligations, and as subsequent chapters will show, nearly every one of the obligations discussed above was violated, confirming the prophecy of Mexican diplomat Manuel Cresencio Rejón who, at the time the treaty was signed, commented:

Our race, our unfortunate people will have to wander in search of hospitality in a strange land, only to be ejected later. Descendants of the Indians that we are, the North Americans hate us, their spokesmen depreciate us, even if they recognize the justice of our cause, and they consider us unworthy to form with them one nation and one society, they clearly manifest that their future expansion begins with the territory that they take from us and pushing [sic] aside our citizens who inhabit the land.[78]

Conclusion

Manuel Cresencio Rejón affirms the legacy left behind by Anglo conquest and violence. Mexicans were the victims of unjust aggressions and transgressions against them and their nation. Mingled with feelings of Anglo-American racial and cultural superiority, the violence created a legacy of hate on both sides that has continued to the present. The image of the *Tejano* has become that of the obnoxious, rude oppressor throughout Latin America, whereas most Anglo-Americans considered Chicanos as foreigners with inferior rights. As a result of the Texas War and the Anglo-American aggressions of 1845–1848, the occupation of Chicano territory began, and colonization started to take form. The attitude of the Anglo, during the period of subjugation following the wars, is reflected in the conclusions of the noted Texan historian and past-president of the American Historical Association, Walter Prescott Webb:

A homogenous European society adaptable to new conditions was necessary. This Spain did not have to offer in Arizona, New Mexico, and Texas. Its frontier, as it advanced, depended more and more on an Indian population. . . . This mixture of races meant in time that common soldiers in the Spanish service came largely from pueblo or sedentary Indian stock, whose blood, when compared to that of the plain Indians, was as ditch water. It took more than a little mixture of Spanish blood and mantle of Spanish service to make valiant soldiers of the timid pueblo Indians.[79]

A new era had begun, and according to the Anglo-American, it had a homogenous and racially superior people to lead it. The conquest laid the framework of the colony and justified the economic and political privilege established by the conquerors. Most Anglo-Americans, historians and laymen alike, are inflicted with a historical amnesia as to how they acquired it and how they maintained control over the conquered land and people.

Notes

1. Robert A. Divine, ed., *American Foreign Policy* (New York: The World Publishing Company, 1966), pp. 11–18.
2. Cecil Robinson, "Flag of Illusion," *The American West* 5, no. 3 (May 1968): 15.
3. T. R. Fehrenbach, *Lone Star: A History of Texas and the Texans* (New York: The Macmillan Company, 1968), p. 128.
4. Walter Prescott Webb, *The Texas Rangers: A Century of Frontier Defense* (Austin: University of Texas Press, 1965), pp. 21–22.
5. Fehrenbach, pp. 163–164.
6. Eugene C. Barker, *Mexico and Texas, 1821–1835* (New York: Russell & Russell, Inc., 1965), p. 52.
7. Barker, pp. 74–80.
8. Barker, pp. 80–82.
9. Fehrenbach, p. 182.
10. Fehrenbach, p. 180.
11. Fehrenbach, p. 180.
12. Fehrenbach, p. 180.
13. Fehrenbach, p. 181.
14. Fehrenbach, p. 181.
15. Nathaniel W. Stephenson, *Texas and the Mexican War: A Chronicle of the Winning of the Southwest* (New York: United States Publishing Company, 1921), p. 51.
16. Stephenson, p. 52: on Austin's letter, also see Barker, p. 128.
17. Stephenson, p. 52.
18. Fehrenbach, p. 188.
19. Fehrenbach, p. 189.
20. Barker, p. 146.
21. Barker, p. 147.
22. Barker, p. 148.
23. Barker, pp. 148–149.
24. Barker, p. 162.
25. Fehrenbach, p. 189.
26. Fehrenbach, p. 189.
27. Felix D. Almaraz, "The Historical Heritage of the Mexican American in 19th-Century Texas," *The Role of the Mexican American in the History of the Southwest* (Edinburg, Tex.: Inter-American Institute, Pan American College, 1969), pp. 20–21.
28. Walter Lord, "Myths and Realities of the Alamo," *The American West* 5, no. 3 (May 1968).
29. Lord, p. 20.
30. Rafael Trujillo Herrera, *Olvídate de El Alamo* (Mexico, D.F.: La Prensa, 1965).

31. Lord, p. 18.
32. Lord, p. 22.
33. Lord, p. 24.
34. Lord, p. 25.
35. Lord, p. 25.
36. Fehrenbach, p. 232.
37. Marilyn McAdams Sibley, *Travelers in Texas, 1761–1860* (Austin: University of Texas Press, 1967), pp. 108–109.
38. Charles A. Hale, *Mexican Liberalism in the Age of Mora, 1821–1853* (New Haven, Conn.: Yale University Press, 1968), pp. 11–12, 16.
39. Carl N. Degler, *Out of Our Past: The Forces That Shaped Modern America,* rev. ed. (New York: Harper & Row, Publishers, Inc., 1970), p. 107.
40. José María Roa Barcena, *Recuerdos De La Invasión Norte Americana (1846–1848),* ed. I. Antonio Castro Leal (México: Editorial Porrua, S.A., 1947), pp. 25–27. This author reviews historical precedent.
41. Albert C. Ramsey, ed. and trans., *The Other Side or Notes for the History of the War Between Mexico and the United States* (reprint ed., New York: Burt Franklin, 1970), pp. 28–29; and Ramón Alcaraz *et al., Apuntes Para La Historice Del La Guerra Entra Mexico y Los Estados Unidos* (Mexico: Tipografia De Manuel Payno, Hijo, 1848), pp. 27–28.
42. J. D. Richardson, *A Compilation of the Messages and Papers of the Presidents,* 10 vols. (Washington, D.C., 1905), 4: 428–442, quoted in Arvin Rappaport, ed., *The War with Mexico: Why Did It Happen?* (New York: Rand McNally & Company, 1964), p. 16.
43. Grady McWhiney and Sue McWhiney, eds., *To Mexico with Taylor and Scott, 1845–1847* (Waltham, Mass: Praisdell Publishing Co., 1969), p. 3.
44. Glen W. Price, *Origins of the War with Mexico: The Polk-Stockton Intrigue* (Austin: University of Texas Press, 1967), p. 7.
45. Rappaport, p. 16.
46. Rappaport, p. 16.
47. Justin H. Smith, *The War With Mexico,* vol. 2 (Gloucester, Mass.: Peter Smith Publisher, 1963), p. 310.
48. Ramón Eduardo Ruíz, ed., *The Mexican War: Was It Manifest Destiny?* (New York: Holt, Rinehart and Winston, Inc., 1963), p. 1.
49. Ruiz, p. 1.
50. Abiel Abbott Livermore, *The War With Mexico Reviewed* (Boston, Mass.: American Peace Society, 1850), p. 8.
51. Livermore, p. 11.
52. Livermore, p. 12.
53. T. B. Thorpe, *Our Army on the Rio Grande;* quoted in Livermore, p. 126.
54. Alfred Hoyt Bill, *Rehearsal for Conflict* (New York: Alfred A. Knopf, Inc., 1947), p. 122.
55. John Y. Simon, *The Papers of Ulysses S. Grant,* vol. 1 (London, England, and Amsterdam, Holland: Feffer & Simons, Inc., 1967), p. 102.
56. Livermore, p. 140.
57. Quoted in Livermore, pp. 148–49.
58. Smith, vol. 1, p. 550, fn. 6.
59. Smith, vol. 2, p. 385, fn. 18.
60. Livermore, p. 160.
61. Samuel E. Chamberlain, *My Confessions* (New York: Harper & Brothers, 1956), p. 75.
62. Chamberlain, p. 87.
63. Chamberlain, p. 88.
64. Chamberlain, p. 174.
65. Chamberlain, p. 174.
66. Chamberlain, p. 176.

67. Chamberlain, p. 177.

68. Alfonso Zabre, *Guide to the History of Mexico: A Modern Interpretation* (Austin, Tex.: The Pemberton Press, 1969), p. 300.

69. Dexter Perkins and Glyndon G. Van Deusen, *The American Democracy: Its Rise to Power* (New York: The Macmillan Company, 1964), p. 237.

70. Robert Selph Henry, *The Story of the Mexican War* (New York: Frederick Ungar Publishing Co., 1950), p. 390.

71. See John D. P. Fuller, *The Movement for the Acquisition of All Mexico* (New York: Da Capo Press, 1969).

72. Letter from Commissioner Trist to Secretary Buchanan, Mexico, 25 January 1848, Senate Executive Documents, no. 52, p. 283.

73. Wayne Moquin *et al.,* eds., *A Documentary History of the Mexican American* (New York: Frederick A. Praeger, Publishers, 1971), p. 185.

74. Lynn I. Perrigo, *The American Southwest* (New York: Holt, Rinehart and Winston, Inc., 1971), p. 176.

75. Moquin, p. 181.

76. Perrigo, p. 176.

77. *Compilation of Treaties on Force* (Washington, D.C.: U.S. Government Printing Office, 1899), p. 402; quoted in Perrigo, p. 176.

78. Antonio de la Peña y Reyes, *Algunos Documentos Sobre el Tratado de Guadalupe-Hidalgo* (Mexico, D.F.: Sec de Rel Ext, 1930), p. 159; quoted in Richard Gonzáles, "Commentary on the Treaty of Guadalupe Hidalgo," in Feliciano Rivera, *A Mexican American Source Book* (Menlo Park, Calif.: Educational Consulting Associates, 1970), p. 185.

79. Walter Prescott Webb, *The Great Plains* (New York: Grosset & Dunlap, Inc., 1931), pp. 125–126.

33

Chapter Two

Remember the Alamo: The Colonization of Texas

The stereotype of the Texan with high-heeled boots, white hat, and swaggering manner symbolizes to most Mexicans and other Latin Americans all that was and is bad about Anglo-America. His dress, for example, represents the theft of the *vaquero's* (the Mexican cowboy's) land and heritage. The Anglo-American cowboy did, in fact, learn his trade from and borrow the dress of the Mexican *vaquero*. The Texas cowboy is further stereotyped as a crude, aggressive bully who hates Mexicans. He, in short, has become the prototype not only of the colonization of Texas and the Southwest, but also of Anglo-America's economic colonization of all Latin America. Individual feelings toward Anglo-*Tejanos* are intense and, many times, are translated into sentiments of blind hatred. The expression of these feelings is often crude, as, for example, in the saying: "You pour hot water over an Anglo-*Tejano* and you get instant *caca* [excrement]." The legacy of the conquest undoubtedly influenced this attitude, but the bitter conflict between Anglos and Mexicans in the occupied territory has increased the animosity.

As we discussed in chapter 1, Texan-Mexican hostilities did not end after 1836. Mexico refused to recognize the Republic of Texas. The issue of the prisoners of war continued to burn. According to the Texas historian T. R. Fehrenbach:

> The treatment of these soldiers was shameful by any standards and has generally been ignored by American historians. Whatever indignities Santa Ana had earned, these were not due Juan Nepomuceno Almonte, his staff, or the common soldiers under the President's command. Many died in captivity, and all were eventually repatriated in poor condition.[1]

The boundary question also remained an issue. The Texans claimed the republic included all of the land to the Rio Grande, whereas the Mexicans said the border was at the Nueces River. In the years that followed, the territory between the two rivers continued to be disputed. Meanwhile, Anglo-American immigration into the Republic of Texas increased.

To escape the discrimination of the Anglos, whose chauvinism had been intensified by the victory and who continued to view the Mexican as an enemy, the Mexicans were forced to move further and further into the southern portion of the new republic. Substantial numbers settled in the disputed territory.

In the years before annexation to the United States, Texans actively warred on the Indians and also stepped up their diplomatic front against Mexico. President Mirabeau B. Lamar had dreams of expanding the republic, and in 1839 and 1840, he took advantage of Mexico's problems with France. He pressed for a settlement of the boundary question, offering Mexico $5 million if it would accept the Rio Grande as the territorial border. In 1841 he involved himself in Mexican internal affairs by signing a treaty with Yucatán, a southeastern Mexican state, which was attempting to secede from Mexico. That same year Lamar sent the ill-fated Santa Fe Expedition into New Mexico in a scheme to add that area to the republic (see chapter 3).

During the late 1830s, tension was acute along the border. The situation was aggravated by Black Texan slaves who crossed into Mexico to freedom. The owners demanded their return, and the Mexican authorities refused. When the hostilities erupted into war, South Texas became the gateway for Zachary Taylor's invasion of northern Mexico, and Mexicans in that portion of Texas suffered greatly from Anglo-American violence.

Technically, after the Mexican-American War, the Mexicans who remained in Texas became citizens of the United States. In reality, however, they continued to consider themselves Mexicans. The proximity of the border and the attitude of the colonizers reinforced this nationalism. In addition, Anglo-Americans believed they had won special rights to the land and its bounty by right of conquest and because of their racial and cultural superiority. Mexicans were treated as conquered people who had to pay tribute. The Mexican way of life was replaced by Anglo laws, administration, language, and values—all of which were alien to the conquered people. Although the Mexican was in the minority throughout the state, he enjoyed a majority in Southeast Texas; yet it was in that area that the superimposition became most repugnant. His large numbers presented a threat to the new order, which had to be supported by an army of occupation. Each time a conflict between Mexicans and Anglos erupted, U.S. troops supported the occupiers.

A caste system developed that condemned Mexicans, because of their race and culture, to the lower stratum. In other words, a colonial relationship developed between Anglos and Mexicans. T. R. Fehrenbach likened it to that of the Boers in South Africa and the native population there. The Mexican became the servant, the low-paid worker, but seldom the boss. Fehrenbach writes that tensions were "natural" and stemmed from the fact that two radically different peoples had been brought under a single government. He states that ethnic conflict comes about "historically . . . in only three general ways: conquest of one race or culture by another, the imposition of arbitrary boundaries combining different groups within one political unity, or the importation of foreign stock by a more highly organized society for labor."[2] The Mexican was victimized by each of these processes, which are attendant to the establishment of a colonial society.

The Apologists

Most histories dealing with the relations between Mexicans and Anglos have been one-sided, written by Anglo-American historians who are apologists for the *gringo's* treatment of the Mexican. These historians have attempted to shift responsibility for the conflict to the Mexican. They ignore the economic motives of the Anglo-American encroachers.

The first task of the Chicano historian is to expose the apologists, who have influenced beliefs about the Mexican. We do not attribute base motives to these historians, but we maintain that they represent the attitudes of Westerners toward Mexicans. One of the leading Texas historians to advance the apologist point of view was Walter Prescott Webb. Until his death in March 1963, he was considered dean of the Texan historians. The most respected professor of history on the faculty of the University of Texas at Austin and past-president of the American Historical Association, he wielded considerable influence among scholars and graduate students. His most important works were *The Texas Rangers, The Great Plains, Divided We Stand,* and *The Great Frontier;* in addition, he wrote countless articles.[3]

Webb's writings have had considerable impact on the historiography of the West. Recently, however, a crack appeared, and some scholars have begun to question many of his conclusions, implying that they are racist. Among these scholars are Américo Paredes, Llerena B. Friend, and Larry McMurtry.

McMurtry writes of Webb's *The Texas Rangers:* "The flaw in the book is a flaw of attitude. Webb admired the Rangers inordinately, and as a consequence the book mixes homage with history in a manner one can only think sloppy. His own facts about the Rangers contradict again and again his characterization of them as 'quiet, deliberate, gentle' men."[4] McMurtry then points out some of the inconsistencies. He faults Webb's description of the Rangers role in the seige of Mexico City: "A sneak thief stole a handkerchief from them. They shot him."[5] One Texas Ranger was shot, and the Rangers retaliated by killing 80 Mexicans.[6] McMurtry concluded: "[These] are hardly the actions of men who can accurately be called gentle."[7] McMurtry also questions Webb's description of Ranger Captain L. H. McNeely as a "flame of courage."[8] McMurtry states of McNeely, "He did a brilliant, brave job, and his methods were absolutely ruthless."[9] McNeely tortured Mexicans and shot them down in cold blood. Once he crossed the border with 30 men and attacked a ranch that he thought housed Mexican troops. However, he was mistaken, and he murdered a number of innocent Mexican workers. When he discovered his error, he merely rode off. Webb's apology for the Rangers is that "Affairs on the border cannot be judged by standards that hold elsewhere."[10] McMurtry responds: "Why they can't is a question apologists for the Rangers have yet to answer. Torture is torture, whether inflicted in Germany, Algiers, or along the Nueces Strip. The Rangers, of course, claimed that their end justified their means, but people who practice torture always claim that."[11]

Webb had ceased being a historian and had become a Ranger by proxy. While he must have surely seen the brutality of these violent men, he closed his eyes to it. McMurtry sheds more light on the situation, writing: "The important point to be made about *The Texas Rangers* is that Webb was writing not as an historian of the frontier, but as a symbolic frontiersman. The tendency to practice symbolic frontiersmanship might almost be said to characterize the twentieth century Texan, whether he be an intellectual, a cowboy, a businessman, or a politician."[12] McMurtry's work, in fact, explores the effect of this frontiersmanship. It is also significant that Webb was a scholarly man who did not have evil motives. His works are, however, racist.

By the end of Webb's long career, his viewpoint of the Chicano had changed.[13] When he published an article, in *True West* in October 1962, "The Bandits of Las Cuevas," he received a letter from Enrique Mendiola of Alice, Texas, whose grandfather owned the ranch that the Rangers under McNeely, mistakenly attacked. Mendiola stated, "Most historians have classified these men as cattle thieves, bandits, etc. This might be true of some of the crowd, but most of them, including General Juan Flores, were trying to recover their own cattle that had been taken away from them when they were driven out of their little ranches in South Texas. They were driven out by such men as Mifflin Kenedy, Richard King and [the] Armstrongs."[14] Walter Prescott Webb's reply was revealing: "To get a balanced account, one would need the records from the south side of the river, and these are simply not available." He stated that there was stealing back and forth, but that "The unfortunate fact is that the Mexicans were not as good at keeping records as were the people on this side. . . . I have often wished that the Mexicans, or some one who had their confidence, could have gone among them and got their stories of the raids and counter raids. I am sure that these stories would take on a different color and tone."[15]

Mexicans did, in fact, record their story in *corridos* (ballads), that glorified the deeds of men who stood up to the oppressors. These *corridos* are still sung in the Rio Grande Valley and in other places in the Southwest. *Corridos* to Juan Cortina were composed when he resisted the *gringo* in the 1850s, and even today, Chicano leaders such as César Chávez, Reies López Tijerina, and Ruben Salazar have had *corridos* composed in their honor and memory. One of the best known is *El Corrido de Gregorio Cortez,* a man unjustly pursued by the Rangers and Texas authorities in 1901. In his book, *With His Pistol in His Hand,* Américo Paredes* analyzes this *corrido,* as well as reviewing the history of the *corridos.* They convey the Mexican attitude, which is one of defiance, toward *los rinches,* as the Mexican call the Rangers:

> Then said Gregorio Cortez
>   With his pistol in his hand,
> "Ah, how many cowardly rangers,
> Against one lone Mexican!"[16]

Paredes wrote that: "The official Texas Rangers are known as the *rinches de la Kineña,* or Rangers of King Ranch, in accordance with the Borderer's belief that the Rangers were the personal strong-arm of Richard King and the other 'cattle barons.' "[17]

What has been the traditional view of the Texas Ranger as portrayed in U.S. history? Rip Ford, a Ranger himself, wrote: "A Texas Ranger can ride like a Mexican, trail like an Indian, shoot like a Tennesseean, and fight like the very devil!"[18]

T. R. Fehrenbach, in 1968, wrote in his *Lone Star: A History of Texas and Texans:*

> To fight Indians and Mexicans, Ranger leaders had to learn to think like both, or at least, to understand what Mexicans and Indians feared. The collision between the Anglo-American and the Mexican on the southern frontier was inevitable, but some aspects of this were unfortunate. Contact did not improve either race; it seemed to strengthen and enhance the vices of both. The Ranger arrived with instinctive Teutonic directness, preferring the honest smash of the bullet to the subtlety of the knife. But against the Mexican, bluntness turned into brutality, because it was almost impossible for the Protestant Anglo-Celt to understand the Hispanic mind. Impatient with Mexican deviousness, the Ranger reacted with straight force. But the Mexican, to keep the records straight, slipped from deviousness to outright treachery; history records that Mexicans killed more Texans by the result of parleys than on all the battlefields. Each side felt themselves justified because of the incomprehensible and despised cultural attributes of the foe. The Rangers seemed barbaric Nordics, void of all gentlemanly

*Paredes is a Chicano scholar from the Rio Grande Valley who became a professor at the University of Texas.

intrigue or guile; they saw the Mexicans as treacherous, lying people, who never wanted to do the obvious, which was to call their play and fight.[19]

Walter Prescott Webb, who was even less objective in his analysis of the cultural differences between the Rangers and the Mexicans, wrote of the Ranger: "When we see him at his daily task of maintaining law, restoring order, and promoting peace—even though his methods be vigorous—we see him in the proper setting, a man standing alone between a society and its enemies." Conversely, he wrote of the Mexican:

> Without disparagement it may be said that there is a cruel streak in the Mexican nature, or so the history of Texas would lead one to believe. This cruelty may be a heritage from the Spanish of the Inquisition; it may, and doubtless should, be attributed partly to the Indian blood.[20]

This type of reasoning justified the Ranger's violence to many Anglo-Americans; the "vigorous methods" were necessary in dealing with "savage adversaries."

Américo Paredes gives another viewpoint of the Rangers. He looks upon them as the representatives of Anglo ranchers and merchants who controlled the valley of the Rio Grande. Their commitment was to keep order for the Anglo oligarchy. They recruited gunslingers who burned with a hatred of the Mexican, shooting first and asking questions afterwards. Paredes writes: "That the Rangers stirred up more trouble than they put down is an opinion that has been expressed by less partisan sources."[21]

Paredes was one of the first Chicano scholars to attack the Rangers and, by inference, Webb. He expressed the feelings of the Mexican, which were based, for the most part, on the Mexicans' oral traditions and their experiences. His facts refuted those of Webb. An example is the differing interpretation by the two men of the facts surrounding the murder of the Cerdas, a prominent family near Brownsville. Paredes writes:

> The Cerdas were prosperous ranchers near Brownsville, but it was their misfortune to live next to one of the "cattle barons" who was not through expanding yet. One day three Texas Rangers came down from Austin and "executed" the elder Cerda and one of his sons as cattle rustlers. The youngest son fled across the river, and thus the Cerda ranch was vacated. Five months later the remaining son Alfredo Cerda crossed over to Brownsville. He died the same day, shot down by a Ranger's gun.[22]

Paredes' account is not based on secondary sources, but on eyewitness accounts. Marcelo Garza, Sr., of Brownsville, a respected businessman, told Paredes that a Ranger shot unarmed Alfredo, stalking him "like a wild animal."[23]

Webb's version is based on Ranger sources, which resemble some contemporary police reports. According to Webb, the Ranger surprised a Mexican branding a calf that belonged to the King Ranch. The Mexican, Ramón De La Cerda, shot at the Ranger, and the latter shot back, killing Ramón in self-defense. The Ranger was cleared at an inquest, but the Mexicans did not accept this verdict and disinterred De La Cerda's body and conducted their own inquest. They found

> "evidence" [Quotes are Webb's] . . . to the effect that De La Cerda had been dragged and otherwise maltreated. Public sentiment was sharply divided. . . . The findings of the secret inquest, together with wild rumors growing out of it, only served to inflame the minds of De La Cerda's supporters.[24]

Again, Webb's sources were secondary, and he based his conclusion that the people were being inflamed on Ranger reports. Webb admitted that a double standard of justice operated as to Mexicans and Anglos. Therefore, it was natural that they should question the findings of the inquest, especially the facts behind this particular shooting. The Cerda family was a well-known and respected family whose land the Kings coveted. More telling is Webb's quote as to who posted bail for Baker, the Ranger who shot De La Cerda: "Captain Brooks reported that Baker made bail in the sum of ten thousand dollars, and that he was supported by such people as the Kings, Major John Armstrong —McNeely's lieutenant—and Lyman Brothers."[25]

The historian wonders why Webb did not question the support of the Kings. It is no wonder that the Mexicans were inflamed. Shortly afterwards, the younger brother of Ramón, Alfredo, was also shot by Baker.

The importance of the Cerda affair is that it exposes the use of violence to take over land and then to legalize murder through the court system. It was not an isolated instance; it merely mirrored the activity of the Rangers throughout the century. During the Cortina uprising, hundreds if not thousands of Mexicans were victimized because they were relatives of partisans or because they were suspected of being associated with the revolutionaries. The Rangers, who operated independently of the traditional law enforcement agencies, were proud of their efficiency in dealing with Mexicans.

Hatred of *los rinches* burned among the Mexicans during the nineteenth century. In the *corrido* the feelings of the people were recorded:

> The "rinches" are very brave
> that cannot be denied;
> they hunt us like deer
> in order to kill us.[26]

A partial explanation for the terrorism by the Rangers was the overwhelming number of Mexicans compared to *gringos* in the valley; the latter lived in terror of a mass uprising. In 1915, when a band of 40 Mexicans led by Aniceto Pizaña raided the town of Norias on the King Ranch, the revolt was quickly suffocated, but not before a reign of terror was touched off in South Texas.[27] Anglo-Americans believed that it was a conspiracy—blaming it on the Germans, the IWW (Industrial Workers of the World), or the Japanese. Between 1915 and 1920, according to an estimate by Walter Prescott Webb, 500 to 5000 Mexicans were killed by local posses, peace officers, and Texas Rangers. Webb wrote: "The situation can be summed up by saying that after the troubles developed the Americans instituted a reign of terror against the Mexicans and that many innocent Mexicans were made to suffer."[28]

Paredes reports an account by Josefina Flores D. Garza, who was a victim of the Rangers' wrath. *Los rinches* invaded her home during the 1915 blood-bath. They murdered her father and teenage brothers. Josefina, with her mother and several other children, witnessed the assassinations. The family was then left with the corpses for several days, afraid to leave the house. Later, U.S. troops removed the bodies. Josefina went temporarily insane.

Rangers even today display their arrogance by brutally bullying Mexicans. One of the most hated Rangers was Captain A. Y. Allee, who retired at the end of 1970. A newspaper account described him:

> Paunchy, crusty, with a face like a sunburned potato, Alfred Allee is the most controversial policeman in South Texas. The son of a former New Mexico senator—Dennis Chavez, Jr.—has testified to a House Agriculture subcommittee that Allee is "a known killer, a professional Mexican-hater whose saying is 'Shoot first and ask questions afterwards.' "[29]

Allee carried a chrome-plated pistol and was always ready with his fist. On one occasion, when he beat up a suspect, he stated that he thought the man had a concealed weapon and, after all, "The guy was only hit once."

In 1967 Allee put down what he considered a rebellion. Followers of César Chávez led a strike against agribusiness in the valley for better wages and conditions. Allee's Rangers harassed and physically abused the strikers. The Council of Churches filed an injunction against him, but this did not slow him down; he bragged that he had been sued many times but had never been reprimanded.[30] This is probably true. His job was to protect the political and economic privilege of the colonizers. With the use of organized violence through forces like the Rangers, the Mexican was kept in his place.

The events of 1967 show all too clearly that the Rangers have changed little in their reaction to Mexicans. McMurtry, a non-Chicano, reports the reaction of Anglo-*Tejanos* to the strike:

> One gains no popularity there [South Texas] by suggesting that Mexicans have rights to something other than air, *frijoles,* and goat's milk. The farm-labor disputes of 1967—disputes in which the Texas Ranger played a suspect role—made this very clear. I know a farm manager, a man but recently migrated from the Valley to the High Plains, who was sincerely shocked by the fact that Mexicans were beginning to want houses to live in. Tents and truck-beds, fifty-cents an hour cash, and a free goat every week or two no longer satisfied them. They had come to consider themselves human beings, an attitude which filled the manager with astonishment and vague dismay. When Mexicans become thus aberrated it is time, in Texas, to call the Rangers.[31]

The Texas Rangers facilitated the continued subjugation of the Mexicans by a handful of unscrupulous and brutal men who corrupted local and state authorities, making a mockery of democracy. To gain their ends, they assassinated their opposition, stole their homes, and appropriated their cattle. To understand how this happened, we must look at the life of the *Mexicano* in Texas before the coming of the *gringo.* Américo Paredes described this life in the Rio Grande Valley:

> In the days before upriver irrigation projects, the lower Rio Grande was a green, fertile belt, bounded on the north and south by arid plains, situated along a river which, like the Nile, irrigated and fertilized the land close to its banks and periodically filled countless little lakes, known as *resacas* and *esteros.* [32]

Before 1848, the area supported many thousands of cattle. It had towns, such as Laredo, Guerrero, Mier, Camargo, and Reynosa, that had been founded before 1755. Paredes described the life of the border Mexican:

> The simple pastoral life led by most Border people fostered a natural equality among men. Much has been written about the democratizing influence of a horse culture. More important was the fact that on the Border the land owner lived and worked upon his land. There was almost no gap between the owner and cowhand, who often was related to him anyway. The simplicity of the life led by both employer and employee also helped make them feel that they were not different kinds of men, even if one was richer than the other. [33]

The valley supported communities that were self-reliant and that raised corn, beans, melons, and vegetables. The people also tended sheep and goats. Commerce between the people on both sides of that river helped to bind them together. It was not the highly organized and profit-yielding ventures that Anglos were accustomed to and considered productive. If we use the technological standards of the United States, the economy of the valley was underdeveloped.

While life among the Mexicans in the other sections of Texas did not exactly mirror the life style of the Rio Grande people, it greatly resembled it. Life had a communal rhythm rather than the individualistic beat of Anglo-American civilization. The destruction of this culture and the hammering out of a civilization became a fetish with the colonizer.

The Mexican in Texas had an established culture and life style that fitted his needs, and that was supported and complemented by his political and economic system. The Anglo occupation was designed to replace both his life style and these economic and political pillars. Ironically, although the pillars were destroyed by the Anglo-American in much the same way as the forests had been, the Mexican tenaciously held on to his traditions, which were literally rooted in the soil. The destruction of the Mexican's political and economic system, nevertheless, robbed him of control over his economic mobility and determined his role and social status. How the Anglo-American gained his position of dominance is strikingly similar throughout the Southwest. In the Rio Grande Valley, the prototype of the "Robber Baron" was Charles Stillman.

Stillman arrived in the valley in 1846 and started a trading center in a cotton field across the river from the Mexican town of Matamoros. Within four years the town of Brownsville developed. This town was full of warehouses, wharves, and a booming trade with Mexico. This boom drove land prices up and attracted more Anglo-Americans, who came without their families and who were ready to capitalize on the prosperity.

A substantial number of the newcomers were war veterans who still remembered the war and looked upon Mexicans as a conquered race. They felt that Mexicans had done nothing to improve the land, and that they benefited from the Anglo-American occupation. These men did not recognize Mexican land titles and felt few qualms about taking property from them. Racial and nativist arguments justified their chicanery. At first, Stillman and others feared that the state of Texas would protect Mexican land claims, so they attempted to separate the valley from the rest of Texas in order to create their own state. They played on the Mexicans' regional feelings and got them to support their scheme. This group enlisted powerful congressional allies such as Henry Clay and William Seward. The separatists were led by Richard King, James O'Donnell, Charles Stillman, Captain Mifflin Kenedy, and Sam Belden—all prominent members of the privileged elite. Their plans for separation proved unnecessary because it was soon evident that the state of Texas supported the Anglos' encroachments.

Charles Stillman was from New England, the descendant of Puritan merchants. Conditions in the valley and the trusting nature of the Mexicans proved to be a bonanza to him. He used unscrupulous means to build up his annual earnings to $50,000. His trading post was built on land that did not belong to him; the land around Brownsville belonged to the descendants of Francisco Cavazos. After 1848, the Cavazos family's title was known as *El Espiritú Santo* Grant. Stillman wanted the land, but he did not want to pay for it. He purposely confused the ownership of the land. Squatters moved onto the Cavazos' land and claimed it. They based their action on veterans' as well as squatters' rights. These actions violated the Treaty of Guadalupe Hidalgo and its Statement of Protocol; however, this meant little to Stillman. He purchased the squatters' claims, as well other questionable titles, but refused to deal with the Cavazos family, knowing he had the support of the troops at Fort Brown.

The Cavazos family was not intimidated and fought Stillman in the courts, but Stillman was confident about the outcome of the case. Judge Waltrous, the presiding judge, was his personal friend. Moreover, many Anglos believed that the "whole *Espiritú Santo* Grant should be thrown out on the grounds that the owners were Mexicans."[34] Stillman, however, had made many enemies who lobbied the judge to decide against Stillman. On January 15, 1852, Judge Waltrous ruled in favor of the Cavazos family, validating the

Espíritu Santo Grant. But then, Stillman had his lawyers, the firm of Basse and Horde, offer $33,000 for the grant, which in 1850 was evaluated at $214,-000.[35] Stillman had made it known that he would appeal the decision, so the Cavazos family accepted the offer; the legal costs to defend the grant would have been prohibitive. Moreover, the Cavazos family knew that Stillman had influence in the political and judicial structure of the state. After the sale, the law firm transferred title to Stillman, yet he did not pay the $33,000; neither did the law firm, since it went bankrupt.

Stillman's tactics were duplicated throughout Texas. The Mexican's land and wealth quickly passed into the hands of the colonizers. By 1860 the Anglo-American completely dominated the Texas economy. A census taken in.that year showed that 263 Texans owned over $100,000 in real property; 57 of these wealthy men lived in southeast Texas; only two were of Mexican extraction and their holdings were in Cameron County. Bexar County had seven wealthy Texans, not one of which was a Mexican. Of significance is that the real property value and the personal worth of the 261 Texans was roughly in balance, while the two Mexicans' personal worth was far below their real wealth.[36]

Stillman's associate, Richard King, was the arch-robber baron of South Texas. His career is difficult to assess since his descendants control his records and have carefully censored them. Richard King amassed over 600,000 acres of land during his lifetime, and his widow increased the family holdings to over 1,000,000 acres.

The King Ranch Corporation commissioned a professional author and artist, Tom Lea, to eulogize Richard King in a two-volume work entitled *The King Ranch*.[37] Lea portrays King as a tough-minded, two-fisted Horatio Alger who brought prosperity to South Texas. In the process, Richard King, according to Lea, never harmed anyone, except in self-defense. Lea denies charges against King and ignores the allegations that he unscrupuously drove out small Mexican ranchers to get their land and was brutal to those who opposed him. When referring to Mexican resentment toward Anglos like King, Lea writes:

> In their encounter, Americans were apt to feel superior and Mexicans were apt to feel abused. An ordinary American was more prosperous—because he paid more attention to "prosperity"—than an ordinary Mexican, so that an economic division generally conformed with racial cleavage to more sharply align the border's array of old resentments and mistrusts.[38]

The upshot is that Lea whitewashed King and his kind, much in the same manner that Alan Nevins did when he rechristened the robber barons of the East as the "captains of industry."

Historians writing about King undoubtedly have been influenced by Lea's work. Few have relied on what Mexicans feel about him. In our portrayal of King, we use the Lea work in order to expose the inconsistencies. It is hoped that someday a Chicano scholar, using Mexican sources, will document the

Mexican version of the story—that men such as King and Mifflin Kenedy were cattle rustlers who operated with the protection of the state to increase their holdings.

Richard King was born in 1824 in New York City of poor Irish immigrant parents. As a youth he ran away to sea, eventually becoming a pilot on a steamboat that was mastered by Mifflin Kenedy.[39] The two men became fast friends. The Mexican-American War took them to the Rio Grande, and after the war, they remained to cash in on the boom. King ran a flophouse at Boca del Rio[40] and later bought a vessel from the U.S. government and went into the freighting business.[41] Much of his business consisted of smuggling goods to the Mexican ranchers and miners in northern Mexico.

Although at first the principal competitor of King and Kenedy was Charles Stillman, in 1850, they joined him.[42] The association prospered, soon monopolizing the water-borne trade into northern Mexico.[43] In 1852, King purchased the *Santa Gertrudis* Grant; according to Lea, King knew that the holdings were abandoned since they were under the *gringo* flag, which he knew the Mexicans distrusted.[44] Title to 15,500 acres cost him less than two cents an acre.[45] King also entered into a land purchasing partnership with Gideon K. Lewis, later buying Lewis's shares.

Although Lea says that many Mexican cattle were stolen, he does not implicate King.[46] It is, however, common knowledge among Mexican border settlers that King did participate in these operations. King was also involved in the chase of Juan Cortina, which we shall describe later in this chapter.

During the Civil War, King was pro-South and profited from the war trade by selling cattle, horses, and mules to the troops. He continued his freighting operations, running Union blockades by flying the Mexican flag.[47] In 1866, Stillman left the border area, and King and Kenedy took over many of his operations.

In 1872, the Mexican Border Commission reported that much of the border friction was caused by Texas thieves. The report claimed that Mexicans raided the Nueces area to retrieve their stolen cattle, and that Richard King branded calves "that belonged to his neighbor's cows."[48] Lea discounts the report, however, because the Mexicans were condemned for the raids by the citizens of Brownsville and by a U.S. congressional committee.[49] During this period, King became president of the Stock Raisers Association of Western Texas. It was formed by Texas ranchers to protect their "interests." They organized Minute Companies to fight the so-called Mexican bandits. Later they disbanded when Ranger Captain McNeely took over the fight for them. McNeely's methods have already been discussed.

Although Lea attempted to exonerate King of wrongdoing by interpreting his actions as justifiable, nonetheless, certain facts emerge. King made his money as a smuggler; he associated with a band of cutthroats and, in fact, played a leading role in their operations; he was accused of cattle rustling and of murdering small land owners to get their land; and he paid bonuses to the Rangers. We can only rest our case on T. R. Fehrenbach's statement:

45

In the 1850s, the border towns of El Paso and Brownsville, and San Antonio itself, were dominated by a handful of leading merchants or financial men, none of whom were born in Texas or the south. This peculiar politico-social system, in which ethnic Mexicans usually possessed numerical superiority but remained politically inert as individuals, became a lasting feature of south-Texas life. . . . The early entrepreneurs . . . became ranchers. In this way Richard King and Mifflin Kenedy, who with a few others at one-time dominated all Texas south of the Nueces from Brownsville, became two of the largest landowners in the South. In the 1850s the nucleus of the immense King Ranch was formed.[50]

The Revolt of Cheno Cortina

King's method of subjugation of the Chicano was repeated throughout the Southwest. Collectively Mexicans became the poor, the powerless, and the oppressed, whereas the Anglo-Americans were the symbol of the wealthy oppressor. This process produced a reaction on the part of Mexicans and resulted in intense banditry. While a few Anglo-American historians have conceded that often the Mexican *bandido* was driven to the highway, most of the chroniclers justify his repression; they rationalize that the *bandido's* behavior was criminal, or at the least, it was the outgrowth of frontier conditions.

The system was, however, the main cause of Mexican outlaw activity, because law enforcement authorities often were the thieves and the assassins. E. J. Hobsbawm, in his *Primitive Rebels: Studies in Archaic Forms of Social Movement in the 19th and 20th Centuries,* sheds considerable light on the *bandido's* motives. Taking Mexican banditry in the context of history, this writer concludes that it represented "in one sense . . . a primitive form of organized social protest, perhaps the most primitive we know."[51]

In studying the California outlaw Tiburcio Vásquez (see chapter 5), we see that in order to retain his honor, he broke an Anglo-American law. Once this happened he became an outcast who was forced to steal to survive. Like other Mexican *bandidos,* his activities were directed against the Anglo-American and only in time of dire need did he steal from his own people. In this way, he retained the support of the Mexican people, who considered him a hero, a Robin Hood of sorts, even though he never gave to the poor. To the Mexican, the *bandido* killed just for revenge. In this way, he became "The tough man . . . unwilling to bear traditional burdens of the common man in a class society, poverty and meekness."[52] He revolted against the *gringo* and was admired by his people for doing what they were unwilling to do.

Vásquez and other Mexican bandits easily fit the Hobsbawm model of the primitive rebel; however, Juan N. Cortina, who has been called the "Red Robber of the Rio Grande," goes beyond the *bandido* model. Unlike the social bandit, he had an organization with a definite ideology and organization that led guerrilla warfare against the *gringo* Establishment. As with so much of the Chicano's history, the Mexican records must be examined, especially those of Tamaulipas, to understand the rise of Juan Cortina.

As in the case of most social rebels, an attempt has been made to discredit

Cortina's motives. Most Anglo-American historians have labeled him an outlaw. They portray him as an illiterate rogue who came from a good family but "turned bad."[53] Lyman Woodman, a retired military officer, wrote a biography of Cortina, describing him as a "soldier, bandit, murderer, cattle thief, mail robber, civil and military governor of the State of Tamaulipas, and general in the Mexican army" who was, in short, a *gringo* hater.[54]

In contrast, Mexicans have eulogized his exploits in *corridos*. Cortina conducted guerrilla warfare against Anglo domination and was supported by the common people. A recent study sums up the reaction of the few Mexicans who opposed him:

> Some members of the patron class opposed Cortina because their commercial interests required peace with the Americans; others feared that the United States would not be satisfied with Texas, New Mexico, Arizona, and California, and would use Cortina's war as a pretext to "liberate" all of Mexico. It was admitted, however, by Major Heintzleman that "the marauders have active sympathy of the lower classes of the Mexican population."[55]

Juan "Cheno" Cortina, a product of Mexico's northern frontier, was born on May 16, 1822, in Camargo, located on the Mexican side of the river. His parents descended from the upper classes, and his mother owned a land grant in the vicinity of Brownsville.[56] Cortina and his family moved to that grant while the hostilities of the War of 1846 raged. He did not return to Mexico, and, under the terms of the Treaty of Guadalupe Hidalgo, became a U.S. citizen.[57] Cortina was a regionalist who identified with northern Mexico and who had fought to protect the land from the Anglo-Americans. He also resented the abuses, insults, and plundering that marked the Anglo-American occupation. It was a matter of time before he rebelled against it.

An insignificant and commonplace incident began Cortina's revolutionary career. On a hot July morning in 1859, while returning to his mother's ranch, he saw Marshall Bob Spears pistol-whipping a Mexican who had had too much to drink. The victim had worked for Cheno's mother. When Cheno offered to take responsibility for the offender, Spears replied: "What is it to you, you damned Mexican?" Cortina fired a warning shot, and then:

> Cortinas [sic] promptly shot the marshall in the shoulder, took the Mexican behind him and galloped out of town in the grand style of an American cowboy or a Mexican *vaquero* on a holiday. This episode had about it the dramatic qualities that any rising young bandit—or hero—could desire. Cheno, popular member of the wealthy class, a Mexican, had shot down a representative of American law, rescued the humblest member of Mexican society, and carried him boldly away to a safe retreat on his mother's Santa Rita Ranch.[58]

Cheno knew he could not get a fair trial, so he prepared to leave for Tampico, Mexico. Before his departure, he learned about further Anglo-American transgressions. Later, with a small group of friends, he returned to Brownsville to bring the oppressors to justice. On September 28, they rode into that city and raised the Mexican flag. Cortina's detractors claim that he plundered the city; however, his partisans point out that he did not rob and steal when he had the city at his mercy as he certainly would have done had he been a bandit."[59] Whether Cortina did or did not plunder Brownsville is still a point of contention.

Cortina did not plan to lead a revolution. Nevertheless, from his mother's *Rancho del Carmen,* he issued a circular justifying his actions. The crux of his "declaration of grievances" was the injustice that the Mexican people suffered at the hands of the occupiers. He said he had gone to Brownsville solely to punish those guilty of terrorizing Mexicans, and he appealed to the Anglo-American government to bring the "oppressors of the Mexicans" to justice and not to protect them. Cortina, after issuing his statement, again prepared to emigrate to Mexico.[60]

Seeking revenge, the Brownsville citizens took Tomás Cabrera prisoner. Cabrera was a man of advanced age whose only crime was that he was Cortina's friend. When the *caudillo* (regional strongman) learned that his friend had been arrested, he recruited an army of 1200 men. He demanded the old man's release, threatening to burn Brownsville if the townspeople did not comply. The Brownsville Tigers (the local militia) and the Mexican army at Matamoros attacked him, but Cortina defeated them in battle, whereupon the *gringos* lynched Cabrera. The Rangers were called in, and they chased Cortina, but he defeated them on November 22.

Flushed by his victories, he "envisioned raising an army powerful enough to force the Texas authorities to grant the Mexicans those rights . . . guaranteed them by the Treaty of Guadalupe Hidalgo."[61] He issued a notice that "reviewed the crimes against Mexicans" and suggested that the colonized form a secret society to achieve justice. The document is a classic example of the motivations of a liberator. In it he charged that the Mexicans' land had been stolen from them by "flocks of vampires, in guise of men," who "came and scattered themselves in the settlements, without any capital, except the corrupt heart and the most perverse intentions. Some brimful of laws, pledged us their protection against the attacks of the rest; others assembled in shadowy councils, attempted and excited the robbery and burning of the houses of relatives on the other side of the river Bravo; while others, to the abusing of our unlimited confidence, when we entrusted them with our titles [of land] . . ." robbed the Mexicans. Cortina condemned the Anglo justice law, stating, "It would appear that justice had fled from this world, leaving you to the caprice of your oppressors. . . ." The liberation leader continued, "This race has never humbled itself before the conqueror." He exclaimed, "Mexicans! My part is taken; the voice of revelation whispers to me that to me is entrusted the work of breaking the chains of your slavery, and that the Lord will enable me, with powerful arm to fight against our enemies." Cortina called for the liberation of Mexicans and the "exterminating [of] their tyrants."[62]

The colonial government then intensified its oppression. Many innocent people were the victims of the colonizers' wrath; they were murdered in cold blood. Well-trained and well-equipped federal troops poured into the valley, forcing Cortina across the border. This did not end the threat, and a state commissioner wrote Governor Sam Houston: "The Mexicans are arming everything that can carry a gun, and I anticipate much trouble here. I believe that a general war is inevitable. . . . New arms have been distributed to all the *rancheros,* so I apprehend trouble."[63] Houston appealed to the federal government for assistance and wrote to the secretary of war in Washington, D.C.:

> I will deplore the situation in Texas, an empty treasury, the Indian troubles, unexampled for the last 10 years, and the forays from Mexico on our southern borders, are well calculated to impress the mind of the executive of the State of Texas with the intricacies of the attitude which he has in justice to his fellow-citizens and humanity, to assume, should not the Federal arm be speedily raised and extended in behalf of our suffering frontier.[64]

Washington responded in February 1860 by sending Robert E. Lee to Texas to lead the expeditions against Cortina. Mexican authorities cooperated with Lee.

> Throughout the month of March, as in all his black career, there were many conflicting ideas about Cortina's activities and whereabouts. Even Lee, an honored veteran of the Mexican War, ex-superintendent of the Military Academy, and an officer with considerable experience in chasing Indian raiders all over Texas, was confounded by the wily bandit; he wrote back to his wife, Betsy, in Virginia, of "that myth Cortina."[65]

Rumors raged that Cortina threatened all strategic points, but by May 8, Lee believed that Cortina had abandoned the frontier and he left Texas.

Cortina, however, did not abandon his war with the *gringo;* he merely shifted his base of operations. He became active in the affairs of Tamaulipas, defending that state against the French intervention that began in 1861 and ended in 1867. After the war, he settled in Tamaulipas, where he allegedly made and unmade governors.* He allegedly led rustling operations against the Anglo-Americans and had a flourishing trade with Cuba, thus hitting at the heart of Anglo-American concerns—its economy.** Rip Ford, the journalist, politician, and sometime Ranger, reported: "Cortina hates Americans, particularly Texans. . . . He has an old and deep-seated grudge against Brownsville."[66]

In the meantime, Cortina cleaned up banditry in Tamaulipas. Anglo-Americans claimed that he "told thieves in Mexico that he would hang them

---

*Cortina had been the military governor of that state, as well as a general in the Mexican army.

**Woodman, p. 99, reports that King and Kenedy lost 200,000 head of cattle and 5300 horses from 1869 to 1872.

for stealing in that country, but that there was plenty for them to take in Texas."[67]

Anglo-American influence in Mexico increased during the 1870s and pressure was brought to get rid of Cortina. He remained active, however, and had his private troops called *Los Fieles de Cortina* and *Los Exploradores.* In the valley, he had a network of spies and partisans called *las aquilas negras.* Charges were brought against him, and investigations were conducted; but he was untouchable until 1875, when he was taken to Mexico City and jailed on charges of cattle rustling. When Porfirio Díaz seized power, Cortina was exiled to Mexico City. He did not return to the border until the spring of 1890, when he visited the area for a brief time, receiving a hero's welcome. With the growing awareness of the struggle of Chicanos for liberation, Cortina is recognized today as one of the precursors to the movement.

The People's Revolt

The El Paso Salt War of 1878 is an example of a people's revolt. Mexicans in the country banded together along the lines of race and class, taking direct action to effect an economic and political change in response to the political chicanery of foreigners who took away a traditional right. The mob's action had no seeming ideology behind it, other than an emotional response to the oppression. It was, nevertheless, a class struggle against the rich, powerful *gringo* Establishment.[68] In this manner, it became a primitive insurrection—a people's revolt—against the foreign occupier's domination.

The El Paso area was settled by Mexicans in the early 1600s, and until the 1840s most of the population lived south of the Rio Grande. After the Mexican-American War, settlements sprang up north of the river, capitalizing on the Chihuahua-Texas-New Mexico trade. Even then, the population on the north side was overwhelmingly Mexican. Soon a handful of Anglo-Americans arrived in El Paso County. They immediately took control of the county's politics, managing the Mexican vote through agents who were rewarded through patronage. They were aided by the distribution of the Mexican population, which was dispersed in small hamlets around the present-day city of El Paso. Moreover, Mexicans were not familiar with Anglo politics, and the politicians purposely did not include or educate them. By 1870 the population of El Paso County had grown to 12,000, "all but eighty of whom were Mexican."[69] Despite this fact, Anglo-Americans held the majority of elected offices as well as the wealth of the county.

The Mexicans were almost all poor and Spanish-speaking. In 1862, the lives of these marginally subsisting people were lightened by the discovery of salt at a location about 100 miles from the area where most of the population was clustered. People made trips to the salt beds to obtain salt for their own use as well as for sale to Mexicans south of the river. It had not occurred to them individually to claim the beds. However, Sam Maverick from San Antonio soon staked out a substantial portion of the salt beds. Still, the Mexicans continued to use the remaining portion, content to take out what they could use.

The salt beds came to the attention of Anglo politicos who conspired to gain control of the portion of the beds being used by the Mexicans in order to derive profit. The conspirators became known as the Salt Ring. The scheme might have succeeded if a split had not occurred in their party ranks. The contention crystallized during the election of 1870, when A. J. Fountain ran against the Salt Ring's leader, W. W. Mills, for a seat in the state senate. He ran with the support of Antonio Borajo, an Italian priest, and campaigned on the promise that the salt beds would be made public. Fountain defeated the ring.

Fountain attempted to keep his campaign promise, but he had a falling out with Borajo, who wanted him to stake out the beds and share the profits with him. The state senator's refusal led to the end of his political career in El Paso, with Borajo joining Louis Cardis, another Italian, to back Charles Howard in 1875 for county judge. Cardis, it was agreed, would run for state senator. Both men were elected. Borajo and Cardis's power rested in their ability to speak Spanish, allowing them to cultivate the Mexican majority. Moreover, Borajo used his powers as a priest. It appeared that the three men would control the county's politics, but Howard defected, staking out the salt beds for himself in his father-in-law's name.[70] This ended his political career in 1877, when the two Italians opposed him; however, he still had control of the beds.

Howard then attempted to profit from the "legal" claim by charging the Mexicans for the salt they removed. Borajo tried to incite the people from the pulpit, but he was removed by the bishop for meddling in politics. The friction continued, however, and two Mexicans were arrested when local authorities learned that they intended to remove salt in violation of the law. When one of the Mexicans was imprisoned, several hundred of his *paisanos* (countrymen) from San Elizario and Ysleta forcibly freed him, calling mass meetings to demand their rights. Soon afterwards, they seized Howard and held him prisoner for three days. He was not released until he promised to leave the county and to post a bond to insure that he would not return.

Although Howard left El Paso, he had every intention of returning. He knew that the authorities would enforce his claim and that a double standard existed. His conduct defies comprehension, for he returned to El Paso and shot Cardis down in cold blood. Authorities did not prosecute Howard, nor did they forfeit his bond. In fact, Major John B. Jones of the Texas Rangers actively cooperated with him. Meanwhile, he wrote a friend that he "did not wish to see general punishment visited on the rioters, who were ignorant as mules and misled, but thought that the leaders should be punished and made to respect the law," concluding that, "If the governor don't help us, I am going to bushwacking. . . ."[71]

In 1878, Howard returned to El Paso, where authorities released him on bail. Local authorities moved to support his claim, and Rangers set out with him to see to it that Mexicans did not take the salt. This action triggered a response, and 18 Chicanos led by Chico Barela captured them. At first they hesitated in taking direct action, but when word arrived from Borajo to "Shoot the *gringos* and I will absolve you,"[72] they shot Howard. The local authorities

51

moved to punish the Mexicans, touching off several days of rioting, which were ended when Rangers, joined by other *gringos,* suppressed the Mexicans. This revolt was clearly racial and was caused by extreme economic exploitation.

Conclusion

The events in the Rio Grande Valley and in El Paso County were not unique. The same process of economic and political subjugation took place in other areas of Texas. For example, in San Antonio, the Mexican city of Texas, Mexicans were pushed out and those remaining were employed as maids, servants, and other low-paid workers. Caroline Remy writes about this subjugation:

> In 1837 all but one of the forty-one candidates of the municipal election were of Spanish-Mexican descent; a decade later there were only five. Erosion of the land base which formed the principal wealth of the Spanish-Mexican began almost immediately after the Texas Revolution. From 1845–1860 the fine houses and buildings erected belonged to the Irish, American, German, and French citizens. The Mexicano had little economic influence. While San Antonio seemed Mexican in appearance and ways, the population increase during these years was largely non-Mexican.[73]

The colonization of Texas continued throughout the nineteenth century and exists to this day. In 1932, Jovita González, an activist, summarized the Mexicans' reaction to the subjugation:

> Mexicans considered Americans in Texas as intruders . . . vandals . . . aggressors, waiting for the opportunity to deprive them of their personal possessions as they had deprived the mother country of a whole province. On the other hand, the Americans looked upon the Mexicans as a conquered, inferior race, despised because of their inability to check American advances. Because they were the conquered race the Mexicans were considered cowards . . . while the big ranchmen prospered and profited, the small Texas-Mexican landowner was forced to abandon his property and either became a peon or leave the country.[74]

The Chicanos' struggle to regain self-determination and to retain their culture during these years was not told, because Texas historians, writing from an Anglo perspective, legitimized the suppression directed by a handful of *gringos.* Until recently, the conclusions of men such as Walter Prescott Webb were taken as gospel. Nonetheless, the Chicano's story was kept alive by *corridos* and oral tradition that glorified the exploits of men like Juan Cortina and Gregorio Cortez, who resisted the oppressors "with pistols in their hands." The Mexican's role during these years was confined collectively to that of the low-skilled wage earner. In fact, it has been conceded that his labor made the growth of Texas possible, much in the same way that the Black's sweat contributed to the Southeast's economy. The Mexican, meanwhile, organized *mutualistas,* and from them trade unions and civic and political organizations, which have kept the resistance alive. Today this struggle is paying off in successes such as, for example, *La Raza Unida* party (see chapters 9 and 10) taking over Crystal City, Texas, signaling the beginning of the thrust toward political self-determination. Mexicans in Texas have also won their struggle to retain their cultural identity, and the majority speak Spanish, identifying with their Mexican past. Nationalism has become the unifying thread in this struggle.

Notes

1. T. R. Fehrenbach, *Lone Star: A History of Texas and the Texans* (New York: The Macmillan Company, 1968), p. 465.

2. Fehrenbach, p. 677.

3. Larry McMurtry, *In A Narrow Grave* (Austin, Tex.: Encino Press, 1968), p. 39.

4. McMurtry, p. 40.

5. McMurtry, p. 40.

6. McMurtry, p. 40.

7. McMurtry, p. 40.

8. McMurtry, p. 40.

9. McMurtry, p. 40.

10. McMurtry, p. 41.

11. McMurtry, p. 41.

12. McMurtry, p. 43.

13. Llerena B. Friend, "W. P. Webb's Texas Rangers," *Southwestern Historical Quarterly,* January 1971, p. 294.

14. Friend, p. 321.

15. Friend, p. 321.

16. Américo Paredes, *With a Pistol in His Hand* (Austin: University of Texas Press, 1958).

17. Paredes, p. 169.

18. Editorial by John Salmon Ford in the *Texas Democrat,* 9 September 1846, quoted in Fehrenbach, p. 465.

19. Fehrenbach, pp. 473–474.

20. Walter Prescott Webb, *The Texas Rangers: A Century of Frontier Defense* (Austin: University of Texas Press, 1965), p. xv.

21. Paredes, p. 31.

22. Paredes, p. 29.

23. Paredes, p. 30.

24. Webb, p. 463.

25. Webb, ·p. 464.

26. Paul Jacobs and Saul Landau, with Eve Pell, *To Serve the Devil,* vol. 1 (New York: Vintage Books, 1971), p. 240.

27. Paredes, pp. 25–26.

28. Webb, pp. 477–478.

29. Tom Tide, "Chicanos Won't Miss Ranger," *New Chronicle* (Thousand Oaks, California), 4 November 1970.

30. Tide, *New Chronicle,* 4 November 1970.

31. McMurtry, pp. 41, 42.

32. Paredes, p. 7.

33. Paredes, p. 10.

34. Charles W. Goldfinch, *Juan Cortina 1824–1892: A Re-Appraisal* (Brownsville, Tex.:

The Bishop's Print Shop, 1950), p. 21.

35. Goldfinch, p. 36.

36. Ralph Wooster, "Wealthy Texans," *Southwestern Historical Quarterly,* October 1967, pp. 163, 173.

37. Tom Lea, *The King Ranch,* 2 vols. (Boston, Mass.: Little, Brown and Company, 1957).

38. Lea, vol. 1, p. 457.

39. Lea, vol. 1, pp. 8–9.

40. Lea, vol. 1, p. 42.

41. Lea, vol. 1, p. 45.

42. Lea, vol. 1, pp. 58–59.

43. Lea, vol. 1, p. 73.

44. Lea, vol. 1, pp. 100–101.

45. Lea, vol. 1, p. 104.

46. Lea, vol. 1, pp. 107–108.

47. Lea, vol. 1, pp. 179–180.

48. Lea, vol. 1, p. 275.

49. Lea, vol. 1, pp. 275–276.

50. Fehrenbach, p. 289.

51. E. J. Hobsbawm, *Primitive Rebels: Studies in Archaic Forms of Social Movement in the 19th and 20th Centuries* (New York: W. W. Norton & Company, Inc., 1965), p. 13.

52. Hobsbawm, p. 13.

53. Webb, p. 176.

54. Lyman Woodman, *Cortina: Rogue of the Rio Grande* (San Antonio, Tex.: The Naylor Company, 1950), p. 8.

55. Jacobs and Laudau, p. 235.

56. Goldfinch, p. 17.

57. José T. Canales, *Juan N. Cortina Presents His Motion for a New Trial* (San Antonio, Tex.: Artes Graficas, 1951), p. 6.

58. Webb, p. 178.

59. Goldfinch, p. 44.

60. Goldfinch, p. 45.

61. Goldfinch, p. 48.

62. Wayne Moquin *et al.,* eds., *A Documentary History of the Mexican American* (New York: Frederick A. Praeger, Publishers, 1971), pp. 207–209.

63. Woodman, p. 53.

64. Woodman, p. 55.

65. Woodman, p. 59.

66. John Salmon Ford, *Rip Ford's Texas* (Austin: University of Texas Press, 1963), p. 371.

67. Woodman, pp. 98–99.

68. Hobsbawm, pp. 110–112.

69. Carey McWilliams, *North From Mexico* (New York: Greenwood Press, 1968), p. 110.

70. Webb, p. 350; Jack C. Vowell, Jr., "Politics at El Paso: 1850–1920" (M.A. thesis, Western College at El Paso, Texas, 1952), pp. 65–66.

71. Webb, p. 356.

72. Webb, pp. 360–361; Vowell, pp. 69–70.

73. Caroline Remy, "Hispanic Mexican San Antonio: 1836–1961," *Southwestern Historical Quarterly,* April 1968, p. 570.

74. Jovita González, "Historical Background of the Lower Rio Grande Valley," *Lulac News* (San Antonio, Texas), September 1932, p. 5.

Chapter Three

Freedom in a Cage:
The Expansion into New Mexico

In a speech at the University of California at Los Angeles in 1968, Chicano activist Reies López Tijerina summed up the grievances of the Mexican people in New Mexico:

> We are angry because they have stolen our lands and language. They gave us the "freedom" a man gives to a bird in a cage. They took the scissors and clipped both wings [land and language]. Language is our freedom—language which is the result of the accumulated centuries—the food left us by our forefathers.[1]

The suppression of Mexican culture and the land robbery in New Mexico is well documented. The injustices have, however, been obscured by the socialization process whereby many Mexicans have come to accept myths about their role in the political, economic, and cultural life of the state, taking for themselves the values of the conquerors and forgetting about their past, present, and future. In his speech, Tijerina was reminding the Chicanos of this cultural genocide.

Many New Mexicans have found security in the belief that they were assimilated into the new culture and that they became effective participants in the democratic process. This belief has been articulated often enough that the colonized have come to deny their oppression and have thus even evaluated their failures as successes. The reality that a small oligarchy of Anglo-Americans established their privilege at the expense of the Mexican masses has been submerged by the desire of New Mexicans to believe in their acceptance in the new society. Even the knowledgeable Fray Angelico Chávez, a prominent New Mexican Catholic priest, historian, and writer, stated as late as 1970:

> In short New Mexico quickly became a willing enclave of the United States, all of her citizens of whatever economic or social level deeming themselves true and loyal American citizens. And what they evidently liked best, the poor as well as the more affluent, was the game of politics within the framework of the Democratic and Republican parties. It has become New Mexico's chief indoor and outdoor sport with all the shenanigans connected with it.[2]

Although Fray Angelico's perspective defies history, it is at the crux of our task to correct New Mexican myths. In order to survive economically, many of the descendants of the original New Mexican settlers found it necessary to separate themselves from other Chicanos. This led many New Mexicans to label themselves Spanish-Americans, as distinguished from other Mexicans. They rationalized that they were the descendants of the original settlers, who were Spanish *conquistadores* (conquerors). According to them, New Mexico was isolated from the rest of the Southwest and Mexico during the colonial era; thus, they remained racially pure and were European, in contrast to the *mestizo* (half-breed) Mexican.

By this process, they believed that they could separate themselves from the intense discrimination against Mexicans, allowing them to better their economic and, in some cases, their social situation. George Sánchez, Arthur L. Campa, Carey McWilliams, and others have exploded this "fantasy heritage." Indeed, the *Hispanos* were Mexicans, for the majority of the original settlers from Mexico in 1598 were males who, over the years, mixed with the Pueblo Indians of the region, as well as with Mexican Indians who settled in the area. During the nineteenth century, although the label Spanish-American was used throughout the Southwest and Latin America, the New Mexican was commonly referred to by Anglo-Americans as Mexican. Nancie González wrote that it was not until the twentieth century that the New Mexican consciously removed himself from his Mexican identity. The cause was that during the 1910s and 1920s there was a large influx of Mexican laborers into New Mexico, and at the same time, many Texans, Oklahomans, and other Southerners settled in the eastern plains, intensifying discrimination against Mexicans. The more affluent New Mexicans, believing they were Caucasians, rationalized to the Anglos: "You don't like Mexicans, and we don't like them either; but we are Spanish-Americans, not Mexicans."[3] By this simple denial of their heritage, New Mexicans thought they could escape discrimination and become eligible for higher paying jobs.

The Myth of the Bloodless Conquest

Fray Angelico also expounded the myth that New Mexicans peacefully joined the Anglo nation and "became a willing enclave of the United States." This is known as "the myth of the bloodless conquest of New Mexico," which has been repeated by a majority of historians and is believed by most people. With this sleight of hand New Mexicans were no longer the victims of history and, consequently, the enemies, but were the willing friends of the Anglo-Americans. This was not the case, however, since the 50,000 to 60,000 people who lived in New Mexico were not enthusiastic about the United States' invasion of their land; only a handful of merchants saw it as an advantage. Anglo historian of New Mexico, Lynn I. Perrigo, explodes the myth of the bloodless conquest, writing:

> The legend that the occupation of New Mexico was peacefully accomplished has a foundation only in the circumstances surrounding the original *entrada* of Kearny. Before the territory was brought fully under American administration, the conquest precipitated considerable bloodshed. Altogether at Santa Cruz, Taos, Mora, Las Vegas, and El Brazito, nearly three hundred Mexicans had been killed and thirty-some Americans lost their lives.[4]

Actually, the hostilities began many years before Kearny's entrance into New Mexico in 1846. Texans claimed that their boundary followed the Rio Grande and included a sizeable portion of New Mexico. After 1836, tensions between the New Mexicans and the Texans increased. New Mexicans knew that Anglo-Texans hated them, and they resented the treatment Mexicans suffered at the hands of Anglo-Americans. They had cause for alarm when the controversial Santa Fe venture threatened them in 1841.

Some Texan historians allege that the situation started with a simple trading expedition to New Mexico. New Mexicans, however, viewed the incident differently. The facts are that General Hugh McLeod led an expedition of about 300 Texans, divided into six military companies, into New Mexico. Governor Manuel Armijo sounded a general alarm. His militia was badly equipped, but he succeeded in tricking the Texans into believing he had a large army, with the result that the Texans surrendered.

The fate of the Anglo-Americans caused considerable controversy. One source charged: "Many of the prisoners were shot down in cold blood, others cruelly tortured, and most of them forced into a death march southward apparently as dreadful as the march of Bataan."[5] However, historian Hubert Howe Bancroft's version differed. He gave little credence to the atrocities, writing that, to the New Mexicans, "They [the Texans] were simply armed invaders, who might expect to be attacked, and if defeated, to be treated by the Mexicans as rebels, or at best—since Texan belligerency and independence had been recognized by several nations—as prisoners of war."[6] Bancroft concluded: "There can be no doubt that Governor Armijo was fully justified in seizing the Texan invaders, disarming them, confiscating their property, and sending them to Mexico as prisoners of war."[7]

The Texans retaliated: they raided, plundered, and murdered Mexicans in the aftermath of the Santa Fe filibuster. A nasty guerrilla war with racial overtones followed, with both sides guilty of atrocities. The problem, however, is that historians, wanting to justify Anglo aggression and absolve the United States of guilt, have ignored the activities of the Texans while concentrating on the excesses of Mexicans.

By the time Zachary Taylor led his attack on northern Mexico, no love was lost between Anglo-Texans and New Mexicans. Colonel Stephen Watts Kearny, in June 1846, prepared volunteers of the "Army of the West" to invade New Mexico and ultimately California. His instructions were to use peaceful persuasion whenever possible, force when necessary. By late June, he was ready to march his army west from Fort Leavenworth along the Santa Fe Trail. Governor Manuel Armijo had prepared to defend New Mexico. As Kearny approached New Mexico, he sent James W. Magoffin with an ultimatum to Governor Armijo, stating that if the New Mexicans surrendered they would not be disturbed; otherwise, they would suffer the consequences. Magoffin, a merchant, was well known and liked in New Mexico.[8] Some sources claim that the negotiators bribed Armijo to sell out the province. In fact, Magoffin later submitted a $50,000 bill to Washington, D.C., for "expenses," of which he received $30,000.[9] There is no proof that Armijo took the bribe, but there can be little doubt that his subsequent actions were highly suspicious, especially since Magoffin later boasted that he bribed Armijo.[10]

Armijo, despite the fact that he had a shortage of arms and trained men, could have defended the province. By August 1846, Kearny had taken Las Vegas, New Mexico, and prepared to attack Santa Fe. He had to pass through Apache Canyon, a narrow passage southeast of Santa Fe, where Armijo could easily have ambushed him. Surprisingly, he met no resistance at the canyon. Armijo had fled south without firing a shot, allowing the Army of the West to enter the capital. The governor had in all probability sold out his people.

The myth of a bloodless conquest stems largely from Armijo's inaction. Kearny was lulled into thinking that there would be no further resistance, and on September 25, he left for California. In mid-December, Colonel Alexander W. Doniphan was sent south to conquer Chihuahua. In actuality, the resistance had gone underground, but by the fall of 1846 it crystallized. Colonel Doniphan observed: "A people conquered but yesterday could have no friendly feeling for their conquerors, who have taken possession of their country, changed its laws and appointed new officers, principally foreigners."[11] Warren A. Beck, an authority on New Mexico, wrote: "The natives, especially those from the better classes, would not have been human had they not resented the overbearing, rowdy, and insulting Americans, who lost no opportunity to show their contempt of the 'greasers.' "[12] In fact, a movement to expel the hated *gringo* was afoot.

Influential New Mexicans conspired to drive their oppressors out of the province. The patriots included Tomás Ortiz; Colonel Diego Archuleta, a military commander; the controversial Padre Antonio José Martínez; and the Reverend Juan Felipe Ortiz, the vicar general of the diocese and brother of Tomás. The conspirators planned to attack the Anglo authorities during the Christmas season when many of them would be in Santa Fe and when the Anglo-American soldiers could be expected to be drinking heavily; the plan failed because a woman confidante informed Colonel Price, the military commander, of the impending revolt.

After this, the original leadership did not take part in further conspiracies. Anglo-Americans, moreover, believed that the spirit of the New Mexicans had been broken. They were, however, mistaken. The resentment of the masses smoldered. Pablo Montoya, a Mexican peasant, and Tomasito Romero, a pueblo Indian, emerged as the resistance leaders, attacking the colonials and killing Governor Bent, along with five other important persons. Soon afterwards New Mexicans killed several dozen more of their enemy. The revolt was spontaneous.

Meanwhile, Padre Martínez attempted to deter the rebellion. A realist, he knew that an unorganized revolt would be disastrous; he also knew the consequences of failure. The people, however, would not listen to him; conditions had become intolerable. Under the leadership of Colonel Price, well-armed soldiers retaliated by attacking some 1500 Mexican and pueblo Indians armed with bows, arrows, and lances. The army slaughtered the rebels on the snow-covered ground outside the insurgent capital of Taos. The defenders retreated into the pueblo's church, fighting bravely in the face of intense artillery fire.

> About 150 Mexicans were killed; some twenty-five or thirty prisoners were shot down by firing squads; and many of those who surrendered were publicly flogged. Colonel Price's troops are said to have been so drunk at the time that the Taos engagement was more of a massacre than a battle.[13]

The trial of the surviving rebels resembled that in other occupation situations: "One of the judges was a close friend of the slain governor and the other's son had been murdered by the rebels. The foreman of the grand jury was the slain governor's brother and one of the jurors a relative of the slain sheriff."[14] The town was so emotionally charged that it was surprising that the defendants received any kind of trial at all. Fifteen rebels were sentenced to death—one for high treason. After this, it became evident that armed revolt on a limited scale could not succeed.

The question of the land is at the heart of Mexican grievances against the United States. Anglo-American control of New Mexico did not just happen; an organized seizure of land followed the conquest. To understand how this took place, the Anglo-American and the Mexican pioneering experiences must be contrasted. The Anglo-American experience was largely based on the movement of individuals into new areas with the accoutrements of civilization following; the Mexican moved into the northwest collectively. The land was arid and, in order to survive, communal cooperation was necessary. The settlement of New Mexico was planned in advance. The principal institution was the pueblo; its plazas, *acequias* (water canals), and communal economy resembled those in other villages throughout the Spanish Americas. The government furnished new settlers with the basic equipment to farm their lands. They became members of a village and, in return, acquired rights to farm a plot of land and to use the communal pasturelands and forests. The villager had water rights, and necessity bound him to other members of the community. An interdependency existed among the villagers, with the settlers relying on each other for entertainment and assistance in building their homes, tending crops and animals, maintaining the village, and caring for the sick and the aged, as well as in burying the dead.

Life in the pueblos was not idyllic, for the privilege of a few was established by tradition. Some exploited their fellow villagers as well as the surrounding native Indians; however, even with the obvious flaws of the Mexican system, the small man shared in the land and Mexican law protected him. Many small farmers grazed their flocks on land that belonged to the state. Some Mexicans owned large land tracts, and many poor families lived on these *haciendas* (estates), free to use the land and the water as needed. After the initial confrontations between the Mexicans and the sedentary native Indians, both groups lived in relative harmony, with miscegenation taking place.

Despite the injustices, the society provided for a wider use of the land base than under the tenure system of the United States—supposedly more democratic because it favored the individual rather than the community. The Anglo-American system separated the Mexican from his land and heritage, placing the land almost exclusively in the control of a few.

The Anglo-American cycle of land grabbing resembled the one, described previously, that took place in Texas. The difference was that in New Mexico the Chicano settlements were more extensive. The province had many villages and some cities. Santa Fe had grown into a trade center. Extensive agriculture existed. Sheep raising gave the people their principal contact with the outside world. A definite life style had taken root, which changed little despite the concerted efforts by U.S. officials to change it. This life style exists in many small New Mexican villages, where Spanish is still spoken in spite of programs to replace it with English.

After 1848, Anglo-American opportunists moved into New Mexico to enjoy the spoils of conquest. Victory meant the right to exploit the territory's resources. These opportunists established their privilege, controlling the territorial government and administering its laws to further their political, economic, and social dominance. In the process, the Mexican lost his land. The Anglo-Americans systematically took the land by legal and illegal methods. A brief discussion of these methods is necessary to understand why so many New Mexicans are angry.

First, the Anglo-American superimposed his law and administrative rules upon the Spanish-speaking majority. Many were antithetical to the New Mexican's traditions. Authorities in many instances required Mexicans to register their land, and when they did not meet the deadline, they lost their land. Often the requirements were inadequately posted.

Second, Anglo-Americans taxed the Mexicans' land heavily, a practice that contrasted to Mexican custom. Many Mexicans lacked the capital to pay these impositions, and their land was sold at auction. Soon after the auction, unscrupulous officials, in collusion with the privileged, lowered the tax assessments.

Third, the Anglo-American economic system made access to capital imperative. The Anglos owned the banks, the prime sources from which Mexicans could obtain capital. The bankers charged excessive interest rates, and foreclosures followed the Mexicans' inability to meet the payments.

Fourth, the post–Civil War boom ushered in unprecedented greed and exploitation. Hoards of speculators arrived in New Mexico in search of easy money, caring little about the land or the natural grasses. Overuse and overgrazing of the land led to erosion of the soil, and with the range destroyed, the demise of the small farmer was hastened. In addition, timberlands were ruthlessly cut out, resulting in runoffs that further destroyed the soil.

Fifth, the government made large tracts of land available for agriculture, but contrary to popular belief, reclamation projects in general did not help the small farmer. They favored corporate agriculturalists who raised crops in large quantities. The efficiency of these combines completed the decline of the small farmer, who could not compete. Moreover, the reclamation projects changed the balance of nature, greatly affecting the Rio Grande. They reduced the supply of water in many areas and, in other places, provided too much water. The communal villages no longer had priority as they had under Mexican law. The people had no say as to where the government would build dams. New Mexican farmers had to pay for "improvements" whether they wanted them or not. When the farmers could not pay for these impositions, their land was taken from them in lieu of tax payments.[15]

Nancie L. González, in *The Spanish-Americans of New Mexico*, documents other examples of how government projects displaced the Mexican farmer. Dr. González states that increased use of the Rio Grande waters by farmers in Colorado lowered the water supply in northern New Mexico, depriving the small farmers of needed irrigation, while projects in the Mesilla Valley in southern New Mexico further displaced the small farmer. One example of the disastrous effects of a reclamation project is the Elephant Butte Dam, built in 1919. Large farm corporations were granted extensive land tracts, and using mechanized methods, they led in the production of cash crops, such as cotton. The small farmer could not compete, because he did not have the capital to mechanize. The dam raised the water level of the river in the Middle Valley, so when the rains came in the 1930s, much of the area was flooded, and the entire village of San Marchial was wiped out. In addition, the overflow along the banks of the river converted much of the small farmers' land into marshes, and once more the Chicano was the victim of "*gringo* progress."[16]

Sixth, the federal government granted large concessions of land to railroad corporations and to some institutions of higher learning. The history of fraud and exploitation of the nation's railways is well documented. On the other hand, public education in the United States traditionally has been a sacred cow that no one has ever really challenged. Funds allocated to public education in the past were automatically approved, and it was not until educational institutions became centers and advocates of change that they have come under fire. In the past as well as in the present, colleges and universities have not benefited the Chicano. Most *Mexicanos* have not reached high school, let alone institutions of higher learning, which have been reserved for the few. Moreover, these institutions produced teachers who Americanized many Chicanos, a traditional function of schools in the colonies, where education is used to socialize the colonized. Furthermore, the universities served as centers for research to develop machines for the benefit of big business, especially agribusiness. This has been at government expense, with machines and improved agricultural techniques used to replace Mexican labor. The tragedy is that the small man has had to pay for these gains, since the railroads received land belonging to the public domain and the universities were tax-supported.

Seventh, at the turn of the twentieth century conservationists, concerned over industry's rape of timber and recreation land, moved to create national forests. In retrospect, who paid for conservation? New Mexicans can answer that question; many blame their poverty on the creation of the U.S. Forest Service: "The most far-reaching event [in destroying communal lands] was the establishment of the National Forest early in this century. It diminished sheep and goats by preempting grazing lands and pasture; thus indirectly eliminating spinning, weaving and related skills."[17]

As a result of conservation and the frauds described in this section, the Mexican in New Mexico lost 2,000,000 acres of private lands and 1,700,000 of communal lands.

The New Mexicans' antiforester sentiment is vehement to this day. Stan Steiner, in *La Raza: The Mexican Americans,* quotes a New Mexican who denounces the forestry service and the government: "Our poverty is made and created by the Government of the United States. . . . The problem of the poor is that the Government of the United States creates poverty in the villages."[18] The accusation is substantiated by the fact that the federal government owns 34.9 percent of the land in New Mexico, the state government owns 12 percent, while federal Indian reservations own 6.8 percent. The state and federal governments together, therefore, own 53.7 percent of New Mexico, with the forestry service controlling one-third of the state's land.

Government ownership would be desirable if it were managed for the benefit of the majority, but this has not been the case. Bureaucrats manage the land as their private domain, giving preferential treatment to large interests. Moreover, the forestry service fenced off the forests and separated them from the villages to which they once belonged. The same New Mexican, quoted above by Steiner, laments: "We are almost in a concentration camp. . . . The Forest Service is fencing all around the villages, so that in a few years we will all be in a concentration camp. In other words, we are oppressed. . . ."[19] It is ironic that the U.S. government, which urged Latin American nations to reform their land policies for more equitable land distribution, is itself taking the land away from its citizens and placing it in the hands of modern day *latifundistas* (owners of gigantic plantations).

Foresters defend their actions, claiming that they are doing what is good for the greatest number of people, and that grazing permits in national forest land have been issued. This is so much rhetoric, since grazing permits have been issued only to large stock raisers. In fact, the government has consistently discouraged small operators by raising grazing fees, adding new fees, and shortening the grazing season. This policy is inequitable, since the land once belonged to the villagers. Peter Nabokov writes that U.S. government policy "is making them [the Chicanos] receive the loathed ten-pound brown bag of welfare powdered milk." As a consequence, New Mexicans still carry the memory "difficult for an Anglo to understand, that this land was a Spanish Pueblo's holding, never to be sold, always to be enjoyed and to yield communally."[20]

Makeshift solutions were advanced. After 1906, permits were issued for limited grazing in the national forests. They were codified by the Taylor Grazing Act of 1934. Stockmen were issued permits to graze on government land according to the number of animals they owned, so of course, the large operators got more. The permits could not be sold, but could be given away when the owners sold their animals. The big stockmen built up their stocks by buying out small operators.[21] Thus the small man was squeezed out and was unable to return to sheep raising.

An interesting postscript to the land grant question is that most archives housing important New Mexican documents were destroyed around 1870. The story goes that then Governor William A. Pike wanted additional office space, so he ordered the state librarian to remove old documents from the room where they were housed. The librarian sold some of the documents for wrapping paper and disposed of the rest as trash.[22] Valuable documents that might have shed some light on the land claims were thus destroyed, working to the advantage of the unscrupulous land grabbers. The motive behind Pike's action is not known. Many charged that he intentionally had the records destroyed because he was implicated with the infamous "Santa Fe Ring" that defrauded Chicanos out of millions of acres of land. Others say it was a serious blunder. Still others claim it was simply an act of stupidity.

Closely related to the Chicano's economic plight is his political exclusion. Until 1912, the federal government appointed the governor, and he was often a political hack who was appointed with the backing of the political machine in New Mexico. Anglos held the key appointive offices. In the state legislature, Chicanos were in the majority, but more often than not they were controlled by the Anglo oligarchy. In spite of this, the myth of "Spanish-American self-determination" persists.

New Mexico has, indeed, produced more Chicano leaders of national reputation than any other southwestern state. New Mexico has had two governors of Mexican extraction (but each was in office for less than a year). In addition the state has had three Chicano senators and a number of Chicano congressmen, mayors, judges, and other minor office holders. Some New Mexicans point to this as proof that they have more self-determination and political success than have their counterparts elsewhere. Many attribute this success to the political acuity—an ability to play the Anglo game—of the Mexican in New Mexico. However, their success is not surprising, considering their numerical majority in the state. During the 1850s the population of New Mexico was estimated at 60,000, the vast majority of which was Mexican. The quality of representation is questionable, for most elected representatives served through the grace of the Anglo Establishment and supported the latter's colonial rule. It would have been virtually impossible for the colonizers to keep so many dissatisfied Mexicans in check if the Mexicans' own leaders had not been involved in governing. This token representation, on the other hand, led many Chicanos to rationalize that "It's not the government but our own leaders who exploit us." Chicanos in office could also be held up to other Chicanos as success models to emulate. They could be lulled by these representatives' occasional protests on their behalf. The fact is, however, that the poor quality of representation by Mexican elected officials facilitated the land grab. If the New Mexicans had actually had self-determination, it is doubtful that they would have been bilked out of over four million acres.

The Americanization of the Catholic Church

In his speeches and writings, Tijerina has dwelt at length on the attempted suppression of the Chicanos' language, which, despite concerted opposition, the community in general has retained. In many of the New Mexican villages it is still the people's primary language, symbolizing their refusal to be Americanized. The Mexicans' reaction was not the same as other ethnic groups who, through the passage of time, have forgotten their language and have attempted to "outdo" the Anglo-American in his way of life. In the case of the North Africans and Asians, religious institutions served as a consolidating influence, as these institutions often were comprised exclusively of the colonized. The church was a place where the people congregated and aired their grievances, serving as a base for organizational resistance. The church's religious mission became a mission to improve the quality of life of its congregation, and gradually it became involved in social action.

The Roman Catholic church was the most important institution to the New Mexican; it most directly touched the masses, following them from the cradle to the grave. However, unlike the Irish clergy who provided unifying support for their congregations when Irish-Americans were faced with repression in the eastern United States, the New Mexico clergy became a passive ally of the state. Soon after the occupation, the church limited its functions to tending strictly to the spiritual needs of the people. With few exceptions, it did not champion the rights of the poor; instead, it worked to Americanize New Mexicans. Before the conquest, the New Mexican clergy had actively participated in championing the people. After 1850, control of the church went from the Mexicans to an Anglo-American hierarchy. It was an alien clergy that related more to the power Establishment and a few rich Anglo-American parishioners than to the masses of people. In actuality, it became a pacifying agent, encouraging the Mexicans to accept the occupation. It might be argued that these conclusions are not fair, since the church's responsibility was to Rome and not to Washington, D.C.; it might also be argued that accommodations were made in order to survive the anti-Catholic currents in Anglo-America during this period. This may be true. However, we must question whether the primary responsibility of priests and bishops—taking precedence over the interests of Rome, the vagaries of national politics and economics, or the construction of imposing edifices—is not to God and those made in his image.

Prior to and during the years of the occupation of New Mexico, there was one man who ministered to the people as a true man of God. His devotion to the Catholic church was deep and abiding, but he saw it as an institution for the benefit—not the enslavement—of mankind. Padre Antonio José Martínez was one of the most important figures in New Mexican history, as well as one of the most beloved. Although he was criticized because he was not a celibate, having had several mistresses and a number of children, his courageous defense of and loyalty to the humble people of New Mexico reduces the criticism to a triviality.

The "priest of Taos," as he was known, was born in Abiquir in Rio Arriba County, on January 7, 1793. He married in 1812 and had a daughter, but when his wife died, he entered the priesthood and was ordained in 1822. His daughter, Luz, died in 1825.[23] In 1824, Martínez took charge of a parish in Taos, where after two years he established a seminary. This school furthered Martínez's influence in relation to the New Mexican priests who graduated from the institution, since they became great advocates of his philosophy. He taught grammar, rhetoric, and theology, as well as law. From 1830 to 1836 he was a member of the Departmental Assembly. In 1835, he published a newspaper called *El Crespusculo* (*The Dawn*). He also wrote and printed books and pamphlets. During this period, he took a progressive religious stand, refusing to collect tithes from the poor and opposing large land grants, claiming the land should go to the people.[24]

After the Anglo-American occupation, Martínez continued his activism and was involved in the first liberation movement. He served in the legislature from 1851 to 1853. Known as a fighter against both church and state, he criticized the church for "its policy of allowing the clergy to exact excessive and oppressive tithes and fees for marriages, funerals, and like services."[25]

In 1851, however, Padre Martínez's liberal, people-oriented philosophy of the role of the church was challenged with the arrival in New Mexico of a new vicar general. Fray J. B. Lamy, although French by birth, worked under the Baltimore diocese. In the mid-1850s, he became a bishop.[26] His partisans claimed that he revitalized religion by founding schools, building churches, and increasing the number of priests in his diocese from 10 to 37.[27] His critics contended, however, that he did this at a tremendous cost, and they condemned him for his failure to speak out against the injustices suffered by the people. Perhaps this should be no surprise, since Lamy had excellent relations with the Anglo-American leaders and was a close personal friend of Kit Carson, who was infamous for his exploitation of Mexicans.

Soon after Lamy's arrival, a power struggle erupted between him and the Mexican clergy, many of whom were Martínez's former students. The issue of celibacy emerged, but the most important disagreement concerned the involvement of the Mexican clergy in temporal matters, especially their functioning as advocates for the people.

At first, Martínez avoided an open rift with Lamy, remaining silent even when close friends were excommunicated. Gradually, however, Lamy's edicts became more obtrusive. Finally, when he sent a letter to all the parishes insisting that priests collect tithes and first fruits, and telling them to withhold the sacraments from those who did not comply, Martínez rebelled. He believed it immoral to take from the poor. Lamy finally excommunicated Martínez, but the padre defied the bishop by continuing, until his death in 1867, to minister the sacraments. Other Mexican priests continued his work.

The Anglo-American priests did not involve themselves with the material welfare of the Mexicans. Instead, they cooperated with Anglo-Americans in Americanizing New Mexicans to accept the colonization.

The Great Land Robbers

After the conquest, New Mexico attracted more than its share of opportunists. Many were professional bureaucrats who were especially adept at manipulating government and the law. In fact, "one out of every ten Anglos in New Mexico in the 1880s was a lawyer."[28] During the occupation, these vultures completely dominated the government, using its powers to steal the land from the people. To facilitate these thefts, they formed small political cliques, which resembled the political machines of the eastern United States. Most of these cliques were associated with, and subservient to, the Santa Fe Ring, which Carey McWilliams described as "a small compact group of Anglo-American bankers, lawyers, merchants, and politicians who dominated the territory through their ties with the *ricos* [upper-class Mexicans] who in turn controlled the votes of the Spanish-speaking."[29] The network woven by the ring paled its eastern counterparts.

The leaders were Thomas B. Catron, Stephen B. Elkins, and Le Baron Bradford Prince, all of whom were prominent Republicans. A number of Democrats as well as rich Mexicans in New Mexico were also members of the ring. The ring controlled the governor and most of the office holders in the state. In addition, it was supported by Max Frost, editor of the *New Mexican,* the territory's most influential newspaper:

> Frost, who was at one time during his active career indicted in a land fraud prosecution, acted as the journalistic spokesman for the Ring, effectively using the press to discredit foes of the Ring and to place its activities in the best possible light.[30]

It would be impossible in this brief space to trace the entire network of the ring, but a brief description of its principal leaders is enlightening.

Thomas B. Catron was the ring's titular leader, its axeman, and the mastermind of its New Mexico operation. He came to New Mexico in the late 1860s, eventually becoming U.S. attorney general for the territory. "Throughout his life in New Mexico, Catron wielded more power than any other single individual in the Territory. Through land grant litigation and by purchases he acquired more than one million acres of land. . . ."[31]

Stephen Elkins, a close friend of Catron, came to New Mexico in 1863. He was a lawyer and, in 1871, president of the First National Bank of Santa Fe. He represented the ring's interests in Washington, D.C., becoming a delegate to the U.S. Congress, and later serving as secretary of war under President Benjamin Harrison.[32] In 1884, he became chairman of the executive committee of the National Republican Committee.

Le Baron Bradford Prince came from New York, where he'd had experience in machine politics. He had powerful friends in Washington, D.C., and was offered the governorship of New Mexico, but turned it down to become chief justice of New Mexico in 1879. Later, in the 1890s, he became governor.

Governor Edmund Ross, appointed by President Grover Cleveland, described the ring's network and influence:

> From the Land Grant Ring grew others, as the opportunities for speculation and plunder were developed. Cattle Rings, Public Land Stealing Rings, Mining Rings, Treasury Rings, and rings of almost every description grew up, till the affairs of the Territory came to be run almost exclusively in the interest and for the benefit of combinations organized and headed by a few longheaded, ambitious, and unscrupulous Americans.[33]

One of the ring's most infamous capers was its takeover of the Maxwell Land Grant, which was formerly the Beaubien-Miranda Grant, given to the grantees in 1841. When the parties requested execution two years later, Fray

Martínez objected on the grounds that part of the grant belonged to the people of Taos.[34] Over the next years, various other groups claimed parts of the Beaubien-Miranda Grant: Indians, Mexican tenant farmers, pueblos, and Anglo squatters.

Lucien Maxwell was the son-in-law of one of the original grantees, Charles Beaubien. In 1858, Maxwell bought Guadalupe Miranda's share of the grant, as well as a tract from his father-in-law's share. Some years later, after the death of his father-in-law, Maxwell began to buy up other shares. His total outlay was not more than $50,000.

In 1868 Maxwell sold his grant to a British-Dutch combine.[35] The sale created problems because a number of tenant farmers lived on the property. Another complication was that Maxwell did not know how much land was included in the grant.

After it took control of the Maxwell Land Grant, the British-Dutch combine ran into many problems. In 1867–1868, gold was discovered on the grant, bringing in many prospectors. Later, when it was learned that the federal government had laid claim to a portion of the Maxwell grant for reservation and park land, squatters moved onto the land, believing it would become public domain and that under U.S. law, they would be entitled to it.*

Finally, the British-Dutch combine sold the grant to (or merged with) the Santa Fe Ring, which evicted the squatters.

Lucien Maxwell probably estimated the size of the grant at between 32,000 and 97,424 acres, but once the ring got control from the British-Dutch combine, the grant was expanded to 1,714,765 acres.[36] The residents of Colfax County began to feel threatened as the boundaries of the grant moved outward and threatened to engulf even those lands to which the owners held legal title. At many times, open warfare erupted. For example, on September 14, 1875, T. J. Tolby, a Methodist minister and a leading opponent of the ring, was killed. Cruz Vega, a Mexican and constable of the Cimarron precinct, was accused of the murder; although he denied any involvement, he was lynched. The vigilantes believed that he was hired by the ring. But according to some sources, the lynching seems to have had racial overtones in that the vigilantes took advantage of the situation to get themselves a "meskin."[37] The result of the murder and lynching was that all-out warfare raged in Colfax County, where more people died than in the Lincoln County War.[38]

The Maxwell case finally went to the courts which were controlled by the ring.

Throughout the violence, the Santa Fe group continued its relentless drive to gain control of the land through manipulations of the law. It influenced the territorial legislature to enact legislation that "authorized the courts to partition grants or put them up on the sale block, even when the smallest owner

---

*The Indians involved were the Utes and Jicarilla Apaches. At the insistence of the ring, they were finally moved off their hunting ground and to reservations.

petitioned such action. Another territorial law, enacted in January 1876, annexed Colfax County to Taos County for political purposes for at least two court terms."[39] Thus, where the ring owned even a small portion of land, it could force a sale; and since the ring also controlled Taos judges, the annexation was a great boon to it. During this period the ring received the cooperation of the appointed governors, who refused to intervene even though there was considerable bloodshed. Moreover, when the government surveyed the Maxwell grant, John T. Elkins, a brother of Stephen B. Elkins, was appointed as one of the surveyors. Finally, on April 18, 1887, a decision was reached by the U.S. Supreme Court, which completely disregarded the rights of the Indians, the Mexicans, or the squatters. It found for the Maxwell Company[40] (which the ring now owned), thus dispossessing the Indian and the Mexican tenant farmers (both of whom had lived on the land included in the grant until the land grabbers moved in), and marking the end of an era.

The Lincoln County War

The Lincoln County War was similar in origin to the troubles in Colfax County. The struggle was complex, involving the Santa Fe Ring, but centering on a smaller ring and a group of its challengers. The power blocs in this rivalry, which dominated the 1870s, were led by Anglo-Americans—one a Republican and the other a Democrat. The losers, as always, were the poor—principally Mexican sheepherders and farmers.

Lincoln County was in the plains area of New Mexico, and contrary to myths perpetrated by historians such as Walter Prescott Webb in his book *The Great Plains,* Mexicans had moved into the area. Prior to the 1870s, when the Anglos began arriving in large numbers, Mexicans had established small villages and farms in the county. Charles L. Kenner, in *A History of New Mexican–Plains Indian Relations,*[41] attests to the fact that the Chicano was a first-rate plainsman and, incidentally, explodes the myth of the cowardly Mexican:

> In combating the Commanches, the New Mexicans, when well led and adequately armed, were more than able to hold their own. Had they been as timid and cowardly as many Anglos have claimed, their province could never have endured two centuries of constant exposure to Indian attacks.[42]

The Mexicans herded sheep on the open range, a practice that was resented by the Anglo-American adventurers who encroached in Lincoln County. The Anglos not only wanted the land for cattle grazing but also wanted dominance of the entire area. During the 1870s, the main town was Lincoln, formerly the Mexican pueblo of *La Placita.*

The Lincoln County War (1876–1878) often has been portrayed as a cattle or range war, with the conflict growing out of cattle rustling and range rights. The focus also has been limited by some historians to a personal feud. Robert

N. Mullin, editor of *Maurice Garland Fulton's History of the Lincoln County War,* has clarified this, writing:

> The Lincoln County War was essentially a struggle for economic power. In a land where hard cash was scarce, federal contracts for the supply provisions, principally beef, for the military posts and for the Indian reservations, were the grand prize. Since the early 1870's Laurence Gustave Murphy had been the Lincoln County sub-contractor for William Rosenthal and the political clique at Santa Fe which enjoyed a near-monopoly in supplying the government with beef, even though neither Rosenthal nor Murphy himself then raised or owned any significant number of cattle. They were challenged by John H. Chisum, owner of the largest herds in the territory, who declined to do business through Rosenthal but instead bid direct on the beef contracts. Thus began Chisum's struggle with Murphy and his successors along with their backers at Santa Fe—a struggle out of which grew the Lincoln County War.[43]

For the Mexican, however, the only significance of the Lincoln County War was its affect on the people—the utter disregard for life.

Soon after the arrival of the Anglo-Americans, Lincoln County became a haven for outlaws. Corrosive elements from Texas spilled over into New Mexico. The Murphy group, led by Laurence Gustave Murphy, who was the Santa Fe Ring's beef subcontractor, encouraged lawlessness by hiring Anglo-American gangs as rustlers for their beef-supply business, thus bringing into the territory men who had little concern for law or life—especially Mexican life.

One outlaw band, the Harrell clan, rode into Lincoln in 1873 and began to entertain themselves by abusing the townspeople. When Constable Juan Martínez attempted to restrain them, a gun fight followed in which three of the marauders and Constable Martínez were killed.

The outlaws retaliated for the deaths of their friends by attacking the town and shooting indiscriminately into a crowd of townspeople attending a dance. Four Mexicans were killed. Although troops finally chased the Harrells out of the county, enroute they killed José Haskell because he had a Mexican wife. As they rode toward Texas, Ben Turner, a member of the gang, was shot from ambush, whereupon they went on another rampage, killing five Mexican freighters.

In the power play between the Murphy group, who controlled Republican party politics in Lincoln, and John H. Chisum, who represented the Democrats, Juan Patrón emerged as the Mexican leader in Lincoln. His father had been killed by the Harrell clan. Patrón, a native of *La Placita,* was born in 1855 and attended parochial schools in New Mexico, eventually graduating from the University of Notre Dame in Indiana. Friends described him as "honest, studious, and industrious."[44] In 1878 he served as a delegate to the state House of Representatives, where the deputies elected him speaker of that body. He also functioned, without pay, as the town's only school teacher.

Patrón's emergence as a leader began in 1875, when he was employed as a clerk of the probate court. John Copeland, an Anglo rancher, and his neighbor, John Riley, a member of the Murphy clan, accused two Mexican workers, who had run away because of threats by Copeland, of stealing property from their ranches. They pursued the two, killing one and capturing the other. They decided to take the captured Mexican to Fort Stanton, seven miles away, and these "cowboys," who were accustomed to riding, set out *on foot* with the prisoner in front of them. When the unarmed Chicano allegedly attempted to escape, the two Anglos shot him. They reported their version of the incident to Probate Judge Laurence Murphy, an associate of Riley and leader of the Murphy ring, who acquitted them.

Patrón investigated the incident and concluded that the men were shot on the ranch and not, as alleged, on the road. His demand for a grand jury investigation was denied. Determined not to allow this injustice to go unpunished, Patrón, as probate clerk, signed a warrant for the arrest of Copeland and Riley, enlisted a posse, and rode to the Copeland ranch. They eventually found both men, took them prisoner, and interrogated them. Concluding that the two Mexicans had been shot in cold blood, many in the posse wanted to shoot the accused murderers, but Patrón calmed them. When troops arrived from Fort Stanton (their aid had been sought by one of Riley's friends), the posse released the two *gringos*. Riley went into his house, got a gun, and shot Patrón in the back. The army arrested the Mexicans.

Patrón was taken prisoner and held in the post hospital, where he remained in critical condition for some time. Although, on the demand of John Riley, Patrón was indicted, he did not go to trial. He recovered to lead the Mexicans during the Lincoln County War.

Throughout the trouble leading to the Lincoln County War, Juan Patrón and most Mexicans sided with Chisum and against the Murphy ring, probably because they considered the latter to be the principal and most immediate threat to them. The Murphy group's involvement with the Harrell gang and the Riley-Copeland affair undoubtedly influenced the Mexicans' decision to support the opposition. In addition, James Dolan, a violent man who committed many atrocities, became the leader of the Murphy group.[45]

The causes for the Lincoln County War were set in motion in the spring of 1877 when an Englishman, John H. Tunstall, opened a mercantile store in competition with the Murphy establishment. Alexander McSween, a lawyer, and John Chisum, the cattle king, were Tunstall's associates. In addition, the Chisum-Tunstall group opened a bank that competed with the First National Bank, which was controlled by Stephen B. Elkins and T. B. Catron.

When Dolan threatened Tunstall, two armed camps formed. Most of the Mexicans joined Juan Patrón in backing the Tunstall group. Tensions mounted and bloodshed followed. Dolan employed the Jesse Evans gang to do the dirty work. Even though the gang had a few Mexican members, it viciously murdered and persecuted the Mexican community. Finally, Tunstall was murdered by Dolan's men, and revenge was immediately sought by the

Englishman's associates and supporters, among whom was the notorious William Bonnie, alias Billy the Kid. During the hostilities Dolan attacked Patrón in the *New Mexican,* charging that he was the leader of the county's lawless Mexican element. As far as the Murphy group was concerned, all Mexicans were in the Tunstall camp.

The lawlessness in Lincoln County attracted outlaws from throughout the West, and both groups recruited gunmen from their ranks. Among the newcomers to the territory were John Selman and his so-called scouts. Selman was a well-known cattle rustler, and soon after his arrival, he was hired by Dolan. According to Maurice Fulton, "During the latter part of September [1878], Selman's group moved to the vicinity of Lincoln and inaugurated a worse type of terrorism than heretofore known." With the Dolan forces, they committed "apparently motiveless deeds of violence."[46] Sam Corbet, in a letter to Tunstall's father, wrote: "They killed two men and two boys [Mexicans] only about 14 years old, unarmed and in the hay field at work. Rode right up to them and shot them down."[47] Maurice Fulton commented: "[These actions] roused the ordinarily docile Mexicans; some even determined to visit retaliation on the first *Americanos,* in particular *Tejanos,* that came their way."[48]

Throughout most of the Lincoln County War, Governor Samuel B. Axtell sided with the Dolan faction, remaining silent, and maintaining that the situation in the county did not require intervention. Many people believed he was a member of the Sante Fe Ring. However, the murders of Reverend Tolby in Colfax and of Tunstall, a British subject whose death attracted international attention, signaled Axtell's political demise. On September 4, 1878, over the protests of Catron, Elkins, and other prominent ring members, General Lew Wallace was appointed governor by President Rutherford B. Hayes. Wallace was a Republican, so New Mexicans waited nervously to see if he would prove to be another Axtell. President Hayes, however, had given him a mandate to clean up the trouble in Lincoln County, and he took vigorous action to do so. He formed a local militia, led by Juan Patrón, to clean up the county, and peace was restored in 1879.

Dolan, however, continued to exercise considerable power in the county and eventually became influential in territorial politics. Chisum left the county, and because of harassment, Patrón finally moved to Puerto de Luna, several hundred miles away. Misfortune hounded him. While in a saloon having a drink with a friend, a cowboy named Mitch Maney shot him. Many believed Dolan had hired Maney as an assassin and certainly the subsequent trial raises some questions. Although Maney was a penniless cowboy, one of the most expensive legal firms in the territory defended him. Moreover, the main prosecutor was Thomas Catron, leader of the Sante Fe Ring. The outcome was a hung jury, and Maney was never retried.[49]

Juan Patrón was an effective and honest leader, and as such, he was a threat to the Establishment in the county and to the ring in New Mexico. One can speculate that if his challenge had gone unpunished, other dissidents might have been encouraged to rebel. His violent death, therefore—whether there was evidence of design or not—served to intimidate incipient rebels.

Some might argue that these acts of violence were committed by violent men—Anglo-Americans who killed their own kind as well as Mexicans. But it cannot be disregarded that the Mexican populace was the main target of the violence, with hundreds of Mexicans being murdered throughout the course of the Lincoln County War. Patrón symbolized the Mexican resistance to this oppression.

As an epilogue to the violence of the Lincoln County War, and further signaling the end of the old way of life, after 1879 the railroads arrived in New Mexico. This had been dreaded and even opposed by many New Mexicans, because it meant the arrival of more *gringos,* who would eventually outnumber the original settlers. When the railroads inevitably did arrive, wool shipments were spurred, and soon nearly three million head of sheep roamed the territory, most of which belonged to the Anglo-Americans. A thousand ewes brought $15,000 a year, whereas a Mexican herder could be employed for less than $200 annually.[50]

The Resistance

The land, as we mentioned previously, is at the crux of the Mexicans' grievances against the United States government. The latter allowed and abetted a few unscrupulous men to take the land away from the people. The story of Mexican resistance to the appropriation of the land, and with it a way of life, is today emerging. *Las Gorras Blancas* (the White Caps), which operated in San Miguel County in the 1889–1891 resistance to the Anglo and rich Hispano land grabbers, was one of the many societies formed in New Mexico to resist privilege. This group used offensive tactics, sabotaging the efforts of the land grabbers to carve up their land and to shut them out.[51]

San Miguel County is located in northern New Mexico, a mountainous land. Its principal town is Las Vegas. "The tract of land that came to be known as the Las Vegas Grant contained 500,000 acres of fine timber, agricultural and grazing lands, the meadows in the area of the future town of Las Vegas being especially rich."[52] As early as 1821, grants to portions of this region had been awarded to individuals; however, because of Indian attacks, most of the grantees failed to settle on their grants. Nevertheless, by 1841, 131 families were living in the area known as Las Vegas. "On June 21, 1860, Congress confirmed 496,446 acres as the grant of land made to the town of Las Vegas."[53] Also confirmed was the grant given to Luis María Cabeza de Baca in 1821. The population of Las Vegas at the time was a communal one, with many subsisting by grazing sheep and farming. The land, in accordance with Mexican law and traditions, belonged to the people in common and could not be sold. Not until after the Civil War was this way of life challenged by land-hungry Anglo-Americans, who were accustomed to squatting on the public domain. They had little knowledge or respect for village lands or the open range. In the 1880s, these Anglo-Americans began to buy tracts from the original settlers, which according to Mexican law, the users of the land could not sell, since in many instances they conflicted with communal interests.[54]

The land grabbers claimed an absolute right to the lands and fenced their claims, enclosing as many as 10,000 acres. This action denied the Mexicans access to timber, water, and grazing lands. Naturally the Mexicans resented the action, especially when Anglo land grabbers brought a suit, Milhiser versus Padilla, in 1887 to test ownership of the land. The court found that the land belonged to Las Vegas, which in reality left that town at the mercy of the cattle and lumber companies. Fencing continued, as did other encroachments. The favorable court decision did nothing to dissuade the land grabbers.[55] The attitude of the territorial authorities was one of apathy and indifference.

On November 1, 1889, Mexicans moved to defend themselves. "Armed with rifles and pistols, draped in long black coats and slickers, their faces hidden behind white masks . . ." 66 horsemen rode into Las Vegas.[56] They converged on the jail, asking for Sheriff Lorenzo López, and then on the home of Miguel Salazar, the prosecuting attorney. No property was damaged at this time, but the action climaxed a year of fence cutting by night riders. The offensive actions were blamed on *Las Gorras Blancas,* and indictments of Mexicans were issued. During this time, however, the White Caps had public support, and on December 16, 1889, 300 persons marched through the town in support of releasing suspected White Caps. The secrecy of the organization was also an advantage, making it difficult to identify and bring charges against the participants of the raids.

Las Gorras Blancas claimed a membership of 1500, and on March 11, 1890, they made a tour of East Las Vegas, leaving copies of their platform, which read:

Nuestra Platforma

Our purpose is to protect the rights and interests of the people in general and especially those of the helpless classes.

We want the Las Vegas Grant settled to the benefit of all concerned, and this we hold is the entire community within the Grant.

We want no "land grabbers" or obstructionists of any sort to interfere. We will watch them.

We are not down on lawyers as a class, but the usual knavery and unfair treatment of the people must be stopped.

Our judiciary hereafter must understand that we will sustain it only when "justice" *is* its watchword.

We are down on race issues, and will watch race agitation.

We favor irrigation enterprises, but will fight any scheme that tends to monopolize the supply of water sources to the detriment of residents living on lands watered by the same streams.

The people are suffering from the effects of partisan "bossism" and these bosses had better quietly hold their peace. The people have been persecuted and hauled about in every way to satisfy their caprices.

We must have a free ballot and fair court and the will of the Majority shall be respected.

We have no grudge against any person in particular, but we are the enemies of
bulldozers and tyrants.
If the old system should continue, death would be relief to our suffering. And
for our rights our lives are the least we can pledge.
If the fact that we are law-abiding citizens is questioned, come to our houses and
see the hunger and desolation. We are suffering; and "this" is the result of the
deceitful and corrupt methods of "bossism."
The White Caps, 1,500 Strong and Growing Daily.[57]

Of course, many Anglos and Establishment Mexicans condemned the
platform as anti-American and revolutionary, and there is no question that the
theme of the document was resistance to oppression and the right of the people
to the land.

Las Gorras continued fence cutting and destruction of property during
the 1890s. By this time, others were emulating them in venting their frustrations over grievances, but, in general, most of the incidents were blamed on
Las Gorras. The town newspaper portrayed them as a destructive influence
in the community, and the government stepped up activities against them.

Another enemy of *Las Gorras* and the people was the railroad. Land was
appropriated for railroad rights-of-way, and the incursion of people and commerce destroyed the old way of life. The White Caps, consequently, also
destroyed railroad tracks. This action put hundreds of Anglo citizens out of
work. *The Optic* played up this latter theme.[58] Governor Le Baron Prince
threatened to move troops into the area if the local authorities did not stop
Las Gorras, and, in fact, went to the area to talk to the members. Felix
Martínez, a leader among the poor Mexicans, confronted him, stating, "On
one hand, you have the power of money—the rich land grabbers—on the
other, the physical might of the people. True, the innocent with good titles are
made wrongfully to suffer on account of the land thieves."[59] These remarks
met with the general approval of the Mexicans of Las Vegas. Governor Prince
responded that the grievances of the people could not be righted until "law and
order" was reestablished.[60]

Russel Kistler, editor of *The Optic,* was not totally insensitive, and he
condemned the land grabbers who bought small claims for $5 and expanded
these holdings to 5000 acres.[61] However, to many Mexicans *Las Gorras Blancas* symbolized an extreme solution, for it operated outside the law. Many did
not realize that to achieve reform, action was needed; peaceful reform had
failed.[62] Moreover, many were lulled by the favorable decision in the Milhiser-
Padilla suit and hoped for official action. History has proved them wrong.

Alternative solutions also defused *Las Gorras* movement. The Knights
of Labor, an early national trade union, capitalized on the interest. They issued
a declaration on August 25, 1890: "A cry of discontent has become general
among the people of San Miguel County on account of party abuses against
the sovereignty of the people, and public and private interests of the same,
especially the interests of the working people."[63]

The principal signer of the declaration was Juan José Herrerra, a district

75

organizer of the Knights who had been suspected of being a ringleader of *Las Gorras.* As a trade unionist, however, Herrerra did want to separate the Knights from illegal activity, so it has been speculated that the alleged tie between the White Caps and the Knights may have been a device to smear the union. In any case, the declaration launched the United People's party, which operated entirely within the system, and at the same time, delivered a death blow to *Las Gorras.* Schlesinger concludes:

> The paisano [peasant] was not a political animal, nor was he trained in the intricacies of democracy as applied on the American scene. Moreover, he lived under constant economic pressure which was increasing as the society was changing. In such a situation, he was an easy target for political bosses who, at a price, could guarantee him a subsistence.[64]

There is no question of the effect of the White Caps on the Mexican, and if allowed to evolve, they might have had a far reaching impact. The political process led down a one-way street, which could easily be manipulated by the politicos. Some leading Chicanos defected to the People's party when it nominated candidates for offices in 1890, and significantly, fence cutting decreased.

The Republicans who controlled the territory, however, played up the issue of the White Caps:[65] A vote for the Democrats or for the People's party was said to be a vote for *Las Gorras Blancas.* Nonetheless, the People's party swept the county elections throughout the territory.[66] It won four seats in the Assembly. Soon afterwards, however, a People's party assemblyman, Pablo Herrerra, announced his disillusionment. Speaking before the legislature in February 1891, he said:

> Gentlemen . . . I have served several years time in the penitentiary but only sixty days in the legislature. . . . I have watched the proceedings here carefully. I would like to say that the time I spent in the penitentiary was more enjoyable than the time I spent here. There is more honesty in . . . prison than . . . [in] the legislature. I would prefer another term in prison than another election in the house.[67]

Pablo Herrerra returned to San Miguel and attempted to revive *Las Gorras Blancas,* but he was harassed at every turn and eventually was fatally shot by Felipe López, a deputy sheriff. Reforms at the county level were frustrated and attacks on the White Caps continued. However, symptomatic of the New Mexican *paisanos'* resentment, new organizations similar in purpose to the White Caps sprang up.[68] The White Caps faded away; too many of its leaders had defected to politics, perhaps to further personal ambitions.

Conclusion

Toward the end of the century, many mines were developed in New Mexico; copper, coal, zinc, and other minerals were mined in substantial quantities. Again the owners were the Anglo-Americans, and again the Mexicans were the low-paid workers who generated large profits. Irrigation brought large-scale agriculture to New Mexico, changing the life style of the residents to the detriment of the *paisano*, who provided the bulk of the labor force in that industry as well. By 1900, the economic privilege of a handful of Anglo-Americans had become permanent: with few exceptions, the Mexican did not share in the control of production. Meanwhile, more Texan cowboys entered New Mexico, reinforcing discrimination. By 1912, when New Mexico achieved statehood, Anglo-American mining, ranching, and transportation combines owned the state.

This chapter has merely provided an overview of the colonization of New Mexico. Much more research, such as that of Andrew Bancroft Schlesinger on *Las Gorras Blancas,* must be conducted so that the history of the Southwest can be viewed through the eyes of the Chicano and those sympathetic to his story. We can no longer tolerate historians' justification of Anglo-American aggression. Only through broader understanding of history will we appreciate the protests of men like Tijerina. To perpetuate many of the myths, such as the myth of the New Mexican's self-determination, is to reinforce the oppression that exists today. Men like Juan Patrón and J. J. Herrerra were the precursors of today's breed of rebels or insurrectionists. In understanding them, as well as the Catrons, the Dolans, and others of their kind, we shall better understand the present, and the words of Reies López Tijerina will take on more significant meaning:

The U. S. is violating the UN Charter!
Down with Land Grabbers!
Down with Treaty violators!
U. S. Violates International Law![69]

Notes

1. Patricia Bell Blawis, *Tijerina and the Land Grants* (New York: International Publishers, 1971), p. 156.

2. *Albuquerque Journal,* 18 December 1970.

3. Nancie González, *The Spanish-Americans of New Mexico: A Heritage of Pride* (Albuquerque: University of New Mexico Press, 1967), p. 205.

4. Lynn I. Perrigo, *The American Southwest* (New York: Holt, Rinehart and Winston, Inc., 1971), p. 168.

5. Warren A. Beck, *New Mexico: A History of Four Centuries* (Norman: University of Oklahoma Press, 1962), pp. 126–127. It is ironic that references should be made to the infamous Bataan death march in the Philippines during World War II, since a sizable proportion of the marchers were Chicanos of the New Mexican National Guard.

6. Hubert Howe Bancroft, *History of Arizona and New Mexico 1530–1888* (Albuquerque, N. Mex.: Horn & Wallace, Publishers, 1963), p. 327.

7. Bancroft, p. 324.

8. James Magoffin met with President Polk before the march, giving him a considerable amount of information about New Mexico. Stella M. Drumm, ed., *Down the Santa Fe Trail and Into New Mexico* (New Haven, Conn.: Yale University Press, 1962), p. xxiv.

9. Perrigo, p. 164; Drumm, p. xxiv.

10. Drumm, p. xxiv.
11. Quoted in Beck, p. 134.
12. Beck, p. 134.
13. Carey McWilliams, *North From Mexico* (New York: Greenwood Press, 1968), p. 118.
14. Beck, p. 138.
15. González, p. 52.
16. González, pp. 121–122.
17. Quoted in González, p. 53.
18. Stan Steiner, *La Raza: The Mexican Americans* (New York: Harper & Row, Publishers, Inc., 1969), p. 7.
19. Steiner, p. 8.
20. Peter Nabokov, *Tijerina and the Courthouse Raid* (Albuquerque: University of New Mexico Press, 1969), p. 65.
21. González, p. 53.
22. Nabokov, p. 48.
23. William A. Keleher, *Turmoil in New Mexico, 1846–1868* (Santa Fe, N. Mex.: The Rydal Press, 1952), p. 132, fn. 71.
24. William A. Keleher, *The Maxwell Grant* (Santa Fe, N. Mex.: The Rydal Press, 1942), p. 15.
25. Keleher, *Maxwell*, p. 133.
26. Robert W. Larson, *New Mexico's Quest for Statehood, 1846–1912* (Albuquerque: University of New Mexico Press, 1968), p. 82.
27. Perrigo, pp. 219–220.
28. Armando Váldez, "Insurrection in New Mexico: The Land of Enchantment," *El Grito*, Fall 1967, p. 21.
29. McWilliams, p. 122.
30. Larson, p. 144.
31. Keleher, *Maxwell*, p. 152.
32. Larson, p. 143.
33. Quoted in Howard R. Lamar, *The Far Southwest, 1846–1919* (New Haven, Conn.: Yale University Press, 1966), p. 150.
34. Keleher, *Maxwell*, p. 150.
35. Keleher, *Maxwell*, p. 82.
36. Keleher, *Maxwell*, p. 29.
37. Keleher, *Maxwell*, p. 79.
38. F. Stanley, *The Grant that Maxwell Bought* (Denver, Colo.: World Press, 1953), p. i.
39. Larson, p. 138.
40. Keleher, *Maxwell*, pp. 109–110.
41. Charles L. Kenner, *A History of New Mexican–Plains Indian Relations* (Norman: University of Oklahoma Press, 1969).
42. Kenner, p. 41.
43. Maurice G. Fulton, *History of the Lincoln County War*, ed. Robert N. Mullen (Tucson: University of Arizona Press, 1968), p. 8.
44. Fulton, pp. 406–407.
45. Fulton, pp. 45–47.
46. Fulton, pp. 291, 292.
47. Quoted in Fulton, p. 292.
48. Fulton, p. 294.
49. Fulton, pp. 405–409.
50. Perrigo, p. 279.
51. This account is based on Andrew Bancroft Schlesinger, "Las Gorras Blancas, 1889–1891," *Journal of Mexican American History*, Spring 1971, pp. 87–143.
52. Schlesinger, p. 93.

53. Schlesinger, p. 44.
54. Schlesinger, p. 95.
55. Schlesinger, pp. 96, 99–100.
56. Schlesinger, p. 97.
57. *The Optic,* 12 March 1890, quoted in Schlesinger, pp. 107–108.
58. Schlesinger, p. 113.
59. *The Optic,* 18 August 1890, quoted in Schlesinger, p. 115.
60. Schlesinger, p. 115.
61. *The Optic,* 7 August 1890, quoted in Schlesinger, p. 116.
62. Schlesinger, p. 116.
63. *The Optic,* 25 Ausust 1890, quoted in Schlesinger, p. 117.
64. Schlesinger, p. 117.
65. Schlesinger, p. 121.
66. Schlesinger, p. 122.
67. Schlesinger, p. 123.
68. Schlesinger, p. 125.
69. Blawis, p. 57.

Chapter Four

Sonora Invaded:
The Occupation of Arizona

More words have been written about the shootout at the OK Corral than have been written in all the combined works on the Mexican in Arizona. Arizona historians have elected to ignore the role of the Mexican, forgetting about his contributions and tribulations during the territorial period. The violence of the men from Tombstone and their kind has been immortalized, romanticizing the deeds of savage men who were brutal toward one another and those around them. Considerable attention has also been paid to the economic development of the territory by a handful of Anglo-American entrepreneurs. In the process, the Mexican has been made almost invisible. For example, a recent work by Jay J. Wagoner, *Arizona Territory 1863–1912: A Political History,*[1] refers only fleetingly to individual Mexicans, ignoring the plight of the group. Arizona works in general are infected by a Western-corral-buff mentality and have been dedicated to building the myth of the glories of the "Wild West." The result has been to create an Anglo-American success syndrome, which is difficult for Mexicans to overcome. The Chicano's history has to be pieced together from between the lines of diaries, papers, newspapers, and secondary sources, most of which are Anglo chauvinistic, making it difficult to forge the Mexican's side of the story. Nevertheless, this chapter brings to the surface the Chicano perspective: as definitive research is conducted, this perspective will become bolder.

Another problem is that even Marxist historians refuse to recognize that much of the violence directed toward the Mexican derived its strength from the colonization of the territory by the Anglo-American. They confirm that racism was, and is, a fact of life, and that exploitation was not unique to the Mexican. However, they contend that the Mexican would have been a victim of racism and economic exploitation even though colonialism had not occurred.

The acquisition of southern Arizona is a major point of contention between the Chicano historian and his Anglo-American counterpart. The latter is a captive of his sources, believing that the territory south of the Gila River was purchased by the United States solely for the purpose of building a southern railway route. Additionally, citing Mexican historians who write from a national perspective, many allege that Mexico sold the territory, which included parts of southern New Mexico, because President Antonio López de Santa Anna needed money and believed that Mexico would lose the land anyway. These historians deny that a prime motive was the desire of the United States to obtain the area for its mineral wealth. They ask: How would the Anglo-Americans know of mineral wealth in an area far to the west and south —an area considered uninhabitable? These historians have not consulted newspapers and other sources in the Mexican state of Sonora.

First of all, it is not true that the land was almost uninhabited: Pimas, Papagoes, and Apaches lived there. Moreover, Tucson had a permanent population of about 1000 settlers. Secondly, Mexicans as well as foreigners in Sonora knew of the mineral potential of southern Arizona. For example, Juan A. Robinson, a merchant and at times the U.S. consul in Guaymas, was a long-time resident, and he knew the conditions in Sonora well. He lived in the state long before the signing of the Gadsden Treaty. Many other Anglo-Americans in Sonora were well versed concerning the potential of southern Arizona. Before Mexican Independence, extensive ranching and farming existed there. In 1736, *bolas de plata* (nuggets of silver) were found ten miles southwest of Nogales, Arizona. The mine, which yielded large amounts of silver, significantly was called *Arizonac* or *La Mina Real de Arizona.*[2] As early as 1760, ore was also found in Cananea, just across today's U.S. border. Sonora was, in fact, a land renowned for its mineral wealth. Southern Arizona's topography resembled that of the rest of Sonora, and citizens from that state never doubted its potential.

The French had shown considerable interest in Sonora. In January 1852, *Jecker-Torre y Cia,* a company with French connections, signed a contract with the local government to exploit northern Sonora. The exploring company was called *La Mineral de la Arizona.* An ill-fated expedition made up of Frenchmen was launched from San Francisco, California. The French, however, never abandoned their interest in the rest of the state, and it is said that this interest encouraged the intervention of Napoleon III in Mexican affairs in the 1860s.[3]

The economic motive for the seizure of southern Arizona makes further sense when the negotiations are reviewed. James Neff Garber wrote what has been called the definitive work on the Gadsden Treaty.[4] However, the weakness of the work is obvious. He deals with the political history of the negotiations and almost totally ignores the motivational factor. We concede that the United States wanted a southern railroad route, but in order to make this route economically feasible, the Sonoran port of Guaymas was essential. Gadsden knew this and negotiated for more than southern Arizona, wanting Sonora down to and including Guaymas. When Gadsden could not purchase this area, he settled for the mineral potential of southern Arizona and New Mexico. He finalized the deal by using heavy-handed methods, threatening Mexican ministers that, if they did not sell southern Arizona and parts of New Mexico, "we shall take it."[5] Mexico gave up over 45,000 acres, of which some 35,000 acres were in southern Arizona. Ten million dollars was a large amount to pay for land that was considered worthless and uninhabitable and through which a railroad route was no longer feasible with Guaymas excluded from the purchase. The economic motive for the purchase of southern Arizona sets the tone for the area's colonization.

The Anglo-American migrants or colonizers to Sonora were immediately confronted with an economic problem. They needed a constant supply of cheap labor. Frontier conditions made it virtually impossible to attract white labor in sufficient quantities to fill labor needs. Climate, the lack of transportation, and hazardous conditions discouraged Anglos from flooding into Arizona. From the beginning it was necessary to rely on Mexican labor; and from the beginning, to make the mines and other industries of the territory pay, Mexican wage scales had to be kept below subsistence.

The Drive on Sonora

Arizona's geographical isolation presented a barrier to its economic development. In order to survive, it needed cheap labor and inexpensive transportation. Vast deserts separated the Arizona mines from California ports, and eastern routes were even more hazardous. The Anglo-American capitalists who came to the territory knew of these liabilities and realized that Sonora, Mexico, was essential to their economic survival. The Mexican state had a good supply of experienced miners and manual laborers, and the Sonoran seaport of Guaymas was one of the finest on the Pacific Coast. This economic dependence led to conspiracies to annex Sonora in order to gain Guaymas, and to an active policy of gaining dominance over the Mexican state to insure a ready flow of labor.

Sonoran historians, as well as contemporary sources, charged that Anglos in Arizona encouraged the Apaches to raid the Mexican state in order to weaken it and make it vulnerable for annexation. Laureano Calvo Berber, a Sonoran historian, charged: "The North American government permitted unscrupulous traders to trade with the Apaches at various crossings on the Colorado River, buying property that they stole [in Sonora] and supplying them with equipment, arms, and munition."[6]

On January 25, 1856, Joaquín Corella, head of Arizpe's *ayuntamiento* (city council), wrote a letter to the Sonoran governor:

> The Gadsden Treaty, we repeat, has again brought misfortune to Sonora; it has deprived the state of its most valuable land, as well as resulting in the protection of the Apache who launch their raids from these lands [Arizona] and to North Americans [bandits] who live among them, because in less than twenty-four hours they can cross the boundary; there the robbers and assassins remain beyond punishment; in our opinion it is vital as well as indispensable to garrison the border with sufficient troops that are always alert, since only in this way can their operation be successful and [only in this way] can they defend the integrity of a state threatened by filibusters.[7]

There is considerable evidence that private treaties were negotiated by Anglo-Americans with Apache bands. Arizona miners and ranchers made bargains with the Apache, giving them sanctuary in Arizona in return for immunity from Apache raids, "providing economic ends [the Apache's] could be served by raiding elsewhere."[8] Charles D. Poston, owner of the Sonora Exploring and Mining Company and later called the "Father of Arizona," made such a treaty with the Apaches. He negotiated the treaty through Dr. Michael Steck, an Indian agent. Poston admitted that Steck instructed the Apaches "that they must not steal any of my stock nor kill any of my men. The chiefs said they wanted to be friends with the Americans, and would not molest us if we did not interfere with 'their trade with Mexico.' "[9] Steck made other treaties for Anglo-Americans during this period. This problem was compounded by the inactivity of the U.S. Army, which ignored the Apache raids into Mexico. In fact, Captain R. S. Ewell, the commanding officer at Fort Buchanan, was more interested in exploiting the Patagonia Mine, of which he was part owner, than in tending to his duties as military and civil administrator.[10]

The cynical disregard of Anglo-Americans for Mexican life was demonstrated in the private treaty provisions of noninterference with "the Apache's trade with Mexico." However, a welcome side effect for the Anglo-American was that this forced many Sonoran citizens to seek refuge in Arizona, making cheaper labor more available, and depopulating the Mexican state. Annexationists knew that the population drain weakened Sonora so that it became difficult for it to defend itself. Thus, many Anglo-Americans publicly stated that they hoped the Apaches and the Mexicans would club one another to death. Sylvester Mowry, a prominent miner, stated this philosophy, in hopeful terms, before the Geographical Society in New York on February 3, 1859:

The Apache Indian is preparing Sonora for the rule of a higher civilization than the Mexican. In the past half century the Mexican element has disappeared from that which is now called Arizona, before the devastating career of the Apache. It is every day retreating further south, leaving to us (when the time is ripe for our own possession) the territory without the population.[11]

Not every Anglo-American agreed with this policy of genocide by proxy. The *Weekly Arizonian,* on April 28, 1859, strongly condemned the use of the Apache to annihilate Sonorans: "It is, in fact, nothing more nor less than legalized piracy upon a weak and defenseless state, encouraged and abetted by the United States government. . . ." The prominent miner and soldier Herman Ehrenberg echoed the *Arizonian:* "If we hate Mexicans, or if we want to take their country, we want no blood-thirsty savages to do the work for us, or to injure them." Although Ehrenberg was a realist who knew that Mexican labor as well as trade with Sonora was essential to the growth of Arizona, he condemned the policy of making separate treaties with the Apaches.[12]

There were two factors at the crux of the annexationists' "Sonora-without-Mexicans" goal: they wanted title to all of the Sonoran mines without having to worry about the former owners; and they were Anglo-American racists, who looked upon the Sonoran as a half-breed who was not assimilable into the superior Anglo-Saxon population. John Ross Browne, in his *Adventures in Apache Country,* sums up the antipathy of the Anglo-American toward Sonorans:

For this reason I think Sonora can beat the world in the production of villainous races. Miscegenation has prevailed in this country for three centuries. Every generation that population grows worse; and the Sonorans may now be ranked with their natural comrades—Indians, burros, and coyotes.[13]

The Anglo-Americans were caught in a dilemma: while they did not want Mexicans as citizens, they needed them as laborers. This fact hit close to home during the Henry Crabb filibuster of 1857. Crabb had led approximately 100 Californians into Sonora on what he claimed to be a peaceful colonizing expedition. The party marched into the state in military formation. Sonoran authorities ordered them to leave, but Crabb disregarded the order and marched ahead. The Sonorans ambushed the Californians, executed Crabb, and cut off his head and preserved it in alcohol. Anglo-Americans retaliated against Mexicans in Arizona, and small-scale warfare broke out. President James Buchanan condemned the Mexican "brutality" and attempted to use it as an excuse to invade Mexico. Many Mexicans fled across the border, abandoning Arizona, and paralyzing the mines and Arizona's economy. Owners and supervisors of the mines used their influence to cool emotions on both sides.

Expansionist forces were active in Washington, D.C., where Senator Sam Houston sponsored a resolution to make Mexico a protectorate. Twenty-two years later, Charles D. Poston wrote:

Among other secrets, it may now be told that President Buchanan and his cabinet, at the instigation of powerful capitalists in New York and New England, had agreed to occupy northern Sonora by the regular army and submit the matter to Congress afterwards. Ben McCullough was sent out as agent to select the military line, and Robert Rose was sent as consul to Guaymas with an American flag prepared expressly to hoist over that interesting seaport upon receiving proper orders.[14]

Although Poston's quote does not conclusively prove that there was official U.S. action toward acquisition, the evidence is strongly indicative. In 1859 Buchanan sent an armed vessel, the *St. Mary's,* to Guaymas to precipitate a fight, an action that resembled Commodore Stockton's adventure in Texas.* His pretext was the refusal of Governor Ignacio Pesqueira to allow Charles P. Stone to survey the public lands of Sonora. The Mexican government had entered into a contract with Jecker-Torre Company and a group of Anglo-American capitalists, in which, in return for the survey, the foreigners would get one-third of the public lands. Pesqueira, resenting Stone's arrogant manner, challenged the contract. Since Stone's party resembled a military operation more than a survey team, Pesqueira ordered him out of the state.

Stone made no secret of his desire to annex Sonora and encouraged Washington, D.C., to take action:

> I have carefully studied the country and people for eight months past, in which time I have had an excellent opportunity of gaining information from my position in the Survey of the Public Lands, and I feel confident that the only means of saving this state from a return to almost barbarism will be found to be its annexation to the United States. In this opinion I only agree with the most intelligent inhabitants of the State, both native and foreign.[15]

Captain William Porter of the *St. Mary's* demanded that Pesqueira allow Stone to continue his survey and, in May, protested Stone's expulsion. The Anglo-American partners, meanwhile, pressured Buchanan to intervene. Captain R. S. Ewell, of Fort Buchanan, later a well-known general, entered Sonora and further increased tensions by his insolent manner. Finally, in November 1859, Captain Porter threatened to bombard Guaymas. Pesqueira replied that if one bomb fell on Guaymas he would not be responsible for Anglo-American property or lives in the state of Sonora. The *St. Mary's* sailed away, but the incident did not end. On December 19, 1859, Buchanan complained that the Mexicans had expelled peaceful Anglo-Americans, violating their personal and real property rights. He requested the U.S. Congress to approve occupation of Sonora as well as Chihuahua.

---

*Filibustering was hardly the domain of U.S.-Sonoran situation; it was popular in the United States during the 1850s, when Anglo-American adventurers dreamed of emulating Sam Houston's success in Texas. In any case, it is indicative of the imperialist dreams of the times, with Anglo-Americans seeing the economic benefits and glories of acquiring more land.

The Anglo-Americans failed to annex Sonora, but their continuing attempts kept the state in constant flux. In addition to the problems of Apache raids and the outlaw conduct of U.S. agents, Sonora was plagued by Anglo-Americans who bred dissatisfaction within the state in much the same way as had been done in Texas and New Mexico. In the process, Sonora's northern frontier was depleted, with many of its citizens killed or abandoning the northern frontier. Because of the internal chaos, caused in great part by Anglo-American actions, Mexicans fled from the disorder to relatively safe conditions in Arizona. After 1876, this policy became passé, since Anglo-American capitalists were given preferential treatment in Sonora.

From Peonage to Poverty

From the start, Anglo-Americans in Arizona were the masters and the Mexican majority became the servants. The news media, the historians, and the schools supported this relationship, and, whether intentionally or not, they helped the colonizers to indoctrinate the Mexican masses to accept it as natural.[16] Joseph Park, curator at the University of Arizona Library, criticizes the role of the historian in creating myths like that of the "Murderous Apache, and the Mexican Outlaw, [who] rivalled each other in their deeds of pillage, robbery, and slaughter."[17] The portrayal of the Mexican as a negative participant automatically made him unworthy of leadership. He had to be controlled by an orderly race. A further justification for the permanent caste system was racism. Arizonian historian Rufus Wyllys readily admitted that it existed:

> The American never loved the Spaniard when the two met along the Mississippi and on the borders of Florida. How much less did the American love the Mexican, who seemed to be, (and in fact, often was) less white in blood than the Spaniard had been. Right or wrong, the prejudice would not last indefinitely without breaking into violence. The feeling was especially strong after Anglo-American Texas achieved practical independence from Mexico in 1836 and after California had made a vain bid for independence in the same year. During the forties, this inter-racial dislike reached a crisis.[18]

There were many instances of discrimination in the annals of Arizona history.

Peonage, the practice of legally binding a debtor or members of his family to a creditor until the debt was paid, was carried over from the Mexican period and practiced by the Anglo-American in Arizona. For a number of reasons, it did not become a permanent institution. First, the proximity of the border made it easy for a runaway to cross into Sonora. Second, the threat of Apache attack discouraged runaways. Third, it was cheaper to pay a man wages and cut him loose when there was no work. Fourth, peonage resembled slavery, and soon after that institution had been abolished, peonage was made illegal. Nevertheless, the practice did continue *de facto* for many years in Arizona as well as in other places in the United States.

Many mines, ranches, and businesses practiced peonage during the 1850s and 1860s. Sylvester Mowry called the institution ideal and praised Mexican labor:

> The question of labor is one which commends itself to the attention of the capitalist: cheap, and under proper management, efficient and permanent. My experience has taught me that the lower class of Mexican, with the Opata and Yaqui Indians, are docile, faithful, good servants, capable of strong attachment when firmly and kindly treated. They have been "peons" (servants) for generations. They will always remain so, as it is their natural condition. The master, if he consults his own interest, and is a proper person to carry on extensive work, is (in their own language) their "*amo y patrón*"—guide, philosopher, and friend. They depend upon him, and serve him willingly and well.[19]

Raphael Pumpelly, in his book *Across America and Asia,* wrote: "The substitution of white labor for peon (Mexican) would probably be a failure, owing to the debilitating influence which the climate exerts on Northerners. The Mexican labor is good when properly superintended; but, to render it advantageous, the recognition of the traditional custom of peonage is necessary."[20] Mowry and Pumpelly's rationales are representative of the thinking that justifies the master-slave pattern. Peonage becomes a natural state for Mexicans.

Peonage was protected by law until it was abolished by the 14th Amendment to the Constitution. If a peon ran away, the law would hunt him down, try him, and punish him. The punishment, in many instances, was inhumane. Witness, for example, the following cases: N. B. Appel owned a mercantile store in Tubac. His servant was indebted to him for $82.68. The latter ran away and allegedly took a rifle and other articles of worth. The law returned the peon to Appel and prosecuted him. He was found guilty and publicly received 15 lashes.[21] A similar episode occurred on the Riverton Ranch where seven peons escaped, but were returned and charged with debt and theft. The overseer, George Mercer, whipped them and cut off their hair as punishment. Mercer's shears got out of control and he took some skin with the hair. Stories of the "scalping" spread as far as San Francisco. Mercer publicly denied the charge, but readily admitted the whippings; nonetheless, the stories were widely believed.[22]

Another example of the institutionalization of the master-servant relationship in Arizona was the double wage standard that existed between Mexicans and Anglos. In the mines, Mexicans' wages were: 30 cents a day for wood choppers or ore sorters (this was called peon's wages); $12.50 to $15 a month for pick and crowbar men (*barrateros*) and ore carriers (*tantateros*); and $25 to $30 a month for skilled workers, such as furnace tenders or smelters. They worked for 12 hours a day, six days a week. In addition, the mine operators paid the Mexicans with 16 pounds of flour weekly. These wages prevailed through most of the 1800s and were slightly above those paid in Sonora. Actually, the wage outlay by the operators was even lower, because they ran company stores and recovered most of their capital. The operators extended liberal credit to the miners and charged them outrageous prices—the stores made as much as 300 percent profit on their goods. The stores were also invaluable to the mine owners because they insured a stable work force; indebted miners had to remain in order to pay off their debts.[23]

Anglo-American workers, because they were white and members of the occupying caste, demanded wages that were double those received by the Mexican and received from $30 to $70 a month.[24] The Mexicans were always assigned the dirtiest jobs—"Mexican work"—and were the first fired. When the Anglo-Americans did not receive preferential treatment, they spread the word that "the managers . . . employed foreigners and greasers, and would not give a white man a chance."[25]

As in other colonial situations, there were some Mexicans who were self-employed. Some started small mercantile businesses, and others freighted ores and other goods. Around the Yuma area, some Mexicans, returning from the California diggings, realized that the wealth was not in the mines, but in services. Felipe Amabisca and Antonio Contreras arrived in Arizona City in 1858, and Amabisca opened a mercantile store. In partnership with Contreras, he also started a freighting business, making hauls from Tucson to Los Angeles.

In spite of these exceptions, Mexicans collectively remained at the bottom of the economic and social ladder and were stereotyped as "peons." Occasionally, an Americanized Mexican was referred to as "Spanish." But to the overwhelming majority of the Anglo-Americans, he remained a "greaser." Other than the small businesses they pioneered, Mexicans were rarely found in industries requiring a large outlay of capital or in supervisory positions.

As agriculture developed in Arizona, Mexicans formed the work force. The Anglo-American farmer, arriving in the Phoenix-Mesa-Florence area, was especially antagonistic to Mexicans. Discrimination increased as new settlers arrived from Utah, Colorado, and points east. The new settlers were mostly farmers who came to plow their own lands. They concentrated primarily in the San Pedro, Salt River Valley, and Yavapai County sections of the territory. These were "peace-loving and God-fearing" settlers who practiced strict puritanical ethics. But they were also bigoted toward Mexicans and considered them intruders. In the Anglos' eyes, colonialism, resulting from the conquest, legitimized the racism and economic exploitation of the Mexican in Arizona. However, it is fair to speculate that substandard wages and conditions would have prevailed even if the conquest had not taken place; the capitalistic system abetted racism and exploitation in relation to European and Asian immigrants, even though they were not conquered peoples.

Violence and Polarization

Anglo-Americans stereotyped the Mexican as lazy, apathetic, dirty, and as a passive person who did not contribute to the economic growth of the territory. For all intents and purposes, he was not considered a citizen, although many Mexicans were U.S. citizens under the provisions of the Treaty of Guadalupe Hidalgo. Census takers in 1860 did not make a distinction between noncitizens and U.S. citizens.

As mentioned previously, however, Mexican labor continued to be indispensable to the development of modern Arizona. In the late 1850s, Mexicans began to move out of the Santa Cruz-Sonoita region, pioneering new areas around the junction of the Gila and Colorado rivers. As placerers, men who panned for gold, they went into western Arizona and worked many new strikes, followed by an avalanche of Anglo adventurers. Even after the boom, Mexicans lingered on to rework abandoned Anglo diggings. Mining treasures of the Black Canyon mines, Bradshaw District, and Walnut Grove yielded to the Mexican's *batea* (a cone-shaped placering pan).

During this period, relations between Anglos and Mexicans were often strained. California Chicanos drifted into the area, fresh from the California diggings and, according to many Anglos, prone to "forget their place." As Mexicans began to dominate the sites, nativism cropped up and developed to exclude them from the diggings—notably, Walker's diggings at Lynx Creek, where, according to one literate Anglo, the Mexican was not a "sitizen." In spite of these harassments, the Mexican placerer continued to push the frontier back.

The 1870s brought changes that directly affected the Mexican. Machines began to replace the Mexicans in mining and agriculture. No longer were as many Mexicans needed to perform the all-purpose skills. In the mines, the *arrastra* and the *patio* processes* began to phase out. Steam engines and the ten-stamp mills appeared, relieving the miners of much of the back-breaking work. The Mexican miner, however, did not enjoy the benefits of the new well-paying jobs (smelters, blacksmiths, carpenters, millwrights, etc.); the mine owners imported Anglo-Americans from places such as San Francisco to reap the harvest of the Mexican's early labors. Adding to the Mexican's plight was that during the 1870s the mines frequently shut down because of mechanization, a change of owners, the declining value of metals, and the fluctuation of the economic cycle. Mexicans were always the first affected during these periods—the last to be hired and the first fired. For a time, placering offered a safety valve, with many Mexicans turning to prospecting when no other work was available. They would work exhausted ground, literally wringing ore from the land. The Mexican's ingenuity demonstrated itself in many ways. Many started small smelting enterprises and subcontracted work from the mines.** This allowed many Mexicans to become more independent.

Throughout Arizona, mining towns such as Clifton, Arizona, stood as

---

Arrastra refers to a burro- or horse-drawn mill where ore was pulverized; *patio* refers to a court or levelled yard where ore was spread out and then pulverized.

**See Joseph Park for the best account on the role of Mexican labor during the territorial period.

tributes to the Mexican's abilities. Although Mexicans had known about copper in the mountains north of the Gila, this area had not been worked. In 1864, Henry Clifton rediscovered the body of ore, but many Anglos believed that the area was too isolated to develop, and Clifton himself left the site. Several years later, another Anglo-American filed a claim for the mine and, in turn, sold it to Charles and Henry Lesinsky, who incorporated the Longfellow Copper Company. They recognized the Mexican's skill in smelting and hired an experienced Mexican crew. The owners then left the Mexicans alone, later returning to find the settlement of Clifton "built entirely by Mexican labor." Within a few years, the mines at Clifton produced thousands of tons of ore. But, in spite of the Mexican's contribution, a double wage standard persisted.

Mexicans resented their oppressors. In Arizona, as in other places in the Southwest, "acts of lawless violence, including murders, robberies, and lynching . . ." were all too common and "too often . . . [there was] a clamor for the expulsion of all Mexicans."[26]

Mexicans were blamed for every crime imaginable, as attested to by Hubert Howe Bancroft, a research historian and compiler whose works are a capstone for the study of the West:

> Mexican outlaws of a peculiarly vicious class frequented the frontier districts, easily escaping after the commission of crimes into Sonora, where their punishment, by reason of endless complications of international red tape, was generally impracticable. These Mexicans, bad as they were, had like the Indian to bear the responsibility for hundreds of offenses they never committed. The native population of Spanish race, here as in other border regions of the United States, has often been the object of most unfair treatment. Innate race prejudice being aggravated by the acts of a few outlaws, and then being utilized by designing desperadoes or politicians of another race for the carrying out of their various designs.[27]

This was manifested during the Crabb expedition, which has already been described: "There were public meetings held to urge the expulsion of the hated 'greasers' from the mines and from the country. A war of races at times seemed impending."[28] Most evidence points to the existence of two societies in Arizona: Mexican and Anglo-American. Bancroft, himself, often falls into the trap of stereotyping the Mexican laborer: "Sonoran laborers of a vicious class were employed in the mines, and were accused of many robberies and murders, being hardly less feared than Apaches."[29] Like other historians, he based his conclusions on sources that were antagonistic to the Mexican; for example, Pumpelly had written that Mexicans felt "only hatred [of the *gringo*], giving full play to the treachery of their character."[30] Major S. P. Heintzelman wrote that the Mexican as a group "all cheat and steal, from the Priest to the Peon."[31] In contrast, however, Charles Poston stated that peace prevailed in Arizona during the first years of the occupation when the Mexicans were in the majority.[32] The conquest mentality of the Anglo-Americans complemented their racism and underlay the exploitation of the Mexican.

Anglo-Mexican conflicts many times created international incidents, since Mexicans fled into Sonora. Mexican authorities often refused to extradite the alleged criminals, because they knew that the crimes were committed in self-defense and that there was little chance of justice. The Mission camp affair was typical. On December 24, 1870, according to Arizona officials, some Mexicans killed Charles Reed, James Little, and Thomas Oliver and wounded Reed's wife. The dispute arose from the fact that the Mexicans allegedly had stolen some furniture and five horses. The culprits fled into Sonora, and Arizona authorities wanted them back. The Mexicans' version differed. According to their account, the Mexican workers had been abused, complaining that the employer had beaten one of them severely. The other Mexicans then defended themselves, fearing that they would be injured or killed.[33] A group of *gringos* did not wait around for answers. Greasers had killed Anglo-Americans, and reprisals were in order. In February 1872, a group of Anglos went to the ranch of Francisco Gándara, brother of the former governor of Sonora. They accused him of stealing a mule, which he denied. A shootout between the Anglos and Gándara's men ensued. Gándara was murdered, but not before killing one of the assailants—James Bodel. The Anglo gang then left the ranch and hunted down and killed a Mexican who had vowed to avenge Gándara.

The hostilities continued, with the press of each state hurling accusations at the other. Naturally, the Sonoran press brought up the issue of discrimination in Arizona.[34] Governor Pesqueira continued to refuse to extradite the accused Mexicans, although he carried on lengthy negotiations with the Arizona governor, A. P. K. Safford. Similar occurrences continued throughout the 1870s, heightening tensions. Anglo-Americans used the incidents to justify attacks on Mexicans, and the Mexicans reacted to the violence by resisting both defensively and offensively.

The antipathy toward Mexicans reached its highest pitch in places where there were "cowboys." In Tombstone, Arizona, famous for harboring the most corrosive outlaws of Texas, businessmen and mine owners would not hire Mexicans because they did not want to incur the wrath of the cowboys who controlled the town. The cowboys formed gangs to raid defenseless Mexican villages. The shooting of Mexicans became commonplace, with the cowboys showing little respect for women or children.[35]

As in other territories and states in the Southwest, Mexicans in Arizona had to fight the land-grant battle, although on a smaller scale. The controversies resembled those in California, with the pattern of fraud and delay again being followed to rob the Mexican of his land. Bancroft stated in *Arizona and New Mexico,* published in 1889:

Most of the claims are doubtless equitably valid and will eventually be confirmed, though since 1879 the surveyor-general has investigated fourteen of them or more, and recommended them for approval or rejection. This delay on the part of the government has been entirely inexcusable, as the matter might have been easily settled fifteen years ago. Since that time lands have increased in value; conflicting interests have come into existence; probably fraudulent schemes have been concocted; and even a hope has been developed that all the Mexican titles might be defeated. Owners have no real protection aginst squatters, cannot sell or make improvements, and in fact have no other right than that of paying taxes; while on the other hand the rights of settlers are jeopardized by possibly invalid claims, and a generally unsettled and unsatisfactory system of land tenure is produced.[36]

In short, the Mexican played a major role in the development of territorial Arizona, but his impact was minimized by physical and legal violence. His role was, moreover, conditioned by this colonized status and the attendant racism and economic exploitation.

Competition Among the Oppressed

Oppressed groups within a society separate themselves, one believing that it is better than the other. Frantz Fanon, writing about the Algerian experience, says:

Colonial Algeria being an eminently racist country, the different mechanisms of racist psychology are to be found there. Thus the Jew, despised and excluded by the European, is quite happy on certain occasions to identify himself with those who humiliate him to humiliate the Algerian in turn. But it is very rare, except in the region of Constantine where many poor Jews find shelter in the shadow of the colonial reign, to see Jews, in broad daylight, affirm their membership in Algeria's extremist groups.[37]

In Arizona, the oppressed Mexican similarly turned on the Chinese who were brought in by Anglo-Americans in the late 1870s to exploit their labor. The colonizer, by design, kept these groups apart, playing on the pecking order psychology. In addition, they played on racial differences and on each group's need for economic survival. Many Anglo-Americans believed the Chinese would totally replace the Mexican as the dominant work force of Arizona. Anglos had attempted to edge Mexicans out, but they were unable to survive the blistering heat, which did not bother the Chinese. The railroads brought many Chinese laborers, and it is probable that had it not been for the white fear of the yellow man, he would have replaced the Mexican as the major labor force. Popular feelings ran high against the Asian, however, and nativists rekindled old fears of a "Mongolian invasion" of Arizona. Exaggerated tales filtered in from California, a seat of bigotry. Nevertheless, many small Anglo-American capitalists used Asians in jobs that not even Mexicans, according to Arizona sources, would accept. They sent Chinese into the desolate mountainous areas of the territory to burn wood for charcoal and then, like pack animals, to carry the black fuel out. Employers could not help but be impressed by these hardy workers, but they yielded to public opinion and began to exclude them.

Big business, in contrast, has held the traditional view that "the public be damned." The Southern Pacific Railroad was too big to be intimidated by the chants that "The Chinese must go!" All that mattered to this huge organization was that the Chinese worked cheaper than others. They could be exploited at will. Nevertheless, there were not sufficient numbers of the yellow men to perform all the work to be done, and finally, in the 1880s, immigration legislation totally excluded them. The Southern Pacific managers then turned to the next most logical source of cheap labor—Mexico. After the Chinese exclusion, Mexicans dominated the railroad crews. To solve the problem of moving entire families—a problem that did not exist with the Chinese— Mexicans were outfitted with old box cars, which they converted into homes and which were crated from one work site to the next. So thorough was the Mexican involvement with the railroads that there are few Mexican families in the United States that cannot trace back one relative who worked for the Southern Pacific.[38]

In short, Mexicans complained about the Chinese challenge, fearing their jobs might be taken from them. They joined the peckers in the pecking order, calling for the yellow man's exclusion. In turn, the Chinese were used to depress the Mexican's wage. Yet the Mexican found solace in the fact that he was paid more than the Asian. This playing of ethnic minorities against each other is typical of colonial administrations.

The Paradox of Mexican Immigration

The growth of mining and agriculture and the exclusion of the Chinese created a pressing demand for more Mexican labor. This labor could not be furnished entirely by Sonora. Anglo-American capitalists had to dip further into Mexico, which had become an economic colony of the United States. The increase of the area covered by Mexican railroads made this importation of Mexican labor feasible.

In the 1880s, the railroad also brought new prosperity to Arizona. However, it also brought more of the hated colonizers. With this inundation, the prejudice against Mexicans increased. More and more, the Mexicans located in the southern half of the territory, with the citizens of many northern towns taking pride in the absence of "greasers." Agitation for separate territorial status from New Mexico had racial implications, for many white Arizonians feared that if the overwhelming Mexican majority in New Mexico joined the Mexicans in Arizona, they would dominate state politics. After Arizona became a separate territory in the early 1860s, many feared that the Mexicans would still out-vote the whites. On June 30, 1859, the editor of the *Weekly Arizonian* summed up the fears of the white population:

> Let us look at the matter in a fair and candid manner. If organized, and the Mexican population admitted to citizenship, we should be completely under their control, which, considering the character of a large portion of the Mexican residents, would be far from agreeable.

This antipathy for the Mexican population was also reflected in the sometimes bitter rivalry as to where the territorial capital should be located. On October 5, 1867, the *Daily Arizona Miner* observed: "Tucson has not a white population sufficiently numerous to be an exponent of the wishes of the majority of the inhabitants." Ironically, the Mexican population was in the majority.

A paradox had developed. Many whites wanted statehood for Arizona, and they needed Mexican residents to increase the territory's population sufficiently to make the territory eligible. However, they did not want Mexicans to vote. This dilemma contributed to the late admission of Arizona into the Union and is indicative of the attitude of the colonizers.

Gradually, the Mexican-born population further increased, and the 1880 census reported 9330 Mexicans in the territory; in 1900, 11,544; and in 1910, 29,452.[39] It was estimated unofficially, however, that the number was double, if not triple, the official count. The development of the territory had encouraged the importation of Mexican workers to such an extent that Sonora, the traditional supply depot, could not furnish them. El Paso then became a clearing house for Mexican labor.

Although the immigration acts of the 1880s prohibited foreign contracted labor, the practice of contracting Mexican labor became widespread. Anglo-American agents in El Paso hired Mexican agents, called *enganchadores* (hookers), who traveled into the interior of Mexico, usually to the cities, and recruited Mexicans. The *enganchadores* paid the train fare of the worker, and the amount was later deducted from the worker's wages.[40] The agent acted as a subcontractor and sold his contracts to Anglo-American employers. Sometimes problems developed. Often the Mexican worker signed up to get a free train ride, and just before the destination was reached, he would jump the train; he then did not have to pay back the fare and could contract for better wages than the *enganchadores* had offered him. To prevent this, the *enganchadores* hired armed guards, and they locked the workers into box cars.

The U.S. government did little if anything to protect Mexicans exploited by these practices. It even ignored the fact that it was illegal to bring contract labor into the United States. The need for cheap labor and the demands of capitalists in the Southwest overrode the legal infractions.[41] Meanwhile, the influx of large numbers of poor and unorganized Mexicans, who had none of the rights of citizenship, cemented the master-servant relationship that already existed.

Unionism Comes to the Southwest

As noted earlier, the Mexicans physically resisted Anglo-American violence. This resistance became more difficult as the number of Anglo-Americans increased in the territory; by the 1920s, the Anglos were in the majority. Moreover, the attitude of the Mexican government changed. In the 1850s and 1860s, and even during the early 1870s, Mexicans could find refuge in Mexico, but as Anglo-American control increased during the Díaz years, this safety valve was turned off. Mexicans then turned to defensive measures such as collective bargaining. The pro-management attitude of the territorial government made this activity hazardous. The pecking order that separated Mexican, Anglo-American, and Asian workers prevented any effective unity in the laboring ranks.

The latter part of the nineteenth century saw considerable labor organization throughout the Southwest. In general, the unions were most successful in the mining industry. Mexican aliens presented a problem to the union organizers, because they were often used as "scab" strike breakers. At first, union officials attempted to restrict Mexican immigration by using strike breaking as an excuse, clearly differentiating between Mexican aliens and Chicanos. Later, however, their arguments became increasingly racist. To understand the role of organized labor in relation to the Chicano, it must be remembered that the main interest of the trade union movement in the United States traditionally has been to obtain higher pay and better working conditions for its members. Few trade union leaders have been intellectuals and the majority of the rank and file has conspicuously lacked any ideology whatsoever. Thus, instead of educating members, unions often have reflected some of the most base prejudices of their memberships. Increasingly, the Anglo mine workers became anti-Mexican—not only on the strike-breaking issue, but also on the race question and even 'on the right of Mexicans to work in the mines. They jealously guarded the privileged double wage standard that they enjoyed. Moreover, the Anglo viewed the Mexican as a competitor and believed his own economic survival depended on the latter's exclusion, lumping Mexican labor into the category of "cheap labor." The Mexican, on the other hand, increasingly resented the higher wages paid to the Anglo for the same work. Fights erupted between members of the two groups.

Two opposing camps developed. The Western Federation of Miners (WFM), a union led by radicals, actively recruited in Arizona. Although they recruited Mexicans in other parts of the Southwest, in Arizona the strategy at first was to concentrate on Anglo-Americans, a policy pursued because of the growing rivalry between the two groups. For a while, the WFM was fairly successful. Arizona legislators feared the union's presence and passed special legislation in 1901 that created the Arizona Rangers, an organization that closely resembled the infamous Texas Rangers. The intended role of the Rangers was to assist cattlemen in ending rustling and to assist local law officers. In reality, the mine owners used them as strike breakers and to help maintain their privilege.[42] Labor's power had, however, increased, forcing the legislature to pass pro-labor legislation, which went into effect in 1903, making the eight-hour day in Arizona mandatory. Joseph Park observed:

> While the eight hour law constituted a major victory for union men in their efforts toward better working conditions, their principal satisfaction came in seeing an effective blow delivered to mine operators who sought to employ alien Mexicans wherever possible because they would submit to working ten to twelve hours a day at a wage that undercut the union scale by almost fifty percent.[43]

Mine owners complied with the law, but they sabotaged it by cutting the workers' wages by 10 percent. On the morning of June 3, three days after the law had gone into effect, miners walked off the job, shutting down the smelters and mills; the strike affected 3500 people.[44] The walkout at the mines in the town of Clifton was 80 to 90 percent effective. It was evident that the Mexicans were in control of the strike, since, as in later strikes, many of the leaders came from the ranks of Mexican *mutualistas* (mutual aid societies). The *Bisbee Daily Review* of June 3, 1903, stated: "The Mexicans belong to numerous societies and through these they can exert some sort of organization stand together."[45] At first there was an alliance between Mexicans and other ethnic groups. The main leaders were Abraham Salcido, the president of a Mexican society, Frank Colombo, an Italian, and W. H. Laustaunau, a Rumanian.[46] Two days later, however, the *Bisbee Daily* observed: "The strike is now composed almost entirely of Mexicans. Quite a number of Americans have left."[47] During the *huelga* (strike), tempers rose and racial animosities heightened.

The governor called the Arizona Rangers into action in an effort to intimidate Mexican workers, and on June 9, 1903, the workers responded by staging a demonstration of solidarity. In direct defiance of the Rangers, 2000 Mexicans marched through the streets of Morenci in torrential rains. A clash seemed inevitable, but nature delayed it when the rains grew worse and the demonstration broke up. A flood threw the city into panic, killing almost 50 people and causing some $100,000 worth of damage.[48] As so often happens, the poor were the hardest hit by the flood.

In the meantime, the local sheriff reported that the Mexicans had armed themselves and requested additional assistance from the governor. The Mexican consul in Arizona, a tool of Porfirio Díaz, was sent "to talk some sense to the Mexicans." Federal troops, along with six companies of national guardsmen, were sent to the troubled area, and martial law was declared.[49] This action was not necessary, since the disastrous flood had hit the Mexican community hard, and had ended the strike.

The strike leaders were rounded up, tried and convicted, and interned in the territorial prison at Yuma. This ended Arizona's first major strike. Officials with an army larger than it had taken to fight the Indian wars insured that the Mexican did not challenge the mine owners' privileged status.[50] The *huelga,* while it failed, went a long way in politicizing miners throughout Arizona; the Clifton-Morenci strike became known as the "Mexican affair."

While the WFM took notice of Mexican tenacity and capitalized on the drama by issuing a statement of support, it actually had abandoned the Mexicans. The violence of the Arizona Rangers continued unchecked, and in 1906, the Rangers even crossed the international border into Mexico to suppress Mexican strikers during the Cananea mine strike. Mexican workers there had the audacity to defy Anglo-American interests, protesting the double wage standard (see chapter 8).

The strike did not end labor difficulties in the Clifton-Morenci district, which was the first major copper producer in Arizona.[51] The WFM began to organize *all* workers in the area after the 1903 strike, and by 1915 strike activity had mounted. The miners had many grievances:

> In spite of the existence of some private businesses in the Clifton-Morenci district, over 80 percent of the workers were constantly in debt to their employers because of the trading with the mercantile departments, wither at the "urging" of the company or because credit was easy to obtain. Moreover, independent merchants were in no position to undersell the company stores. They existed at the pleasure of the town-owners, and were dependent upon the Arizona Company railroad to bring supplies to Clifton. Furthermore, few people would complain about being forced to make bigger profits.[52]

In addition to the company store, the company also monopolized the water; the owners deducted the water fees from the workers' wages.[53] The Mexican miners were subjected to extreme discrimination:

> The inarticulate Mexicans suffered silently the dishonest and often brutal yoke of many of these lesser officials. Often workers complained among themselves of being compelled by petty foremen to buy chances on worthless, or nearly worthless, items, but what they particularly resented was the bribery required by minor officials to get or keep a job. Shift bosses collected from $5 to $15 a month for such services.[54]

Foremen also made money by renting shacks to the workers for $10 a month. This was a high rate, considering that Mexican miners only earned $2.39 for a 7½-hour shift.

By August 1915, the union had gained sufficient power that it could make demands on the mine owners. Significantly, a $3.50-per-day minimum was demanded for all underground miners, regardless of their race. Once again, Mexican leadership was prominent. In September, when the owners rejected the WFM's demands, the miners went on strike. The strike lasted five months, but involved no major violence. This time, Arizona had a governor who was not appointed by Washington, D.C., and who was beholden to labor. The miners won a raise of $2.50 per day for surface workers and $3 for men working underground. The workers, however, were forced to abandon the radically led WFM, an affiliate of the Industrial Workers of the World (IWW), for the milder Arizona State Federation of Labor, an affiliate of the American Federation of Labor (AFL).

At the state constitutional convention in Phoenix on October 10, 1910, labor organizers exposed their true colors. While the reasons for the limitation of aliens—based on the rationale that alien labor offers unfavorable competition and drives wages down and that it stifles union organization—are understandable, what cannot be understood is the racism that appeared. At the convention, labor men introduced a resolution to exclude non-English-speaking persons from hazardous occupations, a resolution that technically would have driven the Mexican from the mines. It also stated that all mines had to employ 80 percent U.S. citizens. These resolutions, if they had been passed, would have caused hardships among the Mexican population. As one mine owner pointed out, 50 percent of the 1000 Mexican miners he employed would have to be fired, even though they had been with the company for as long as 25 years. Union leaders replied that during that time the workers should have learned English or declared their intention to become citizens. The owners' representatives prevented these resolutions from becoming law—probably because they realized the importance of Mexican labor to the continued growth of the state.

Conclusion

The occupation of Arizona institutionalized the second-class status of the Mexicans, reinforcing Anglo-American racism and feelings of cultural superiority. Although the population remained overwhelmingly Mexican in the nineteenth century, the government and economy of the territory was Americanized. By 1912, Arizona's Anglo-American population had increased sufficiently that, under the countenance of the economic power interests, it could attain statehood. The master-servant relationship had become firmly implanted. Throughout this time, the Mexican was tolerated, but was far from accepted as an equal.

By the 1920s, the preponderance of Arizona's population was Anglo. The Mexican's political exclusion became more complete than in Texas, New Mexico, or California. In Arizona, the Mexican office holder has been the exception rather than the rule. Further, trade unions have been weaker in that territory than in most states, making the Mexican's wage-earner status even more depressing.

Much more could be written about the Chicano's role in Arizona and his political emasculation. For example, the Tucson Ring, sometimes known as the "Federal Ring," manipulated the Mexican vote to maintain power during most of the nineteenth century. Much more could also be written about the effects of colonialism, as well as capitalism, on the lives of the people, and about the progressive movement in Arizona. The problem is that most sources, in emphasizing the state's political history, report from a perspective that is alien to the Chicano. By concentrating mainly on two areas—that of the Anglo expansionist mentality and the exploitation of Mexican labor—this chapter has attempted to lay the foundations for questioning Anglo histories of Arizona.

Notes

1. Jay J. Wagoner, *Arizona Territory 1863–1912: A Political History* (Tucson, Ariz.: University of Arizona Press, 1970).

2. John B. Brebner, *Explorers of North America, 1492–1806*, p. 407; Francisco R. Almada, *Diccionario de historia geografía y biografía sonorenses* (Chihuahua: n.p., 1952), pp. 140–144.

3. Jack A. Dabbs, *The French Army in Mexico, 1861–1867* (The Hague: Mouton Co., 1963), pp. 14, 65, 241, 283.

4. James Neff Garber, *The Gadsden Treaty* (Gloucester, Mass.: Peter Smith Publisher, 1959).

5. J. Fred Rippy, "A Ray of Light on the Gadsden Treaty," *Southwestern Historical Quarterly* 24 (January 1921): 241.

6. *Nociones de Historia de Sonora* (Mexico, D.F.: Librería de Manuel Porrua, 1958), p. 50.

7. Fernando Pesqueira, "Documentos Para la Historia de Sonora," *Segunda Serie, Tomo III* (Manuscript in the University of Sonora Library, Hermosillo, Sonora).

8. Joseph F. Park, *The History of Mexican Labor in Arizona during the Territorial Period* (Tucson: University of Arizona Press, 1961), pp. 15–16.

9. Charles D. Poston, "Building a State in Apache Land," *Overland Monthly* 24 (August 1894): 204.

10. See P. G. Hamlin, ed., *The Making of a Soldier: Letters of General R. S. Ewell* (Richmond, Va.: Whittel & Shepperson, 1935); and Clement W. Eaton, "Frontier Life in Southern Arizona, 1858–1861," *Southwestern Historical Quarterly* 36 (January 1933).

11. Sylvester Mowry, *Arizona and Sonora* (New York: Harper & Brothers, 1864), p. 35.

12. Quoted in Park, p. 20.

13. John Ross Browne, *Adventures in Apache Country* (New York: Harper & Brothers, 1869), p. 172. It is ironic that a considerable number of the *gringos* did marry Mexican females. They, in fact, sang the praises of the *señorita* and contrasted her to the unreliable and sneaky male. However, it is observed that the first Anglo-American females, who became permanent settlers, did not arrive until 1870. Thus, we can only conclude that the biological urge rose above the *gringo's* conviction.

14. *Arizona Weekly Star;* quoted in Park, p. 29.

15. Stone to Lewis Cass, Guaymas, 23 December 1858, "Dispatches from United States Consuls in Guaymas."

16. See Ivan Illich, *Deschooling Society* (New York: Harper & Row, Publishers, Inc., 1971). Illich draws a similar analogy.

17. Thomas Farish, *History of Arizona* (San Francisco: The Filmer Brothers, 1915), p. 346; quoted in Park, p. 40.

18. Rufus Wyllys, *Arizona: The History of a Frontier State* (Phoenix, Ariz.: Hobison & Herr, 1950), p. 81.

19. Mowry, p. 94.

20. Raphael Pumpelly, *Across America and Asia,* 4th ed. rev. (New York: Leypodt & Holt, 1870), p. 32.

21. *Weekly Arizonian,* 30 June 1859.

22. *Weekly Alta Californian,* 28 May 1859.

23. *Report of Frederick Brunckow to the Sonoran Exploring and Mining Company upon the History, Prospects and Resources of the Company in Arizona* (Cincinnati, Ohio: Railroad Record, 1859), pp. 17–18; *Fourth Annual Report of the Sonora Exploring and Mining Company March 1860* (New York: W. Minns & Co., 1860), pp. 12–14.

24. Pumpelly, p. 32.

25. Park, p. 78.

26. Hubert Howe Bancroft, *History of Arizona and New Mexico* (San Francisco: The History Co., 1889), p. 575.

27. Bancroft, p. 575.

28. Bancroft, p. 503.

29. Bancroft, p. 503.

30. Pumpelly, p. 37.

31. *Third Annual Report of the Sonora Exploring and Mining Company, March 1859* (New York: W. Minns & Co., 1859), p. 29.

32. Charles Poston, *Overland Monthly* 24 (August 1894): 207.

33. Editorial, *La Estrella de Occidente,* 12 April 1872.

34. "La Prensa de Arizona y los Horrores Perpetados en el Río Gila," *La Estrella de Occidente,* 22 March 1872; "Asesinator en el Gila," *La Estrella de Occidente,* 22 March 1872; "Trouble Ahead," *Arizona Citizen,* 24 June 1871.

35. Douglas D. Martin, *Tombstone's Epitaph* (Albuquerque: University of New Mexico Press, 1951), pp. 139–165.

36. Bancroft, pp. 599–600.

37. Frantz Fanon, *A Dying Colonialism* (New York: Grove Press, Inc., 1965), p. 154.

38. See *Arizona Sentinel* (1878–1886); *Arizona Weekly Star,* 1880s; and Park, chapter 6.

39. Park, p. 220.

40. Park, p. 190.

41. See Victor S. Clark, *Mexican Labor in the United States,* U.S. Department of Commerce Bulletin no. 78 (Washington, D.C.: U.S. Government Printing Office, 1908).

42. Carl M. Rathbun, "Keeping the Peace Along the Mexican Border," *Harper's Weekly,* 50 (17 November 1906): 1632.

43. Park, p. 256.

44. Park, p. 257.

45. Quoted in Park, p. 257.

46. Wagoner, p. 386.

47. *Bisbee Daily Review,* 5 June 1903; quoted in Park, p. 257.

48. James H. McClintock, *Arizona: The Youngest State,* vol. 2 (Chicago: S. J. Clarke Publishing Co., 1916), p. 424.

49. Park, p. 258.

50. Wagoner, pp. 387–388.

51. James R. Kluger, *The Clifton-Morenci Strike: Labor Difficulty in Arizona 1915–1916* (Tucson: University of Arizona Press, 1970), p. 9.

52. Kluger, p. 20.

53. Kluger, pp. 22–23.

54. Kluger, p. 23.

Chapter Five

California Lost:
America for Anglo-Americans

When Anglos first arrived in California, they were welcomed by the native population. Feelings soon changed, however. In 1855, Juan Bandini, a *Californio,* lamented, in biblical terms, the fate of his people:

> Our inheritance is turned to strangers—
>   our houses to aliens.
> We have drunken our water for money—
>   our wood is sold unto us.
> Our necks are under persecution—
>   we labor and have no rest.[1]

Of all the territorial conquests in the Southwest, the colonization of California was, perhaps, the most tragic. The prize was great: a climate that was conducive to a wide variety of crops and a long growing season; lumber-rich forests; a wealth of minerals in the ground; broad rivers fed by plentiful mountain streams; and seaports convenient for the growing trade with the Orient.

The tragedy was compounded by the character of the *Californios* themselves. For the most part, they welcomed the Anglo-Americans, often granting them large sections of land. When Spanish colonialism ended in 1821, California became part of the Mexican republic, and thereafter the number of foreigners entering the province increased. The first Anglos to arrive—often trappers and traders who were tired of wandering—intermarried with the Mexicans and lived in peace. The *Californios,* therefore, did not view the Anglos as enemies and were not prepared for the violence that ultimately was visited upon them.

In the 1840s, Anglo-Americans with families began to arrive in substantial numbers, and between 1843 and 1846, about 1500 Anglos reached California. This later wave mixed less readily, and less intermarriage took place. Not surprisingly, the Texas adventure had an affect on Mexican attitudes toward the immigrating Anglos.

Anglo-American trade with the Orient increased, and the ports of California became even more valuable. Moreover, the discovery of gold by Francisco López in 1842 at San Feliciano Canyon in southern California focused attention on a fact already known by the Mexicans: there was gold in California. The events prior to the 1840s left no doubt about the nefarious intentions of the Anglos. Since 1829, President Andrew Jackson and the U.S. presidents who followed him had attempted to coerce Mexico into selling California. In 1842, Commodore Thomas Jones slipped and raised the stars and stripes over Monterey. He believed that the United States had already started the war with Mexico. The excuse made by many Anglo historians is that "the United States did not intend to be caught unprepared in any ruse between the great powers to acquire California."[2] The expansionist fever drove many Anglo-Americans to a paranoiac pitch. Meanwhile, John C. Frémont led three expeditions for the U.S. Army's Topographical Engineers. Although these expeditions were supposedly scientific, they were heavily armed. On his second expedition in 1843–1844, Frémont "mapped, surveyed, and charted the trails ..." to and in California.[3] Thomas Oliver Larkin, the U.S. consul at Monterey, California, served as an agent, reporting conditions in California and fomenting discontent among the natives. President James K. Polk conspired to pull off another Texas adventure in California.

The last link in the United States' Bismarckian conspiracy was the third expedition of John C. Frémont, who had left St. Louis for California in May 1845. A portion of the peaceful scientific expedition reached California in December 1845, whereupon Frémont went to Monterey to purchase supplies. There, he met with Larkin. José Castro, the commander of the garrison in Monterey, was highly suspicious and watched Frémont closely. Frémont asked to be allowed to quarter in California for the winter, and permission was granted, with the stipulation that the expedition stay away from the coastal settlements. By March 1846, the main body of Frémont's expedition entered California. Emboldened by the additional soldiers, Frémont raised the U.S.

flag at Hawk's Peak, about 25 miles from Monterey. His actions give credence to Leonard Pitt's conclusion: "The United States connived rather cynically to acquire California, provoked the native Californians into a dirty fight, and bungled a simple job of conquest."[4] Castro, understandably, ordered Frémont to leave California. Just as the expedition was about to leave, Lieutenant Archibald H. Gillespie, a marine, reached Frémont and gave him personal letters in addition to verbal instructions from Polk. Frémont was told that the war with Mexico was near and to hold in readiness. Frémont returned to the Sacramento Valley. This was a hostile act intended to create an incident, since he was blatantly ignoring Castro's orders to leave.

Anglo-Americans in California rallied to Frémont's lead; they knew that an uprising was at hand. Frémont and his men already had taken on the aura of the swaggering conquerors, antagonizing their few friends. In June 1846, they struck, taking Mexican General Mariano Vallejo prisoner at his ranch in Sonoma. It is ironic that Vallejo had been sympathetic to the Anglo-Americans. Frémont's marauders took as their symbol the bear flag. Acting in the customary racist manner, they took Vallejo and his brother to Sutter's Fort, where they were subjected to indignities; the Anglo-American soldiers intimidated and harassed them and referred to them as "greasers."[5]

The Bear Flaggers spread a reign of terror, confiscating cattle and horses, looting homes, and wounding and murdering innocent people. On one occasion, a scouting party under Kit Carson came upon José de los Reyes Berreyesa and his twin nephews, Francisco and Ramón de Haro, who were occupied with landing in a rowboat. The men were unarmed, but the Anglos shot at them anyway. They killed Ramón, whereupon Francisco "threw himself upon his brother's body." One of the assassins then shouted, "Kill the other son of a bitch!" Seeing his two nephews killed, the old man said to the Anglos: "Is it possible that you kill these young men for no reason at all? It is better that you kill me who am old too!" The Bear Flaggers obliged by killing him.[6] It is of significance that the Berreyesa killings had no military value. Not only were the Mexicans mistreated and raped, but so were the California Indians.

The Mexicans resisted in the face of the violence. They were at a disadvantage because they were caught by surprise and had limited arms. Commodore John Drake Sloat arrived in July, landed 250 marines at Monterey, and raised the Anglo-American flag. He was soon replaced by Commodore Robert F. Stockton who was a well-known expansionist. (See chapter 1.) Frémont was promoted to the rank of major and placed in charge of the California Battalion of Volunteers, and the Anglo-American flag was raised over key California cities. Naval forces entered Los Angeles harbor, and Captain Archibald Gillespie was placed in charge of the occupation of the area.

At Los Angeles, the Anglo troops humiliated and intimidated the Mexicans, whereupon a resistance movement was led by José María Flores. His band of guerrillas chased the *gringos* into the hills. The patriots were poorly armed, but they defeated Gillespie and forced him to surrender. Six thousand Angelinos cheered Flores' men during the battle.

In the meantime, Kearny approached California with a token force of his Army of the West. He believed California had been conquered, so he left most of his soldiers in New Mexico, bringing only 125 men on the march. Kit Carson had advised him to do so, saying the Mexicans were "cowardly" and could be easily subdued. On December 5, 1846, the invaders met the 150 Mexicans, led by Andrés Pico, at San Pasqual Pass, northeast of San Diego. The Mexicans, armed with lances, attacked the Army of the West. Although outnumbered, they won the battle, killing 18 Anglos and suffering no losses. Kearny and many of his men were wounded. The conquerors, however, had warships, marines, and a well-armed cavalry, so Kearny soon received reinforcements. The Mexicans continued to fight against great odds. The regrouped Anglos, led by Kearny, marched north to Los Angeles in late December. Frémont approached Los Angeles from the north. Flores led the Mexicans, but this time they were overwhelmed—nonetheless, they continued to resist. Kearny's army, however, entered Los Angeles on January 10, 1847. Meanwhile, Frémont reached the outskirts of Los Angeles. At the Cahuenga pass, Andrés Pico surrendered to him and signed the Treaty of Cahuenga, ending the *organized* resistance. After the conquest, more conquering troops poured into California, securing their occupation.

The Occupation of California

California in 1848 resembled the typical colonial situation, with the Mexicans outnumbering their new masters. The army of occupation kept the natives in their places as the occupiers went about Americanizing California. It appeared for a while that the Anglo-Americans would be forced to accommodate to the firmly entrenched Mexican ways. However, the times conspired against this; on January 24, 1848, before the signing of the Treaty of Guadalupe Hidalgo, James Wilson Marshall discovered gold on John Sutter's property. When the news of the bonanza leaked out, almost overnight thousands of outsiders flooded into California, overwhelming the Mexicans and ending any hope they might have had of salvaging their way of life.

By 1849, almost 100,000 people lived in California, 13,000 of whom were Mexicans. This substantial population qualified the territory for statehood. A constitutional convention took place in August of that year at Monterey, California. Eight of the 48 delegates to the convention were *Californios* who had the opportunity, if they had voted as a bloc, to champion the rights of the masses. However, they acted like elites in other colonial situations: they attempted to ally themselves with the colonizers to salvage the little power they had. At this point, their relations with the colonizers were cordial. They allowed themselves to believe that they were different than the *cholo* masses (pejorative term for low-caste Mexicans). Thus, they were separated from their base. They were swayed by the possibility of prestigious positions within the new order. Instead of voting as a bloc, the *Californios* voted for their own self-interests. Of the eight Spanish-speaking delegates, only José A. Carrillo voted for the admission of free Negroes into California, and he did this out of political expediency, since he believed that it would enhance California's chances for early admission as a state. The *Californios,* moreover, could have voted as a bloc to split the territory into north and south. This would have given Mexicans control of the southern half. Again, the *Californios* voted for their self-interests: many of the delegates were from the propertied class and wanted lower taxes. Generally, the Constitution established laws favorable to the Anglo-Americans. Mexicans won only token victories: suffrage was not limited to white males (the Mexicans were half-breeds), the laws would be printed in Spanish and English, etc. On the other hand, they even accepted the "California Bear," the symbol of the conquest, as the state seal.

The Mexicans' Economic Subjugation

The capitulation at Monterey set the stage for the Mexicans' decline. In 1851 a Land Law was passed that set in motion the mechanism through which the Mexican could be legally robbed of his land. The Anglo-American, as elsewhere in the Southwest, entered California believing that he had special privileges by right of conquest. He was infuriated to find that 200 Mexican families owned 14 million acres of land. To him, it was undemocratic for greasers to own 35,000 acres, and he schemed to take it away from them. In the process, the Mexican landowner was lynched, kicked off his land by armed squatters, taxed out of existence, or insidiously bled by the costs of litigation imposed by the Land Law of 1851. Finally, nature and the economic cycle finished his demise.

Although the Treaty of Guadalupe Hidalgo and its Statement of Protocol had given the Mexican specific guarantees, like other Anglo-American treaties, it was ignored. William Gwinn, who was notoriously anti-Mexican, sponsored the Land Law of 1851. The law gave the Anglo-American an advantage, and, in fact, it encouraged him to homestead Mexican-owned land. While on paper the law appeared just, in practice it was tyrannical. Its ostensible purpose was to clear up land titles, but it placed the burden of proof on the landowners, who had to pay exorbitant legal fees to defend titles to land that was already theirs. Moreover, the judges, the juries, and the land commissioners were open to intrigue and were guided by their prejudices. The hearings were held in English, which put the Spanish-speaking grantee at an additional disadvantage. The result was that, although the commission reviewed 813 titles and only rejected 32, the Mexican lost most of his land during this period of harassment.

The Land Act, by implication, challenged the legality of the Mexican land titles. It told land-hungry Anglo-Americans that there was a chance that the *Californio* did not own the land. This encouraged many squatters to move onto the California *ranchos.* They knew that local authorities would not or could not do anything about it. Like locusts, they swarmed over the land, harassing and physically intimidating many landowners. By standing by and doing nothing, law officers condoned the violence that followed: "José Suñol was killed somewhere on confirmed land, shortly after his family had acquired title."[7] In 1858, 200 squatters and 1000 "gun-carrying settlers" ambushed surveyors and held Domingo Peralta hostage. Salvador Vallejo sold his Napa ranch for $160,000; he had paid $80,000 in legal fees to secure title. Moreover, squatters burned his crops while they appealed the case. Vallejo, rather than lose everything, sold Napa. Manipulators like Henry Miller, a former German butcher, used numerous schemes to steal the land. One of his favorite devices was to buy into ranches owned by several owners. Even though he was a minority owner, he could then graze as many head of cattle as he wished. But more important, according to California law, if one of the property owners— even one owning the smallest share—called for a partition of the land, the property would be sold at auction. Miller would then buy cheap. This Anglo-American rape disillusioned even the most pro-Anglo Mexicans.

The disasters of the 1860s took the little that was left to the *rancheros*. In 1862 a flood devastated California ranches. Two years of drought, followed by falling cattle prices, made it necessary for ranch owners to mortgage their property at outlandish interest rates, resulting in foreclosures. Legal fees and taxes did the rest. Prior to 1860, *Californios* owned all the land valued at over $10,000; by the 1870s, they owned only one-fourth of this land. By the 1880s the Mexican was relatively landless in California.[8]

As the Mexican lost his land, he was also politically emasculated. Only in Southern California, where the Mexican had an absolute majority, did he retain some local representation, but even there the Anglo dominated the political offices. The gigantic increase of Anglos statewide crowded the Mexican out of government. Mexicans were not experienced in competing in the crooked game of Anglo politics, which was especially bad in California. Pro-slavery Democrats and anti-Mexican politicians dominated the California legislature. By 1851, all native Mexicans had been excluded from the state Senate; by the 1860s, only a few Mexicans remained in the Assembly; and by the 1880s, people with Spanish surnames could no longer be found in public offices. During this period, many Anglo politicians represented themselves as friends of the Mexican.

California, like other colonial states, passed legislation that legally excluded the colonized from participating in the state's wealth. In 1850, the California state legislature passed its first Foreign Miner's Tax, which imposed a miner's tax on all foreigners. In reality, the tax was primarily directed at Mexicans and other Latins. At the crux was the racism of the Anglo-American, who resented foreign competition, believing that only Anglo-Americans should share in the fruits that God had given their nation. General Persifor F. Smith expressed the Anglos' feelings in a circular published in 1849:

> Sir: The laws of the United States inflict the penalty of fine and imprisonment on trespassers on the public lands. As nothing can be more unreasonable or unjust than the conduct pursued by persons, not citizens of the United States,

who are flocking from all parts to search for and carry off gold from lands belonging to the United States in California, and as such in direct violation of law, it will become my duty, immediately upon my arrival there, to put those laws in force, and to prevent their infraction in future, by punishing by the penalties provided by law, all those who offend.

As these laws are probably not known to many about to start to California, it would be well to make it publicly known that there are such laws in existence, and that they will in future be enforced against all persons, not citizens of the United States, who shall commit any trespass over the land of the United States in California.[9]

Anglo miners hailed the Smith "Doctrine." They believed that if the foreigners were allowed to continue to mine, they would take all of the gold out of the United States of America and strengthen some other nation at the expense of Anglo-America. They brutalized the foreigners at the mines and pressed the politicians to exclude them.

Considerable support for exclusion existed in the California legislature. G. B. Tingley of Sacramento described Mexicans and Latins:

Devoid of intelligence, sufficient to appreciate the true principles of free government; vicious, indolent, and dishonest, to an extent rendering them obnoxious to our citizens; with habits of life low and degraded; an intellect but one degree above the beast of the field, and not susceptible of elevation; all these things combined render such classes of human beings a curse to any enlightened community.[10]

Tingley warned of a foreign invasion.[11] Many others shared Tingley's views and would have voted for total exclusion. However, a compromise bill was proposed by Thomas Jefferson Green, who was a Texan, a hater of Mexicans, an expansionist, and a white supremacist. Green was responsible for seeking new sources of revenue for the state government, so he hit on the plan of taxing foreigners $20 per month. The legislators knew that if a direct tax were placed on all miners for the right to mine, there would be trouble. The foreigners, however, did not have a vote. Moreover, the Anglo legislators rationalized that the tax would prevent violence, since foreigners who had licenses would have the right to mine and would be accepted.

The act was a failure; neither the foreigners nor the Anglo-Americans reacted as they should. The foreigners, who were for the most part Mexicans, objected to the arbitrary tax. Rather than pay the exorbitant fee, they abandoned their diggings, and many former boom villages turned into ghost towns. This crippled commerce in mining-related businesses. Violence in the fields increased: foreigners were harassed, beaten, driven off the sites (license or no license), and lynched. It is also significant that after this series of events, so-called Mexican banditry flourished. The tax itself was repealed less than one year after it was passed—not because the legislators cared about the Mexicans or other foreigners, but because the merchants pressured Sacramento for repeal. During this lobbying period, even the *Daily Pacific News* of October

19, 1850, wrote: "The Mexican is, so far as the development of the resources of the country is concerned, the most useful inhabitant of California." In the end, money power talked.

Methodically, the Mexican was made more dependent on the colonizer, and he lost whatever control over his life that he may have had. There was little doubt that the conqueror-conquered relationship existed, for by the 1850s, even the elite publicly recognized their subjugated status and economic demise. Pablo de la Guerra condemned the Land Law before the state Senate, saying:

> Who are the claimants? They are the conquered prostrate before the conquerors asking his protection for the few things that his bad fortune has left him. They are the ones who have been sold like slabs of meat—they are the ones who were abandoned and sold by Mexico. They are strangers in their own country. They have no voice in this Senate, except those which are today so weakly speaking in their favor.[12]

De la Guerra demanded that the state protect the rights of the *Californios,* and accused the Anglo-Americans of acting in bad faith. The disenchantment of the former elite was almost complete.

Violence in Occupied California

The Mexican has been victimized by military and police powers from the beginning. Police and military violence, as mentioned, is a key to maintaining order among the colonized.* An important continuation of this organized violence is the individual or group violence that the colonizers perpetrate on the colonized. These actions are condoned by the colonial administration, which turns the other way until the colonized resist; then it intervenes. This process mentally conditions the colonizers so that they believe it is permissible to take advantage of the conquered. The colonizer's experience is similar to that of the white-Black relationship during slavery. The white could brutalize the Black, but the Black would be severely punished if he defended himself. In a colonial situation, the conqueror attempts to set up this kind of master-slave, or servant, relationship—a relationship perpetrated not only because of the racial prejudice of the colonizers, but also because of the economic benefits they derive from it.

Mob violence manifested itself in many forms in California. Most Anglo-

---

*Critics may argue that the violence directed against the Mexican was more the product of the savagery of the frontier and the Anglo-American character, than the nature of colonizers per se. Although I agree with them in principle, I would emphasize that the frontier situation and the colonial situation complement each other. Tunisia and Algeria, for example, were considered by the French as frontier areas, and perhaps the racism and violence that attended France's presence in those countries can be attributed simply to frontier necessity. But in a very real sense, the French were also colonizers—in the same way that the Anglo-Americans were colonizers of the Southwest by virtue of the conquest.

Americans believed that they were the champions of right and justice, and they moved quickly to promote it for themselves.* In California, local law enforcement was especially corrupt. Vigilante committees sprang up and took the law into their own hands. On occasion, they used their power prudently, but on most occasions they were nothing but a mob that acquired a mystique of legality.

The vigilante mobs set the tone for a kaleidoscopic series of violent experiences for Mexicans and Latin Americans. Following are some of the tragic incidents that were recorded. On June 15, 1849, a "benevolent, self-protective and relief society" called the Hounds attacked a Chilean *barrio* in San Francisco. The drunken mob of trespassers rioted, killed a woman, raped two, looted, and plundered. This action aroused the ire of many Anglo-Americans who condemned the Hounds and moved to control them. In 1851, when the Foreign Miner's Tax was passed, Antonio Coronel was leaving the diggings when he ran across a mob that was about to lynch five foreigners accused of stealing five pounds of gold. Coronel offered to pay them that amount for the release of the prisoners. They refused, and they whipped three of the men and hung two.[13] At Downieville in 1851, an Anglo was killed by a lover of a Mexican prostitute named Juanita. After a kangaroo (mock) trial, the lover was exiled and Juanita was hanged. After this, lynching became commonplace[14] and Mexicans came to know Anglo-American democracy as "linchocracia."[15]

On July 10, 1850, four Sonorans were charged with the murder of four Anglos near Sonora, California. A group of Anglo-Americans had come upon the Mexicans while they were burning two of the Anglo corpses, which were already in a decomposed state. The Mexicans explained that it was their custom to burn the dead (three of the four belonged to the Yaqui tribe). Justice of the Peace R. C. Barry believed the men innocent and attempted to forestall violence, but the mob had its way. The four men were hanged.[16]

During this time, public whippings and brandings were common. To the Anglo-American, "Whether from California, Chile, Peru, or Mexico, whether residents of 20 years' standing or immigrants of one week, all the Spanish-speaking were lumped together as 'interlopers' and 'greasers.'"[17]

Mexicans resented the discourteous attitude of Anglo-Americans toward Mexican women. While many Anglo-Americans courted the sexual favors of Mexican women, considerable racism accompanied miscegenation. If an Anglo married a Mexican, he immediately lost prestige. For example, John S. Barclay married Marta Carlos and was libeled in the press and later lynched when he shot an Anglo who had thrown a chair at his wife when she rejected a sexual overture.[18] On the other hand, instances of wife stealing were common. In these triangle situations, the Anglo-American mob supported their fellow colonizers. Professor Leonard Pitt writes:

---

*An interesting sidelight is that about one-fourth of the Anglos in California were not U.S. citizens; however, they rated as a class apart from Mexicans, Latin Americans, or Frenchmen.

The situation had certain parallels in the South of the United States, where Negro and white men struggled for the attentions of unprotected Negro women, except that the defense of feminine honor among Spanish Americans could be a deadly cult.[19]

As in other colonial situations, relationship between a male of the colonized peoples and a female of the colonizers was taboo.

Violence had to be justified. In the case of vigilante action, the stance was that the mob championed the law and was attempting to rectify conditions by demanding "an eye for an eye." Another justification was that the Mexicans' criminal nature had to be controlled; to Anglo-Americans, every Mexican was a potential outlaw, and Anglos used the outlaw activity as an excuse to rob and murder peaceful Mexicans.

This pattern was evident when Juan Flores (to be discussed later) escaped from San Quentin Prison in 1856 and rallied 50 Mexicans to his cause. During the time Flores was chased, assassinations were common. For example, near San Gabriel, two Mexicans were stopped because they looked "suspicious." When the *gringos* began mistreating the Mexicans, the latter attempted to escape, and during the chase one Mexican was killed. The *gringos* then went after the other escapees, and a massive roundup of Mexicans followed.

The El Monte gang (a group of Anglos dominated by Texans from El Monte, California) arrested Diego Navarro, who was seen riding away from the gun battle. Navarro claimed that he was on his way to San Gabriel when he saw the gun fight; he rode away because he knew that all Mexicans became victims of the Anglo wrath. The gang threw hot tar on his family home and broke into the house. They dragged him out and executed him, along with two other Mexicans who were accused of being members of the Flores gang.

Shortly afterwards, it was disclosed that Encarnación Berreyesa had been lynched in San Buenaventura. The pretext for the hanging was that Berreyesa was a member of the Flores gang; however, the truth was that the family had been victims of continual persecution. On March 28, 1857, a letter by José S. Berreyesa, reprinted in *El Clámor* from the *San Francisco Daily Herald,* reminded Californians of the terrible series of tragedies that had visited the family since the arrival of the Anglo-Americans. The troubles started, the letter said, with the Bear Flaggers' assassination of the elder Berreyesa and his two nephews. The family's tribulations were compounded when, in July 1854, the body of an Anglo-American was found on the San Vicente Ranch, which belonged to the Berreyesa family. A band of Anglos from Santa Clara, suspecting that the Berreyesas had murdered the man, invaded the house of Encarnación Berreyesa, dragged him out while his wife and children looked on, and suspended him from a tree. When he did not confess to the killings, the vigilantes left him half dead and turned on his brother Nemesio. The latter's wife fled to San José to summon friends to help. When the friends reached the ranch, they found Nemesio dead, dangling from a tree. Encarnación took his family to San Buenaventura to be with relatives and friends. However, when the Flores affair broke out, a vigilante committee went into action. Though

Berreyesa was not officially accused of being a follower of Flores, he was charged with the murder of an Anglo in Santa Clara. Under the cover of night, Anglos lynched Encarnación. The writer then listed members of the Berreyesa family who had been assassinated: "Encarnación, José R. Berreyesa, Francisco de Haro, Ramón de Haro, Nemesio Berreyesa, José Suñol, José Galindo, Juan Berreyesa—fathers, brothers, cousins. . . ." Similar incidents occurred during the early 1850s when the legendary Joaquín Murietta was hunted down.

Throughout this time, there was considerable police brutality. A double standard of justice existed between Mexicans and Anglos. A case in point is the Ruiz incident. On July 26, 1856, Francisco Ramírez wrote in *El Clamor Público* that conditions had never been so bad. Six years of assassinations had created armed camps in California. "The criminals have always escaped. Justice is almost never administered." Ramírez attacked the Anglo-Americans' indiscriminate murder of Chicanos. He demanded an immediate cessation of the violence. Nevertheless, Ramírez was temperate, although his patience was strained when Antonio Ruiz was murdered by William W. Jenkins, a deputy sheriff. Jenkins alleged that Ruiz had interfered in an argument between the deputy and Ruiz's landlady. When Ruiz protested the deputy's mistreatment of the landlady, the armed Jenkins turned on Ruiz and shot him in the chest. As is so often the case, the defense, which had the support of the court, attempted to discredit the reputation of those who had witnessed the Mexican's death. Police officials backed Jenkins. It took the jury only 15 minutes to return a verdict of not guilty. Soon afterwards, Jenkins returned to the task of maintaining "law and order" in Los Angeles.

Currents of Resistance

A colonized community defends itself in various ways: It rises in armed rebellion; it protests the oppression through the press or other publications; it forms trade unions and other confrontation organizations; or it uses political encounter. Californians during the occupation did resist physically; however, as mentioned, they were overwhelmed numerically. Here, we shall focus on resistance currents led by two men: Francisco Ramírez, a journalist, and Tiburcio Vásquez, a bandit. In different ways, these men kept the Mexican nationalism alive and underscored the frustrations of the oppressed.

There were few newspapers dedicated to the Chicano's cause, but for a time, from 1855 through 1859, *El Clamor Público*, published in Los Angeles by the aforementioned Francisco P. Ramírez, took up the banner. Ramírez, a 20-year-old Chicano, had been a compositor for the Spanish page of the *Los Angeles Star*. Tiring of *gringo* chauvinism, he began publishing his own Spanish-language newspaper solely committed to the advancement of the Chicano. The young editor was unpopular with the Anglo populace because of his anti-Establishment views. In 1859, because of lack of money, the newspaper went out of business. After working variously as state printer, postmaster, and the official translator for the state, he tried a comeback in 1872 as editor of *La Cronica* in Los Angeles. Thereafter, he dropped out of sight.[20]

Ramírez was indeed a champion of the Chicano cause. More important, however, he reflected the Chicano's disappointments with Anglo justice. On June 19, 1855, his newspaper editorials began on a moderate tone by calling for justice within the system and recognizing that California was now part of the United States:

> Today we respectfully greet the public. We ask our patrons for the liberal subscriptions they have favored us with. Even though it is difficult to say, the foreigners have demonstrated much more fervor in subscribing to the paper than the Californios themselves.[21]

He asked the Californians for financial support, writing that a free press was their best guarantee of liberty. He pledged his paper to an independent course, promising that the newspaper would "Uphold the Constitution of the United States, [being] convinced that only through it will we obtain liberty. . . . We shall combat all those opposed to its magnanimous spirit and grand ideas."[22]

Ramírez's editorials soon changed, however, and his coverage became more partisan. Only two months later, on August 28, in an article on the filibuster William Walker, Ramírez commented: "World history tells us that the Anglo-Saxons were in the beginning thieves and pirates, the same as other nations in their infancy . . . [but] the pirate instinct of old Anglo-Saxons is still active." Throughout the paper's existence Walker remained the special target of the newspaper's editorials, as did the other "pirates"—politicians and filibusters alike—who had designs on Mexico or Latin America. In September, Ramírez reprinted an article that questioned:

> What is the foreigner in California? He is what he is not in any other place in the world; he is what he is not in the most inhospitable land which can be imagined. . . . The North Americans pretend to give us lessons in humanity and to bring to our people the doctrine of salvation so we can govern ourselves, to respect the laws and conserve order. Are these the ones who treat us worse than slaves?[23]

The article then condemned lynchings of Chicanos. By October 1855, he encouraged Mexicans and Chileans to join Jesús Isla's *Junta Colonizadora de Sonora* and return to Mexico. He promoted this emigration society to the end, even when it was evident that it was not getting the proper support from Mexico. Ramírez's loss of faith in the U.S. government is beyond question.

On May 10, 1856, Ramírez protested Anglo-American nativism, writing: "California has fallen into the hands of the ambitious sons of North America who will not stop until they have satisfied their passions, by driving the first occupants of the land out of the country, villifying their religion and disfiguring their customs." Ramírez encouraged Mexicans to return to Sonora. One reader objected to Ramírez's "return-to-Mexico" stance, saying: "California has always been the asylum of Sonorans, and the place where they have found good wages, hospitality, and happiness."[24] The writer implied that Mexicans never had it so good. Ramírez caustically replied that the letter did not merit comment and asked: "Are the Californios as happy today as when they belonged to the Republic of Mexico, in spite of all of its revolutions and changes in government?"[25]

The pages of *El Clamor Público* also reveals a schism between the Establishment Mexicans and the lower-caste Mexicans, or *cholos*. The oppression and its attendant discrimination was obvious; however many of the elites continued to work within the system and cooperated with the Anglo-American to frustrate, not only resistance movements, but the Mexicans' justifiable demands. The Juan Flores story, mentioned earlier, is a case in point. Juan Flores, 21 years old, broke out of San Quentin Prison where he was serving a term for horse stealing. He returned to Los Angeles and rallied almost 50 Chicanos, including Pancho Daniel, to his flock. Many of these so-called *desperados* had grievances against the Anglos. They operated around San Juan Capistrano. When Los Angeles Sheriff James Barton and a posse went to investigate, the Flores gang killed the sheriff. Soon, rumors spread that the Flores gang intended to kill all whites. A vigilante committee was organized to deal with the situation. Anglos flooded into Los Angeles for protection. Although many *Californios* aided and abetted Flores and his followers, some joined in the preparations to arrest the "criminals" as proof that they were good citizens and loyal patriots. Even Ramírez condemned the "bandits" in an editorial dated January 31, 1857, calling for *Californios* to join in the protection of their families and the enforcement of the laws. Tomás Sánchez, the Chicano *cacique* (boss) of the Democratic party, and Andrés Pico led the posse comprised of Anglos and Chicanos. They joined with the El Monte *gringos* to pursue Flores.

El Monte was the *gringo* stronghold—the only community in the Los Angeles area that was predominately Anglo-American. Many inhabitants were former Texans (some were even ex-Rangers from that state) who were notorious as "Mexican busters." In almost every incident involving friction between Mexicans and Anglos, the El Monte crowd posed as defenders of white supremacy. Many Mexicans, however, considered them outlaws.

The El Monte force, which operated separately from the Los Angeles posse, captured Flores and Pancho Daniel, but the two escaped. The Anglos then insured "justice" by hanging their next nine captives. Andrés Pico emulated the *gringos* and hanged two of his countrymen whom he had captured. Finally, with the exception of Pancho Daniel, the entire gang was captured. During the hunt, 52 men were crammed into the jails. *El Clamor* lauded Andrés Pico in an editorial published on February 7 and congratulated him for cooperating with the citizens of El Monte. Ramírez praised the spirit of togetherness and even wrote that *Californios* had vindicated their honor. Flores, not surprisingly, was hanged after being convicted by a kangaroo court.

Many Chicanos, however, did not share the enthusiasm of *El Clamor* and the *ricos* (rich *Californios*), and condemned their participation in suppressing the Flores-Daniel rebellion. As Professor Pitt noted, "Sánchez and Pico, who gladly rode with Texans to track down 'their own kind,' thereby won the gringo's everlasting gratitude."[26] They were rewarded; Sánchez became sheriff and Pico was made a brigadier in the California militia and was also elected to the state Assembly.[27]

Why had Ramírez backed this action? The only explanation is that he believed the cooperation of Mexicans with the Anglos would bring the two peoples together. These hopes were shattered by the lynchings of innocent Mexicans throughout the state, and Ramírez had a change of heart. He had applauded the hanging of Flores, but several months later when Pancho Daniel, a member of the gang, was hanged, Ramírez called it a "barbaric and diabolic execution" and then lambasted the Chicano population, writing: "And you, imbecile Californios! You are to blame for the lamentations that we are witnessing. We are tired of saying: open your eyes, and it is time that we demand our rights and interests. It is with shame that we say, and difficult to confess it: you are the sarcasm of humanity!" He scolded the readers for not voting and for putting up with the indignities, calling them "cowards and stupids." He warned *Californios* that until they cared, they could never cast off the "yoke of slavery."[28] In less than four years, Ramírez had changed from an assimilationist to a nationalist.

In many ways, Ramírez's evolution reflected that of many *Californios* and Mexicans. Once the annexation of California became a reality, they sincerely sought to become good citizens; however, when it became evident that they were not considered nor treated like first-class citizens, they turned to separatism. Atrocities committed against the Mexican population intimidated and alienated them. Mexicans were not treated as individuals, and when some Mexicans took to the highway, forced into a life of crime, they were collectively guilty in the eyes of most *gringos* in California. Protests against the current injustices appeared in newspapers like *El Clamor,* but gradually those voices were silenced as the Mexican population grew too poor to support newspapers. Therefore, the California of the Mexican and the Anglo grew further and further apart, with the *Mexicano* growing more resentful of the *gringo.* He was able to release his frustration only through extralegal activities, because as we have seen, the courts and the system favored the Anglo and discriminated against the Mexican.

Resistance also manifested itself in antisocial behavior. When the colonized cannot earn a living within the system, or when they are degraded, they strike out. The most physical way is to rebel. This can be done in an organized way, as was done by Juan Cortina in Texas, or it can express itself in bandit activity. An analysis of the life of Tiburcio Vásquez clearly demonstrates that, while in the strict sense of the word he was a criminal, at the same time his underlying motivation was self-defense. Some Anglo-American folklorists have attempted to portray Tiburcio Vásquez as a comical and oversexed Mexican bandit. In stereotyping Vásquez, Anglos have purposely or unconsciously attempted to use satire to dismiss the legitimate grievances of Chicanos during the nineteenth century. While it is true that Tiburcio Vásquez was an outlaw, many Mexicans still consider him a hero.

Tiburcio Vásquez was born in Monterey, California, on August 11, 1835. His parents had a good reputation, and Vásquez had an above-average education for the times. Vásquez never married but acknowledged that he fathered a child in Monterey County. In about 1852 or 1853, he attended a dance in Monterey where he was involved in the shooting of a constable. He fled to the hills, but charges were never brought against him. Vásquez at the end of his career explained the incident and his reasons for turning *bandido:*

> My career grew out of the circumstances by which I was surrounded. As I grew to manhood I was in the habit of attending balls and parties given by the native Californians, into which the Americans, then beginning to become numerous, would force themselves and shove the native born men aside, monopolizing the dance and the women. This was about 1852. A spirit of hatred and revenge took possession of me. I had numerous fights in defense of my countrymen. The officers were continually in pursuit of me. I believed we were unjustly and wrongfully deprived of the social rights that belonged to us.[29]

In the second half of the 1850s, the "people" indicted Vásquez in Los Angeles for horse stealing and sentenced him to five years in San Quentin Prison. He broke out in 1859, but the law apprehended him in Amados County —again on a charge of horse stealing. After serving more time in San Quentin, he was finally released in 1863. For a time he became a gambler, but in 1864 he returned to the life of a highwayman. In 1867, the state again sentenced him to San Quentin, this time for cattle rustling, and he remained there until June 4, 1870. This date marks the start of Vásquez's legendary exploits. Contemporaries described him as "elusive, clever, and highly skilled in horsemanship." In the next years, Vásquez was so successful in eluding the Anglo that his exploits were advertised widely among Chicanos. Many believed that he was ambitious toward effecting an uprising or revolution against the "Yankee invaders" of California.[30] The *Los Angeles Express* (date unknown) quoted Vásquez as claiming: "Given $60,000 I would be able to recruit enough arms and men to revolutionize Southern California."

In the fall of 1871, Vásquez and his men robbed the Visalia stage. His reputation as a *desperado* grew, and he was even blamed for crimes that he did not commit. The magnitude of the manhunts increased. Authorities paid informers in an effort to locate Vásquez, who was by this time a hero among the Chicano populace. Throughout 1871 Vásquez not only continued his activities, but also avoided arrest. Once in the mountains above Santa Cruz, a marshall seriously wounded him, but he managed to escape nonetheless. Meanwhile, Cleovaro Chávez and a Chilean, Abdon Leiva, joined him, rounding out his gang to six members. The band operated out of Leiva's ranch in La Canteca, not far from the New Idria Quicksilver Mine. Vásquez had made a deal with the mine's owners and employees that he would not bother them if they would not inform about his movements. Both kept their bargains. The

Chicano populace continued to aid Vásquez, for "to some, Vásquez must have seemed a hero dealing out his own particular brand of justice. Certainly his reputation was growing fast."[31]

In the summer of 1873, Vásquez planned his most daring caper—robbing the Southern Pacific payroll train between San José and Gilroy. The gang was not able to derail the train as planned, so they turned instead to the Twenty-One Mile House, a well-known hotel and restaurant on the railroad line and successfully raided it. After this, Vásquez planned the Tres Piños robbery; on August 26, 1873, he and his men converged on Snyder's store in Tres Piños and robbed it of $1200. Needless to say, newspapers sensationalized the Vásquez raids, and wanted posters were circulated. Vásquez prudently decided to shift his activities to Southern California.

At this point, Vásquez's indiscretions caught up with him in a way that the manhunts were never able to do. He had been carrying on a secret affair with Leiva's wife, Rosaria. The Chilean caught the two *in flagrante delicto* and would have shot Vásquez if it had not been for the intervention of another of the gang members. Leiva got his revenge by surrendering to Deputy Sheriff W. W. Jenkins in Los Angeles, and telling the full story of Vásquez's activities and the whereabouts of the gang. Vásquez abandoned Rosaria, and much later, when he was finally captured and tried, both she and Leiva were star witnesses for the prosecution.

On December 26, 1873, Vásquez sacked the pueblo of Kingston. He boldly entered the town, tied up 35 men, and robbed all of them in less than ten minutes. All of the stores in town were robbed simultaneously. In an exchange of fire, Vásquez was wounded in the knee; however, he collected $2500 in cash and jewelry. The press again spread the news of Vásquez's exploits:

> Vásquez seems determined to excel even the dare-devil exploits of the famous brigand chief Joaquin Murietta. After having been hunted for months like a wild beast from lair to lair—the banditti under his command either killed, captured or dispersed—and successfully eluding the most vigilant and indefatigable pursuit to which an outlaw was ever subjected in this state, has placed himself again at the head of a band of Mexican cut-throats and ex-prison convicts, and has entered upon another campaign of pillage and murder.[32]

Mexicans, oppressed and degraded, felt a gleeful identification with the anti-Establishment escapades of Vásquez.

On February 25, 1874, Vásquez, accompanied by a lieutenant, struck again. In broad daylight, they held up the Coyote Holes stage station, which lay between Los Angeles and the Owens River, as well as the stage. The legislature appropriated $5000 to finance an expedition against Vásquez. The governor offered a reward of $8000 alive or $6000 dead. While Vásquez hid at La Brea Rancho—the guest of George Allen, better known as "Greek

George"—Sheriff Harry Morse covered 2720 miles in 61 days searching for him.

The authorities learned where Vásquez was hiding out, and a posse surrounded the ranch. A special correspondent for the *San Francisco Chronicle,* George A. Beers, accompanied them. When Vásquez attempted to escape through a window, Beers shot him. Although captured, Vásquez remained cool; he told his captors: "If you dress my wounds and nurse me careful, you boys get $8000. If you let me die, you only get $6000. You get $2000 for being kind!" He then congratulated the posse for a job well done. An all-Anglo jury found him guilty, and he was sentenced to hang.

A partial explanation as to why Vásquez captured the imagination of the Mexican populace is advanced by George Beers, who wrote:

> Vásquez turned to the life of a bandido because of the bitter animosity then existing, and which still exists, between the white settlers and the native or Mexican portion of the population. The native Californians, especially the lower classes, never took kindly to the stars and stripes. Their youth were taught from the very cradle to look upon the American government as that of a foreign nation.
>
> This feeling was greatly intensified by the rough brutal conduct of the worst class of American settlers, who never missed an opportunity to openly exhibit their contempt for the native Californian or Mexican population—designating them as "d——d Greasers," and treating them like dogs. Add to this the fact that these helpless people were cheated out of their lands and possessions by every subterfuge—in many instances their property being actually wrestled from them by force, and their women debauched whenever practicable—and we can understand very clearly some of the causes which have given to Joaquin [Murietta], Vásquez, and others of their stripe, the power to call around them at any time all the followers they required, and which secured to them aid and comfort from the Mexican settlers everywhere.[33]

Conclusion

Tiburcio Vásquez's death ended the era of intense Chicano banditry. Anglo-Americans, who in the first years had lived in fear of a Chicano uprising, soon numerically overwhelmed the Chicanos throughout the state. The impact of the conquest had resulted in an alien government occupying the area. The violence and the bigotry of the Bear Flaggers and the other occupiers set the tone for the captivity of the Chicano. The gold rush brought in a people who were not concerned with assimilating the native Californians into their society, but were intent upon erasing the Mexican past and establishing their own privilege. Because the Anglos were the majority, the state government reflected on their objective, which was to replace the "undemocratic" greaser system with an administration that promoted the Anglo-American interests.

The state legislature and courts aided the Anglo nativists* in this endeavor, passing laws that stripped Chicanos of their economic base and excluded them from an opportunity to build a new one through mining. The era's two most significant laws, the Land Act of 1851 and the Foreign Miner's Tax, have already been discussed. The former took the land from the Chicano, resulting in most of the land passing to the Anglo-Americans by the 1870s. The latter encouraged violence, establishing the principle of "America for Anglo-Americans."

During this time, the Chinese were used as an alternative to the Chicanos as California's labor force. Chicanos were pushed to the southern half of the state and were literally forced out of California in order to escape the lynchings, abuses, and colonized status to which they had been condemned. Their political decline paralleled their economic reduction. Fewer and fewer Chicano representatives were found in the state Senate. Even at the local government level, Anglos replaced Chicanos. In areas where Chicanos still formed a high percentage of the population, they were rarely represented on juries, and thus the accused Chicano was denied the right of trial by his peers. Moreover, their number in the prisons increased; from 1854 through 1855, they represented 16 to 20 percent of the inmates in San Quentin.[34]

Most Anglo-Americans believed that, based on their right of conquest, they were entitled to special privileges and special citizenship status; this was reinforced by a belief in their cultural and racial superiority. The Chicano, in contrast, was a conquered person, an alien, and a half-breed. When a small number of Chicanos turned to highway banditry, Anglo-Americans did not bother to investigate why they committed antisocial acts or why the Chicano masses supported them. They merely stereotyped the entire group as criminal, justifying further violence against the Mexican American community. These factors created the colonization of the Chicano in California, with the Chicano becoming dependent on the Anglo-American majority, having no political or economic control, and being forced to adhere to an alien culture and government.

---

*In this monograph, the terms nativist and nativism are used in the historical rather than in the sociological or anthropological sense. In U.S. history, nativism refers to the policy of favoring citizens of Anglo or Nordic extraction as opposed to immigrants with other backgrounds. Immigration restrictions and violence directed against foreigners have been an outgrowth of nativist sentiment in the United States, for Anglos have feared that aliens (and, at different times, Catholics and radicals) would endanger their distinctly "American" way of life. Nativists have not only been exceedingly ethnocentric, but have also nurtured strong cultural antipathies against those they regard an inferior. See John Higham, *Strangers in the Land* (New York: Atheneum Publishers, 1971).

Notes

1. Leonard Pitt, *The Decline of the Californios* (Berkeley and Los Angeles: University of California Press, 1966), p. 116. This chapter relies heavily on this work, which is the best history on the Chicano in California. It also draws heavily from *El Clamor Público,* a Spanish-language newspaper that was published between 1855 and 1859. Considerable primary research in this area must still be done—not into the papers of *los ricos,* but into the feelings of the poor Mexicans, who were exploited by the *gringos* and rich *Californios* alike.

2. Andrew F. Rolle, *California: A History* (New York: Thomas Y. Crowell Company, 1963), p. 191.

3. Rolle, p. 182.

4. Pitt, p. 26.

5. Pitt, p. 27.

6. Pitt, p. 30.

7. Pitt, p. 119.

8. Joan W. Moore, *Mexican American* (Englewood Cliffs, N.J.: Prentice-Hall, Inc., 1970), p. 19.

9. Leonard Pitt, "The Foreign Miner's Tax of 1850: A Study of Nativism and Anti-Nativism in Gold Rush California" (M.A. thesis, University of California at Los Angeles, 1955), p. 14.

10. Pitt, "Miners," pp. 49–50.

11. Pitt, "Miners," p. 49.

12. *El Clamor Público,* 26 April 1856.

13. Pitt, *Decline,* pp. 50–51.

14. Pitt, *Decline,* p. 74.

15. *El Clamor Público,* 4 April 1857; 26 April 1857.

16. Pitt, *Decline,* pp. 61–63.

17. Pitt, *Decline,* p. 53.

18. Pitt, *Decline,* pp. 72–73.

19. Pitt, *Decline,* p. 72.

20. See Pitt, *Decline,* chapter xi, for a biography of Ramírez.

21. *El Clamor Público,* 19 June 1855.

22. *El Clamor Público,* 19 June 1855.

23. *El Clamor Público,* 18 September 1855.

24. *El Clamor Público,* 17 May 1856.

25. *El Clamor Público,* 17 May 1856.

26. Pitt, *Decline,* p. 173.

27. Pitt, *Decline,* p. 174.

28. *El Clamor Público,* 18 December 1858.

29. Robert Greenwood, *The California Outlaw: Tiburcio Vásquez* (Los Gatos, Calif.: The Talisman Press, 1960), p. 12.

30. Greenwood, p. 13.

31. Greenwood, pp. 23–24.

32. *The Bakersfield Californian,* 1 January 1874; quoted in Greenwood, p. 39.

33. Greenwood, p. 75.

34. Pitt, *Decline,* p. 263.

Part Two

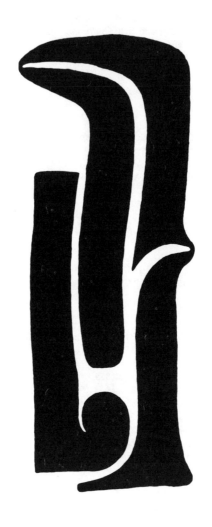

A Radical View
of the 20th Century Chicano

*L*iberation for Chicanos can be achieved only through awareness—awareness of the oppression and injustices Chicanos have suffered in the United States. But this awareness cannot occur without a reexamination of history; we must take a radical viewpoint if we are to correct the myths that have been perpetuated for so long. Through this approach Chicanos can identify, and then confront, the forces that dominate them.

In the first part of *Occupied America,* we challenged the historical myth that the Anglo-American people brought democracy to the Southwest and "liberated" the area from Mexican tyranny. In reality, the Anglo-American conquest and the occupation that followed it reduced the Mexican in the Southwest to a dependent status. As a result of continued exploitation and intimidation, Chicanos by the turn of the century lived in a "nation within a nation." This Chicano nation (which was, in reality, "occupied America") was characterized by visible psychological, political, economic, and social boundaries—as opposed to geographic ones—and those boundaries were shaped by the Anglo conquest and occupation.

The size of the Chicano nation was swelled by Mexican migration to the Southwest in the twentieth century, and the immigrants reinforced the concept of nationalism in the *colonias.* In turn, the *colonias* extended sanctuary to the newcomers, giving them a chance to acclimate gradually to the hostile environment. These twentieth-century immigrants were imported to the United States by the same economic interests that exploited the existing *colonias.* The powerful men who controlled agriculture, mining, and the railroad combines knew that cheap labor was essential to extending their economic domains. As a result of immigration restrictions placed on Asians, as well as other developments in the early twentieth century, Mexico became the logical source for this labor.

The struggle of Chicanos to liberate themselves from their oppression was a difficult one—especially in light of the forces that conditioned their role in the United States. The new immigrants had been brought north as temporary laborers, to serve as a supplement to white labor, and they were supposed to return south once their work was finished. Instead, they stayed, often hidden in the *colonias.* When it became evident that many of these Mexicans would not return to their homeland and their numbers increased, the racism and ethnocentrism of Anglo-Americans grew more pronounced. A movement was mounted in Congress to limit the number of Mexicans entering the United

States. That this movement was not successful is due primarily to the powerful lobby of Southwestern agriculturalists who needed Mexican labor—economic necessity, not moral right, was the determining factor.

Mexican workers were pawns, caught between the racists and the exploiters, and abandoned by union leaders, churches, and educators. In the face of tremendous odds, Chicanos joined together in mutual aid societies and other organizations to try to improve their situation. Many Chicanos attempted to accommodate to the Anglo majority, only to be rejected. The price of acceptance was the surrender of their Mexican identity. But many Chicanos refused to surrender. When their resistance to the forces that exploited them became militant, Anglos reacted with even greater measures of repression: organizers and strikers were jailed, beaten, deported, or murdered. If the Anglo-American public did not entirely approve of these brutal methods, it nevertheless did little to stem the abuse.

In the 1960s Chicanos became increasingly aware that they were collectively subjugated. They realized that they were being manipulated, and that their *colonias* were controlled, for the benefit of privileged Anglos. During the latter half of the 1960s, the drive toward Chicano self-determination and cultural pluralism consolidated. A consciousness of the link between Chicanos and other Third World people also in captivity developed.

A major problem in reexamining Chicano history is the dearth of basic research in almost every area: their leadership in the trade-union movement, their separatism, their continuing "Mexican" nationalism, and the development and effectiveness of their early organizations. Out of necessity, therefore, we have relied on selected secondary sources as well as government records in chapters 6 to 8, whereas chapters 9 and 10 are based largely on the author's own experiences. The perspective that emerges is, indeed, a Chicano perspective, and as such it is filled with the feelings and beliefs—the emotions—of Chicanos. But it is a perspective that must be considered, for it is based on the reactions of Chicanos against continuing repression, against inequities, against second-class citizenship.

Chapter Six

Greasers Go Home

Contrary to popular belief, the Mexican did not come to the United States because he wanted freedom or because he wanted to improve his social life style. Most Mexicans became part of the United States either because of the Anglo conquest or because they were brought here by economic forces over which they had little control. The uprooted Mexican was torn from his homeland "like a nail torn from its finger." And, like so many Eastern and Southern European emigrants, he could not read or write. He, therefore, expressed his anguish through his ballads, called *corridos,* which today offer a clue to the Mexican experience. The "Emigrant's Farewell" relates the feelings of many of the uprooted Mexicans:

> Mexico is my home-land
> where I was born a Mexican;
> give me the benediction
> of your powerful hand.

I go to the United States
to seek to earn a living.
Goodbye, my beloved land:
I bear you in my heart.

For I am not to blame
that I leave my country thus;
the fault is that of poverty,
which keeps us all in want.

Goodbye, fair Guanajuato.
The state where I was born;
I am going to the United States
far, far from you.[1]

This simple *corrido* reflects the intense nationalism of the Mexican peons who came to the United States from the interior of Mexico. After 1910, they migrated from the state of Guanajuato, Jalisco, Mexico, and others, rather than from northern Mexico from where most of the newcomers had come previously.

This mass migration was among the largest mass movements of a people in the history of mankind, eventually shifting one-eighth of Mexico's population "north from Mexico." It is ironic that it was not better documented. This chapter traces the reasons for the Mexican migration, as well as the public and institutional reaction to it when it became clear that the Mexican was here to stay and would not return to Mexico once his intended role as a temporary supplement to white labor was finished. Many Anglo-Americans felt threatened, since, like the Eastern and Southern Europeans, the Mexican did not fit the Anglo-Saxon image of a good Anglo-American citizen. The reaction of the Anglo-American was, in short, "Greaser go home!" Although there are parallels between the exclusion of the Mexican and of other ethnic minorities, the conquest and the proximity of the border set him apart. As we shall see, it is these differences that have contributed to today's defining of the master-servant relationship between the Mexican and the privileged Anglo-American.

Background to the Mexican's Importation

The first U.S. Industrial Revolution had spread to agriculture by the 1850s, and McCormick's machine reaped the grain fields in the lands seized from Mexico. Mining bonanzas in the West attracted large numbers of Anglos. More and more, the Southwest supplied the raw materials for the East, which in turn provided the "colony" with manufactured goods and capital. An era of unprecedented industrial growth began with the Union's victory of the Civil War, and control of the country fell to the nation's industrialists. Capitalists made fantastic profits from war contracts and used the capital to build industrial empires. Railroad interests laid a track linking the East and West in order to open up the virgin lands of the Southwest. Fuel and minerals were needed, as well as food to feed the European immigrants who manned the new factories. The refrigerated car went into service one year before the transcontinental railroads were completed in 1869. Both the railroads and the refrigerated cars proved to be revolutionary in the last quarter of the nineteenth century. Railroad and industrial monopolization gave rise to trusts, and the trend to "bigness" carried over into agribusiness in the Southwest.

Large numbers of Chinese were brought across the Pacific to work on the railroads, farms, mines, and industries of the Southwest. For a time, labor in the region was predominately Chinese. During this period, however, the nativists increasingly abused, lynched, and finally, in the 1880s, excluded the Chinese. Japanese and other Asians filled the vacuum for a time, but they too suffered nativist abuse, mainly because, like the Chinese, they were racially and culturally different. What Anglo-American society wanted was workers who would do the work white men would not, who would accept below-subsistence wages, and who would go home to their native lands when their work was finished. The Anglos wanted this at the minimum of expense and inconvenience. Mexico was the logical source for this kind of labor. Prior to 1880, however, contact between the United States and Mexico was limited to the sparsely settled borderlands of northern Mexico. Although this area did not have sufficient manpower to supply the Southwest's growing labor demands, events in Mexico soon changed this situation.[2]

At the time of the Mexican Independence of 1821, Mexico was a feudal and predominately rural nation, with most laborers bound to the land through either tradition or peonage. A struggle between conservative forces intent on maintaining this status quo and liberals intent on making Mexico a modern or capitalist nation broke out in the 1850s. The liberals won. Widespread civil war broke out, called the War of the Reform (1858–1861), during which Benito Juárez became president of Mexico. Juárez was not a popular champion of the masses, even though he was romanticized as such. He has been portrayed as a great president—and he did keep the nation together. However, supported by the rising middle class of Mexico, he became one of the nation's first capitalistic presidents.

Mexican feudalism was far from equalitarian, for the church and a few *hacendados* (landholders) owned most of the land; still, many communal Indian villages had been allowed to exist. The new capitalist presidents of Mexico, on the other hand, were greatly influenced by *científicos* (positivists), who believed in the industrial development of Mexico, and they openly condemned the Indian as a barrier to this development. The reformers passed the Laws of the Reform to end the special privileges of the church and the military, but these laws were used to take the Indians' lands from them. In other words, although the targets of the laws were the special-interest groups that benefited from feudalism—the church and the *hacendados*—in the end, the Indian and the peon lost more. Confronted by the War of Reform and the French intervention (1861–1867), Juárez did not implement his economic program, and it was not until the rise of Porfirio Díaz in 1876 that an all-out assault on feudalism began. Feudalism then was replaced by an even more exploitive system.

At the heart of Díaz's economic program was railroad construction. "Economically, railroad building and industrialization were the two most important innovative processes generating social change in Mexico during the Porfiriato."[3] Díaz gave tangible support to both. Anglo-American and other foreign capital financed the building of 15,000 miles of track between 1880 and 1910.[4] These lines ran from north to south, providing access to the mineral deposits of Mexico's interior, then being used to carry the ore north to the United States. Díaz, moreover, promoted interstate commerce, abolishing state import taxes as well as municipal taxes. This brought about a transition in Mexico, with many old haciendas becoming profit-making enterprises. They were now forced to modernize their operations in order to show a profit. The capitalist farmers bought machines, borrowed money to purchase them, and grew cash crops to pay for the loans. In short, agriculture became a capitalist venture and, therefore, was more dependent on the domestic and international marketplace.

In the process many *peones* were uprooted, either because they were displaced from the hacienda by machines taking their jobs, or because they were attracted to better-paying jobs on the railroad construction crews, in the booming mines, or in the nascent industries. Peonage, however, was not abolished, since the new capitalist agriculturalists protected the institution to insure a generous supply of cheap labor. Many of the uprooted went to the cities searching for work; others moved simply to escape from the oppressive peonage that had bound them to the land.

The decline of ruralism in Mexico began before the Revolution of 1910, and even before that time, the Mexican cities served as employment centers for both domestic and foreign employers. Meanwhile, in their quest for profit, the new capitalists subverted the Laws of the Reform, especially *La Ley Lerdo*, which had intended to break up the church holdings by specifying that the corporations must sell excess lands. They twisted the law to give the *hacendados* the right to encroach on the *ejidos*, the communal lands of the Indian villages. As in the United States, the Mexican farm family was doomed: "Private property holders like the Zapata family lost their lands, as did the communal land holders (*ejidatarios*), to big commercial farmers interested in expanding the sugar industry in Morelos by developing large plantations with cheap labor and by constructing sugar mills on the plantations themselves."[5]

These developments had a profound effect on the poor Mexican worker. In a sense, the hacienda had protected him, as had the *ejido*. He always had something to eat and shelter of one kind or another. But, under capitalism and the liberal party, he became a wage earner who had to have capital in order to survive. Professor James Cockcroft notes that "between 1876 and 1910, maize prices increased 108 percent, bean prices 163 percent, and chile prices 147 percent; since wages increased only 60 percent during the same period, real income for the masses declined an estimated 57 percent."[6] This decline in purchasing power encouraged proletariat discontent and many Mexicans moved north, which was not, in all cases, to the United States. Considerable Anglo-American capital had moved into northern Mexico where Anglo-Americans operated large mining and agriculture enterprises. Economic development in northern Mexico required additional labor, which was obtained from the interior. The economic growth of northern Mexico served to make the area a way-station for workers migrating to the Anglo-American Southwest.

Meanwhile, the U.S. federal government had gradually changed its policy from encouraging European and Asian immigration to restricting it. It all boiled down to the determination of most Anglo-Americans to "preserve their [Anglo-Saxon] political and religious ideals."[7] Legislation of both a qualitative and quantitative nature was passed. The qualitative restrictions involved, in general, mental, moral, and economic "disabilities" of the would-be immigrants. Restrictions of a quantitative nature were more important to the Mexicans, for it reduced the number of aliens allowed to enter the United States. An example of this kind of legislation was the Immigration Exclusion Act of 1882, which eliminated Chinese immigration to the United States. The exclusion of other Asians followed a pattern similar to that of the Chinese: at first, the new arrivals were welcomed as a needed labor supply, but as their numbers increased, so did the nativist sentiment against them.[8] Organized resistance to the foreigners sprang up, and the nativists successfully pushed for stricter immigration laws. As we have mentioned earlier, however, economic necessity demanded a supply of cheap labor; thus, Mexicans became dubious beneficiaries of the ban on Asian immigration as Southwestern Anglos turned to Mexico for their labor force.

The Importation of the Mexican

Most students of Mexican migration into the United States support Carey McWilliams' thesis that economic conditions in Mexico pushed Mexicans north, while the economic growth of the United States and the need for cheap labor pulled them there. They correctly point out that "Mexico's population growth rate is among the highest in the world"[9] and that its economic growth lags behind, contributing to the push as did the upheaval of the Mexican Revolution. The result was that eight to ten percent of Mexico's population migrated to the United States after 1900. McWilliams graphically described the underlying motivation for the migration:

> Irrigation was the magic key that unlocked the resources of the region. Irrigated farming is intensive farming: with high yields per acre, heavy labor requirements, year-round production, and crop specialization. Small in area, the "winter gardens" of the Southwest have offset, by their exceptional productivity, many disadvantages of an arid environment. Throughout the region, the distribution of Mexicans in rural areas is largely determined by the location of irrigated crops. As an economic empire, the Southwest dates from the Reclamation Act in 1902,

which outlined a development policy for the West and made possible the use of federal funds for the construction of large-scaled irrigation and reclamation projects. Irrigation has had more to do with the economic growth of the Southwest than any single factor.[10]

We agree with McWilliams' thesis, but feel that it should be taken one step further.

Economic studies usually have ignored the United States' role in the push process. In fact, more traditional Anglo-American economic histories of Mexico have dwelt upon the capital investment in Mexico and the industrial imbalance. They have not researched what happens once U.S. capital creates a dependency or when Anglo business collaborates with Mexican capitalists to exploit labor and resources. A study of the effects on the Mexican people and how these conditions have forced Mexicans north is needed. From the facts available, however, we can conclude that Mexican labor was imported into the United States, and that by the 1900s a dependency relationship between the United States and Mexico existed. U.S. interests manipulated the Mexican economy to keep it underdeveloped, insuring to U.S. corporations the advantages of cheap labor and privileged treatment in Mexico, a policy that is not uncommon in relations between developed and underdeveloped nations. U.S. dominance in Mexico cannot be denied. Victor Alba, a Mexican historian, states that U.S. corporations owned three-quarters of the mineral holdings in Mexico and that by 1910, "U.S. investment amounted to more than $2 billion, more than all the capital in the hands of Mexicans."[11] Alba points out that the Díaz government gave foreign investors preferential treatment: Edward L. Doheney bought oil-yielding tracts in Tampico for $1 an acre. The companies exported all the oil they wanted and did not pay taxes.[12] Furthermore, the Mexican government intervened on the side of management during these years. In the next chapter, we shall discuss the Cananea strike of 1906, which is an example of the preferential treatment that the *gringo* investors received. Only the most naive would deny that the United States interfered in Mexican affairs.

Mexican economic dependence on the United States caused resentment, which contributed to the Mexican Revolution of 1910. Alba notes this resentment:

> No serious study was given to this situation. The people did not dare speak out against foreign capital for fear of reprisals by the investors, but a flood of resentment was cresting. This was reflected in a number of cartoons in various newspapers, which were quickly suppressed—cartoons directed not so much at foreign capital as at the Mexicans who submitted to it.[13]

In the process of their audacious interference in the Mexican economy, the U.S. capitalists kept Mexico underdeveloped, thus insuring a constant supply of raw materials as well as cheap labor for their parent corporations in the Southwest. Monopolies, such as U.S. Steel, the Guggenheims, Anaconda, Standard Oil, and others, were active in both countries.[14] The U.S. controlled the flow of immigration, as well as indirectly encouraging illegal migration. U.S. business interests built railroads that facilitated the movement of Mexicans to the border areas, and during the early years, in many instances, these interests paid the workers' fares to the United States, even though contract labor was in violation of U.S. law. U.S. business policies also encouraged millions of others to flock to the border cities, which became labor pools for both legal and illegal recruitment by agribusiness and large corporations. At the turn of the century, most border cities numbered about a thousand inhabitants. Since then, the growth of these cities has been phenomenal:[15]

Municipio	1940	1967
Tijuana	21,977	347,501
Mexicali	44,399	540,300
Ciudad Juarez	55,024	501,406
Nuevo Laredo	31,502	140,818

A brief review of Anglo-American economic involvement reinforces our thesis of the importation of the Mexican laborer. After Mexican independence from Spain, England and the United States vied for economic control of Mexico. The reader might contend that other nations, including the United States, did everything possible to attract foreign capital. This is true; however, the flow of foreign capital into the United States never reached the proportions that it did in Mexico or other colonized nations, where it dwarfed domestically owned enterprises and controlled (through bribes and intimidation) elected and appointed authorities. Moreover, in the case of the United States, this investment lessened as the nation industrialized. In Mexico it increased. Furthermore, foreign investment in the United States was primarily in U.S.-owned and controlled corporations, whereas in Mexico and other developing and underdeveloped nations, the foreign corporation moved in directly to exploit the resources and remove them from the nation.

Anglo-American political aggressions against Mexico, for a time, weakened U.S. influence; however, this influence increased after the ascendancy of the Mexican Liberal party and the removal of the French threat. Mexican economic thinkers, impressed by the U.S. and French positivists, encouraged foreign immigration and capital. The immigration failed, but an influx of foreign corporations flooded the nation. In collusion with Mexican authorities and Mexican capitalists, they exploited the resources of the country. They were given free land and special political and economic privileges. At first, Britain had the edge over the United States, but the building of railroads north and south, "with rail connections to seven land ports of entry into the United States and heavy U.S. investments in Mexico, all tended to divert the exports from Europe, which in 1877 took nearly 60 percent."[16] The United States' influence increased: "In 1877 the United States took 42 percent of the Mexican goods, and Great Britain, 35; by 1901, the northern neighbor absorbed 82 percent, and Great Britain, a meager 6."[17] The majority of the goods were in the form of raw materials. The United States was also the heaviest exporter into Mexico during this period; most of the goods were machinery for agribusiness and mines. Meanwhile, foreign interests made heavy investments in Mexico. Charles C. Cumberland, in his history of Mexico, states that this investment gave the Mexican economy a great stimulus, and it certainly indicated great confidence, but some economists hold that Mexico labored under rather than benefited from it. One contemporary estimated that over two-thirds of *all* investments in Mexico came from foreign sources; the nation had become an economic fief of the United States, Great Britain, and France.[18] Anglo-American control of the Mexican economy cannot be denied.

The Mexican economy became so dependent on the United States and other foreign powers that economic reversals in these countries caused disaster in Mexico. The frequency of economic depressions and the antagonism of Mexicans toward foreign domination (i.e., most mining interests were foreign-owned) contributed to the Mexican Revolution of 1910. For a time during the revolution, U.S. investments and influence decreased; however, since the 1940s it has grown, and by 1946, U.S. investment in Mexico climbed to slightly more "than half a billion dollars, spread over nearly 200 different enterprises";[19] by 1965 it totalled over a billion. Mexico has again become a fief of the United States, and in collusion with Mexican authorities and businessmen, Anglo-American businessmen determine the economic present and future of that nation. Like individuals in the United States, Mexicans have had little control over their lives.* Their labor has been imported into the United States as a commodity. They came because conditions in Mexico were bad—a situation created in large part by Anglo-American economic imperialists.

Mexican Migration Patterns

The influx of European immigration from areas other than western Europe did not begin until the late 1880s, with the peak from 1903 to 1913. Because the foreigners departed from the Anglo-Saxon image required for membership to the Anglo-American "country" club, there was an ever-increasing cry to ban their entry into the United States. Nevertheless, the newcomers were accepted, for better or worse, as permanent residents. Initially, most of the immigrants settled in ghettoes that were located in urban centers, and in time, the ghettoes became stable communities. Contributing to the stability was the fact that Europeans worked in urban factories and did not have to move constantly to find work.

---

*A similar analogy could be made in the United States' relations with Canada; however, conditions were different in that U.S. influence in Canada, while significant, was softened by Canada's membership in the British Empire and then in the Commonwealth. Moreover, the attitude of Anglo-Americans toward Canadians has been different from their attitude toward Mexicans. Anglo-Americans have looked upon Canada as an extension of the United States and her citizens were, after all, an Anglo-Saxon people. Lastly, the United States did not conquer Canada.

Like the European, the Mexican came to the United States because of his hunger; but unlike the European, he did not intend to stay, nor did his masters intend him to remain. He came as a temporary worker. Moreover, he did not stay in one place and was constantly shuttled throughout the Southwest and Midwest. When working on the railroad crews, he moved from site to site, many times taking his family with him; this created box car *colonias*. In the mines, he was the last hired and the first fired and was paid half the wages paid to a white man for doing the same work. Southwestern employees considered the Mexican the perfect solution to labor problems; he would work in temperatures over 100°, would not demand an equity in society, and would return to Mexico when the work was finished.

Relatively few Mexican immigrants entered the United States until the twentieth century. Since there were no border controls, most of the migrants merely walked into the United States, then crossed back when they wished. As in the case of the Eastern and Southern Europeans, Anglo-American reaction to the Mexican did not become antagonistic until his numbers increased to such an extent that he became a threat to Anglo-Saxon homogeneity. This process becomes evident in a study of the census figures indicating the number of Mexican-born persons in the United States:[20]

	1880	1890	1900	1910
Arizona	9,330	11,534	14,172	29,987
California	8,648	7,164	8,068	32,694
New Mexico	5,173	4,504	6,649	11,918
Texas	43,161	51,559	71,062	125,016

These figures must be qualified, since they represent only those Mexicans who were officially counted. It should be mentioned that Mexicans were elusive when it came to dodging census takers, because they were afraid of being apprehended or harassed by them. Thus, the actual number of Mexicans in the United States probably was much higher.

One of the few studies on the Mexican immigrant during this period was conducted by Victor S. Clark.[21] He paints a graphic picture of the networks developed by the "captains of agribusiness" to entice and transport Mexicans to the Southwest. As discussed in chapter 4, the railroads provided the key to actual importation of the Mexican, and business interests developed a sophisticated system to recruit the Mexican and bring him to the United States.

In the first decade of the twentieth century, Mexicans began to deviate from their traditional areas of settlement. In 1908, Clark stated: "As recently as 1900, immigrant Mexicans were seldom found more than one hundred miles from the border. Now they are working as unskilled laborers and as section hands as far east as Chicago and as far north as Iowa, Wyoming, and San Francisco."[22] The incoming Mexicans settled permanently only in Texas; Clark estimated that prior to 1908 about 60,000 entered the United States annually, with most Mexicans remaining only for a brief period in the United States, principally in the Southwest.

In 1910, the *Report of the Immigration Commission* stated: "They as a rule, do not come as settlers, but as a transient and migratory unskilled labor supply." The report also made obvious conclusions; for example: most Mexicans worked in former Mexican territory; the majority returned to Mexico after only a few months; and they were the lowest-paid of any laborers in the area. It is significant that the report observed that the Mexican, who was a temporary laborer and not intended to become a permanent resident, was confined to nonskilled and "dirty" work. The report also reflected the biases of the Immigration Commission:

> The assimilative qualities of the Mexicans are slight. Because of the backward educational facilities in their native land and a constitutional prejudice on the part of the peones toward school attendance, the immigrants of this race have among them a larger percentage of illiterates than is found among any race immigrating to the western country in any considerable number. . . .

> Because of a lack of thrift and a tendency to regard public relief as "pension" . . . many Mexican families in time of industrial depression become public charges. . . .

> Thus it is evident that, in the case of the Mexican, he is less desirable as a citizen than as a laborer. The permanent additions to the population, however, are much smaller than the number who immigrate for work.[23]

Anglo-American society, however, would soon be confronted with the dilemma of what to do with the increasing number of Mexicans. Should it restrict their immigration and then be faced with a labor shortage? Or, should it expose itself to the prospect of assimilating the "docile, ignorant, and non-clannish" Mexicans who would "become public charges"? Typically, Anglo-Americans firmly believed that neither situation would develop, since most Mexicans returned to Mexico after the seasonal work had been completed and were "only temporary visitors. . . ."

The Mexican Revolution of 1910 brought the first large wave of Mexicans to the United States. The figures are graphic: from 1910 to 1914, there was a migration of 82,588 to the United States; from 1914 to 1919, there was a migration of 91,075—a total of 173,663 for the decade. The revolution removed the last restraints on the poor Mexican, who was freed from his peonage; moreover, the attendant chaos uprooted him and lessened his attachment to the land. Simultaneously, agricultural and industrial interests in the United States became increasingly dependent upon Mexican labor.[24] In 1909, 98 percent of the crews employed by the Atchison, Topeka, and Santa Fe Railways west of Albuquerque were Mexicans; the Southern Pacific Railroad employed a similar percentage.[25] Although the sharp increase in Mexican population alarmed the nativists, business interests protected the Mexican against the restrictionists' attempts to limit his immigration.

Manuel Gamio, the Mexican anthropologist, reinforces our thesis of importation: "Mexican immigration into the United States is, fundamentally, an economic phenomenon, the automatic result of increasing demand for labor in one country and available supply in the other."[26] The commissioner general's report of 1910 gave substance to Gamio's statement: "The principal reason underlying this increase is the extensive industrial development now taking place in the southwestern part of the United States."[27] The next year, the commissioner noted that agencies were reaping "an enormous profit."[28] The Mexican peon was imported by contractors who, in the process, evaded the law, which prohibited contract labor. In sum, the necessities of survival compelled Mexicans to migrate, conditions made the traffic in Mexicans profitable, and networks were established to capitalize on this situation.

As conditions in Mexico worsened as a result of the revolution, many middle- and upper-class Mexicans entered the United States. In 1913, the commissioner sounded the alarm, indicating that the Mexican might become a public charge:

> Refugees will be found in almost every city and town . . . a considerable number of whom are unfit to perform hard manual labor, and as their funds become exhausted it will be difficult for them to maintain themselves, and unless conditions in Mexico become settled in the near future a satisfactory disposition of the refugees may become a serious problem.[29]

In other words, it was all right for the Mexican to come as a temporary laborer, but he was not welcomed as a potential permanent resident. Only the Mexican who would do the work that the white man would not do was welcomed. However, the situation changed in 1914 with the beginning of the war in Europe. The cry once again was: "We need Mexican labor!"

In 1916, the commissioner general noted the increase of immigration of Mexican workers to the United States and wrote:

> The volume of refugees of a nonpolitical stripe has greatly increased. Fortunately for this, a general revival of industrial activity throughout the Southwest, and even in regions more remote from the border, has created a demand for unskilled labor.[30]

To a large extent, the war in Europe softened efforts to control the Mexican's entry.

In 1917, a substantial number of Mexicans returned to Mexico. The reasons were varied: the Mexican was reluctant to be drafted into a foreign army, the cost of living had increased in the United States, and conditions had improved in Mexico. Moreover, the Mexican government feared the effects of the exodus of so many of its productive workers and began a campaign to entice them back.

Although the Immigration Act of 1917 was primarily aimed at Eastern Europeans, the act also placed a head tax on Mexicans and applied the literacy provision of the act to them. Previous acts had excluded "contract laborers" and "persons likely to become a public charge." Supposedly, the Mexican was regulated by these mandates, but the wording was so broad and vague that Anglo-Americans profiting from the Mexican labor traffic ignored the laws. Moreover, the $8 head tax proved a major obstacle for poor Mexicans, who had no recourse but to remain in Mexico or to enter the United States illegally, paying the smuggler a fee, which usually depended on how much the traffic would bear. By 1917, however, the labor shortage created by the hostilities in Europe threatened to cripple the war effort. Industrialists and growers pressured the federal authorities to waive those sections of the Immigration Act that limited the free flow of Mexican labor. Soon afterwards, exceptions were made to allow illiterate contract workers from Mexico to enter the United States. The head tax also was waived. The secretary of labor excused his actions:

> Hardly had war been declared when representations reached the bureau from numerous sources to the effect that, with the calling of men to military service, and with the simultaneous going into operation of the new immigration act, containing the illiteracy test, the supply of common labor for the farms of the Southwest would be reduced, since the farmers in that section had been in the habit of relying to a considerable extent upon seasonal labor from Mexico. This matter was investigated and the conclusion reached that, while there was considerable hysteria, there was also considerable basis for the alarm.[31]

In other words, Mexican labor was a necessary commodity. In his report, the commissioner affirmed that U.S. employers feared they would have to pay higher wages if the Mexican was excluded. Naturally, the Department of Labor aided agribusiness. It attempted to lay down rules to regulate the exemptions, but the growers resented any kind of regulation. The result was that the Immigration Act of 1917 was temporarily suspended, and the border was opened to Mexicans. In spite of the United States' entanglement in a world war, border control by the military was conspicuously absent during this period.

The Labor Department, meanwhile, assured Congress that these were only "stop-gap" measures; however, the temporary exemptions, as well as the open border, continued until the end of the 1921 fiscal year, when a surplus of labor existed in the United States. The unsuccessful regulation even of the exemptions proved that it was impossible to control Mexican migration effectively. In the four years that the exemptions were in force (1917 to 1921) only 72,862 Mexicans entered the United States legally, whereas hundreds of thousands crossed the border illegally.[32] The influx of undocumented workers was destined to continue as long as jobs in the United States were plentiful, and as long as the U.S. government looked the other way.

Public Opinion Toward Mexican Immigration

Opposition to Mexican immigration crystallized in the 1920s. During this decade reaction to the Mexican reached hysterical levels as his numbers became too large to be ignored by the bigots—nationalists and racists alike. Consider the number of legal Mexican immigration to the United States.[33]

1920 – 52,361	1924 – 89,336	1928 – 59,016
1921 – 30,758	1925 – 32,964	1929 – 40,154
1922 – 19,551	1926 – 43,316	1930 – 12,703
1923 – 63,768	1927 – 67,721	

Nativist efforts to restrict quantitatively the Southern and Eastern European bore fruit on May 19, 1921, with the passage of the Immigration Act. Many wanted to include the Mexican in the provisions of the act, but Congress did not concur because of the opposition of agribusiness and because it did not want this opposition to block passage of the bill. The 1921 act was temporary, and generally it was considered too lenient. (It was replaced three years later by a permanent quota act that excluded most Asians and drastically cut the flow from sections of "racially inferior Europe."[34]) The act of 1921 started a battle between racial and cultural bigots, who wanted to keep Anglo-America "Anglo-American," and the economic colonialists, who set aside their prejudices for low-cost labor. The colonizers of the Southwest realized that the act of 1917 had hurt them financially, and they vehemently opposed any restrictions on the free flow of Mexicans to the United States, especially since the supply of European labor was now limited. In contrast, nativists feared that too many Mexicans would subvert the Anglo-American way of life.

In 1923—a key year—the commissioner of immigration turned his attention more fully to the Mexican: "It is difficult, in fact impossible, to measure the illegal influx of Mexicans crossing the border. . . ."[35] According to restrictionists, Mexican immigration had reached tidal-wave proportions. During the previous two years, there had been an economic depression in the United States, but by 1923, the economy had sufficiently recovered to entice Mexican workers again. In 1924, the number of immigrants jumped to 89,336, as compared to 63,768 in the previous year. This *legal* migration was paralleled by an avalanche of undocumented workers who avoided the head tax as well as visa charges. The new migration differed from that of earlier years, for it became more permanent. The permanency and the large numbers of Mexicans alarmed the nativists, who deplored the fact that the Johnson Bill, which later became the Immigration Act of 1924, did not limit Mexicans. Debate over the issue of Mexican immigration had been vehement in both houses of Congress.

Debate on the 1924 Act

The exclusion of Mexicans from the quota was one of political realism. Albert Johnson of Washington, the chairman of the House Immigration and Naturalization Committee, bluntly stated:

> The committee came to the conclusion that until we could make sure of control of the European immigration situation, and of something to take the place of the

quota law which is about to expire, we would better leave the matter of close restrictions from contiguous territory until we could finish the matters in hand. . . .[36]

Johnson promised that the committee would frame another bill to establish a border patrol to enforce existing laws, and he claimed that a quota alone would not effectively exclude Mexicans. Representative John E. Raker of California seconded Johnson, and he saw no need for further legislation to restrict Mexicans. If existing laws were enforced, their numbers would be cut to 1000 annually, because, according to Raker, "from 75 to 90 percent of all Mexicans in Mexico are illiterate and cannot lawfully come to the United States."[37] Raker concluded that Mexicans could not afford the head tax, and employers who paid it for them were violating the contract labor provision of the immigration code.[38]

The nativists were not convinced. Representative Martin Madden of Chicago, chairman of the House Appropriations Committee prophesied: "The bill opens the doors for perhaps the worst element that comes into the United States—the Mexican peon. . . . [It] opens the door wide and unrestricted to the most undesirable people who come under the flag."[39] Representative John O. Box of Jacksonville, Texas, seconded Madden and demanded a two-percent quota for Mexicans, based on the 1890 population, as well as additional funds for its enforcement. Box supported an amendment to put Mexico alone on a quota basis, exempting the rest of the nations in the Western Hemisphere. The Johnson Bill, however, passed the House without the proposed amendment.[40]

In the U.S. Senate, Frank B. Willis of Ohio echoed restrictionist sentiment: "Many of [them] . . . now coming in are, unfortunately, practically without education, and largely without experience in self-government, and in most cases not at all qualified for present citizenship or for assimilation into this country. . . ."[41] Senator Matthew M. Neeley of West Virginia charged: "On the basis of merit, Mexico is the last country we should grant a special favor or extend a peculiar privilege. . . . The immigrants from many of the countries of Europe have more in common with us than the Mexicanos have."[42] Antirestrictionists countered by arguing that there would be difficulty in enforcing such a quota; that Mexicans stayed only temporarily anyway; that they did work white men would not; and that an economic burden would be the result of their restriction.

The argument of Pan-Americanism proved to be the most effective, however. It became a determining factor in the minds of many senators who wanted to use the organization of a Pan-American union as a vehicle for establishing the United States' political and economic dominance over Latin America. Senator Holm Bursum of New Mexico summed up the feeling of most of the senators, stating that he did not favor disrupting Pan-Americanism; that Mexico was sparsely populated anyway; and "So far as absorbing the Mexican population . . . , that is the merest rot. . . ."[43] In the end, the economic interests supporting the Mexicans' entry overwhelmed the nativists.

In 1924, the battle was won, but not the war. Additional funds for the border patrol were appropriated. Furthermore, the restrictionists continued to fight for the exclusion of Mexicans throughout the 1920s and into the 1930s. Working to their advantage was the fact that the Europeans and the Asians already had been restricted. Johnson's committee, true to its promise, began to occupy itself with the Mexican problem. Although border officials strictly applied the $8 head tax, plus the $10 visa fee, which in the past had been ignored, Mexicans still entered legally and illegally. The reports of the commissioner now devoted more space to the Mexican. In so many words, they stated that the peon was benefiting from the reduction of European immigrants. In 1926 the commission wrote that there were 855,898 Mexicans legally in the United States and predicted, "It is safe to say that over a million Mexicans are in the United States at the present time [counting illegals], and under present laws, this number may be added to practically without limit."[44]

Box Bill

An open fight broke out in Congress in 1926. In that year restrictionists introduced two bills. The best known was called the Box Bill, after Representative Box. This bill simply sought to apply the quota provisions to the whole Western Hemisphere; the other bill, sponsored by Robert L. Bacon of New York, applied them only to Mexico. The Box Bill soon emerged as the main bill before the House. Western representatives opposed any attempt to restrict Mexicans. S. Parker Frieselle of California stated: "We, gentlemen, are just as anxious as you are not to build the civilization of California or any other western district upon a Mexican foundation. We take him because there is nothing else available to us."[45] Representative James Nance Garner of Texas emphasized that the Mexican returned home after the picking seasons: "All they want is a month's labor in the United States, and that is enough to support them in Mexico for six months. . . ."[46] He continued: "In our country they do not cause any trouble, unless they stay there a long time and become Americanized; but they are a docile people. They can be imposed on; the sheriff can go out and make them do anything."[47] Garner praised the contributions of the Mexicans to his state.

The restrictionists were bigots, whereas the antirestrictionists were economic opportunists. When questioned about the merits of the Mexican, antirestrictionists made revealing statements, such as: "The Mexican is a child naturally," and they further stressed that he was in the United States only temporarily.

Box candidly accused the attackers of his bill of attempting to attract only the "floating Mexican peons" for the purpose of economically exploiting them, charging that "they are to be imported in trainloads and delivered to farmers who have contracted to grow beets for the sugar companies, who also agree to import and furnish contract laborers to do the menial farm work. . . . They are objectionable as citizens and as residents."[48] In the committee hearings on immigration, Box questioned a farmer, asking him if what he really wanted was a subservient class of Mexican workers "who do not want to own land, who can be directed by men in the upper stratum of society. . . ." The farmer answered, "I believe that is about it." Box then asked, "Now, do you believe that is good Americanism?" The farmer replied, "I think it is necessary Americanism to preserve Americanism."[49]

The restrictionists, however, could not mount sufficient power to push either the Box or the Bacon bill through Congress. The power of agribusiness and other industrial giants employing Mexicans blocked them. The role of these combines in fighting the restrictionists is similar to the one they played in early efforts to restrict Europeans. They effectively warded off public opinion, which in both cases was against the immigrant. However, there was one big difference. The restrictionist movement against the Mexican centered in the Southwest, which, at that time, had relatively little influence on national politics. Middle-class and lower-class nativists were much more politically powerful on the eastern seaboard. Southwestern nativists attempted to ally with eastern restrictionist groups, but the Mexican was not a visible threat in the nation's most populated centers. Without widespread national support, southwestern restrictionists could not muster sufficient nativist feeling to effect the limiting of the Mexican. Without this support, they were no match for the moneymen of the Southwest.

The 1928 Hearings

In 1928, a congressional fight again loomed. The commissioner general of immigration recommended "that natives of countries of the Western Hemisphere be brought within the quota provisions of existing law. . . ." The commissioner specifically recommended the restriction of Mexicans, stating: "The unlimited flow of immigrants from the Western Hemisphere cannot be reconciled with the sharp curtailment of immigration from Europe."[50] A definite split also developed between the Department of Labor, which called for putting the Mexican on a quota system, and the Department of State, which opposed it.[51] The State Department opposed placing Mexicans on the quota because it knew that such action would seriously compromise its negotiations with Latin American nations for economic trade treaties and privileges for Anglo-American interests. Anglo-American bigotry was a sensitive area. Placing Mexicans on a quota would be a legal affirmation of discrimination toward all Latin Americans. Moreover, State Department officials had been carrying out tense negotiations with Mexican officials, who had threatened to expropriate Anglo-American oil. The State Department, representing Anglo-American foreign investors and exporters, joined the southwestern industrialists to kill restrictionist measures. They attempted to sidetrack the debates, and for a time, congressional debate centered around the enforcement of existing immigration laws. Many congressmen, however, were not satisfied and pushed for quantitative restrictions. Anglo-American labor supported the restrictionists, and questioned, "Do you want a mongrel population, consisting largely of Mexicans?"[52]

In the meantime, the *Saturday Evening Post* ran a series of articles by Kenneth L. Roberts advocating that Mexicans be restricted. The author flatly prophesied that Mexicans would become public charges if their immigration were allowed to continue.[53] J. S. Stowell wrote in the *Journal of Current History:* "While certain interests have pleaded for the United States to invade Mexico, that country has unostentatiously accomplished an invasion of the United States, which is bound to have its effect on our future."[54] Richard Lee Strout wrote:

> The Mexican peons are coming in more rapidly now than did the Asiatics when the Pacific Coast demanded, and secured, complete exclusion. Racial and labor riots introduced the fight to keep out the Asiatics. Hints of such disturbances are already heard against the Mexicans.[55]

He continued: "The crux of our whole problem . . . [is that] the employer along the border does not want *Mexican* labor—what he wants is cheap labor. It is the same old dollar argument . . . that first brought negro slaves into the United States."[56] Despite such arguments in Congress, growers and other interests joined forced with the departments of State, Agriculture, and Interior and formed a solid front to overwhelm the restrictionists.

Meanwhile, the number of Mexican immigrants decreased, partially because of a conference in February 1929 at Mexico City, where Mexican officials agreed to limit the number of visas they would grant, in return for an end to the agitation for restrictive legislation. In spite of this diplomatic coup, the Department of Labor ignored the accomplishments of the State Department. In 1929, the commissioner general once more called for a quota. It became evident that the restrictionists would not compromise, and their attacks reflected this. In a 1929 issue of the scholarly journal *Foreign Affairs,* Glen Hoover wrote that "the Mexican peon is the most unassimilable of all immigrants. Measured by the percentage of those who learn English, become citizens, or adopt American ways, his record is a poor one. New Mexico affords a striking instance." Hoover went on to say that the Mexican was proving himself adept "at assimilating American charity." The article seethed with racist generalizations, stating, for example: "While the social workers are afraid that the peon will not mix with our native population, the eugenists are afraid they will." Hoover warned about the probability of miscegenation, and condemned it in much the same manner as those who oppose Black-white unions. Hoover concluded that the Immigration Act of 1924 had limited immigration to those who were eligible for citizenship, i.e., Caucasians or Africans; therefore, the Mexican could not be legally admitted, since his Indian heritage made him ineligible. Hoover believed it was an error to classify the Mexican as white and thus permit him to circumvent the legal requirements; he termed Mexican immigration as "the greatest Indian migration of all time."[57] Hoover's biased attacks were nevertheless temperate compared to those that followed.

The year 1929 ushered in the Great Depression. Whereas the number of Mexicans entering the United States from 1925 to 1929 was 238,527, from 1930 to 1934, only 19,200 migrated into the country. During the years from 1935 to 1939, this number fell even further—to 8,737. The decline in Mexican immigration did not, however, quiet the restrictionists; they only became more vocal.[58] The House Committee on Immigration and Naturalization again held hearings in 1930. The debates were a replay of previous hearings. Once more, agricultural and industrial interests defended the Mexican's "special standing," and once more, the same interests were against their immigration. Of the several bills introduced in 1930, the Harris Bill loomed as the major one. Three new arguments were advanced for restriction: widespread unemployment; the racial undesirability of the Mexican; and his alleged un-Americanism.[59]

The best example of overt racism can be found in a report prepared for John Box by Dr. Roy L. Garis of Vanderbilt University. As an "authority" on eugenics, Garis wrote:

> Their minds run to nothing higher than animal functions—eat, sleep, and sexual debauchery. In every huddle of Mexican shacks one meets the same idleness, hordes of hungry dogs, and filthy children with faces plastered with flies, disease, lice, human filth, stench, promiscuous fornication, bastardy, lounging, apathetic peons and lazy squaws, beans and dried chili, liquor, general squalor, and envy and hatred of the gringo. These people sleep by day and prowl by night like coyotes, stealing anything they can get their hands on, no matter how useless to them it may be. Nothing left outside is safe unless padlocked or chained down. Yet there are Americans clamoring for more of this human swine to be brought over from Mexico.[60]

Garis continued that the only difference between Mexican women of the lower and higher class was that the high-class Mexican women were just more "sneaky in adultery."[61]

Groups such as the Immigration Restriction League, Inc., of New York, asserted that the Mexican could not be assimilated to Anglo-American institutions. It charged, "It is ridiculous for us to limit European immigration and continue to admit Mexican peon labor. . . ."[62] Moreover, it rightfully stated that Mexicans were not naturalizing and becoming Anglo-American citizens like other immigrants.

Alonzo S. Perales, an attorney from Alice, Texas, summed up the feeling of Chicanos to this rhetoric: "American citizens of Teutonic or northern extraction . . . just simply exclude any other people who do not belong to that extraction; for instance, the Mexicans." He continued by stating that the restrictionists generally characterized Mexicans "as a degenerate and inferior people, incapable of assimilation or good citizenship." He accused the restrictionists of outright bigotry.[63]

In the Senate, the Harris Bill was placed on the calendar without scheduled hearings. This bill obviously discriminated against the Mexican, because he was singled out as the only exemption withdrawn from special status. Harris complained that Mexican immigration was especially offensive, since Mexico was sending the United States the largest number of undesirables. He cited unemployment among Anglo-Americans, using outdated figures to alarm listeners about the number of Mexicans entering the United States: "There are thousands and thousands of Mexicans who are subject to charity now" in the southwestern states. He also erroneously claimed that one-third of the children born in California were Mexicans and warned that in a few years the Mexican would take over.[64] The Harris Bill passed the Senate by voice vote, and on May 15 the bill was referred to the House, where it was placed on the calendar.

Proponents of the bill maintained that Mexican migration had only stopped temporarily and that as soon as the economic situation bettered, or trouble in Mexico broke out, Mexicans would return. Again, agricultural and southwestern interests fought attempts to exclude the Mexican. These interests reemphasized that the Mexican laborer was a temporary resident, claiming:

> The Mexican "peon" is an intense nationalist, but he is an individual nationalist. He has no real conception of a unified national consciousness. Nevertheless, the love of his native land is so strong that practically no Mexican "peon" enters the United States without expecting to return.[65]

After all, they argued, the Mexican was preferable to the "Filipino or Puerto Rican."[66]

Edward Alvin Moore, a retired army officer who had patrolled the Mexican border, joined the furor in 1931 and wrote:

> All in all, he is an extremely pathetic specimen of the human race, from *our point of view.* [Emphasis is Moore's.] But after dealing with his kind for many years, I do not pity them as I did at first. All things are relative; this poor peon's life contains no more suffering and worries than yours or mine. . . . Nature has protected him by endowing him with the stupidity and apparent insensibility to pain of a mule. He lives a life we left behind centuries ago.
> So I regard him as a mere machine, or a clod of clay to be examined.[67]

Unfortunately, this attitude has been prevalent among too many law enforcement officers then and now.

Affecting the congressional hearings was widespread resentment toward the Mexican, which developed during the 1930s. The small farmer unjustly blamed him for the misfortunes caused by the depression and for the takeover of the corporation farms. Remsen Crawford, a journalist, wrote in 1930:

> The small American farmer, who, with his family, lives and labors on his farm, cannot compete with Mexican peon labor cultivating rich, irrigated lands. . . . While the population of the Southwest is being greatly increased, the greater portion of the increase is coming from Mexico, to the ultimate ruin of American

agriculture . . . and to the detriment of the country schools, churches, community life, and political and racial characteristics of the native American people of these regions.[68]

Crawford's sentiments clearly document the nativist feelings of many Anglo-Americans who made the Mexican the scapegoat for the depression.

During the depression, the Mexican's economic and political situation worsened. Exploitation became more intense. Continued unjust treatment was rationalized by one farmer, who said:

> If they were miserable or unhappy, I would say, "All right Mr. Educator, do your damndest." But the Mexicans are a happy people, happier than we are; they don't want responsibility, they just want to float along, sing songs, make cigarettes. . . . By not compelling Mexicans to go to school, we haven't deprived them of anything, neither earning power or happiness. By compelling them to go, we merely increase their tastes for things they can't acquire, that they haven't the intellect, instinct, nor energy to acquire.[69]

A member of the Imperial County school board in California charged that: "The Mexicans are an inferior race, and we mustn't expect them to move up the scale in less than three or four generations."[70] Another who opposed restricting Mexicans stated:

> I am in favor of restricting immigration of "Bohunks," but not Mexicans. The Mexican makes a fair-to-middling citizen and doesn't try to assimilate. . . . Mexicans have sense and innate courtesy, and they don't demand social equality like the Negro. There will never be any race question with the Mexicans.[71]

In the same work, another source is quoted as stating: "The Mexicans are a wonderful people; they are docile; I just love them. I was paying Pancho and his whole family 60 cents a day before the war [1918]. There were just no hours; he worked from sun to sun."[72]

If Mexican immigration had continued at the 1920 rate, restrictionist legislation probably would have passed, since even the champions of the non-quota would have grown nervous at having so many Mexicans living "next door." As it was, the Harris Bill failed to pass the House, and for a time longer, an immigration quota for Mexicans was averted.

Many Mexicans in Mexico were embittered by the Anglo bigotry during this period. Their sentiments are summed up by Enrique Santibañez, who wrote that the Anglo-Saxon American believes that: "he belongs to the highest species of the human race in intelligence, physical ability, and beauty . . ." and that he viewed the Mexican as a Latin person who was "unequal to him and clearly inferior." This train of thought caused the Anglo-American to separate the Mexican into categories, differentiating between "Spanish" and "Mexican." As in the case of the Black man, even the U.S.-born Mexican, according to Santibañez, has never really been considered an American. Santibañez underscored the effect of this prejudice on the Chicano, observing that Anglos' preoccupation with color led "some foolish bronze colored men to insist on being called 'Spanish' for maybe then they could be Americans."[73] Santibañez observed that most Mexicans immigrating to the United States had not been schooled and had difficulty defending their culture against attacks by Anglo bigots. Santibañez considered the fate of the Mexican in the United States and concluded that his coming to the United States had disgraced the "Aztec nation." Santibañez predicted that, although he was an economic asset to the United States, the Mexican would dangerously disturb the Anglo-American nation in the future.

The Restrictionist Victory

Opposition to Mexican immigration continued during the 1930s, but the depression caused the fanfare to die down. Moreover, local authorities enforced the regulations and even sent undocumented workers back to Mexico. In the 1940s, largely as the result of World War II, the United States again needed Mexicans—both on the home front and in the war zones. In addition, in 1942 the growers and the U.S. government entered into an agreement with the Mexican government in which the latter was to furnish farmers in the United States with twentieth-century bond servants. The Mexican government agreed to send a predetermined number of workers to the United States. The latter, in turn, agreed to place them, guaranteeing a minimum wage and good treatment. This temporary agreement lasted into the 1960s, with many former restrictionists supporting it because the government had administrative assurances from the Mexican government that the majority of the workers would return to that country. However, in the 1950s the traffic of both legal and illegal immigrants swelled, and cries for exclusion of the Mexican again became strident. By this time, however, many U.S. congressmen remembered that World War II had, in part, been fought against racism, so their attacks were more subtle, lest they sound too much like Hitler themselves. Meanwhile, during the first half of the 1950s, "operation wetback," as it was insidiously called, indiscriminately rounded up Mexicans and returned them to Mexico, producing a "smashing" success.

In 1965, liberal Anglo-American congressmen sponsored a new immigration and naturalization bill designed to correct the injustices of the past, especially in relation to Asians. Many reformers wanted to scrap the quota system altogether. Instead, the liberals allowed restrictionists to turn the hearings and congressional debates on the bill into a forum that focused on the New World. Without the powerful lobby of Southwestern agriculturists, who had so successfully championed their own self-interest for cheap labor by keeping Mexican immigration off a quota system in the past, the restrictionists did what they could not do 40 years before. Liberal congressmen sold their principles down the river and agreed to a regional quota system for the Western Hemisphere that was clearly designed to keep Latin Americans of Indian and Black extraction out. This new quota provided for 170,000 persons to be admitted annually from the Eastern Hemisphere, but only 120,000 persons from the Western Hemisphere. The liberals, who traded one quota system for another, went along with setting up a Select Commission on Western Hemisphere Immigration to study further what they had already done. The committee was supposed to make further recommendations. Many observers speculated that this was a device to stall for time to see how much opposition to the New World quota would develop. They could always say that the 1965 decisions were not final; however, when the commission brought in negative findings in 1968, the liberals remained silent, allowing the quota ceiling to become effective without even making a fight out of it.*

Institutional Neglect and Abandonment

In the United States the response to exploitation must be institutional, or at least it must be collective. The individual is insignificant unless he controls a power group, is a prominent member of a power group, or has vast amounts of capital. It does not matter how large the group is, but only how well organized it is. Mexicans, generally, entered the United States poor and unorganized. They entered an underdeveloped, rural region and were scattered over large areas. Their experiences are contrasted to those of Europeans who concentrated in urban centers. The relationship of the Anglo and the Mexican was that of lord-serf, rather than employer-employee. It was much more difficult to organize farm labor, or even mine workers, than it was to organize factory workers. Political organizing of a transient population also was more of a problem than it was in urban ghettoes. Thus, the Mexican was more dependent on traditional Anglo-American institutions from which he could reasonably expect support: organized labor, the Catholic church, and the public schools. It is ironic that these institutions failed them. This abandonment greatly affected the Mexican, since these institutions played a major role in determining his course of action or reaction to the exploitation that existed during these years. Labor forestalled the Mexican's upward mobility by restricting him to unskilled jobs, whereas the church and schools determined the attitude of the Mexican to the oppression—to be complacent in the face of exploitation and discrimination. Our interpretation of the institutions' reactions are general and should be analyzed in the context of the ambience we have described—the attitudes of the restrictionists, the exploiters, and the nature of the Mexican's migration.

Anglo-American Labor

Anglo-American organized labor ignored and excluded the Mexican, and with the exception of an occasional radical organizer, offered the Mexican little opportunity for leadership. This is understandable, since Anglo-American

---

*Many liberals defend the 1965 act because it corrected injustices against Asians; however, the fact remains that Mexicans and other Latin Americans were limited for the first time.

labor rarely has been a radical or moral force in the United States. The present leadership of the AFL-CIO (American Federation of Labor and Congress of Industrial Organizations) is a good example. From the beginning, labor's main goal has been to convert its workers into a middle-class "proletariat." Its skilled trade unions, for the most part, have excluded Blacks and Chicanos. In addition, until recently, it placed the organization of farm workers low on its priority list. Moreover, most minority leaders brand Anglo-American labor as part of the Establishment that condemns them to a dependent status.

During the 1920s, labor took an active part in lobbying for a quota for Mexican immigration. It had played a similar role in restricting the Europeans and Asians. Labor used the rationale that unrestricted immigration depressed domestic wages and that the immigrant was used as a strike breaker, which was true in many instances. However, the attacks of labor on the Mexican, as well as on other immigrants, often have degenerated into racial and cultural slurs that have been used as justifications to exclude them. Labor's fight to restrict Mexican immigration has continued until recent times.

An interesting sidelight was that Anglo-American labor conducted negotiations with Mexican labor in 1925 to have the Mexicans put pressure on their government to voluntarily restrict immigration. Mexican labor conceded, but only on the condition that the AFL would promise to guarantee equal treatment of Mexican workers in the United States—in other words, to end discrimination in its locals. It also proposed that Mexican workers be issued international union cards that would be honored by Anglo-American locals. Similar arrangements had been made between Anglo and Canadian unions. Anglo-American labor, however, was not ready to make these concessions to the Mexican. It would have ended the double wage standard between the Anglos and Mexicans in the Southwest, as well as opening locals from which the Mexican had been excluded. Mexican labor charged that an agreement could not be reached because "American labor's racism prevented any effective alliance."[74]

A follow-up conference between Mexican and Anglo-American labor leaders was held in 1927, but again Anglo-American labor was not willing to cooperate in the spirit of international union brotherhood. Mexican labor even promised to encourage, if not coerce, Mexicans to join unions when migrating to the United States. This action would have strengthened Anglo-American unions and prevented the use of the Mexican as a wage depressor or a strike breaker. Instead, Anglo-American representatives forced Mexican labor to sign a written pledge to pressure the Mexican government to *voluntarily restrict* Mexican immigration. Ironically, the Mexicans themselves favored internal restrictions, since they were alarmed by the drain of some of their most productive citizens. They resented, however, the obvious discrimination and the insult of restrictive quotas that singled out Mexicans. But the leadership of Mexican labor lost its political clout after a clash with President Plutarco Elías Calles of Mexico, and so the voluntary restrictions did not occur. After this, American labor launched an intensive program to restrict Mexicans.

In the United States, Mexicans were excluded from many skilled-trade unions. Apprenticeship programs were closed to Mexicans. During this early period, however, the Mexican did take over the leadership in the organization of some unions. This was especially true in agricultural, mining, and processing industries. These movements, for the most part, were individual efforts on the part of the Mexican and received little support from organized labor. In the next chapter, the Mexican's role in labor is narrated in depth. In effect, labor's abandonment of the Chicano actually worked to colonize him internally.

Anglo-American Public Education

Education is important to a colonized people, since it can either be used as an instrument for creating awareness and thus motivating liberation movements, or it can be used as an agent of the colonial government and its economic system to condition the oppressed to accept their status. Unfortunately, Anglo-American schools have traditionally played the latter role, not only at the expense of the Mexican, but also in relation to other have-not peoples. Their primary role has not been to educate or to make the student aware, but to "school" children into accepting and supporting the Establishment. This process has been called Americanization.

At the very core of Americanization is the compelling necessity for Anglo-Americans to remake the unassimilable masses so they can be more acceptable. This is accomplished by erasing their culture, language, and values and replacing them with Anglo-American culture, language, and values. It is a process that has caused considerable cultural conflict for the Chicano and that has resulted in the following: many Chicanos developing negative self-images; many Chicanos accepting the values of the colonizers and rejecting their own heritage; Anglo-Americans justifying the colonization by glorifying the history of the colonizer and erasing that of the colonized;[75] and Chicanos being conditioned to accept their colonized status, limiting their aspirations, and training them to fill low-paying jobs.

The schools have also bred apathy by stifling questioning, for to protest against oppression is not the "American way"—everyone knows that there is equal opportunity for all. To question the good faith of the nation's business and political leaders is also un-American.

Schools, moreover, have perpetuated many stereotypes about Mexicans. The history of Anglo-American education and the Chicano has been one of neglect. In the early years he was segregated and classified as a nonlearner. Teacher attitudes toward Chicanos helped to insure their failure. In addition, schools have systematically separated educated Chicanos from the masses, destroying any commitment of the educated to the Chicano community. During this period, a "no Spanish" rule also was imposed on the Chicano, which actually punished him for speaking his native language on school grounds. This furthered his alienation. The Anglo-American public schools have functioned as an "advertising" agent for the privileged and have helped to maintain the status quo.

In addition, from the 1920s to the present, there have been intensive Americanization programs in the adult population. The Americanization programs have been both public and private. Again, the objective has been to teach the immigrant to speak English and to appreciate and accept Anglo-American values. The private programs were varied, with many capitalizing on the culture of the immigrant, emphasizing the "immigrant gifts." It is fair to say that many educators were well intentioned and idealistic in perpetuating the myth of the melting pot; however, the objectives of the idealist and the nativist in the Americanization programs were similar—assimilation or, better still, absorption of the alien and conditioning him to accept the "American way." Groups such as the American Legion and the Daughters of the American Revolution played a prominent role in the "Americanization" of students and adults. The mission of the Anglo-American public schools was not to educate, or to create social consciousness, but to condition the newcomer as well as the majority of citizens to accept the corporate society.

Religion's Role in Americanization

The two institutions discussed so far—organized labor and public schools —were alien to the Mexican, and their abandonment or neglect could be predicted. The Catholic church, however, was supposed to be universal. Spain's colonization of Mexico had imposed Catholicism on the Mexican. It became an integral part of the Mexican's life, although it was a colonial agent for the Spanish crown. Furthermore, although it participated in the exploitation of the Indian, it did produce a number of idealistic priests of the caliber of Bartolomé de las Casas and Miguel Hidalgo. What was so disappointing in the United States was that the Anglo-American Catholic church was almost totally devoid of any idealism and thus was totally disinterested in the Mexican. This is tragic, since it was the institution with which the Mexican would come into the closest contact. Not all Mexicans went to school or joined labor unions, but most were members of the church.

Catholicism was important to Mexicans. In the small villages and cities from which they came, the church followed them from the cradle to the grave. In the morning, Mexicans could hear the church bells and, in time of stress, could find some solace within the confines of the church building. The priests were of their own nationality and many of the lower clergy identified with the parishioners. It is true that Mexicans were conditioned by many of the churchmen to accept their oppression in Mexico, but again there were exceptions. In the United States, fewer exceptions existed, and the power of that institution worked more actively to oppress him. The Catholic church in Mexico was a part of the Establishment, and an overwhelming majority of Mexicans were church members. In the United States, Catholics were in the minority, and had suffered persecution throughout the nineteenth century. This was especially true in the Southwest, where the population was overwhelmingly Protestant. Anti-Catholicism was vehement among the fundamentalists there. The reasonable man would have expected the church in the Southwest to welcome their fellow Catholics; however, the Catholic church refused to promote social action and limited itself to meeting the minimal spiritual needs of the people.

Although Mexicans comprised the majority of Catholics in the Southwest, they had no power within the institution. Few Mexicans became priests, and until recently, no Mexicans were bishops.* The church in the United States was greatly influenced by an oligarchy of wealthy laymen, who contributed heavily to the church coffers. In contrast, the Chicano had little to give in material terms. In many places, special masses were set aside for him, and he was excluded from the church's social functions. The church thus abetted the bigotry of its wealthy parishioners. The abandonment of the church was especially noticeable in rural areas where the rich parishioners employed Mexicans. There, the clergy knew that if they supported the Chicano's rights, they would lose generous contributions. As a consequence, the church sided with the rich.

By the time Mexicans arrived in numbers in the Southwest, the Catholic church had also acquired a large material stake in Anglo-American society: It owned stocks and a considerable amount of real and personal property.** Gradually, it had also gained more acceptance among the nativists. Because of its experiences as the object of discrimination, the Catholic hierarchy was determined not to become controversial by getting involved in social action: "Religious care was . . . [its] first and primary mandate. . . ."[76] The church fathers set out to prove that they were loyal Anglo-Americans. In fact, "to the Catholic hierarchy in the United States, Americanization was an important strategy for institutional survival." It used Americanization as a "defensive and self-legitimizing strategy."[77] Bishops ordered priests and nuns to condition Mexicans to support the system. Many Catholic priests told Mexicans that God meant them to be poor, and they discouraged protest as un-American.

Most Anglo-Catholics wanted to be accepted as good Anglo-Americans. They did not want to be different. To identify with the Mexican would have identified them with aliens. These Catholics put pressure on the hierarchy to force priests to adhere strictly to the above-mentioned religious-care mandate and to not get involved in activities that would reflect on them as Catholics.

Many priests and nuns, when they got involved with the people, were censored by the hierarchy and ordered to be silent. For example, in 1962, Fathers Donald McDonnell and Thomas P. McCullough were ordered in California to stop their work in agricultural labor and to be silent.[78] Both had worked among Chicano workers for a dozen years. In 1970, Sister Gregoria Ortega was transferred out of the Abilene, Texas, diocese because she worked

---

*There is now one auxiliary bishop who is a Chicano.

**Only order priests take a vow of poverty; the secular priests, who are in the majority, do not.

among Chicanos.[79] This unselfish sister traveled through the small towns, holding meetings and encouraging Chicanos to demand better education and working conditions. Priests attacked her from the pulpit. There are hundreds of similar experiences reported by priests and nuns. On other occasions the church participated in Red-baiting activities.* In short, the Catholic church was a missionary group that, by its silence, tacitly supported oppressive conditions under which Chicanos had to live and work.

The Protestant churches were rooted in rural Anglo-America. In the Southwest these churches were intent on preserving their identities as white men's churches. They also were interested in preserving the status quo while at the same time Americanizing the Mexican. The objective of the Protestant missionaries was "Americanization through evangelization."[80] They were not interested in Christian ideals—in championing rights or promoting brotherhood.[81] In general, the Catholic and Protestant churches played similar roles in attempting to Americanize the Mexican. Since the Mexican was overwhelmingly poor, he relied on religion more than did the middle-class Anglo-American. He was more devout in his humility and, consequently, more susceptible to the church's counsel.

Conclusion

This chapter has sought to outline the conditions in both Mexico and the United States that resulted in one of the largest migrations of people from one nation to another. The Mexicans came to the United States because conditions forced them to uproot from their traditional villages. The inability of Mexico to industrialize left that nation powerless to feed its own people. The failure of Mexico was largely due to its dependence on the United States and other technologically advanced nations. In a sense, most of the immigrants in the first waves to enter the United States were imported to fill the need for cheap labor in the developing Southwest. Although stereotyped and not at all accepted as permanent residents, Mexicans were welcomed as temporary laborers to supplement white labor. However, when their numbers increased, intense public opposition erupted. This was especially evident at times of economic recession. The Mexican also migrated at a time when the restriction movement in relation to Europeans and Asians was at its zenith. Many restrictionists, when they had won the battle to restrict the latter, merely transferred their zeal to restricting Mexicans. The restriction of Europeans and the exclusion of Asians, however, left the industrialists and agribusinessmen in a bind, and through economic and political power, they fended off the efforts of the restrictionists.

Once in the United States, many Mexicans did not return to Mexico, but were absorbed into the existing Chicano *colonias.* Chicanos, having no politi-

---

*There is an increasing minority within the church that is protesting the noninvolvement of the church. Many are now preaching a theology of liberation.

cal or economic control over their own communities, could not defend themselves against the racism and nativism that had increased with the "Mexican threat." During this period the condition of the Chicanos was further depressed by the action (or nonaction) of institutions, such as labor, the schools, and the churches. The following chapter narrates the Chicanos' response, and how they struggled for self-determination.

Notes

1. J. Frank Dobie, ed., *Puro Mexicano* (Dallas, Tex.: Southern Methodist University Press, 1935), pp. 222–224.

2. Max Sylvius Handman, "Economic Reasons for Mexican Immigration," *The American Journal of Sociology* 35 (January 1930): 601–611.

3. James D. Cockcroft, *Intellectual Precursors of the Mexican Revolution, 1900–1913* (Austin: University of Texas Press, 1968), p. 14.

4. Charles C. Cumberland, *Mexico: The Struggle for Modernity* (New York: Oxford University Press, 1968), p. 216.

5. Cockcroft, p. 32.

6. Cockcroft, p. 46.

7. An excellent treatise on immigration legislation and the Chicano is Job West Neal, "The Policy of the United States Toward Immigration From Mexico" (M.A. thesis, University of Texas at Austin, 1941).

8. See Roger Daniels, *Politics of Prejudice* (New York: Atheneum Publishers, 1968), for the reaction of white Americans toward Asians, and toward Japanese in particular.

9. Julian Samora, *Los Mojados* (Notre Dame, Ind.: University of Notre Dame Press, 1971), p. 9.

10. Carey McWilliams, *North From Mexico* (New York: Greenwood Press, 1968), p. 175.

11. Victor Alba, *The Mexicans* (New York: Frederick A. Praeger, Publishers, 1967), p. 106.

12. Alba, p. 106.

13. Alba, p. 107.

14. Alba, p. 106.

15. Samora, p. 10.

16. Cumberland, p. 228.

17. Cumberland, p. 228.

18. Cumberland, p. 233.

19. Cumberland, p. 319.

20. McWilliams, p. 163, and Neal, p. 51.

21. Victor S. Clark, *Mexican Labor in the United States,* U.S. Department of Commerce Bulletin no. 78 (Washington, D.C.: U.S. Government Printing Office, 1908). This is the best contemporary report on Mexican migration available for that period.

22. Clark, p. 466.

23. Quoted in Job West Neal, pp. 58–59, from U.S., Congress, *Report of the Immigration Commission,* 61st Cong., 34d sess., 1910–1911, 1: 41.

24. Neal, p. 104.

25. Paul Shuster Taylor, "Some Aspects of Mexican Immigration," *Journal of Political Economy* 38 (October 1930): 610.

26. Manuel Gamio, *Mexican Immigration to the United States* (Chicago: University of Chicago Press, 1930), p. 30.

27. U.S., Department of Commerce and Labor, "Report of the Commissioner General of Immigration," *Report of the Department of Commerce and Labor* (Washington, D.C.: U.S. Government Printing Office, 1910), p. 288.

28. U.S., Department of Commerce and Labor, "Report of the Commissioner General of

Immigration," *Report of the Department of Commerce and Labor* (Washington, D.C.: U.S. Government Printing Office, 1911), p. 263.

29. U.S., Department of Labor, "Report of the Commissioner General of Immigration," *Report of the Department of Labor* (Washington, D.C.: U.S. Government Printing Office, 1913), p. 337.

30. U.S., Department of Labor, "Report of the Commissioner General of Immigration," *Report of the Department of Labor* (Washington, D.C.: U.S. Government Printing Office, 1916), p. 397.

31. Quoted in Neal, p. 81.

32. Neal, p. 100.

33. Neal, p. 100.

34. The quota was aimed at limiting Central and Southern Europeans.

35. U.S., Department of Labor, *Annual Report of the Commissioner General of Immigration* (Washington, D.C.: U.S. Government Printing Office, 1923), p. 16.

36. Quoted in Neal, p. 106.

37. Quoted in Neal, p. 107.

38. Neal, pp. 107–108.

39. Quoted in Neal, p. 108.

40. Neal, p. 110.

41. Quoted in Neal, p. 112.

42. Quoted in Neal, p. 113.

43. Quoted in Neal, p. 117.

44. U.S., Department of Labor, *Annual Report of the Commissioner General of Immigration* (Washington, D.C.: U.S. Government Printing Office, 1926), p. 10.

45. U.S., Congress, House, Committee on Immigration and Naturalization, Hearing No. 69.1.7, *Seasonal Agricultural Laborers from Mexico,* H.R. 6741, H.R. 7559, H.R. 9036, 69th Cong., 1st sess., 1926, p. 24.

46. *Seasonal Agricultural Laborers,* p. 190.

47. *Seasonal Agricultural Laborers,* p. 190.

48. *Seasonal Agricultural Laborers,* p. 325.

49. *Seasonal Agricultural Laborers,* p. 112.

50. U.S., Department of Labor, *Annual Report of the Commissioner General of Immigration* (Washington, D.C.: U.S. Government Printing Office, 1928), p. 29.

51. Neal, p. 162.

52. Quoted in Robert J. Lipshultz, "American Attitudes Toward Mexican Immigration, 1924–1952 (M.A. thesis, University of Chicago, 1962), p. 61.

53. Kenneth L. Roberts, "West and Other Mexicans," *Saturday Evening Post,* 4 February 1928, p. 146.

54. J. S. Stowell, "Danger of Unrestrained Mexican Immigration," *Journal of Current History,* August 1928, p. 763.

55. Richard Lee Strout, "A Fence for the Rio Grande," *The Independent,* 2 June 1928, p. 518.

56. Strout, p. 519.

57. G. E. Hoover, "Our Mexican Immigrants," *Foreign Affairs,* November 1929, pp. 103–104, 107.

58. Leo Grebler, Joan W. Moore, and Ralph Guzman, *The Mexican-American People* (New York: The Free Press, 1970), p. 64.

59. Neal, p. 172.

60. U.S., Congress, House, Committee on Immigration and Naturalization, "Mexican Immigration: A Report by Roy I. Garis for the Information of the Members of Congress," *Western Hemisphere Immigration,* H.R. 8523, H.R. 8530, H.R. 8702, 71st Cong., 2d sess., 1930, p. 436.

61. *Western Hemisphere Immigration,* p. 436.

62. *Western Hemisphere Immigration,* p. 394.

63. *Western Hemisphere Immigration,* p. 182.

64. Quoted in Neal, p. 194.

65. James Hoffman Batten, "New Features of Mexican Immigration" (Address before the National Conference of Social Work, Boston, 9 June 1930), p. 960. The author was the executive director of the Inter-American Federation at Claremont, California.

66. Batten, p. 960.

67. Edward Alvin Moore, "Problems of Mexican Immigration," *The Overland and Out West Magazine,* May 1931, p. 156.

68. Remsen Crawford, "The Menace of Mexican Immigration," *Journal of Current History,* February 1930, p. 904.

69. Paul Shuster Taylor, *Mexican Labor in the United States: Imperial Valley,* University of California Publication in Economics, vol. 6, no. 1 (Berkeley: University of California Press, 1930): 78–79.

70. Paul Shuster Taylor, *Mexican Labor in the United States: Valley of the South Platte, Colorado,* University of California Publication in Economics, vol. 6, no. 2 (Berkeley: University of California Press, 1930): 197.

71. Paul Shuster Taylor, *An American-Mexican Frontier: Nueces County, Texas* (Chapel Hill: The University of South Carolina Press, 1934), p. 303.

72. Taylor, *An American-Mexican Frontier,* p. 299.

73. Enrique Santibañez, *Ensayo Acerca de la Immigracion Mexicana en los Estados Unidos* (San Antonio, Tex.: The Clegg Co., 1930), pp. 46–47.

74. Harvey Lenstein, "The AFL and Mexican Immigration in the 1920's: An Experiment in Labor Diplomacy," *Hispano American Historical Review,* May 1968, p. 214.

75. For an in-depth study see Thomas P. Carter, *Mexican Americans in School: A History of Educational Neglect* (Princeton, N.J.: College Entrance Examination Board, 1970).

76. Grebler, Moore, and Guzman, p. 456.

77. Grebler, Moore, and Guzman, p. 444.

78. Joan London and Henry Anderson, *So Shall Ye Reap* (New York: Thomas Y. Crowell Company, 1970), see chapter 4.

79. I was with Sister Gregoria at the time she was censured for championing Chicanos' rights.

80. Grebler, Moore, and Guzman, p. 493.

81. See Delbert Lee Gibson, "Protestantism in Latin American Acculturation" (Ph.D. diss., University of Texas at Austin, 1959).

Chapter Seven

The Road to Delano

The conquest, racism, nativism, and the dependence of Mexico's economy on the United States all played a role in relegating the Mexican in the United States to a servant status. To understand the Chicano's struggle within the trade union movement, we must understand the role of Anglo-American labor in the economic system. Industrialists have considered workers as commodities—providing not only cheap labor but also a ready market for goods. Historically, workers have been at a disadvantage, since the industrialists, or "economic royalists," had the power—money, control of government, a partisan press, and, most important, control of the police. The only counterpower of the workers in general has been the power to disrupt—the power to stop production—a power that has been difficult to implement, since it depends on organizing hungry, dependent men who are afraid to put their families in jeopardy. Anglo-American labor, which developed in the face of bitter opposition, fought the economic royalists—who responded by passing antisyndicalism laws, deporting labor leaders, jailing strikers, and assassinating and blacklisting malcontents. Labor men motivated their followers by playing upon their nationalistic feelings, and thus they could present a solidarity of workers against big business interests. These men hated the economic royalists and condemned the exploitation that took place, as well as the police, the press, and "the viciousness of the entire system."[1]

Gradually, the economic royalists made concessions to a segment of the workers and thus helped to create a proletariat with middle-class standards that ultimately supported and bolstered their privileged status. In the process, big labor emerged in the guise of the American Federation of Labor (AFL), which shed its radical fervor in exchange for bigger paychecks (and, correspondingly, larger dues). Labor became big business and, in fact, became an exclusive club that excluded certain minorities such as Blacks, Mexicans, and Asians. There were exceptions; the Industrial Workers of the World (IWW) and the Congress of Industrial Organizations (CIO) had commendable records, but they either vanished or were absorbed into the AFL. Big labor, in short, became an ally of the monopolists to perpetuate the status quo.

The Mexican migrating to the United States worked for big business. His first masters were the agribusinessmen, the mine owners, and the railroad tycoons. The fact that he was intended to be a temporary supplement to white labor conspired against him from the beginning, for established labor wrote him off as a foreigner—and therefore not entitled to the protection given to U.S. workers. The pecking order within the labor community separated him from the other workers. Moreover, agriculture, which absorbed the largest number of Mexicans, was the most difficult area to unionize: the workers were dispersed, they were on the move, and, above all, agriculture ruled the Southwest. "Through outright ownership, corporate understandings, interlocking directorates and the like, agribusiness is directly tied to transportation, finance, warehousing, food processing, wholesale and retail sales, and other ancillary industries."[2]

The large growers had the power to influence politicians and thus the legislation that was enacted at local, state, and federal levels. For example, the Land Grant College Act of 1872 greatly aided the development of scientific approaches to farming and of machines for agribusiness at no cost to the growers.[3] Irrigation projects have provided water at little cost to the expanding agricultural combines. (In California alone, for example, it is estimated "that at least 900,000 acres of California farm land are receiving publicly developed water in violation ..."[4] of government regulations.) In various ways, the growers have accrued vast power and have manipulated the law to their own advantage. Farmers also receive subsidies for not growing crops. "One California farmer received $4.37 million for *not* growing cotton on part of his holdings in 1969; another, $3.41 million."[5] Moreover, agribusiness is exempt from "all major social and labor legislation."[6] Most workers do not have the benefit of unemployment insurance, social security, the minimum wage, and overtime provisions. In other words, the Mexican was confronted by a Goliath, and like David, he had only a slingshot.

The road to Delano began with the collective efforts of a handful of Chicanos in the last quarter of the nineteenth century. The revolts were, for the most part, spontaneous and unrecorded, and they were unsuccessful. Today this story is surfacing as the result of the pioneering efforts of a few Chicano labor historians. Carey McWilliams reports that early strikes were the result of efforts to organize for self-protection, writing that Chicanos first organized "when several hundred cowboys had gone on strike in the Panhandle in 1883—the first attempt to form a union of 'agricultural' workers in the United States—the strike call was signed by one Juan Gomez."[7] The Chinese and Japanese also attempted to organize, but were also repressed. As Mexicans began to enter into the region in large numbers, they joined the Japanese in sporadic revolts. The IWW organized as early as the year 1906; isolated Mexicans joined many of their movements. Meanwhile, radical Mexican exiles entered the United States. The foremost Mexican leader during this period was Ricardo Flores Magón, whose influence in the United States is only today being analyzed.*

A Voice of Dissent

Ricardo Flores Magón wrote in Spanish rather than English, which limited the spread of his ideas. And for many years the Mexican government suppressed the importance of his involvement in the Mexican Revolution of 1910. Flores Magón was born in Oaxaca, Mexico, in 1874. He and his brother Enrique helped found *Regeneración,* a radical newspaper, at the turn of the century and later were among the founders of *El Partido Liberal Mexicano* (PLM). They were jailed for their opposition to President Porfirio Díaz's government and even proved to be too radical for the liberal opposition. In 1904 Flores Magón crossed the border into the United States, where he continued to publish *Regeneración* in San Antonio, Texas. After an attempt on his life, he went to St. Louis, Missouri. There, he and his followers were in contact with Anglo-American radicals, especially the anarchists. By 1906, the circulation of *Regeneración* reached 30,000;[8] most of the copies were smuggled into Mexico, but many issues were read by Mexicans in the United States. Meanwhile, the group of Mexican radicals were harassed by U.S. authorities and by hired Pinkerton detectives. His U.S. experience convinced Flores Magón that the struggle was not confined to Mexico, and many of his followers became increasingly active in organizing Mexican workers in the United States. They were involved in the Cananea, Sonora, mining strike against the William C. Greene mining interests. This strike clearly documents the power Anglo-American industrialists had in Mexico and how they used their power to maintain the master-servant relationship there and used U.S.-based power to preserve it.

On January 14, 1906, 30 workers formed the *Unión Liberal Humanidad,* a union whose charter members belonged to the Liberal Club of Cananea. The

---

*Professor Juan Gomez, History Department, University of California at Los Angeles, is doing significant and in-deph studies on Ricardo Flores Magón.

Liberal Club was an affiliate of the PLM,[9] which was dominated by the *magonistas* (followers of Magón). These workers organized to bargain with the Cananea Consolidated Copper Company (a subsidiary of Anaconda). The issues were clear: Anglo-Americans worked an eight-hour day; Mexicans labored ten to twelve hours. Anglo-Americans earned double the wages of Mexican workers for less work. On the night of May 31, 1906, the Mexican workers walked out at the Oversight Mine. The Mexicans demanded "five pesos daily, and eight hours a day." The *huelga* (strike) spread and was joined by 2000 Mexicans. Colonel Greene enlisted the support of Sonoran Governor Rafael Izabal, who sent state militia to quell the demonstration. The Anglo-Americans in Cananea armed themselves and shot at the Mexicans who, for the most part, were unarmed. When William Metcalf killed three Mexicans, burnings followed. Meanwhile, Greene pressured the Sonoran governor to allow 150 Arizona Rangers to enter the state. A reign of terror ensued that did not end until Mexican federal troops entered the city and demanded that the governor expel the Rangers. Porfirio Díaz then sent his henchman, General Luis Torres, who threatened the mine workers with being drafted into the army if they did not return to work. Torres arrested 100 leaders and participants and sent many of them to San Juan de Aliza Prison. Many citizens were infuriated at the entry of Anglo-American troops into Mexico. Although Izabal blamed the *magonistas* for the disorder, word of Cananea and the presence of the Rangers spread throughout Mexico and the United States.[10]

PLM labor organization increased throughout the United States. Repression of these efforts followed, and in Arizona the Rangers confiscated letters that implicated Ricardo Flores Magón and his followers in strike activity there. Arizona authorities charged Flores Magón with violating United States neutrality laws. In the meantime, Ricardo had moved to Los Angeles, California. Awaiting extradition, he was jailed for 18 months. There, he wrote to his brother and expressed his bitterness toward Anglo-Americans:

> The *norteamericanos* are incapable of feeling enthusiasm or indignation. This is truly a country of pigs. . . . If the *norteamericanos* do not agitate against their own domestic miseries, can we hope they will concern themselves with ours?[11]

In March 1909, Magón and two other *magonistas* were extradited to Tombstone, Arizona, for trial. Mexican officials worked in collusion with U.S. authorities; in Phoenix, Mexican Consul Arturo M. Elías actively lobbied for the *magonistas'* conviction. After the *magonistas* were sentenced, Elías gave U.S. Attorney J. L. B. Alexander a $500 ring "purchased by the Mexican Government as a token of gratitude."[12] The Mexican government also paid the U.S. sheriffs bonuses for the capture of the *magonistas.* The court sentenced the defendants to 18 months.

In September 1910, the publication of *Regeneración* resumed, with more articles reporting on the victimization of Mexicans in the United States: bad working conditions, discrimination, police brutality, and lynchings.[13] In 1911,

Ricardo Flores Magón was again arrested for organizational activities and sentenced to three years' imprisonment. He was released in 1914, but was again arrested in March 1918, after he issued a manifesto calling for a world anarchist revolution. He had allegedly violated U.S. neutrality laws. Ricardo was sentenced to 20 years; his associate Librado Rivera received 15 years. Friends in Mexico worked for their release, but according to Professor Cockcroft: "True to their Anarchist principles, Rivera and Flores Magón refused all such support. When President Obregón finally gained U.S. approval of their return to Mexico in November 1922, Ricardo Flores Magón mysteriously died in his jail cell [on the 21st]—murdered, according to Rivera."[14]

The imprisonment of Ricardo Flores Magón left the Mexican in the United States without a voice, but even more tragically, without an organizer. Many states enacted criminal syndicalism laws, which prohibited the advocacy of a change in industrial ownership or control. For many years these laws were used against union organizers. The Chicano, nevertheless, continued to organize. Each effort was a study in power; the worker had only the power to disrupt—to stop production—while the employer had control of production and could influence local, state, and federal authorities. The cantaloupe workers' strike in May 1928, called by *La Unión de Trabajadores del Valle Imperial*, was a study in the use of power.

The Cantaloupe Strike

The Imperial Valley of California was once a desert that was looked upon as a barrier that had to be crossed before the rich coastal valleys of the state could be reached. The soil contained rich minerals, but it needed water to turn it into a garden. The federal government made this possible by the construction of dams and the promotion of irrigation projects. Intensive truck garden farming was made possible, but cheap labor was needed to convert the area into one of the richest agricultural areas in the United States.

In 1928, the farmers expressed optimism; the crops flourished, and many Mexican workers were available to harvest them.[15] The dependence on Mexican labor had become evident. By 1928, Mexicans comprised 90 percent of field workers. Meanwhile, a pattern emerged. The Mexican population had begun to stabilize, with more and more Mexicans living and working year round as field hands in the Imperial Valley. At the same time, a large number of the Mexicans did not have legal immigration papers.

The valley produced two main crops—lettuce and cantaloupes. Both required highly specialized harvesting methods in picking and packaging. The valley farms required large work crews, and such crews were furnished by labor contractors. The growers paid the contractor, and he paid the workers after subtracting as his fee a percentage from each man's earnings. The contractor withheld the first week's wages from the workers, which he kept until the end of the harvest, and often contractors absconded with workers' funds. Since the Chicano barely earned enough to live, this resulted in a great hardship on him. Dr. Paul Taylor found in 1927 that:

> The average Mexican field worker earned only six to eight hundred dollars per year. Such a worker housed his family in a one- or two-room shack, usually on the outskirts of one of the valley's towns. Most of the Mexican dwellings had no plumbing or sanitation facilities. Mexican children in most Imperial County communities attended segregated elementary schools.[16]

An open border had been encouraged before and after World War I. After 1921, however, stricter regulations forced Mexicans to pay $18 (an $8 head tax and a $10 visa fee) in order to enter the United States. Many poor peons could not afford this amount and entered the country illegally. In 1928 some 75 percent of the valley's Mexicans were illegal immigrants.[17] Many growers preferred this situation, since the workers could not complain for fear of deportation.

No doubt, the relative stability of the Mexican workers contributed to solidifying them. They had organized two *mutualistas* (mutual aid societies) —*Sociedad Mutualista Benito Juárez* of El Centro in 1919 and *La Sociedad Mutualista Hidalgo* of Brawley in 1921. These two societies furnished the leadership of the later union. The catalyst was Carlos Ariza, a Mexican vice-consul at Calexico, California. He heard the complaints of Mexican workers and encouraged them to organize a collective bargaining agency. Undoubtedly it was discussed at the *mutualistas'* meetings. They formed *La Unión de Trabajadores del Valle Imperial.* At an executive committee meeting on May 31, 1928, the union sent letters to the cantaloupe growers and the chambers of commerce at Brawley and El Centro. The politely worded letter requested: that wages be increased to 15 cents per standard crate of cantaloupes or 75 cents an hour; that the grower supply free picking sacks and ice; that the growers deposit the workers' withheld wages in a bank instead of giving it to contractors to hold for them; and that the growers assume the responsibility for paying workmen's compensation (contractors were supposed to pay this, but they didn't).[18] Although the demands were moderate as well as reasonable, the growers refused even to discuss them; they did not want to set a precedent. Ramón Mireles, the union's president, made cordial contacts, but he did not threaten a strike. On May 7, workers at the Sears Brothers Ranch in the Imperial Valley demanded 15 cents a crate—only 1½ cents more than they already earned. When the employer refused, half the workers walked out. Sears called the county sheriff, who arrested four Mexicans for disturbing the peace. Soon, two to three thousand workers supported the strike. Officials of *La Unión de Trabajadores del Valle Imperial* used tactics to confuse growers and authorities. They denounced the strike publicly, but supported it before Spanish-speaking audiences.

The agents of the growers, meanwhile, used naked power to break the strike. On May 10, County Sheriff Charles L. Gillett shut down the union's offices, outlawing all future strikes. He branded the workers and their leadership "agitators." In response, the union changed its name to the "Mexican

Mutual Aid Society." Newspapers sided with the growers, as did public opinion in the valley. The growers, also, could not believe that *their* Mexicans would ever cause any trouble. Local officials, from the sheriff up to the county administrators, blamed it on "Reds and radicals." Meanwhile, local county officials moved to smash the union. The district attorney of Imperial County supported the growers, because "they had millions invested in crops." Sheriff Gillett arrested "uppity" Mexicans, stating that "if they were not satisfied with conditions in the United States, they could go back to Mexico."[19] On May 8, Gillett arrested 30 Chicanos for loitering. On the 13th, he arrested a newspaper dealer in Brawley for placing on his billboard a poster that was critical of Gillett's mass arrests. The number jailed climbed to over 100. Gillett ignored constitutional guarantees and unilaterally prohibited any congregation of Mexicans. The court set bail from $250 to $1000, which was prohibitive for the Mexican workers. The district attorney, in turn, offered to suspend the strikers' sentence if they plead guilty and promised to return to work. Financial pressures forced most to accept, and those who did not were deported.[20] The strike was broken by these tactics. The workers—poorly organized, badly financed, and with no outside support—were not able to stop production for a meaningful period. The power of the growers was too overwhelming for them.

Mexicans continued to organize around areas where stable populations lived. In 1927 in Los Angeles, *La Confederación de Uniones Obreras Mexicanos* (CUOM) was formed. It held its first convention on May 5, 1928. In the following years, CUOM organized 20 locals, with membership of about 3000 workers. It was the first Mexican union to include rural and urban workers. It was, however, plagued by internal problems, especially financial.

The Great Depression of the 1930s only intensified the Chicano's struggle within the labor movement. The Mexican had been brought into the United States to work for wages and under conditions that Anglo-Americans would not work. But, hunger drove many Anglos to the fields to compete with the Mexican, and the Mexican continued to move. A typical Mexican family in California migrated along the following route:[21]

Months	Place	Crops
January–March	Salt River Valley, Arizona	Lettuce
March–June	Imperial Valley, California	Carrots
June	Conejos, California	Apricots
July–August	Tulare County, California	Peaches
September–November	Fresno County, California	Cotton
November–March	Salt River Valley, Arizona	Lettuce

Organized labor abandoned Mexicans in this odyssey. The Communist party, however, moved into the void and, in 1929, formed the Trade Union Unity League. It advertised the plight of the workers, sent organizers into the fields, and unlike the AFL, it did not discriminate.[22]

By January 1930, the fervor of the Mexican workers in Imperial had been rekindled, and they struck again, using the base of the Mexican Mutual Aid Society. This strike, along with most others that followed, failed; nevertheless, that any strike took place at all was a credit to the Mexicans. It is true that the Communist party capitalized on the ferment of the Mexicans and the other poor people. They established a front called the Agricultural Workers Industrial League that led four strikes; however, in July 1931, it changed its name to the Cannery and Agricultural Workers Industrial Union (CAWIU). For several years this union dominated the strike activity.[23] Its failure can be attributed to many causes: first, many of its organizers mobilized temporary crisis-oriented groups instead of organizing stable unions with a permanent base; secondly, the depression created a climate that was not conducive to labor negotiations; and, above all, the repression was intense, especially when it was discovered that the union leadership was dominated by Communists.*

California was at the forefront of the Chicano *huelga* activity in 1933. Joan London and Henry Anderson report:

> No one knows how many small, local work stoppages went unrecorded that year: 37 strikes were important enough to appear in the records of government agencies. An estimated total of 47,575 workers walked off their jobs, or were locked out, with 669,400 man-days lost. Of these 37 major strikes, 24 came under the leadership of the CAWIU, including all the major ones.[24]

One of these strikes was held in El Monte, California, in 1933. It was important because it generated considerable activity among Chicanos in the Los Angeles area. Like the Imperial Valley strike, it politicized a large number of workers, and they spread the ferment.

The Berry Strike of 1933

El Monte, California, had been the citadel of white supremacy, the place where the "Monte Boys" (mentioned in chapter 5) had separated themselves from Mexicans. Gradually, however, some whites moved out of El Monte and nonwhites moved in—a natural process, since the town became an agricultural center. Although El Monte itself had only 4000 inhabitants, it served a trade area of 12,000, of whom 75 percent were Anglos, 20 percent Mexican, and 5

---

*The issue of Communist leadership and influence in the unions has always been a thorny one. Despite the antipathy of most Anglos to the "Reds," it must be remembered that Mexicans had a different perspective: they were reacting to the exploitation of *gringos*. Anglo-American argibusinessmen were the visible oppressors, and the Mexicans needed help in organizing for better wages and working conditions; Communists offered such help.

percent Japanese. Each group segregated itself from the others. The Chicano *barrio,* known as Hick's Camp, was a shack town located across a dry river gulch from El Monte proper.[25] Many of the 1100 Mexicans living there were migratory workers. They comprised the bulk of the town's cheap labor force and were paid about $1.50 for a nine-hour day.

Conditions demanded union organization. The pay scale was low, and whole families had to work just to subsist. In May 1933, a group of workers —Chicanos, Japanese, and Anglos—went to the secretary of the Growers Association and demanded higher wages. He refused their request. The Mexicans then went to Hick's Camp where, during the next few days, general meetings were conducted. On the first of June, 500 to 600 workers voted to strike. This number soon increased to 1500.[26] A strike committee of 60 workers, which included Chicanos, Japanese, and Filipinos from the surrounding communities, was organized. As Charles B. Spaulding, a professor of sociology at Whittier College, pointed out:

> The Japanese farmers were greatly troubled and somewhat confused. They felt that they must harvest their crops, which represented their means of existence. They were angry with the Mexicans for thus causing them to lose their produce, but their cultural backgrounds prevented them from offering physical resistance to the Mexican strikers. In so far as they were not sure of their own legal rights and did not know the techniques for securing aid from existing American institutions, they were confused.[27]

Spaulding observed that the Anglo-American public favored the Japanese because of its antipathy to strikes and Chicanos. The Japanese, however, had experienced considerable discrimination in the past and did not trust the Anglo-American. Moreover, they were caught in the middle, since they had to pay the owners high rents for their land. It followed that they had to keep workers' wages low in order to make a profit.

Initially, strikers demanded 25 cents an hour or 65 cents a crate for berries, but later they lowered it to 25 cents an hour or 50 cents a crate. The growers knew that they had to act quickly, since the berries had to be picked. Their offer of 20 cents an hour or 45 cents a crate was rejected. In the first days, the sheriff left the strikers alone, but as intensive picketing began, the sheriff followed the usual tactic of arresting picketers for disturbing the peace. At the request of Armando Flores, chairman of the strike committee, the Mexican consul, Alejandro Martínez, soon arrived. A power struggle developed between the leadership of the CAWIU, which had first organized the strike, and the Mexican consul. The latter denounced the organizers as "Reds." The struggle ended abruptly during the first week in June when eight of the CAWIU organizers were imprisoned on conspiracy charges.[28] Why the power struggle broke out is not entirely clear. There is some evidence that outsiders came into El Monte to disorganize the work of the CAWIU but there is also ample evidence that the Communist union did not pay sufficient attention either to the nationalism of the Mexican or to their leadership.

The CAWIU was replaced by the newly formed Chicano union, which the Mexican vice-consul at Los Angeles, Ricardo Hill, helped found. This union was influenced by former CUOM organizers, many of whom joined the El Monte leadership. After assessing the situation, the new union recommended that the strike be continued. This action encouraged other new unions throughout Los Angeles County to be organized. More than 5000 workers walked off the celery fields of Santa Monica and Culver City during the second week of June 1933. On July 15, union locals in the Los Angeles area called a convention and founded a permanent organization—*La Confederación de Uniones de Campesinos y Obreros Mexicanos del Estado de California* (CU-COM). By January 1934, the organization's membership multiplied from 5000 to 10,000. It said it was a "cultural organization to educate the Mexicans and to protect them," forecasting that "further strikes would be necessary in order to protect the Mexican workers from exploitation."[29]

Meanwhile, the strikers at El Monte solicited aid from Mexico. They knew that Plutarco Elías Calles, a former president of Mexico, and his puppet president Abelardo Rodríquez had alienated Mexican labor.* Armando Flores, therefore, wrote a letter to Calles asking him for support. The latter sent a donation of $150 and, later, another of $3000. *La Confederación Regional Obrera Mexicana* (CROM), the national Mexican labor union, requested that all members support the strike and threatened to boycott Japanese products if the growers did not agree to the strikers' terms. The strike leaders openly solicited the active support of the Mexican government.[30]

The Los Angeles Chamber of Commerce grew concerned about the strike's duration. Ross H. Gast of the Chamber of Commerce, U.S. Labor Commissioner Marsh, and Conciliator G. H. Fitzgerald urged the growers to compromise and to offer the strikers a package that would make it possible for them to earn between 20 and 25 cents an hour for a ten-hour day. The Chamber and the U.S. officials pressured the strikers to accept the offer. The strikers, however, believed their bargaining position had improved and, therefore, rejected the offer. The mediators could not understand the union's militancy and believed that outside influences were involved. "Gast was convinced that Armando Flores was a Communist. . . ."[31] Meanwhile, the Chamber of Commerce was anxious to settle the strike; it feared that the restrictionists would exploit the strike to limit immigration, and it also feared that the strike would spread. The Japanese consul worked behind the scenes with the Mexican consul to effect a settlement. The Japanese feared public opinion would turn against them.[32]

On July 6, a settlement was reached. The time favored the growers, because the peak of the harvest season had passed. As a consequence, the terms of the agreement were lower than those previously rejected by the union. The terms called for $1.50 for a nine-hour day or, for temporary help, 20 cents an

---

*Although Calles was president of Mexico only from 1924 to 1928, he controlled the Mexican government through puppet presidents to 1934.

hour. It was, nevertheless, a victory, because the union was recognized.[33]

Many of the El Monte strikers migrated north to the San Joaquin Valley in search of work, taking the *huelga* fervor with them. In October 1933, labor conditions reached the boiling point in that valley. The CAWIU organized near Visalia, and when the agricultural labor bureau announced that it would pay 60 cents per hundred pounds for cotton, the organizers demanded $1, the 1930 rate. The growers responded by evicting the strikers from camps and company property. Meanwhile, the union had rented 40 acres near Corcoran where the strikers could take refuge. About 15,000 workers joined the strike; three-quarters were Spanish-speaking. The usual mobilizing techniques were used. The grievances went beyond the employer-servant relationship. Workers complained of racism, poor wages, and bad housing and sanitation.[34] On October 10, 1933, near Visalia, California, the growers reacted by ambushing farm workers as they left a meeting. They shot into the crowd, killing Delfino Dávila and Dolores Hernández[35] and wounding others. The police responded by arresting 17 strike leaders, and they branded the episode the "Pixley riots." Eight ranchers were later arrested, and although Chicanos and other workers claimed they had committed premeditated murder, the district attorney did not ask for the death penalty.[36] They were acquitted. The results were tragic: more shooting took place, 42 were wounded, and 113 strikers were arrested.[37]

Although the CAWIU led ten more strikes in 1934, by the end of that year, the union was dead. Organizers had polarized the camps and encouraged violent actions from usually neutral segments of the Anglo-American community. Moreover, many of the organizers were intellectuals who could not distinguish between theory and practice. They had mobilized the workers but had not organized them adequately to enable them to become self-sufficient. Lastly, on July 20, 1934, the CAWIU's top leaders were arrested under California's criminal syndicalism laws. They were tried and convicted.[38] Meanwhile, the press sensationalized the strike activity and made heroes of the oppressors: on July 13, 1934, the *Los Angeles Times* reported: "Tear Gas Routs 1500 in Brawley Lettuce Strike Meeting." The paper reported that local authorities had declared the strikers' meeting an unlawful assembly; then when the union members failed to disperse fast enough, they shot tear gas into the crowd. The *Times* as well as other newspapers played up the theme of the "impending" revolution. They molded public opinion into believing that radical agitators led the strikes, and they condoned the repressive methods used to break the strikes. These newspapers supported the privileged and failed to condemn the exploitation in the fields.

Furthermore, the *Times* linked the strikes to a Communist conspiracy. On January 15, 1934, from El Centro, California, it reported "Red Strike Aim Fails." The article lauded Imperial Valley police for roughing up the "agitators." Three days later the *Times* again exploited the Communist issue and headlined: "Reds Attack Citrus Work." On January 19, it reported that Congressman Stubbs, a Democrat from California, had demanded federal assistance to halt the "Red Drive in California." Stubbs stated: "We believe in

California that the great majority of the farm workers are satisfied with the progress that is being made toward recovery. Communists are working on them daily, and they must be stopped." The *Times* exploited the Communist issue, while it ignored the plight of the migrant in California agribusiness. Along with other California newspapers, it inflamed public opinion against the strikers, encouraging vigilante activity to break it up. To the newspapers, the strikers were all agitators directed from Moscow, and the strikes should be broken by any means available.

Union organization among Mexicans received a boost when John L. Lewis formed a Committee for Industrial Organization within the American Federation of Labor. Lewis broke with the skilled labor elitism of the AFL. In 1937, he walked out of the AFL and formed the Congress of Industrial Organizations. Many radicals joined this new organization in the hope that labor would finally do something for the have-nots. In that year, the CIO chartered the United Cannery, Agricultural, Packing, and Allied Workers of America (UCAPAWA). This union attracted many Chicanos, and it led organizational activity throughout the Southwest. Its most notable effort was in San Antonio, Texas.

The San Antonio Pecan Shellers' Strike

At the height of the depression many Mexicans abandoned San Antonio for the northern manufacturing cities; many returned, however, without jobs, in need of food, and forced to take any work they could find. The pecan industry primarily employed nonskilled workers.[39] Between 5000 and 12,000 Mexicans were on the payroll. Gustave Duerler, a Swiss candy manufacturer, recognizing the potential profits in the many pecan trees of the area, had begun the industry during the Civil War. He bought pecans from the Indians and hired Mexicans to crack them open and extract the meat. By the 1880s, he was shipping the pecans east. In 1914 he mechanized the cracking phase of his operation, still using Mexican girls to extract the meats by hand. Duerler remained the "Pecan King" until 1926, when the Southern Pecan Shelling Company, with an investment of $50,000, was formed. Ten years later the shelling company's gross business had climbed to $3,000,000. Meanwhile, the company had demechanized because it was cheaper to hire Chicanos than to maintain machines and factories. The depression insured an overabundance of cheap labor.

The employment practices in the pecan industry resembled those of agribusiness. The industry worked through contractors, who employed the crackers and pickers. On many occasions, the contractors employed families and friends to shell the pecans in their own homes:

> Frequently as many as one hundred pickers toiled in a room 25 by 40 feet. Illumination was poor; ventilation was inadequate, and the fine dust from the pecans hung in the air, except when doors or windows were open in warm weather. Inside flush toilets and even running water were a rarity until 1936,

when a city health ordinance compelled all plants to install these conveniences. The statutes also required health examinations for all food handlers. However, at least one case is on record of a known syphilitic who secured a job shelling pecans immediately after successfully passing the health department's physical examination.[40]

Moreover, child labor was employed in violation of a San Antonio city ordinance.

The "average sheller earned less than $2 per week" in 1934.[41] This rate had increased only slightly by 1936, when the shellers could earn from 5 to 6 cents per pound for pecan halves. Meanwhile, a pecan workers' union had been organized, claiming that the pay was even lower. Management admitted that wages were low, but they rationalized that the Chicanos ate many pecans while working; the shellers would not work the necessary hours if they were paid more—they would earn 75 cents and go home, whether it was 3:00 P.M. or 6:00 P.M.; the Chicanos were satisfied; and they had a nice warm place in which to work and could visit friends as they did so. Yet Harold Laski, a British economist, was horrified by the deplorable conditions. He stated that "the pecan workers of San Antonio . . . have all the characteristics of a proletariat."[42]

Conditions were ideal for organizing the workers. *El Nogal,* the largest of the pecan workers' unions, claimed 4000 members between 1933 and 1936. Another union, the Pecan Shelling Workers' Union of San Antonio, was a company union. It was led by Mageleno Rodríguez. A National Recovery Administration (NRA) representative characterized him as "a fugitive from justice, a citizen of Mexico, and a labor agitator who betrays his workers."[43] Rodríguez claimed that he represented 9500 workers, yet he sided with the shelling companies before the NRA. Up to this time (1938), both of these unions were ineffective.

On February 1, 1938, at the peak of the pecan shelling season, thousands of shellers walked off their jobs. This action was triggered by a one-cent-per-pound reduction in rates. Workers abandoned 130 plants throughout the West Side of San Antonio. Local law authorities backed management and arrested over 1000 pickets. The charges included blocking the sidewalks, disturbing the peace, unlawful assemblies, etc. "Within the first two weeks tear gas was used at least a half-dozen times to disperse throngs that milled about the shelleries."[44] City officials even dug up an obscure city ordinance aimed at the sign-carrying picketers, which made it "unlawful for any person to carry . . . through any public street . . . any advertising . . ." until a permit had been obtained from the city marshall.[45] It was a ludicrous situation, since the office of city marshall had been abolished some years before. Since the picketers did not have the necessary permit, they were arrested and fined $10. It is of significance that, in contrast to the chief of police, the county sheriff did allow picketing.

Police Chief Owen Kilday was determined to break the strike. When CIO organizer J. Austin Beasley arrived in San Antonio, Kilday promptly arrested him. Kilday alleged Beasley was wanted in El Paso and held him on suspicion for 24 hours. When the strikers attempted to get a court injunction to restrain Kilday from harassing the pickets, the judge held: "There can be no doubt about the right of the strikers to cease work and to also attempt peaceably to persuade others to cease their work and to also attempt to dissuade persons from entering into the employ of their former employers."[46] However, the judge decided that:

> The assembling in one place of a large number of pickets incensed by a spirit of resentment to grievances, whether real or imaginary, tends to produce disorder and become a menace to the public peace, as well as an interference with orderly traffic and use of the streets by others. . . .[47]

Based on this rationale, the judge refused the injunction.

Chief Kilday refused to recognize that a strike existed. He called the UCAPAWA "disturbers of the peace." In spite of Kilday's attitude, the union recruited 6000 of the 12,000 shellers. The polarization increased. The special target of the city officials was Mrs. Emma Tenayuca Brooks, "a fiery little Mexican woman about twenty years old," who was a leader among the strikers and allegedly an admitted Communist.[48] Although the union leadership replaced her, the attacks continued: "The police, assisted by 125 club-wielding firemen, continued to use tear gas and clubs to disperse the crowds of pickets . . ."[49] Kilday continued to issue inflammatory press releases: "[It's a] Communist revolution . . . I branded the leadership as communistic and I still think so . . . It is my duty to interfere with revolution, and Communism is revolution."[50] The chief stated that if he did not act, and if the strike were won, "25,000 workers on the West Side would fall into the Communist party." His definition of a Communist was "a person who believes in living in a community on the government and tearing down all religion . . ."[51]

Nevertheless, Kilday ran a prison more deplorable than the "Communism" he denounced. He packed 33 women in cells designed for 6. He denied strikers privileges accorded to convicted criminals, and in spite of the fact "that 90 percent of the prostitutes suffered from infectious venereal diseases, all cellmates [picketers and prostitutes] shared a single toilet and the lone drinking cup."[52]

Mexican organizations such as the Mexican Chamber of Commerce and the League of United Latin American Citizens, as well as the Catholic archbishop, refused to support the strike under its current leadership. The archbishop went so far as to commend the police for acting against "Communistic influences." In all fairness to the archbishop, he did urge the pecan owners to pay higher wages, because, in his view, lower wages bred Communism. Ironically, Reverend John López, a Roman Catholic priest, urged the workers to return to the true friend of the working masses—the church. The San Antonio Ministers' Association called for a settlement and for a purge of "all Communistic, Fascist, or any un-American elements ..."[53] Many observers considered the CIO as an arm of Moscow and any protest by Mexicans as Communist inspired.

Federal and state officials disapproved of Kilday's methods. The National Labor Relations Board stated that "there has been a misuse of authority in handling the strike." Meanwhile, the governor of Texas condemned Kilday's refusal to allow picketing. He also lamented the beatings, and "forcing Mexicans to become scabs under the threat of deportation."[54] Nonetheless, Chief Kilday continued his repression and even closed down a soup kitchen offering free food to the strikers. He alleged that was in violation of city health ordinances.[55]

After 37 days of Kilday, the dispute was submitted to arbitration. In spite of overwhelming odds, the pecan workers had stopped production and had called national attention to the exploitation. Although the decision of the arbitration board was partial to the owners, it did recognize Local 172 as the sole bargaining agent. This was, however, a short-lived victory. Although the Fair Labor Standards Act* required owners to pay the workers the minimum wage of 25 cents an hour, management complied only temporarily and then mechanized, replacing Mexicans with machines. Without members the unions faded, and by 1948, disappeared from the scene. Victory had come too late since mechanization soon made hand labor obsolete in this industry.

During the 1930s the Mexican government supported Mexican workers in the United States, and on occasion, vice-consuls and consuls actively participated in union organization. This activity, however, gradually decreased as the Mexican revolution became more "institutionalized," and the country entered into a period of consolidation. World War II took the steam out of the agricultural labor organizations, since many of the Chicano labor organizers and workers were drafted and others migrated to the city. Moreover, the *bracero* (helping arms) program retarded organization, since workers from Mexico would be used as organized strike breakers. (See section on *braceros* that follows.)

The Struggle Continues

Much of what we know about the struggle of the 1940s comes from Ernesto Galarza, who wrote a trilogy on the struggle of Mexican workers with the agribusiness of the Southwest. His last book, *Barrio Boy,*[56] is autobiographical and traces his own migration to the United States. It has an "I-was-there" flavor and tells of a boy leaving his native village of Jalcocotán, Nayarit, his feelings as he was uprooted, and his family's tribulations during their odyssey. The Mexican family is featured—a mother, a son, and the mother's two brothers—moving as a unit. (Sometimes the uncles scout ahead in order

---

*The act was passed on June 25, 1938.

to earn enough money to take the family over the railroad *al norte*.) At first, they have no intention of leaving Mexico, but gradually the magnet pulls them —the family being moved more by circumstances than by its own volition. There are also the impressions of a small boy who first discovers a new world —a toilet in a closet. Once, in the *barrio* of Sacramento, the family reaches back into Mexico to help the family members who were left behind come to the United States. The family's strife is told in a gripping style. Like Oscar Handlin's *The Uprooted,* it is a documentary of migration to the United States and deals with people's frustrations and unfulfilled promises.

The second book of the trilogy, *Merchants of Labor,*[57] deals with the *bracero* program in the United States. Galarza wrote this work to expose the evils of the *bracero* program and the power employed by agribusiness to maintain the system. Until the 1960s the prospects of ending it seemed futile because the Mexican government guaranteed that the *bracero* (a temporary contract worker on loan from Mexico) would return to his native country. Not even the restrictionists supported the few labor organizers who worked toward its demise. Big labor officially opposed the *bracero* program; however, farm labor issues were low on its priority list. When unions lobbied in Congress for labor legislation, the farm workers took a back seat to the needs of the large-city proletariat. In many instances, in order to get concessions for the urban worker, the national unions abandoned their demands for the farm laborer. It amounted to simple opportunism. Principles be damned; the urban worker paid dues, whereas the farm laborers did not.

World War II created a labor shortage in the United States. Many Chicanos volunteered for the armed forces. Moreover, they were drafted into the armed forces in large numbers, since they were poor and since they were not as likely to qualify for exemptions. Also, they were not likely to be as vital to the war effort at home as was the son of a rich farmer or factory owner. The Chicano farm workers joined many other migrants in the cities, where they obtained jobs that had previously been closed to them, and where they were paid much higher wages than in their former farm employment. The farm labor shortage became even more acute when the Japanese Americans were placed in concentration camps, because the Japanese included owners of small farms as well as farm workers. With the United States requiring food not only for its domestic market, but for its allies as well, maximum farm production efficiency was vital to the war effort. Once more, the U.S. growers turned to Mexico. They had two alternatives: simply to open the border and allow the Mexican worker to come into the United States unencumbered, or enter into an agreement with Mexico for an agreed-upon number of Mexican *braceros* to be furnished to the United States. The growers preferred the first alternative, since Mexican workers then would not be protected and the grower could hire him at the lowest possible wage. The Mexican government, however, would not permit this and insisted on a contract that protected the rights of its workers.

Mexico had not been enthusiastic about sending large numbers of workers to the United States, but Mexican officials wanted to contribute to the war effort. Therefore, they entered into a preliminary agreement under which the United States and Mexico would supervise the recruitment of *braceros*. Furthermore, the two countries agreed to a contract guaranteeing the workers' rights. The agreement provided, among other things, that the Mexican workers would *not* displace domestic workers, they would be exempted from military service, and discrimination would not be tolerated.[58] It also regulated the transportation, housing, and wages of the *bracero*. Under this agreement, from 1942 to 1947 about 220,000 *braceros* were imported into the United States.

At first, farmers did not unanimously favor the *bracero* agreement. Texas growers, in particular, merely wanted the government to insure an open border. Only a handful of growers participated during the first year, for many resented any form of government regulation. Historically, states like Texas had all the "illegals" they could handle, so they did not want the federal government to regulate the Mexicans' wages and housing. They wanted a "free market" that they controlled. The growers especially disliked the 30-cents-an-hour minimum wage, charging that this was the first step in federal farm-labor legislation. The Texas growers, therefore, boycotted the program in 1942 and moved to circumvent the agreement.[59]

The executive branch of the U.S. government did not receive congressional approval for the *bracero* program until 1943, when Congress gave it authority under Public Law 45. As a result of lobbying by the powerful American Farm Bureau, an escape clause, found in section 5(g), was written into the act. Under this clause, the commissioner of immigration was empowered to lift the statutory limitations of the act, on the condition that such an action was vital to the war effort. Almost immediately, farmers pressured the commissioner to use the escape clause; he relented, and the border was left open and unregulated. Mexicans flooded into the border areas, where farmers employed them without having to worry about federal regulation. It became evident that the United States had breached its agreement, and the Mexican government threatened to retaliate. In Washington, some officials bluntly advocated that the United States disregard Mexico's complaints. In the face of pressure, the Mexican government compromised and allowed workers not covered by the agreement to remain for one year. Mexico, however, made it clear that she would not tolerate uncontrolled migration in the future, and if the farmers wanted a steady supply of labor, they would have to adhere to the bilateral agreement.[60]

In the summer of 1943, Texas growers finally asked for *braceros*. The Mexican government, however, refused to issue permits for Texas-bound temporary workers. Extreme and intolerable race discrimination existed in Texas. Anglo-Texans, notoriously bigoted and narrow-minded, committed brutal transgressions against Mexican workers, including murders. On the other hand, if the Mexican authorities had continued to oppose sending *braceros* to Texas, a labor crisis might have developed. With this in mind, Texas governor Coke Stevenson induced the Texas legislature to pass the so-called Caucasian

Race Resolution, which affirmed the rights of all Caucasians to equal treatment within Texas. However, since most Texans did not consider Mexicans as Caucasians, the law had no relevance. Governor Stevenson further attempted to ameliorate tensions by publicly condemning discrimination. The Mexican government seemed on the verge of relenting when further cases of discrimination were reported from Texas. On September 4, 1943, the Good Neighbor Commission of Texas, financed by federal funds, was organized. The commission would supposedly end discrimination toward Chicanos through better understanding. The Mexican government did not relent, and Texas growers were forced to finish the season without Mexican labor.[61]

During the next four years, the Mexican government refused to accede to the Texas requests, for rampant discrimination continued in Texas. After the war, Texas growers no longer needed *braceros*, since the *veteranos* (war veterans) returned to the fields; the number of undocumented workers entering the United States also increased. Finally, in October 1947, the Mexican government relented and agreed to issue permits to Texas.* The Mexican authorities, through their resistance, had improved the lot of the Mexican workers in the United States. It demonstrated the importance of economic and political pressure from a foreign nation. Unfortunately, this kind of Mexican pressure became more and more infrequent.

Although the labor shortage ceased after the war, the *bracero* program continued. The U.S. government acted as a labor contractor at taxpayers' expense. It also assured nativists that workers would return to Mexico after they finished picking the crops. Moreover, the growers did not have to worry about labor disputes. The *braceros*, meanwhile, were used to glut the labor market and to depress wages; *braceros* were also used as strike breakers. The U.S. government fully cooperated with the growers, even intentionally allocating insufficient funds to the border patrol and, therefore, insuring a constant supply of undocumented laborers.

Labor organizations and Chicano leaders opposed the open border and the *bracero* program. The Chicanos' opposition to Mexicans entering the United States was not based on the restrictionist philosophy of shutting the gates on them. They wanted Mexicans to enter the United States as immigrants, fully protected by the rights that all immigrants have, so that exploitation would be diminished. The undocumented worker was easy prey for unscrupulous employers, since he feared deportation and therefore did not complain about abuses.

In 1951, Public Law 78 renewed the *bracero* agreement. Growers appreciated the advantages of the *bracero* and knew that a spirit of revolt was increasing among domestic workers. In California, the *braceros* were used for "tomatoes, lettuce, strawberries, sugar beets, lemons, melons, asparagus, mis-

---

*Of the 291,420 *braceros* entering the United States in 1961, 117,368 ended up in Texas. The narrative will demonstrate why.

cellaneous vegetables, grapes, and cotton, in that order."[62] In other crops, domestic labor supplemented the *bracero*. The growers benefited from the *bracero* program and protected it.* Under the Republican administration of the 1950s, the farmers had increasingly more to say about the administration of the program, while the Mexican government had less voice. Ernesto Galarza's *Merchants of Labor* cited an incident in which the federal government coerced Mexican authorities to do their bidding:

> In the negotiations of the fall of 1953 for the renewal of the international agreement, the Mexican government had taken a hard position on wage determination. It resolved to use its bargaining power on this and other issues to the best advantage. The Americans, as officials and private employers, were not prepared to abandon the *bracero* program entirely. An impasse was clearly brewing, and a radical answer was taking shape in executive minds in Washington. This answer was to open the border again to all who might wish to step across it and be signed up as regular *braceros*.

> The plan was announced in a joint press release of the departments of State, Justice, and Labor dated January 15, 1954. By way of the newspapers Mexico was informed that beginning on January 18 the United States would institute an interim program at the border because certain major issues between the two governments remained unsettled.

> On January 23 hiring of illegal entrants got under way at Calexico. Hundreds of men who had been waiting impatiently in Mexicali for contracts rushed the gates of the American immigration post. Mexican police squads closed on the mob. Some of the runaways were pulled back bodily as they tried to step over the line onto American territory. Border patrolmen extended a helping hand from their side of the open gates. At Calexico, San Ysidro, and San Diego approximately 3,500 men broke through and were signed up. During the three days of hustling for bodies, border recruiting, as the Imperial Valley Press described it, was 'a riotous success.'[63]

The actions of Anglo-American authorities were a flagrant violation of international law, which supports our labor importation thesis. The opening of the border ended the labor shortage, and it served notice to Mexico that it damn well better negotiate because the United States had the power to get all the workers from that country it wanted—agreement or no agreement. Short of shooting its own citizens, Mexico could not prevent the workers from crossing the border. Mexico, therefore, had no other choice but to sign a contract favorable to the United States.

The increasing dependence of Anglo-American growers on the *bracero* is reflected in the following figures:[64]

---

*Growers did not have to furnish housing for the *bracero* family. Also, the company store recovered a high percentage of their salaries. In some camps, the growers even acted as pimps to recover wages.

1942 – 4,203	1950 – 67,500	1958 – 432,857
1943 – 52,098	1951 – 192,000	1959 – 437,643
1944 – 62,170	1952 – 197,100	1960 – 315,846
1945 – 49,454	1953 – 201,388	1961 – 291,420
1946 – 32,043	1954 – 309,033	1962 – 194,978
1947 – 19,632	1955 – 398,650	1963 – 186,865
1948 – 35,345	1956 – 445,197	1964 – 177,736
1949 – 107,000	1957 – 436,049	

The Di Giorgio Strike at Arvin, California

The *bracero* program presented the major obstacle to unionization of farm workers; the growers knew it and so did the union organizers. With this knowledge, the first major strike against the Di Giorgio Corporation at Arvin, California, began in 1947. This strike is important, because it exposes the power of agribusiness in the United States.[65]

The facts are simple. On October 1, 1947, workers picketed the Di Giorgio farm near Arvin, California. Some 860 workers, an overwhelming majority of the workers at the farm, participated in the strike. The only workers who did not strike that day were 130 *braceros* who were locked in their bunkhouses and 30 illegals who allegedly left as soon as the strike broke out. Local 218 of the AFL led the strike, and the demands were: a 10-cent-an-hour increase in wages, seniority rights, a grievance procedure, and the recognition of the union as the sole bargaining agent.

Joseph Di Giorgio, who founded the Di Giorgio Fruit Corporation, refused the union's requests. The Di Giorgio family's holdings were so vast that Joseph Di Giorgio was dubbed by *Fortune* magazine as "Kublai Khan of Kern County." He had arrived penniless from Sicily, built an enormous fortune, and now seemed unchallengeable. Like many self-made men, he was shrewd and ruthless. He was not all bad, but certainly not all good. Di Giorgio had power and an immense ego, and he used the former to feed the latter. In the strike events that followed, he assembled this power and made the puppets dance.[66]

Di Giorgio's adversary, it must be remembered, was not the entire Anglo-American labor movement; the AFL's commitment amounted only to about $6000 a year in support of its affiliate Local 218, which became popularly known as the National Farm Workers Union (NFWU). It was difficult to organize the workers at the Di Giorgio farm, partially because of the varied ethnic and racial groups there. Mexicans, Filipinos, and Anglos were purposely segregated, and each group had deep-rooted resentments against the others. (Di Giorgio did not hire Blacks.)[67] Bob Whately, a veteran organizer, did much of the preliminary work. When he was ready, he appealed to H. L. Mitchell, president of the NFWU, for help. Mitchell, in turn, sent Henry Hasiwar and Ernesto Galarza to Arvin.[68] Local 218 was chartered in 1947, and its main mission was to organize Di Giorgio farm workers. When the

172

demands were refused, the effort to stop production began.

The press and local law enforcement officials supported Di Giorgio. He used the typical management strategy to break the strike. He evicted workers from their homes on Di Giorgio property, and goons and police attacked the picketers, injuring and hospitalizing them. When acts of vandalism occurred, police blamed the strikers and arrested them.[69] Meanwhile, the Associated Farmers sent an "impartial" investigating team that Red-baited the union.[70] The NFWU, in turn, attempted to stop production by picketing. The Di Giorgio Corporation countered by using undocumented labor. The union even attempted to launch a national boycott, but this failed because it had limited resources. A technique that was too new to be countered effectively was introduced: growers relabeled their products in order to circumvent the boycotts.[71] Meanwhile, in the spring of 1948, the Hollywood Film Council (an AFL affiliate) produced a film called *Poverty in the Land of Plenty,* which highlighted living conditions in the San Joaquin Valley.[72] While the film did not identify the scenes in the film to be those of the Di Giorgio Corporation, the latter claimed that the identification was there by inference.

As the strike continued, Joseph Di Giorgio became more obsessed with winning at any cost. On February 9, 1948, he issued a press statement to the *Los Angeles Examiner,* stating: "We all know this agitation is Communist-inspired by subversive elements."[73] The next day, Hugh M. Burns, California state senator and member of the Senate Committee on Un-American Activities, announced that his committee would investigate the charges. Jack Tenney, cochairman of the committee, led the investigation, but it failed to uncover any evidence of Communist involvement.[74]

Di Giorgio next mobilized friends in Washington, D.C. Congressman Alfred J. Elliot took the fight to the chambers of the House of Representatives, and on March 22, 1948, he read a document, allegedly signed by 1160 Di Giorgio employees, stating that the workers did not want Local 218 to represent them. The document was padded with names not involved in the dispute. Congressman Elliot demanded a federal investigation.[75]

Lack of funds hurt the strike's effectiveness. Strikers moved from Arvin to find employment in order to support their families. In November 1949, federal hearings were conducted at Bakersfield, California. Congressman Cleveland M. Bailey from West Virginia presided over the hearings of the subcommittee of the Committee on Education and Labor. Representatives Richard M. Nixon (California) and Tom Steed (Oklahoma) joined him. The two other members of the subcommittee, Thruston B. Morton and Leonard Irving, did not attend the hearings. The proceedings took two days—hardly enough time to conduct an in-depth investigation. The hearings were nonetheless dramatic, for the Di Giorgio Corporation had filed a $2-million suit against the union and the Hollywood Film Council, claiming that the film, *Poverty in the Land of Plenty,* libeled the corporation. The Di Giorgios wanted the subcommittee to substantiate their charge.[76]

The subcommittee followed the usual procedure. The Committee of the

Whole, having so many matters pending, divided the workload by forming subcommittees. The committee chairman gave a specific charge to the subcommittee, and the members conducted an investigation, which often took the form of hearings. The subcommittee chairman then drafted a report, submitted it to the subcommittee members, and then sent it to the Committee of the Whole. If the findings and suggestions of the subcommittee were accepted, an official report then would be submitted to the House, with recommendations for specific action.

In the case of the subcommittee investigating the Arvin strike, Congressman Bailey pigeonholed the findings; the subcommittee found nothing, so the congressman made no move to file an official report on the strike. Nor did Bailey mention the controversy between the union and Di Giorgio in the report that the subcommittee eventually made to the Committee of the Whole.[77] (A partial explanation is that Bailey, although a good union man, considered the Arvin strike of secondary importance, especially since he realized that the union had lost the strike.) Nevertheless, Joseph Di Giorgio was intent on getting an official condemnation of the union. On March 9, 1959, he had Representative Thomas H. Werdel, from Kern County, file a report, signed by the Honorable Tom Steed, Thruston B. Morton, and Richard M. Nixon, in the appendix of the *Congressional Record.* The appendix serves no official function other than to provide congressmen a forum in which to publish the trivia sent them by constituents. The report—a very clever piece of deceptive literature—was entitled "Agricultural Labor at Di Giorgio Farms, California."[78] Representative Werdel did not state that the report was official, but in the preface, he wrote: "I am, therefore, including herein a copy of the majority report which has been signed by three members of the five-man subcommittee No. 1."[79]

Werdel's report stated that *Poverty in the Land of Plenty* was libelous. The body of the Werdel Report included a letter from John Lesinski, chairman of the Committee on Education and Labor, to Representative Cleveland M. Bailey, which gave him the authority to form the subcommittee and to conduct the investigations at the Di Giorgio farms. Actually, the Lesinski letter had nothing to do with the report itself, but it was an attempt to give it an aura of legitimacy. The report contained a favorable biography on Joseph Di Giorgio, followed by a scathing denunciation of Local 218. It said, in essence, that "This strike was solely one for the purpose of organization." The workers, therefore, had no grievances, for "wages, hours, working conditions, and living conditions have never been a real issue in the Di Giorgio strike." It claimed that the film presented by the union was "designed to represent living and working conditions at the Di Giorgio farms," that the film did not represent the truth, and therefore, that "All of these representations are false." It concluded that the pickets were ineffectual, and the majority of the workers continued to perform their jobs in spite of the strike.[80]

The report further charged that taxpayers' money had been misused by holding the hearings, since they publicized "the leadership of a labor organization which has no contracts, no grievances, no strike, no pickets, and only a handful of members; its only reason for existence is its valuable leaders."[81] It concluded that it would be against the public good to introduce new laws or extend present laws to protect farm workers.

The report delivered a death blow to the NFLU, because it purported to be official, and because its condemnation of the film was used as proof that *Poverty in the Land of Plenty* was, in fact, libelous. The prefatory remarks were the most damaging.

> I recommend as the majority report of the subcommittee, signed by three members thereof, to all Members of this House who have any doubt about the libelous nature of the film, as narrated by Mr. Harry W. Flannery and his associates, [who] deliberately fabricated falsehoods. The officers of the National Farm Labor Union then admittedly used the fabrication to collect hundreds of dollars from workingmen throughout the country to finance a purported strike that did not exist. The majority report is another disclosure of corrupt men deliberately bearing false witness to do untold damage to employers and employees, as well as disservice to the legitimate American labor movement, for a pittance by way of gain for themselves.[82]

The news media echoed Werdel's unsubstantiated accusations. Congressional immunity shielded Werdel from charges of libel and slander.

The California Federation of Labor hierarchy met with the officers of Local 218 and ordered them to settle the suit (the CFL would not pay the defense costs) and also demanded that the strike be ended. Big labor had been scared off by a phony report that purported to be an official record—one that had been published in the "wastebasket" of the *Congressional Record*. The report was issued on March 9, and by May 8 the strike ended. The Di Giorgios agreed to settle the suit for $1, on the following conditions: that the NFLU plead guilty to the judgment, thus admitting libel; that they remove the film from circulation and recall all prints; that they reimburse the corporation for attorney fees; and that they call off the strike.[83]

The Arvin strike and its sequel provided labor organizers with important data. Most of the findings are documented in Ernesto Galarza's *Spiders in the House and Workers in the Field*, which is a case study in the misuse of power by agribusiness. Galarza spent 18 years researching his work. This was made necessary by nine subsequent suits brought by the Di Giorgio Corporation against labor and its officials. The suits were filed whenever *Poverty in the Land of Plenty* was shown or whenever a union official said something critical about the 1947 strike. The Galarza work proved that the Werdel report had no official standing; that the Di Giorgio Corporation had a copy of the report on the same day that the *Congressional Record* was given the report by Werdel, and, in fact, the copy that purportedly came from Washington, D.C., was typed on the Di Giorgio attorney's typewriter; and that Werdel and the signers of the report did not know who drafted the report and signed it without questioning its source.[84] It is reasonable to conclude, therefore, that Werdel,

Steed, Morton, and Nixon all knew that the report was, at best, an opinion and that it had no official status. In other words, they knowingly deceived the public to break the strike. This leads us to the conclusion that agribusiness had enough power to induce four respected congressmen to endorse a blank check in order to satisfy the whim of a very powerful man. Farm workers did not have countervailing power.

The NFLU functioned during the 1950s, but it was a dying union. Labor abandoned it, and its staff eventually dwindled to one man—Ernesto Galarza. Nevertheless, in July 1952, the melon pickers of the Imperial Valley struck, and the union stopped production (the harvesting). The growers, however, imported *braceros,* claiming a "labor shortage," and the state Farm Placement Service certified this claim, even though the *braceros* were displacing domestic labor.[85] During these years, Public Law 78 continued as the main obstacle to the organization of the farm worker. Meanwhile, the NFLU was phased out when, in February 1959, the AFL-CIO decided to form the Agricultural Workers Organizing Committee (AWOC). The NFLU surrendered its charter in June 1960, and the AWOC took over where it left off. It had only limited success among Mexican workers.[86]

The Beginning of the Crusade

On September 16, 1965, the National Farm Workers Association (NFWA) voted to support the Filipinos in the AWOC in their strike against the grape growers of the Delano area. The Filipino grape pickers had won a victory in the spring of 1965 in California's Coachella Valley. The U.S. Labor Department had decreed that *braceros* would be paid $1.40 an hour. The domestic pickers received 20 to 30 cents an hour *less.* Joined by Mexicans, the Filipinos walked out, and ten days later they received a guarantee of equivalent pay with *braceros.* In the San Joaquin Valley, the Filipinos requested the same guarantee, but were refused. Led by Larry Itlong, they voted to strike on September 8, 1965. César Chávez, of the NFWA, did not want to strike; he did not believe the union was ready for a prolonged strike. Nonetheless, the rank and file voted on September 16 to join the Filipinos.

The strike demands were simple: $1.40 an hour or 25 cents a box. The Di Giorgio Corporation, a prominent grower in the Delano area, was again a major target. César Chávez emerged as the central figure in the strike. Events converted him into a Gandhi-like Mexican leader, although from the beginning it was emphasized that this was not a Mexican fight, but rather one for the rights of all humans.[87] For reasons made obvious during the first Di Giorgio strike, the *huelga* could not be limited to Chicanos; outside help was imperative. The logical source for volunteers and money was the contemporary civil rights movement. An important factor was that in December 1964 Public Law 78 had expired. This strengthened the union's hand.

César Chávez was born in Yuma, Arizona, in 1927. He spent his childhood as a migrant worker and knew, from first-hand experience, the tribulations of the farm workers. His father had belonged to farm labor unions and was indoctrinated with the importance of collective bargaining. He had been a member of the NFLU and had seen its mistakes. In the 1940s he moved to San José, California, where he married Helen Fávila. While there, he came into contact with Father Donald McDonnell, who tutored him in the papal encyclicals of Pope Leo XIII, which supported labor unions and social justice. Through Father McDonnell, César Chávez also met Fred Ross, of the Community Service Organization (CSO). Ross was a protégé of Saul Alinsky, so the CSO was heavily influenced by Alinsky's Industrial Areas Foundation.[88] Chávez became an organizer for the CSO and learned grass-roots organizing while working with that organization. In the course of his travels through California, establishing chapters in the cities and hamlets, he met Dolores Huerta, who later became his chief ally in the NFWA. Chávez became general director of the national CSO, but in 1962 he resigned when the CSO turned down a plan that would have committed the organization to a farm labor program. Chávez then moved his family to Delano and began to organize his union with no outside support. He built his union by going from door to door in the *barrios* where the farm workers lived.

Chávez concentrated his efforts on the Mexican field hands, for he knew the importance of nationalism in solidifying an organization. Moreover, many of his first recruits were Mexican *cursillistas.* *[89] Chávez also charged the members relatively high dues of $3.50 per month.** He wanted members who were committed to the union and who looked at it as their organization. He also built it around the family, which is important in organizing Mexicans. Moreover, the credit union and benefits to the members closely paralleled the oldest kind of Chicano organization—the *mutualista.* In addition, Chávez chose his lieutenants carefully, and he recruited a loyal cadre of proven organizers, such as Dolores Huerta. He avoided quixotic fights, and by the middle of 1964, the NFWA was self-supporting.[90]

By this time, organizers like Chávez knew the tactics the growers would use and the extent of their power in countering the union's tactics—which consisted mainly of stopping production by peaceful picketing. Certain actions by growers could be expected. There would be wholesale evictions of the strikers from homes rented from the growers. Workers sympathetic to the strike would be laid off. Undocumented workers and other scabs would be imported to work in the fields. There would be harassment and, in many cases, physical abuse of picketers. Local police power would be used, and their agents would refuse to prosecute the agents of management until the latter's actions

---

*The Cursillo movement began in Spain in 1947. It is very popular among Mexicans in Texas and in the rural sectors of the Southwest. The members attend a three-day meeting in which they rededicate themselves. The whole bent of the group is social action, and members are encouraged to participate in church life.

**It must be remembered that most workers averaged less than $2000 per year, and that they had large families.

became too flagrant to ignore; even then, prosecutions would be effected only under extreme provocation. Investigative committees would harass strikers. Rumors of fraud and embezzlement within the union would be spread; growers would organize countergroups who would claim that they had the right to work without union representation. The growers would rely heavily on the use of the emerging Mexican middle class in the Delano area, which based its newly found prosperity on keeping growers happy by furnishing them cheap labor; many earned a substantial second salary working as labor contractors. The strikers would be Red-baited. In addition, growers had an almost inexhaustible source of money, which in the United States means power. They controlled local state, and federal politicians, as well as the newspapers, the radio stations, and the television corporations. They also controlled the Catholic church and the best lawyers in the valley. In fact, the growers owned Kern County.

Chávez, on the other hand, had a union with no money, one that was made up of poor Chicanos and Filipinos, who traditionally had been the most discriminated and exploited people in the San Joaquin Valley. Chávez must have known that he had to depart from the conventional trade union methods of halting production. He was a realist who warned volunteers coming to Delano that if they believed that the union was all good and that the growers were all bad, they were naive. To him the growers were not entirely bad, nor were they literally devils. They represented men with power, who, in order to gain that power, denied the benefits of the nation's bountiful resources to the most neglected segment of Anglo-American labor—the farm worker.

Chávez built on a rich history of labor organization and had a good grasp of power relationships and organization. His union, started in 1962, had some 1700 members at the beginning of the strike.[91] But no matter how efficiently organized it was, it was not powerful or affluent enough to conduct a prolonged strike against agribusiness. Others had tried the tactic of a long strike and had failed. Chávez, therefore, put religion and civil rights into his labor dispute. Early in the strike, he appealed to church and civil rights groups for support.

It was easy for the civil rights workers to recognize the master-servant relationship between the growers and the farm workers. Volunteers, fresh from civil rights activities in the South, joined the NFWA at Delano. Protestant groups, who had been evangelized by the civil rights movement, championed the workers. A minority of Catholic priests, inspired by an inner revival, began to take seriously the *Rerum Novarum,* the papal encyclical on social justice. They spoke out to condemn the exploitation of the Mexican workers, who, after all, made up the majority of the church's membership in the Southwest.* With a possibility of victory and nationwide notoriety, and perhaps with some shame for its many years of neglect, Anglo-American labor also jumped on the bandwagon.

In Chávez's favor was the growing number of Chicano workers living in

---

*Many allege that the church had not taken an active stand up to this time because of its considerable financial stake in the agribusiness of California. Many growers were also large contributors to church coffers.

the United States. In 1960, Chicanos legally amounted to almost four million. Over 80 percent lived in the cities, and many belonged to unions. Many, in fact, belonged to big labor; many locals of the United Auto Workers (UAW), for example, which became one of Chávez's major supporters, had a Chicano majority. Paul Schrade of the UAW of southern California stated in the middle 1960s:

> Most of the union and minority strength is in the cities. They can exert the kind of pressure that urban senators are susceptible to. So now it's possible to envision the kind of legislation that can really benefit farm labor, like the collective bargaining rights industrial workers have.[92]

Schrade's locals were, and still are, heavily Chicano and very pro-Chávez. Saul Alinsky also held a similar viewpoint; he maintained that Mexican Americans, by the sheer force of their numbers, already had the means to change social conditions.[93]

The times worked for Chávez. The tail end of the major civil rights thrust in the South had ended. The Black movement had become more independent, and its growing separatism alienated many white supporters. These activists gravitated toward Delano. Chávez's nonviolent approach attracted many others who would not confront Establishment groups through sit-ins, large-scale demonstrations, etc., but who would picket a local market, boycott table grapes, or contribute money.

Last, but not least, was Chávez himself. Many leaders before him had attempted to organize Chicano workers but had not succeeded. Chávez was the right man to get the nationalistic Mexicans together with other workers and friends. Chávez put them all under the red flag with the distorted eagle and a banner of the Virgin de Guadalupe and led the march. His approach gave him a national forum and publicity in media such as the *Wall Street Journal* and *Life*; even *Time* magazine featured him in a cover story.

El Teatro Campesino, a theatre company directed by Luis Váldez, whose actors were the workers themselves, traveled throughout the nation, dramatizing to the Anglo-American people the story of the migrant and his struggle. The NFWA or the AWOC was by no means secure, but the spirit and momentum of the strike increased. The Teamsters Union loomed as a very powerful ally, even though it was known as an opportunistic organization which would not hesitate to cut the throats of Chávez and his followers.*

Without doubt, the most spectacular and profitable strategy was the

---

*The Teamsters is one of the largest American unions and is noted for participating in jurisdictional fights and then signing sweetheart contracts with management. Leaders such as Jimmy Hoffa run the union as a business—for a profit. They maintain a strong base with the truck drivers, whose loyalty is rewarded by good pay. In return, the membership has ignored the leadership's corruption and unfair labor practices in relation to brother union men. Union officials are astute enough to know that mechanization is coming to agriculture. Although pickers are not an attractive ally at present because they can neither exert effective pressure nor pay high dues, the skilled operators of the future will be. Thus, the Teamsters' tactic is to sell out the workers today by signing contracts favorable to management—betting on future power and profits. It is fair to speculate that Chávez realized the potential perfidy of the Teamsters even while he dealt with them.

boycott. It began slowly, and supporters were urged *not* to buy Schenley products or Di Giorgio grapes. The first breakthrough came when the Schenley Corporation signed a contract in 1966. It came about when the Teamsters unexpectedly refused to cross picket lines in San Francisco. Rumors of a bartenders' boycott reached 75-year-old Lewis Solon Rosensteil, its president, who decided that a settlement was advisable. Soon afterwards Gallo, Christian Brothers, Masson, Almaden, Franzia Brothers, and Novitiate signed contracts.

The next opponent was the Di Giorgio Corporation, one of the largest grape growers in the Central Valley. The ruthless, tough patriarch and founder of this corporation, Joseph Di Giorgio, recently had died. The corporation was in the process of diversifying its operations; it had become a modern-day trust, with processing and canning operations as well as stocks in other companies. Executives realized that the times had changed and they were concerned about the corporation's public image. Robert Di Giorgio, the new president, was more concerned about public relations than his Uncle Joseph had been. At the same time, he was much more dangerous, because he knew how to use public relations firms to win public opinion.[94]

In April 1966, Di Giorgio unexpectedly announced that he would allow the workers at Sierra Vista to vote on whether or not they wanted the union as its bargaining agent. If the majority of the workers voted that they recognized the NFWA, it would become the legal bargaining agent for the workers and the Di Giorgio Corporation would have to negotiate with the union. The NFWA, however, wanted Di Giorgio to recognize its union unilaterally as had the Schenley Corporation, and for the next two months it attempted to win this concession. Chávez knew that Di Giorgio had the advantage, since many of the original strikers, out of necessity, had moved from the area to find jobs to feed their families. During this negotiating period, Di Giorgio agents openly intimidated picketers, and a security guard beat a woman picketer.

Unexpectedly, the Teamsters became the NFWA's opposition at the Di Giorgio Sierra Vista Ranch. The Di Giorgios now looked upon the Teamsters as saviors. Di Giorgio then dealt in "bad faith," calling for a vote without consulting with the NFWA as to the voting date. The union urged its followers to abstain from the elections, since it did not have time to campaign or to participate in establishing the ground rules. Furthermore, it had to have enough time to return eligible voters to the Delano area. Out of 732 eligible voters only 385 voted; 281 voters specified that they wanted the Teamsters as their union agent.[95] The NFWA immediately branded the election as fraudulent and placed pressure on Governor Edmund G. Brown, a personal friend of Robert Di Giorgio, to investigate the election. Brown needed the Chicano vote as well as that of the liberals who were committed to the farm workers. Therefore, more out of political necessity than moral commitment, the governor reluctantly agreed to investigate. His investigator recommended a new election, and the date was set for August 30, 1966.[96]

That summer an intense campaign took place between the Teamsters and the NFWA. A state senate committee harassed the NFWA, investigating charges of Communist infiltration. The committee found nothing to substantiate the charges.[97] As the election grew closer, Chávez became more and more somber. He had numerous problems. He had to keep the eligible voters in Delano, and he had the responsibility of feeding them and their families as well as the army of strikers and volunteers. Big labor pressured Chávez to merge with the AWOC. He previously had rejected offers of support because he wanted to remain independent. Purists within his ranks demanded that he not sell out to Establishment labor. But the Di Giorgio campaign had drained the union's financial resources. Chávez, moreover, did not consider this campaign a quixotic adventure; he had to keep the organization alive if Delano were not to become another page in the annals of unsuccessful strikes. Therefore, some weeks before the strike vote, he reluctantly merged the NFWA and AWOC into the United Farm Workers Organizing Committee (UFWOC). Many volunteers termed this "Chávez's Munich" and believed it heralded his demise as a moral leader.[98] Subsequent events, however, have since absolved him.

The Teamsters, meanwhile, Red-baited the UFWOC and circulated free copies of Gary Allen's John Birch Society pamphlet. The NFWA passed out excerpts from *The Enemy Within,* where Robert Kennedy, in scathing terms, indicts Hoffa and the Teamsters; association with the Kennedy name helped. Finally the vote was taken. The UFWOC won the election, receiving 573 votes to the Teamsters' 425. More significant was the count breakdown among the field workers, who had voted 530 to 331 in favor of Chávez and his followers. The Teamsters' vote came from the skilled workers. Soon afterwards, the Di Giorgio Corporation and the UFWOC signed a contract.[99]

After the signing with Di Giorgio, the boycott evolved as the union's major weapon. The use of the secondary boycott would not have been possible if the farm workers had come under the jurisdiction of the National Labor Relations Board. Growers had fought the inclusion of agricultural labor under the provisions of the National Labor Relations Act (NLRA), which extended to other workers privileges such as the eight-hour day, the national minimum wage, unemployment insurance, etc. It also set up the mechanism for arbitration of a strike and the right of the workers to form a union. Under later provisions, secondary boycotts were prohibited. This meant that other unions could not support the striking union by boycotting the employer's products, nor could the strikers picket the merchandisers of the products. The rationale was to prevent collusion among unions, as well as to prevent a widening of the conflict area. Proponents of this provision wanted to limit the power of unions in order to prevent their having an unfair advantage—the capability for what many called "blackmailing" management. If the growers had not fought the attempts of unions and liberals to extend benefits to the workers under the NLRA, the UFWOC would have been prohibited from conducting the now-famous grape boycott.

The other growers prove to be more difficult. In 1967 the first target was Giumarra Vineyards Corporation, the largest table-grape producer in the

United States. When Giumarra used other companies' labels to circumvent the boycott, in violation of the Food and Drug Administration rules, the union extended its boycott to all California table grapes. In spite of protests, Chávez increased boycott activities, which spread into Canada and Europe. Grape sales definitely decreased. Some of the slack was, however, taken up by the U.S. Defense Department, which began to buy more grapes. At the start of the boycott, the U.S. troops in Vietnam were shipped 468,000 pounds of grapes; in the following year, 555,000 pounds; in 1968, 2,000,000 pounds; and in 1969, more than 4,000,000 pounds.[100] Although many private citizens protested the Defense Department interference with the boycott at the taxpayer's expense, the practice continued. In fact, the Defense Department extended this practice to buying lettuce when that industry was the object of a strike by Chávez and the UFWOC.

In the summer of 1970 the strike approached its fifth year. Many believed that the grape growers would never give in. That summer, Chávez intensified picketing in the Coachella Valley of California. As in previous years, he invited student groups and other organizations to help; many Chicano organizations responded to his call. In June 1970, a group of growers agreed to sign contracts. They were followed by a majority of Coachella growers. Crates containing union grapes displayed the UFWOC flag with its eagle; sales of union grapes jumped as many markets requested the "eagle." Soon the growers of the San Joaquin Valley also wanted what at one time they had labeled the "Trotsky eagle."[101] These growers also signed with Chávez, and soon the majority of the California table-grape industry had signed contracts.

Chávez then moved into the Salinas Valley, where he is attempting to organize lettuce industry. Again he has been confronted with standard management opposition and attempts to break the lettuce strike. He was jailed on December 4, 1970, when he refused to obey an injunction, and was held without bail. This arbitrary action gave the boycott considerable impetus. Dignitaries visited Chávez in jail; he was finally released on December 23, 1970.[102]

At Salinas, the Teamsters were again the "enemies within." They again challenged the UFWOC for jurisdiction. After negotiations in the spring of 1971, Chávez and the Teamsters signed a pact that gave the UFWOC jurisdiction over the field workers and the Teamsters jurisdiction over the food-process workers. Chávez then turned his attention to attempting to stop lettuce harvesting and to organizing the international boycott of California lettuce.

César Chávez is accomplishing what many believed to be impossible—the organization of farm labor. A victory in the lettuce field would give him a springboard to other agricultural products. What his victory will mean cannot be measured, since agriculture is becoming more mechanized. The dependency on farm labor, consequently, is diminishing. It is true that more skilled jobs are becoming available, but competition for jobs, as well as competition between unions for the right to represent these workers, will also increase. Chávez must be aware of the danger that farm workers, after their long struggle for fair working conditions and wages, could be robbed of the final reward because of the elimination of jobs.

Chávez's main struggle in the future will be to keep his organization together. His main enemies at the present are: factionalism in the union between the two major ethnic groups, the Chicano and the Filipino; the use of undocumented workers by the growers; growing unemployment in agriculture; and the expanding bureaucracy in his own organization, which includes publicity recruitment programs, a credit union, dispatchers, etc. The significance of the UFWOC struggle, meanwhile, has spread beyond the limits of agriculture labor. Chávez and the old NFWA flag have become symbols to the urban Chicanos, who comprise over 80 percent of the Chicanos in the United States. Many Chicanos look to Chávez for leadership in organizing the urban *barrios,* which are relatively new and bursting with impatience. Chávez and other trade unionists have over 75 years of agricultural organizing experience behind them; they are the beneficiaries of the successes and failures of the past unionization efforts. Transferring their experience and methods to the cities is the challenge of the future and will determine, in great part, the route to be taken by the Chicano movement.

Conclusion

The road to Delano has been a long and arduous one. However, although it was the opening of an important front, the victory does not signal success for the Chicano. Our story of the Mexican in trade union organization merely touches the surface of the Chicanos' involvement in the trade union movement. It is, however, enough to explode the "myth of docility," which Carey McWilliams debunked in his *North From Mexico,*[103] and which Dr. Octavio Romano has almost dedicated himself to exposing in *El Grito.*[104] The trade union involvement of the Chicano has been outside the mainstream of organized labor. It has had a handful of sponsors and has been in those industries that traditionally have been the most difficult to organize. Chicanos who worked as agricultural laborers or pecan shellers were contracted laborers, and they had to move to live. They did not have the luxury of remaining in one locale for very long, but when they did, they formed an organization. Many times these organizations took the form of *mutualistas,* which met economic and social needs, and these were expanded into defensive groups that attempted to alter the master-servant relationship that relegated Mexicans to a subordinate caste. The vehicle was a union to bargain collectively with the giants of industry.

As we have seen, these efforts were frustrated by the Goliaths, who simply had too much power. They kept the Chicano at the bottom of the economic scale in order to exploit his labor more easily. A few Chicanos have since improved their material lot by joining established trade unions for skilled and semiskilled workers, but the overwhelming majority remain outside the high-paying labor cycle, which is becoming tighter as unskilled jobs become less abundant.

The importance of the Chicano's labor struggle is that it has shown the Mexican workers that they can organize to fight the oppressor. Although they have lost almost every contest with management, their struggle was at the confrontation level, which greatly personalized the cause and helped to break down workers' fears of their "masters." The losses, moreover, politicized the Chicanos, increasing their awareness of economic exploitation and its role in subjugating them. The strikes further crystallized the workers' grievances, as well as their powerlessness to do anything about them through ordinary channels. They learned that their only power was the power to disrupt—a power they would have to use if they were to achieve economic self-determination. They also learned that they could only exercise this power through collective action. Each strike, moreover, exported its fervor, contributing to the Chicano struggle toward liberation.

Notes

1. Saul Alinsky, *Reveille for Radicals* (New York: Vintage Books, 1969), p. 29.

2. Joan London and Henry Anderson, *So Shall Ye Reap* (New York: Thomas Y. Crowell Company, 1970), p. 2.

3. London and Anderson, p. 3.

4. London and Anderson, p. 4.

5. London and Anderson, p. 3.

6. London and Anderson, p. 5.

7. Carey McWilliams, *North From Mexico* (New York: Greenwood Press, Publishers, 1968), p. 190.

8. James D. Cockcroft, *Intellectual Precursors of the Mexican Revolution, 1900–1913* (Austin: University of Texas Press, 1968), p. 124.

9. Laureano Clavo Berber, *Nociones de Historia de Sonora* (Mexico, D.F.: Publicaciones del Gobierno del Estado de Sonora, 1958), p. 277; Antonio G. Rivera, *La Revolución en Sonora* (Mexico, D.F.: n.p., 1969), p. 139.

10. Rivera, p. 159.

11. Quoted in Ward S. Albro, III, "Magonismo: Precursor to Chicanismo?" (Manuscript, Texas Arts and Industries University at Kingsville, n.d.), p. 5.

12. Cockcroft, pp. 128–129.

13. *Regeneración,* 3 September 1910; quoted in Albro, p. 9.

14. Cockcroft, p. 231.

15. See Charles Wollenberg, "Huelga, 1928 Style: The Imperial Valley Cantaloupe Workers' Strike," *Pacific Historical Review,* February 1969, pp. 45–58.

16. Wollenberg, p. 48.

17. Wollenberg, p. 48.

18. Wollenberg, p. 50.

19. Wollenberg, p. 54.

20. Wollenberg, pp. 55–56.

21. Paul Taylor and Edward Powell, "Patterns of Agricultural and Labor Migration within California," *Monthly Labor Review,* November 1938, p. 982.

22. London and Anderson, p. 28.

23. London and Anderson, p. 29.

24. London and Anderson, p. 29.

25. Charles B. Spaulding, "The Mexican Strike at El Monte, California," *Sociology and Social Research*, July–August 1934, pp. 571–572.

26. Ronald W. López, "The El Monte Berry Strike of 1933," *Aztlán*, Spring 1970, pp. 103–104.

27. Spaulding, p. 577.

28. López, p. 105.

29. Spaulding, p. 575.

30. López, pp. 106–107.

31. López, p. 107.

32. López, p. 108.

33. López, p. 109.

34. London and Anderson, p. 30.

35. *Los Angeles Times*, 12 January 1932.

36. *Los Angeles Times*, 12 January 1932.

37. London and Anderson, p. 30.

38. London and Anderson, p. 32.

39. This section is based primarily on Harold Arthur Shapiro, "Workers of San Antonio, Texas, 1900–1940" (Ph.D. diss., University of Texas at Austin, 1952), and Kenneth Walker, "The Pecan Shellers of San Antonio and Mechanization," *Southwestern Historical Quarterly*, July 1965, pp. 44–58.

40. Shapiro, p. 117.

41. Shapiro, p. 119.

42. *Reflections on the Revolution of Our Time* (New York: Viking Press, 1943), p. 150; quoted in Shapiro, p. 123.

43. Shapiro, p. 124.

44. Shapiro, p. 125.

45. Shapiro, p. 126.

46. Quoted in Shapiro, p. 133.

47. Quoted in Shapiro, p. 133.

48. Walker, p. 51.

49. Walker, p. 51.

50. Shapiro, p. 128.

51. Shapiro, pp. 128–129.

52. Shapiro, pp. 129–130.

53. Shapiro, p. 130.

54. Shapiro, p. 131.

55. Shapiro, p. 132.

56. Ernesto Galarza, *Barrio Boy* (Notre Dame, Ind.: University of Notre Dame Press, 1971).

57. Ernesto Galarza, *Merchants of Labor* (Santa Barbara, Calif.: McNally & Loftin, Publishers, 1964).

58. Galarza, *Merchants*, p. 47.

59. O. M. Scruggs, "Texas and the Bracero Program," *Pacific Historical Review*, August 1962, pp. 251–252.

60. Scruggs, pp. 253–254.

61. Scruggs, p. 254.

62. Ray Gilmore and Gladys W. Gilmore, "Braceros in California," *Pacific Historical Review*, August 1962, p. 272.

63. Galarza, *Merchants*, p. 66.

64. Leo Grebler, Joan W. Moore, and Ralph Guzman, *The Mexican-American People* (New York: The Free Press, 1970), p. 68.

65. Ernesto Galarza, *Spiders in the House and Workers in the Field* (Notre Dame, Ind.: University of Notre Dame Press, 1970). This is the major source for data about this particular strike.

66. Galarza, *Spiders,* pp. 13–18.
67. Galarza, *Spiders,* pp. 20–21.
68. Galarza, *Spiders,* pp. 21.
69. Galarza, *Spiders,* pp. 23–24.
70. Galarza, *Spiders,* p. 27.
71. Galarza, *Spiders,* p. 77.
72. Galarza, *Spiders,* pp. 30–31.
73. Galarza, *Spiders,* p. 25.
74. Galarza, *Spiders,* pp. 25–26, 153.
75. Galarza, *Spiders,* pp. 26, 35.
76. Galarza, *Spiders,* pp. 40–48.
77. Galarza, *Spiders,* p. 48.
78. Galarza, *Spiders,* pp. 288–297.
79. Galarza, *Spiders,* p. 288.
80. Galarza, *Spiders,* pp. 290–295.
81. Galarza, *Spiders,* p. 295.
82. Galarza, *Spiders,* p. 88.
83. Galarza, *Spiders,* pp. 64–66.
84. Galarza, *Spiders,* pp. 231–247.
85. London and Anderson, pp. 120–121.
86. London and Anderson, pp. 46–47.
87. This section is based principally on the following works: Eugene Nelson, *Huelga* (Delano, Calif.: Farm Workers Press, 1966); John Gregory Dunne, *Delano* (New York: Farrar, Straus & Giroux, Inc., 1967); Peter Mathiessen, *Sal Si Puedes: César Chávez and the New American Revolution* (New York: Random House, Inc., 1969); Mark Day, *Forty Acres* (New York: Frederick A. Praeger, Publishers, 1971), p. 39. Also consulted were the numerous anti-Chávez works in the magazine *American Opinion,* as well as *California's Number One Industry Under Attack,* 3d ed. (Glendale, Calif.: California Editors Publishing Co., 1969).
88. London and Anderson, pp. 143–145.
89. London and Anderson, pp. 146–148.
90. London and Anderson, p. 149.
91. London and Anderson, p. 150.
92. Dunne, p. 51.
93. Dunne, p. 53.
94. Dunne, p. 144.
95. Day, p. 42; Dunne, p. 145.
96. Day, p. 42; Dunne, pp. 147–148.
97. I attended the hearings in July 1965.
98. Dunne, p. 156.
99. Dunne, p. 166.
100. *El Malcriado,* 1–15 July 1968.
101. I attended a meeting at La Paz, California, on 4 July 1970, just after the signings. The demand for union grapes was reported.
102. *Los Angeles Times,* 5, 6, 24 December 1970.
103. McWilliams, pp. 189–193.
104. See Octavio I. Romano, "Minorities, History and the Cultural Mystique," *El Grito,* Fall 1967, pp. 3–11.

Chapter Eight

An Era of Repression

The last two chapters traced the Chicanos' migration to the United States and their attempts to defend themselves collectively against the exploitation that resulted. Anglo-American capitalists imported them to work at jobs that "white men would not do." The immigration of over a million Mexicans, marking one of the largest mass migrations of mankind, alarmed many Anglo-Americans, who reacted by attempting to restrict their entry to the United States. However, these efforts failed, since Anglo-American industrialists had become dependent on the brown man's labor; thus, they resisted efforts to exclude him.

Meanwhile, two separate cultural worlds—that of the Anglo-American and the Mexican—crystallized. It was a process similar to the one Albert Memmi described in Tunisia: "Possession of two languages is not merely a matter of having two tools, but actually means participation in two physical and cultural realms. Here, the two worlds symbolized and conveyed by the two tongues are in conflict; they are those of the colonizer and the colonized."[1] Language and culture placed Chicanos in conflict with the Anglo majority, which attempted to suppress their way of life. The Mexicans were considered aliens whenever they looked for a job or a house, and as aliens, they were intentionally denied control of their political, economic, and civil rights.

This chapter elaborates on the *de jure* and *de facto* deportation schemes of many Anglo-Americans, as well as other methods used to subdue Chicanos. Such schemes are important in understanding the creation of a "nation within a nation," which characterizes the Chicano's way of life in the United States. Mexicans were prevented from achieving self-determination by the government's suppression of their movements toward liberation. Mexicans were repatriated, denaturalized, and deported when they threatened the status quo. In times of stress, Mexicans were made scapegoats;[2] an example of this tactic occurred during World War II in the repression of the *Pachuco,* which we shall discuss later in the chapter. Chicanos struggled to adjust to their new environment and to organize to defend themselves against the oppression; too often, they failed, but out of their failures have come increased awareness and an even stronger determination to free themselves from their subservient status.

Early Organizations

Like most immigrants, Chicanos felt alienated. Thus, despite tremendous odds, they attempted to organize their communities. They founded economic, educational, and political associations, which also fulfilled the social needs of the people. The groups were uniquely Mexican, and they revolved around the family unit. Most of the organizations developed spontaneously. For example, a group of people would form a funeral society to insure that the members would receive a Christian burial, rather than being interred in a potter's field far away from their homeland. They organized *mutualistas* that sold insurance and provided limited social welfare benefits. These organizations sponsored social halls, where the members congregated and talked about common problems. At many of these meetings they planned ways of improving their lives or of protecting themselves against police or governmental malfeasance. The *mutualistas* dispelled the prevalent Anglo notion that Chicanos could not organize. Their constitutions (in Spanish and English) were sophisticated, and their meetings were orderly. Since many members of these early societies fully expected to return to Mexico, political issues were not of major concern, but occasionally these organizations did become confrontation groups.

A few *mutualistas* existed in the Southwest before the Treaty of Guadalupe Hidalgo.[3] The most famous of the early organizations was the *Alianza Hispano Americana.* Formed in Tucson, Arizona, in 1894, it provided funeral and insurance benefits. The group was social, with auxiliaries organized for women and youth as well. Family involvement is a characteristic of most of the Chicano organizations that have lasted. *La Alianza* did not limit its activities to social and economic functions, however. It also became involved in political affairs. Tucson, like many southwestern cities, had as residents many Texans, and they dominated the city and discouraged Chicano involvement. *La Alianza* furnished the political base to fight the political chicanery of the Texans. *La Alianza* grew, and 275 lodges were established. The group published its own magazine. In the 1960s, its supreme president, J. Carlos McCormick, became national organizer for the *Viva Kennedy* clubs. Although nationalistic, *La Alianza* has, from the beginning, been an integrationist group, promoting civic improvement projects.

Most of the early organizations sponsored patriotic functions and celebrated Mexican holidays; in their meetings, these first-generation Chicanos spoke Spanish. Later, second-generation Chicanos formed middle-class associations, which promoted goodwill and, in essence, sought to improve the Mexicans' image. However, many Chicanos nurtured deep resentments of Anglo-American expressions of superiority.

Other associations were established to protect the Mexicans against injustices. Deportation was a threat that constantly hovered over the Chicano's head. When there was a business slump, and his labor no longer was needed, he would often be dumped across the border. After World War I, when such a recession occurred, there were rumors that *all* Mexicans would be shipped home. *La Liga Protectiva Mexicana* (The Mexican Protective League) was formed in Kansas City in 1921 in response to the threat of deportation. The association lasted for two years, dissolving once the crisis had passed. *La Liga* differed significantly from other groups, because it was composed mainly of lower-income Chicanos. Low-income Chicano workers in urban areas generally did not form associations. The middle-class integrationist societies, of which most early Chicano organizations were constituted, reacted to specific crises. For example, *La Orden de Hijos de America,* established in San Antonio in 1921, was limited to either native-born or naturalized U.S. citizens. The stated purpose of *La Orden* was "to use their influence in all fields of social, economic, and political action in order to realize the greatest enjoyment possible of all the rights and privileges and prerogatives extended by the American Constitution."[4] *La Orden* fought for the constitutional rights of Chicanos and especially criticized the inequities of the jury system. By the late 1920s it had seven councils. It was the predecessor of the League of United Latin American Citizens (LULAC), formed in 1928 at Harlingen, Texas. LULAC structurally was supposed to incorporate the councils of *La Orden* into one central organization with lodges; however, the older councils refused to subordinate themselves to the new league.

LULAC, unlike most earlier organizations, used an English, instead of a Spanish, name. This association was integrationist, comprised of middle-class Chicanos who were citizens of the United States. Its purpose was "to develop within the members of our race the best, purest and most perfect type of a true and loyal citizen of the United States."[5] It placed major emphasis on learning English and established preschools to teach Chicano children the basic 400

English words, to help them assimilate into the school system, as well as to aid in their eventual Americanization. LULAC councils spread to 21 states, but the organization's main strength remained in Texas, where it served both social and political functions. In general, members identified very closely with LULAC. It survived in the most hostile of environments and kept Mexican American issues in the forefront. LULAC is important because it operated for the benefit of Chicanos.

The Deportation of the Chicano

As long as the Mexicans were needed as laborers, those who needed their services defended their *coming* and *working.* However, even those who fought against an immigration quota for the Mexicans wanted them here only temporarily and maintained that they could easily be sent back to Mexico. In 1929 a national crisis resulted from the failure of the U.S. capitalist economy. Suddenly, the prosperity of millions was a thing of the past. White Americans were desperate for work and even took jobs that they once scorned. They displaced many Chicano farm laborers, and many of the latter migrated to the cities hoping to find work or to obtain money through the relief (welfare) program. Many Anglo-Americans became concerned about the growing cost of welfare and unemployment and resented the "brown men" in their midst who, after all, were not Anglo-Americans. The philosophy of "take care of our own" emerged, as well as the fallacy that the foreigners were responsible for unemployment and that they should return to their homeland.[6] It was decided that money could be saved by shipping Mexicans home, a plan that appealed to many Anglo-American taxpayers. Between the years 1931 and 1934, thousands of Chicanos, many of whom were U.S. citizens, were sent back to Mexico.[7] Official U.S. records put the number at around 300,000, but the figure may well have reached a half million during the course of the repatriation program.

To understand what repatriation meant to Mexicans, Emory S. Bogardus's definition is enlightening:

> In Mexico, a *repatriado* is defined as a person who, having left his country to live a number of years in another country, returns to his own country to reside and to assume the duties of citizenship. According to a leading Mexican official, *repatriados* are regarded in Mexico as Mexicans who have lived in a foreign country and have returned to the Republic "for the purpose of settling down, regardless of whether they came back of their own accord or were deported by foreign authorities."[8]

The Mexican government, therefore, viewed the return of the Chicano favorably. Most Anglo-American officials attempted to emphasize that repatriation was voluntary and was not like deportation—forcible expulsion from the country. To the Chicano, however, the term *repatriation* was synonymous with deportation. Most Chicano experts agree that the line differentiating the two was very thin.

The repatriation of the Chicano differed from city to city.[9] The "send-the-Mexican-back-to-Mexico" movement was inspired by President Herbert Hoover, who, after three years of depression, refused to acknowledge the failure of the U.S. economy. He made countless excuses; a favorite scapegoat was the presence of illegal workers in the United States. He publicly blamed widespread unemployment on the large numbers of illegals, which to many meant Chicanos.

U.S. consuls restricted the number of visas issued and strictly enforced the terms of the Immigration Act of 1924, which excluded those "likely to become a public charge." Hoover's secretary of labor, William N. Doak, stated: "My conviction is that by strict limitation and a wise selection of immigration, we can make America stronger in every way, hastening the day when our population shall be more homogeneous."[10] On January 6, 1931, Doak requested that Congress appropriate funds for the deportation of illegals from the United States. An investigation by his office revealed that an estimated 400,000 aliens had evaded the immigration laws and that at least one-fourth of these illegals were readily deportable. Meanwhile, the representatives of President Hoover requested $500,000 for the expansion of the border patrol. Moreover, the California Senate considered a bill to prohibit "illegal aliens from engaging in business or seeking employment, and making it a misdemeanor to have such an alien as a partner."[11] The antiforeign sentiment reached its zenith during this period of insecurity.

Local authorities throughout the Southwest and the Midwest emulated the actions of the chief executive; they even went one step further and devised a program to encourage even documented immigrants to return to Mexico. They seized on Doak's statements, and newspapers drummed the theme of "caring for one's own." Indeed, the majority of the undocumented workers in the Southwest and the Midwest were Mexican. Moreover, even U.S.-born Chicanos were not considered "real Anglo-Americans," of whom the government should take care. A more truthful view of repatriation was: "In technical language, repatriation refers to the alien who by reason of his age or physical condition is unable to be rehabilitated in the economic situation today."[12]

Los Angeles, meanwhile, served as the model repatriating city. The Los Angeles County supervisors, alarmed at rising unemployment and the number of Chicanos on relief, made the Chicanos the scapegoats. On January 6, 1931, C. P. Visel, the Los Angeles local coordinator for Unemployment Relief, urgently requested guidance in a wire to Washington, D.C.:

> We note press notices this morning, figure four hundred thousand deportable aliens United States. Stop. Estimate five percent in this district. Stop. We can pick them all up through police and sheriff channels. Stop. United States Department of Emigration incapacitated to handle. Stop. You advise please as to method of getting rid. Stop. We need their jobs for needy citizens.[13]

The newspapers exploited the theme of kicking out the illegals. Rumors were circulated in the Chicano community that the deportations would include all Mexicans, legal or illegal. Visel admitted that he had intended to scare illegals and force them to abandon the Los Angeles area. Meanwhile, the Los Angeles Chamber of Commerce vehemently criticized Visel's actions. It warned him that the Mexican community would misunderstand the "wholesale raids." Visel wanted to intimidate the entire *barrio,* and his actions were repeated throughout the United States.[14]

City officials, along with national and state officials, planned the strategy, but the approval of the Mexican government was necessary, since it had agreed to provide transportation from the border to the repatriate's colony. The Mexican government encouraged the Mexican governors and labor unions to welcome the repatriates, and the government promised land and other benefits. Mexican officials cooperated with repatriation, not because they approved of the motives of the U.S. officials (which were a mixture of racism and economics), but because Mexico had lost an estimated one-eighth of its population to the United States.[15] Therefore, Mexican revolutionaries, such as the artist Diego Rivera, took an active role in urging Mexicans to return home. In Detroit, Rivera helped found the League of Workers and Peasants of Mexico. The Mexican government, however, was not able to absorb such a large influx of Mexicans. Economically, Mexico still suffered from the chaos of the Revolution of 1910. It had a difficult time providing for its own masses. As a consequence, the repatriates were neglected and became disappointed with the program.

City officials devised programs to encourage Mexicans to return to Mexico. Charity organizations and the California Department of Unemployment cooperated. When a Chicano approached these departments for assistance, a case worker would call on the family and attempt to persuade the head of the household that he and his family would be happier in Mexico. If he agreed to return, fare and subsistence to the border would be paid for the entire family. In many cases, the local authorities used the Mexican consul to help "persuade" the welfare recipient to repatriate. Generally, the father wanted to return, since he had never intended to stay permanently, but the children had made roots in the United States, were Anglo-American citizens, and opposed the return. Some teenage children bitterly resented being uprooted. The mother was caught between her husband and her children. When the client hesitated, the welfare or case worker became more persuasive.[16]

Just how persuasive officials were is open to conjecture, since local authorities always maintained that the return was voluntary. However, two leading authorities on the Chicano in the 1930s contradict the local authorities' interpretation of "voluntary." Professor Norman D. Humphreys of Detroit wrote:

> Even the families of naturalized citizens were urged to repatriate, and the rights of American-born children to citizenship in their native land were explicitly denied or not taken into account. The case workers themselves brought pressures to bear in the form of threats of deportation, stoppage of relief (wholly or in part, e.g., in matters of rent, or by means of trampling on customary procedures).[17]

In the Los Angeles area, the eminent sociologist from the University of Southern California, Emory Bogardus, charged:

Many Mexican immigrants are returning to Mexico under a sense of pressure. They fear that all welfare aid will be withdrawn if they do not accept the offer to help them out of our country. In fact, some of them report that they are told by relief officials that if they do not accept the offer to take them to the border, no further welfare aid will be given them, and their record will be closed with the notation, "Failed to cooperate." Rumor becomes exaggerated as it passes from mouth to mouth. It takes only an insinuation from an official in the United States to create widespread fear among Mexican immigrants.[18]

The social workers used other subtle measures to persuade the prospective returnee. In Detroit, where winters are cold, Mexican families were placed on a "cafeteria list," forcing them to eat at a local mess hall. There, authorities purposely fed them unfamiliar foods such as sauerkraut instead of the traditional beans, even though the latter were cheaper and contained more nutrients. Case workers continually emphasized that the Chicanos would be much healthier in Mexico. Finally, in some cases, overt threats were made that the rent would not be paid or welfare payments would be cut. Most experts agree that in exerting pressure case workers many times violated the Mexicans' rights.[19] What is more, deceit surrounded the whole affair. The repatriated Mexicans, in most cases, were promised that they could return to the United States if and when they wanted to; however, their exit cards designated that they had been charity cases, which automatically excluded them from reentry.

Although a considerable amount of racism was directed at Mexicans, the repatriation program appears to have been basically a "money-saving device." The program would not have been initiated if it had proved to be more costly to return the Mexicans than to let them remain. In fact, the enthusiasm for the program dissipated as local authorities learned that funds obtained from the Reconstruction Finance Corporation (RFC) could not be used for the transportation of the repatriates.

Los Angeles County provides a documented example of how costs increased. In the first three years of the Los Angeles program (1931–1934) the county shipped 12,668 Chicanos back to Mexico at a cost of $181,228, whereas from 1935 to 1938 it shipped only 3,560 Mexicans at a cost of $160,781.[20]

The attitude of the Los Angeles officials is demonstrated by the following requisition for funds from the RFC to return Chicanos to Mexico.

It will be necessary for the county to furnish transportation for these people in order to move them out. I, therefore, respectfully request that the sum of $6,000 be authorized to be expended in this manner, thus ridding ourselves of a large number of Mexicans who have been or are in danger of becoming dependents upon the county.[21]

Carey McWilliams commented on the dollars-and-cents approach: "It costs the County of Los Angeles $77,249.29 to repatriate one train load, but the savings in relief amounted to $347,468.41"—a net savings of $270,219.12.[22]

In general, the repatriation programs were poorly organized and created bitter feelings. The Mexican families sold or gave away many of the possessions they had accumulated. They took what they could carry—dogs, cats, goats, mattresses, cardboard boxes full of possessions. More terrifying was the general panic that the program and the mass roundup of illegals spread. Dr. George P. Clements of the Los Angeles Chamber of Commerce labeled it as a "reign of persecution" against the Mexican people.[23] In the last analysis, however, President Coolidge's maxim—"the business of America is business" —was applied, and repatriation was profitable—at least in dollars and cents.

The Case of Jesús Pallares

The repatriation, without a doubt, intimidated the Chicano community. During the 1930s, many Chicanos also were deported for their participation in civil rights and organizational work. The story of Jesús Pallares, who was deported on June 29, 1936, as an undesirable alien, is an example of the intimidation.[24] Jesús had emigrated from Mexico to the United States when he was a teenager and was 39 years old when he was deported. Even though he was young, in Mexico he had fought in the revolutionary ranks. He was a skilled miner and a talented musician. From the outset, Jesús was a dedicated union man. In 1923 he opposed the anarchist faction at Dawson, New Mexico, which advocated violence; Jesús convinced the workers that violence would only hurt their cause. Nothing more was heard about him until 1930, when the Gallup-American Coal Company, a subsidiary of the Guggenheim interests, fired him for complaining about working conditions.

Jesús, his wife, and their three children moved to Madrid, New Mexico, a company-owned town. The workers were paid in script that could be used only at the company store. The company owned all the houses. It charged the workers $3 a month for coal, for which they had to pay whether they needed it or not. Moreover, the workers had to contribute to an employee's fund that the company managed, yet workers were not given an accounting of the funds. In the summer of 1933, there were wholesale layoffs. Pressure mounted for the company to comply with the provisions of the National Industrial Relations Act (NIRA), which specified in section 7a that employees had the right to unionize. The company circumvented the requirement and established its own company union. Jesús joined the union, but when he realized that it did not represent the workers, he resigned.

The dissident workers decided to establish their own union, so an organizer from the miners' union was secretly invited to come to Madrid to promote organizational activities. He was smuggled into town, since even the public streets belonged to the mining company, and if he were caught, he would be in physical danger. Elected local union representative Jesús went to the employer and attempted to open negotiations. He failed, so the union appealed to the federal government for hearings conducted under the NIRA code. The hearings were a farce because the chairman of the hearings was pro-management. Company lapdogs (paid cronies of the company) attended the hearings and interrupted the testimony of the workers. The hearings did not advance the cause of the workers, and the union had no alternative but to strike—a maneuver that failed because it was during the company's slack season. Moreover, the company simply had too much staying power.

Jesús could not be dismissed from his job, since the NIRA code specified that a man could not be fired for union activities. Nevertheless, the company had ways of making him uncomfortable. They transferred him to a mine that had been exhausted. He was an experienced miner and knew that he could not earn a living wage there, since he was paid for piece work. His only alternatives were to go into debt or to quit. Company officials, meanwhile, Red-baited Jesús, calling him a Communist agitator. When he could not pay his rent, the company evicted him, even though his wife was expecting a baby at any time. Jesús tried to enter his home and was charged with "forcible entry." He then appealed to federal officials, but his requests were ignored. Blacklisted and unable to find employment as a miner, Jesús and his family moved to Santa Fe where, for the first time, he went on relief.

In 1934, Jesús became an organizer for *La Liga Obrera de Habla Española,* which concerned itself with the problems of the poor Chicanos. In November of that year, the membership was small, but by February 1935, it had grown to 8000. The *Liga* threatened New Mexico politicians, and in January the Democratic state legislature made syndicalism a felony, punishable by 14 years' imprisonment. The law further specified that it was illegal to be seen with an issue of *The Nation* magazine or any other printed material that advocated "any change in industrial ownership." There were only two dissenting votes. *La Liga* assembled 700 pickets and entered the senate galleries protesting the law. The members of the senate changed their votes. Big business interests were infuriated by the defeat. By this time Jesús had been elected organizer for *La Liga.* He was considered a trouble maker, and tremendous pressure was applied on immigration officers to deport him. On April 23, 1935, he was jailed. After three weeks, a secret hearing was conducted by N. D. Collear, a federal immigration inspector, who served as initiator of the case, investigator, prosecutor, judge, jury, and even interpreter. Jesús's past organizational activities were distorted. Meanwhile, Governor Clyde Tingley asked Secretary of Labor Frances Perkins to expedite Jesús's deportation on the grounds that *La Liga* was a Communist organization. This charge was highly unethical, since the governor had no proof. After the hearings, Jesús was released on $1000 bond. Esther Cohen, of the Emergency Relief Appropriation Program in New Mexico, stated that there were repeated attempts to intimidate Jesús, with officials threatening to take his relief away and "starve his family." The outcome of the hearing was predictable. Although the days of the New Deal were in vogue, big business, especially mining, still ruled the state of New Mexico and had considerable influence on the U.S. government. In short, Jesús was deported for organizing Chicanos.

Since the 1930s, Los Angeles has been the center of urban Chicano activism. This is because there are more Chicanos—approximately one million in Los Angeles County—than in any other urban area in the United States, and because Chicano leaders from all over the Southwest have settled there. Los Angeles was the scene of considerable ferment in the 1930s, and several currents led to the later emergence of the Chicano movement.

Many young Chicanos were first exposed to organizational activity at meetings or discussion groups at the local Catholic church. As these groups became more popular, it is alleged that the hierarchy became alarmed at the nationalism within the Chicano parishes. They then conducted intensive drives to recruit Chicano youth to programs sponsored by the Catholic Youth Organization and the Catholic Settlement Houses. These activities gave Chicano youth a consciousness of group action. Moreover, the Young Men's Christian Association (YMCA) expanded its program into the *barrios.* Clubs were formed within the YMCA, which gave the Chicano the opportunity to function in a fraternity-like atmosphere. Many early members were encouraged to go on to college, and a civic attitude developed among these young people.

Another influence was that of the Communist party, which was active in the Chicano community, as it was in most communities during the 1930s. The Communists formed clubs; the number of these clubs was small, but the Communists helped to create an awareness among members of the clubs and the community in general of the horrible conditions in that community.

Finally, there were local unions, especially CIO locals, that conducted extensive organizational drives during this decade.[25] Chicano leaders—such as Bert Corona, today a national organizer for the Mexican American Political Association—received training and experience by working as paid organizers for the longshoremen.

These currents merged into the Mexican Youth Conference, sometimes known as the Mexican American Movement (MAM). This organization was a Chicano college and university student association. Many Chicano students were fed up with the exploitation in the *barrios,* and they banded together to improve conditions. MAM's major emphasis was education. The association published a monthly newspaper called *La Voz Mexicana* (*The Mexican Voice*). The students dedicated themselves to raising scholarships, researching problems, and getting publicity. Students went from *barrio* to *barrio* in an attempt to stimulate and motivate the Chicano community to organize. Many Chicano professionals emerged from this group, and the membership was estimated to be in the thousands. World War II, however, for all practical purposes ended the growth of the MAM, since most of its membership was of draft age. Many key leaders did not return from the war.

Students were also active in another organization. In 1938, *El Congreso de Pueblos de Habla Española* held the first national conference of Spanish-speaking peoples. This was the first nonunion conference—one that was not limited to specific issues. The principal organizer was Luisa Moreno, a leader and national organizer for the United Cannery, Agricultural, and Packing Workers of America, which was involved in the pecan workers' strike in San Antonio. Luisa Moreno traveled throughout the United States and created tremendous interest in the conference to be held in Los Angeles. Representatives came from all over the United States: Spanish and Cuban cigar makers from Tampa, Florida; Puerto Ricans from Harlem; steel workers from Pennsylvania, Illinois, and Gary, Indiana; meat packers, miners, and farm workers from all over the country. Elected officials from New Mexico also attended the conference, including Dennis Chávez, Speaker of the House of Representatives of New Mexico, who later became a U.S. Senator. The Congress was broadly represented: workers, politicians, youth, educators—people from all walks of life.[26]

Everyone was cognizant of the intense Red-baiting that the media aimed at the conference. Local elected officials termed it a "subversive gathering." Nevertheless, the delegates pushed through a radical and progressive platform. Workers were to be organized, and a newspaper and newsletter were to be published. Legislative priorities were set down, and stands were taken against oppressive laws, immigration officials, vigilantes, and police brutality. The right of farm workers to organize was demanded. The extension of the benefits of the National Labor Relations Act to farm workers also was demanded. In short, the conference dedicated itself to "the economic and social and cultural betterment of the Mexican people, to have an understanding between the Anglo-Americans and the Mexicans, to promote organizations of working people by aiding trade unions, and to fight discrimination actively."[27] The Congress was very successful from 1938 to 1940, claiming a membership of over 6000. However, it had committed a strategic mistake in making its aims too sectarian and too specific. Neither the Congress nor the Chicano community had many friends in the media or in positions of power. Moreover, because of its radical stands, it exposed itself to intense Red-baiting, and its members were harassed by the Federal Bureau of Investigation (FBI), as well as by congressional and state investigating committees. After 1940, its effectiveness waned rapidly, and although it continued to function even in the post-war period, it was no longer a viable force.

The Congress was not the only organization that crusaded against the injustices aimed at the Chicano community. During the 1930s a few newspaper editors took stands against discrimination as well as against segregation in schools and public facilities. One such crusader was Ignacio López, editor of *El Espectador* and a graduate of the University of California at Berkeley, who held Master of Arts degrees in both Spanish and history. In the 1930s he was very active, and most observers conceded that he had one of the keenest minds in the Chicano community. In the 1940s, he was instrumental in establishing the Unity Leagues in the area surrounding Pomona, and in the 1960s, he was a moving force behind the Mexican American Political Association (MAPA). Although still active among Mexican Americans today, López is no longer considered a militant, for according to some of his friends, the intense harassment of Chicano leaders during the 1950s blunted his crusading spirit.

López made a reputation by fearlessly attacking any form of discrimination or prejudice against Mexicans. Two typical cases took place in 1939. In February, a Chicano youth and a companion entered the movie theatre in Upland, California. They paid general admission, entered the theatre, and looked for seats near the center. The assistant manager approached them and told them that the first 15 rows were reserved for Chicanos. The Chicano asked if his ticket were not, in fact, general admission, entitling him to sit anywhere. The answer was that Chicanos sat in the first 15 rows. The youths went to Ignacio López. López wrote a stinging editorial condemning the policy of the theatre house and calling for a mass meeting in Upland. Hundreds of Chicanos attended the meeting, which was addressed by the Mexican consul from San Bernardino. The Chicanos decided to boycott the theatre. Shortly afterward, the theatre changed its segregationist policy.[28]

In another incident, López again championed the Chicano's right to use public facilities. In 1939, it was revealed that, although the swimming pool at Chaffey Junior College was used on an integrated basis during the academic year, when it was open to the general public during the summer, Chicanos were allowed to use it only on Mondays. A group of Chicanos, denied admittance, went to López, who again published a scathing account of the incident in his paper. And again, there was a reversal of policy, and the administration declared that the pool would be integrated and available for everyone's use at all times.[29]

World War II

Just as World War II dominated every aspect of the Anglo-American's life in the early 1940s, so it determined the history of the Chicano during this time. Threatened by a foreign enemy, most Chicanos, as well as Anglo-Americans, put aside their self-interest. In the interim, much of the momentum of the movement of the 1930s was lost. Many Chicano leaders entered the armed forces; many were killed; others, when they returned, were frankly tired of crusades. The war took its casualties. Chicanos were the most decorated ethnic group of World War II, yet they were also the least recognized. Raul Morín, in his book *Among the Valiant,* documents the Chicanos' contribution to the war effort.[30] He wrote that at the beginning of the war there were about 2,690,000 Chicanos in the United States and approximately one-third were of draft age.[31] The percentage of Chicanos who served in the armed forces was disproportionate to the percentage of Chicanos in the general population.

The hardships of a community during a war are difficult to translate, since historians must depend upon hearsay, personal experiences, or recorded documents. Historians did not record the feelings of the Chicano because there was little interest in them or in ethnic minorities in general. Chicanos, however, can readily remember how families proudly displayed banners with blue stars (each blue star represented a family member in the armed forces). Many families had as many as eight stars, with fathers, sons, and uncles all serving the U.S. war effort. Everyone of that era recalls the absence of men between the ages of 17 through 30 in the *barrios*. As the war progressed, gold stars replaced the blue (gold representing men killed in action), giving the *barrios* the appearance of a sea of death. One would open a newspaper and read the casualty lists: Gonzáles, Gómez, Sánchez, Ramírez, etc. At that time, few reflected on whether or not it was worth it, even in light of continued discrimination.

Another question that Chicanos did not ask at the time of World War II but, like poor Anglo-Americans, are asking today: How did the war benefit their community? The maze of personal draft exemptions for educational purposes or for numerous other reasons benefited mainly Anglos; the Chicano's social and economic conditions precluded his eligibility for such exemptions. The most insidious exemptions were granted to the sons of farmers so they could remain at home. They were declared vital to the war effort and were left behind to supervise Mexican *braceros*. While Chicanos and other poor migrants fought for their country, the exempted farmer was free to earn a profit. The sons of many rich industrialists also received exemptions so they could contribute to the war effort and were handsomely rewarded through generous government contracts, while the workers were frozen to their jobs with their salaries fixed.

The war, in short, further engrained privilege. Chicanos found both discrimination and acceptance in the armed forces. Their war record, as mentioned, was outstanding. Understandably, during the war and when they returned, many Chicano veterans were proud of their records. They believed that they were entitled to all the benefits and rights of U.S. citizenship. A sort of euphoria settled among many Chicanos, with only a few realizing that the community had to reorganize. Many Chicanos believed the propaganda emanating from World War II about brotherhood and democracy in the United States. They thought that they had won their rights as U.S. citizens. For a time, the G.I. Bill of Rights lulled many Chicanos into complacency, with many taking advantage of education and housing benefits. As a consequence, a few moved out of the *barrios*. But the continued discrimination and exclusion—racism, denial of political participation, economic oppression—shattered the illusions of many returning veterans and reminded them of events that had occurred in the early 1940s, which had turned the Great Anglo-American Dream into a nightmare. These events had been the so-called *Pachuco* riots, which documented both the racism of Anglos and the reaction of a conquered people.

Los Angeles: Confrontation of the Early 1940s

The Chicano's status in Los Angeles during this century has not been very high. He has been segregated in his *barrios* in East Los Angeles and scattered in small islands throughout the county. Before World War II, few Chicano restaurants could be found in the Anglo-American sectors of the city; those that served the traditional Mexican dishes were called "Spanish" restaurants. Segregated swimming pools were common, in which Chicanos and Blacks were allowed to swim only on Wednesday—the day the pool was drained and cleaned. Moreover, schools were segregated. Meanwhile, the Chicano population had grown during the depression when many flocked to Los Angeles to seek relief from hunger. In 1943, some 240,000 to 750,000 Chicanos lived in Los Angeles County, roughly comprising 10 percent of the population.* Fifty-six percent of the people who dwelt in substandard houses were Chicanos, and Mexican Town (as it was called) was located in the unincorporated section of the county. The streets of Mexican Town were unpaved, and many of the services, taken for granted in the city of Los Angeles, were denied to the Chicano community. Suffice it to say that social and economic discrimination against the Chicano was severe, since the attitude of many Anglo-Americans was that these foreigners were a burden to them.

The so-called *Pachucos* were Chicano youth between the ages of 13 and 17. Although many Anglo-Americans at the time claimed that they were organized into a mafia-type association, there is no evidence that the *Pachuco* was a structured organization. The common tie was that most were Chicanos. The *Pachucos* belonged to loosely organized *barrio* clubs that usually carried the name of their particular *barrio* or neighborhood—e.g., the White Fence Gang, Alpine Street, *El Hoyo,* Happy Valley, etc. The fad was to tattoo, on the left hand just above the thumb, a small cross with three dots or dashes above it. Many *Pachucos,* when they dressed up, wore the so-called zoot-suit uniform that was so popular among low-income youths at that time. The *Pachuco* spoke Spanish, but he more frequently used *caló* when he was with his companions. *Caló* was the *barrio* language, a mixture of Spanish, English, old Spanish, and words adapted by the border Mexicans. Many experts say that it originated among Chicanos engaged in criminal activities around El Paso and was brought to Los Angeles in the 1930s. Yet, there is no proof that the so-called gangs were dedicated to "crime"; many were even affiliated with the YMCA.

Like other neighborhood gangs or, for that matter, rival clubs or schools in middle-class Anglo neighborhoods, frequent "rumbles" (gang fights) between Chicano clubs broke out in the streets. Many of the altercations resembled tournaments. The opposing gangs would show up at an empty lot, and with their supporters looking on, the toughest members of each gang would fight it out. Like gangs in other sections of the United States, many of the clubs claimed territorial rights. An invasion of this territory meant war. This is a pattern that developed in ghettos throughout the United States.

It would be in error to consider the *Pachucos* as merely rebellious youth. Although most were second-generation citizens of the United States, most

---

*Statistics are invalid as to the Chicano population; only estimates, at best, can be made.

Anglo-Americans considered them aliens. They lived in two worlds—that of their family and that of the street. While their parents, in many instances, were shielded from the intenseness of the prejudice and insults of society, the second-generation Chicano felt the full impact. His culture was a hybrid one and, therefore, he was caught in the middle. Meanwhile, the schools engrained in him negative self-concepts, which he, as a man, resisted. His resistance took the form of a rejection of the very forces that were attempting to rob him of his own identity. Octavio Paz, the Mexican poet, reported this resistance in the 1940s, writing:

> Since the *Pachuco* cannot adapt himself to a civilization which, for its part, rejects him, he finds no answer to the hostility surrounding him except this angry affirmation of his personality. Other groups react differently. The Negroes, for example, oppressed by racial intolerance, try to "pass" as whites and thus enter society. They want to be like other people. The Mexicans have suffered a less violent rejection, but instead of attempting a problematical adjustment to society, the *Pachuco* actually flaunts his differences. The purpose of his grotesque dandyism and anarchic behavior is not so much to point out the injustice and incapacity of a society that has failed to assimilate him as it is to demonstrate his personal will to remain different.[32]

While Paz's later analysis of the *Pachuco* lacks an understanding of the effects of uprooting and the clash that the first and second generations experienced with Anglo-American society, the quote does offer a clue to the new direction of Chicano resistance—that of separatism, providing a link between past resistance groups and the modern-day Chicano movement. In articles and speeches, Dr. Octavio Romano, editor of *El Grito,* has popularized this thesis that the *Pachuco* was the first large current within the Chicano movement toward separatism.[33]

The *Pachuco* phenomenon is understandable within the context of the colonial experience, where dress and language distinguishes the colonized from the colonizer, and where the difference is emphasized as the former confronts his oppression. The artificial zoot-suit costume was necessary to the *Pachuco,* especially in the United States where dress and behavior have always been standardized. The 1940s were times when a student was ridiculed for even taking a *burrito* to school for lunch. The *Pachuco* was a midway link between the Mexican and the Anglo-American, and the dress gave him an affinity with other disenchanted youth. His separatism was a social expression of rebellion, whereas today the separatism is social as well as political and economic.

During the war, however, the *Pachuco* group seemed more ominous to Anglos, and they looked upon them as a negative influence. Concerned citizens such as Carey McWilliams, the noted journalist and lawyer, and students of the era conclude that the reason the public singled out the *Pachucos* is that the newspapers were anxious for copy and contributed to the hysteria in an already neurotic Anglo-American public. This neurosis was the result of war tensions, which had seen the roundup of Japanese Americans and their internment into camps. What is more, the Japanese had badly defeated the U.S. forces during 1942. Racial xenophobia had heightened in what, at that time, was a racially and culturally homogeneous Los Angeles community. Very few Blacks lived in Los Angeles County, the Japanese had been put away, and Los Angeles did not have the large ghettoes of European immigrants peculiar to eastern cities. Chicanos were the obvious targets for nativists and racists; they were the largest non-Anglo group. Angelinos read with interest accounts of so-called Chicano hoodlums.

The Sleepy Lagoon Case

On August 1, 1942, a party was held at Sleepy Lagoon, which was located in a Chicano section of Los Angeles. Most of the guests were Chicano. There had been a rumble earlier that day, and a member of the 38th Street Club had been beaten up. The members of the 38th Street Club went to the party looking for the perpetrators. The next morning, José Díaz, an invited guest at the party, was found dead on a dirt road near the house. No evidence was found that members of the 38th Street Club had beaten him. Díaz had no wounds and could have been killed by a hit-and-run driver. The police, however, immediately jailed the entire 38th Street gang. Newspapers sensationalized the story. Police flagrantly violated the rights of the accused. Twenty-two of the 38th Street boys were accused of criminal conspiracy. "According to the prosecution, every defendant, even if he had nothing whatsoever to do with the killing of Diaz, was chargeable with the death of Diaz, which, according to the prosecution, occurred during the fight on the Williams Ranch."[34]

The grand-jury investigation of the Sleepy Lagoon case set the tone of the trial that followed. Captain Ed Durán Ayres, head of the Foreign Relations Bureau of the Los Angeles Police Department, presented a report to the jury. Although the report admitted that discrimination against Chicanos in employment, education, schooling, recreation, and labor unions existed, it stated that Chicanos were inherently criminal and violent. The captain cited Rudyard Kipling, stating that the Chicano was an Indian, that the Indian was an Oriental, and that the Oriental had an utter disregard for life. Therefore, since the Chicano was an Oriental and had this inborn characteristic, he was consequently violent. Furthermore, the Chicano was cruel, for he was a descendant of the Aztecs who had allegedly sacrificed 30,000 victims a day![35]

The captain continued by stating that Indians considered leniency a sign of weakness, pointing to the Mexican government's treatment of the Indian, which he maintained was quick and severe. He advocated that all gang members be imprisoned—and that all Chicano youth over the age of 18 be given the option of getting work or enlisting in the armed forces. The Chicano, said the captain, could not change his spots; he had an innate desire to use a knife and let blood, and this inborn cruelty was aggravated by liquor and jealousy.[36]

The Honorable Charles Fricke permitted numerous irregularities in the courtroom. The defendants were not allowed to bathe or shave and were herded into the courtroom, which undoubtedly created a bad impression on the jury members. The prosecution, in its case, failed to prove that the 38th Street Club was a gang; that there was, in fact, any criminal agreement or conspiracy; or that the accused had killed Díaz. In fact, the witnesses testified that there had been considerable drinking at the party before the 38th Street people arrived. One of the prosecution witnesses even testified that a car had run over Díaz earlier in the evening *before* the 38th Street Chicanos arrived at the party. If the theory of conspiracy to commit a crime had been strictly pressed, logically the defendants would have received equal verdicts. This, however, was not the case. In January 1943, the sentences were passed, and they ranged from assault to first-degree murder.[37]

The Sleepy Lagoon Defense Committee, organized by Carey McWilliams and others, was harassed and Red-baited by the press and by government agencies. Members were investigated by the California Committee on Un-American Activities, headed by State Senator Jack Tenney. The Tenney investigation charged that the Sleepy Lagoon Committee was a Communist-front organization and that Carey McWilliams had "Communist leanings" because he opposed segregation and the principle of miscegenation statutes.[38] On October 4, 1944, the committee and its supporters were vindicated when the Second District Court of Appeals reversed the lower court in a unanimous decision. The court stated that Judge Charles W. Fricke had conducted the trial in a biased manner, that he had violated the constitutional rights of the defendants, and it concluded that no evidence existed that linked the Chicanos with the death of José Díaz.[39]

The So-Called Pachuco Riots

The overt Anglo repression of East Los Angeles, the Chicano sector, began in June 1943. The press and the police incited the assault on the Chicano community. Los Angeles police and sheriff's deputies, after the Sleepy Lagoon arrests, intensified their harassment of Chicano youth by indiscriminately putting up road blocks and by arresting large numbers of Chicanos on countless charges, most popular being suspicion of burglary. These arrests were headlined in the press.

During this time, large numbers of servicemen on furlough or on short-duration passes visited Los Angeles. Numerous training centers were located in the vicinity, and the glitter of Hollywood and its famous canteen attracted many servicemen. Also, Navy ships docked in San Pedro and San Diego, so numerous sailors on shore leave came to Los Angeles looking for a good time. Most were young and, perhaps, anxious to prove their manhood. A visible "foe" was the "alien" Chicano, dressed in the outlandish zoot suit that everyone ridiculed. Many in the Chicano community also alleged that the sailors were looking for Mexican girls to pick up, and that many young sailors associated the Chicanas with the prostitutes they had encountered in Tijuana. According to many Chicanos, the sailors, as well as most non-Chicano servicemen, were loud, boisterous, and rude to the females in the Chicano community. The attitude of the servicemen, especially the sailors, was bound to cause trouble. The conduct of the sailors had caused animosity in San Diego as well, where townspeople openly discriminated against them.[40]

In the spring of 1943, tensions increased. Several small altercations had broken out in Los Angeles. In April, marines and sailors in Oakland, California, invaded the Chicano *barrio* and the Black ghetto; they brutalized the people and "de-pantsed" the zoot-suiters. Confrontations elsewhere could be predicted. On May 8, at the Aragon Ballroom in Venice, California, a ruckus between sailors and Chicanos erupted when some high school students told the sailors that *Pachucos* had stabbed a sailor. The sailors, joined by other servicemen, indiscriminately attacked Chicanos. The battle cry was: "Let's get 'em! Let's get the chili-eating bastards!"[41] Twenty-five hundred spectators watched the assault on innocent Chicano youth; the police did virtually nothing to restrain the servicemen. To the contrary, they arrested Chicanos. Moreover, the police charged Chicanos with disturbing the peace. The sole witness at the trial was a policeman who could not identify the defendants. The charges were dismissed for insufficient evidence, but not before Judge Arthur Guerin warned the youths "that their antics might get them into serious difficulties unless they changed their attitudes." In the meantime, the press continued to sensationalize the theme of "zoot-suit equals hoodlum."[42]

The sparks that ignited the "sailors' riots" against the Chicano community were lit on June 3, 1943. Allegedly, a group of sailors had been attacked by Chicanos when they attempted to pick up some Chicanas. The details were vague; the police allegedly did not attempt to get the Chicano side of the story, but took the sailors' report at face value. Fourteen off-duty policemen, led by a detective lieutenant, went looking for the "criminals." They found nothing, but they did get considerable publicity.

The police had sponsored certain Chicano clubs in an effort to improve relations between the youth and the police, and on the night of June 3, the police had invited members of the Alpine Club to a meeting at the Central Street jail. It was speculated that the sailors knew the gang was conferring with the police that night. While the junta took place, the sailors gathered at Chávez Ravine. Heavily armed with clubs, rocks, nickel rolls, etc., they then took taxis and cars to the Alpine district. After the police, who had driven the Alpine boys home in their cars, let the boys out in their neighborhood, the sailors ambushed the youths. The sailors went on a rampage; they broke into the Carmen Theatre, tore zoot-suits off Chicanos, and beat the youths. As a result, many Chicanos were arrested, while the sailors were not charged. Word spread that the *Pachucos* were fair game and that they could be attacked without fear of arrest.[43]

The sailors returned the next evening with some 200 comrades. They hired 20 cabs and cruised up Whittier Boulevard in the heart of the East Los Angeles *barrio,* jumping out of the cabs to gang up on the neighborhood youth, spreading a reign of terror. The police and sheriff maintained that they could not establish contact with the sailors, and when they finally arrested nine sailors, they released them without filing charges. The press sensationalized the incident, portraying the sailors as the heroes. Articles and headlines were openly racist, designed to capitalize on racial hatreds.[44] The sailors, encouraged by the press and the applause of the "responsible" elements of Los Angeles, joined together on the night of June 5 and marched four abreast down the streets, warning Chicanos to shed their zoot-suits or they would take them off for them.

Throughout this time, the servicemen invaded bars and other establishments and victimized Chicanos. By June 6, although the same thing happened again, the police began to be a bit more subtle and at least gave the appearance of chasing the marauders.[45] Conspicuously, the police arrived only after the damage had been done and the servicemen had escaped. Even though the sailors had now wrecked private property, law enforcement officials still did not take action. The Chicano community prepared to defend itself, especially since the law enforcement agencies of the city and county could not or would not do so. However, the police broke up the resistance by arresting Chicanos.[46]

The climax came on the evening of June 7, when thousands of servicemen and civilians surged down Main Street and Broadway in search of *Pachucos.* The mob crashed into bars and broke the legs off stools to use as clubs. The press had inflamed the *gringo* mob with reports that 500 "zoot-suiters" were assembling for battle.[47] By this time the Chicanos were not the only victims; Filipinos and Blacks also became targets. Chicanos had their clothes ripped off, and the youth were beaten and left bleeding on the streets. The mob surged into movie theatres, where they turned on the lights, marched down the aisles, and pulled zoot-suit-clad youngsters out of their seats. Seventeen-year-old Erico Herrera was such a victim. After he had been beaten, the police arrested him. He spent three hours at the police station, where he was found by his mother, still naked and bleeding.[48] A twelve-year-old boy's jaw was broken, but the police still did relatively nothing. Meanwhile, Angelinos cheered on the servicemen and their civilian allies.[49]

Panic gripped the Chicano community; many questioned whether a German or a Japanese occupation could have been any worse. At the height of the turmoil, a Black was pulled off a streetcar and his eyes were gouged out with a knife.[50] Conditions deteriorated so severely that military authorities, realizing that the Los Angeles law enforcement agencies could not or would not do anything to curtail the lawlessness, intervened and declared downtown Los Angeles off-limits for military personnel. Military shore patrols quelled the riot, accomplishing what the Los Angeles police could not.[51]

For the next few days, incidents continued in the suburbs. The police harassed Chicano youth, even raiding a Catholic Welfare Center to arrest some of its occupants.[52] Mass arrests were the order of the day. Meanwhile, the press and city officials continued to inflame the lynch-like mob against the Chicano community. Carey McWilliams in *North From Mexico* narrates a gripping account of the so-called riots. He quotes an editorial, written by Manchester

Boddy, from the June 9 issue of the *Los Angeles Daily News,* supposedly the city's liberal newspaper: "The time for temporizing is past. . . . The time has come to serve notice that the City of Los Angeles will no longer be terrorized by a relatively small handful of morons parading as zoot-suit hoodlums. To delay action now means to court disaster later on."[53] Boddy's statement, taken alone, would not mean much; it could be considered to be just one man's opinion. However, consider that before the naval invasion of East Los Angeles, the following headlines had appeared in the *Times:*

November 2, 1942: "Ten Seized in Drive on Zoot-Suit Gangsters."
February 23, 1943: "One Slain and Another Knifed in 'Zoot' Fracas."
March 7, 1943: "Magistrate 'Unfrocks' Pair of Zoot-Suiters."
May 25, 1943: "Four Zoot-Suit Gangs Beat Up Their Victims."
June 1, 1943: "Attacks by Orange County Zoot-Suiters Injure Five."

During the assault, one can speculate that the marauders were encouraged by other headlines in Los Angeles papers:

Los Angeles Daily News, June 7, 1943: "Zoot Suit Chiefs Girding for War on Navy."

Los Angeles Times, June 7, 1943: "Zoot Suiters Learn Lesson in Fight with Servicemen."

At the time of this crisis, three other major newspapers featured similar headlines and helped to create this ambience of zoot-suit violence. In addition, the radio media reflected the sensationalism.

An important factor in ending the brutalization of the Chicano community was the intervention of the Mexican government. Mexico City demanded answers, and many U.S. authorities feared that the *bracero* program and relations with Mexico and Latin America would be endangered. The Mexican government was blunt. On June 16, an item appeared in the *Los Angeles Times* from Mexico City, headlined: "Mexican Government Expects Damages for Zoot Riot Victims." The article declared that "the Mexican government took a mildly firm stand on the rights of its nationals, emphasizing its conviction that American justice would grant 'innocent victims' their proper retribution." The article further stated that the U.S. government was investigating the matter. By this time, the Los Angeles newspapers had calmed down somewhat and rhetorically asked who had caused the riots, and why. It answered its own question by blaming Chicanos, not by examining the Anglo-Chicano relations of the past century.

In the interim, Mayor Fletcher Bowron assured Washington, D.C., that there was no racism involved.[54] Soon afterwards, Bowron posed as the champion of the law and ordered the Los Angeles police to be firm with delinquents and to stop using "cream-puff techniques." Simultaneously, Bowron, in the long tradition of mediocre Los Angeles mayors, ordered the formation of a committee to "study the problem."[55] City officials and the Los Angeles press became exceedingly touchy about the question of racism, and when Eleanor

Roosevelt commented in her column that the riots were caused by "long-standing discrimination against the Mexicans in the Southwest," on June 18 the *Los Angeles Times* headlined: "Mrs. Roosevelt Blindly Stirs Race Discord." The article denied that racial discrimination was a factor in the riots and charged that Mrs. Roosevelt's statement displayed a similarity to propaganda followed by the Communists. It further stated that the servicemen were looking for "costumes and not races." The article concluded that Angelinos were proud of their missions and of Olvera Street—"a bit of old Mexico." It further said that "We like Mexicans and think they like us."

Significantly, Governor Earl Warren, through his attorney general, Robert W. Kenny, formed a committee with Catholic Bishop Joseph T. McGucken as chairman. It was composed of Walter A. Gordon, Berkeley attorney; Leo Carrillo, screen actor; Karl Holton, director of the California Youth Authority; and the attorney general. Although Angelinos denied that racism existed, the conclusions of this committee and the governor prove that race was indeed on everyone's mind. The governor said that he would do everything in his power to prevent race riots like those in Detroit in 1943 and maintained that "the state means to protect the lives and property of all people, regardless of race or creed." The report recommended the punishment of all persons responsible for the riots—military and civilian alike. It took a left-handed slap at the press and recommended that newspapers minimize the use of names or photos of juveniles. Moreover, it called for a better-educated and better-trained police department to work with Spanish-speaking youth.[56]

Little was done to implement the report, and most of the same conditions still exist today in the city and county of Los Angeles. "The Kid Gloves are off!" approach of Sheriff Eugene Biscailuz has, if anything, hardened since the 1940s.[57] There are countless cases of police brutality and repression. Nevertheless, the riots did politicize as well as polarize the community. Many so-called *gente decente* (decent people) turned their backs on the issue of civil rights and, thus, on the facts of the so-called *Pachuco* riots. They refused to associate with what they called *los pelados* (literally, the vulgar Chicanos). However, many Chicanos realized that this was a repression of the entire community; other Chicanos, for the first time, realized that it was not only Black Americans who were being denied rights under the Constitution and who were second-class citizens. To these and others, the *Pachuco* became the symbol of Chicano resistance.

The so-called *Pachuco* riots of 1943, in the last analysis, were distorted to indict the entire Chicano community. Only a few progressive Anglo-Americans condemned the worst in Anglo-American society; in return they were Red-baited. Time, however, has not only vindicated these fearless citizens, but has in turn condemned the entire Los Angeles citizenry of that time for not speaking out. The press portrayed Chicanos as unpatriotic hoodlums who attacked defenseless servicemen on furlough. Establishment journalists reported that the servicemen, mainly sailors, responded by "cleaning up" Los Angeles. Elmer Rusco, a political science student at the University of California, Berkeley, commented:

[It was determined that] the aggressors in the riots were largely white (although the Mexicans were the ones arrested), that they were mostly sailors or other servicemen, that the riots took place in wartime, and that there were similar riots in other cities (notably Detroit) at about the same time, directed against other minority groups.[58]

Rusco then commented that the Chicanos "were handy and visible targets for aggression."[59]

The roots of this oppression go back much further. In times of stress and fear, the worst inclinations in Anglo-Americans have almost always emerged. John Higham, in *Strangers in the Land,* traces the causes of nativism, clearly documenting this tendency of Anglo-Americans to react violently toward alien cultures and ideas in times of stress and fear. The war put most Anglo-Americans into this type of "pressure-cooker" atmosphere. They first reacted toward the Japanese, putting them into concentration camps. In the Anglos' movies and propaganda, they hit back at the Axis nations. The overt repression of the Chicano was vicariously hitting back at the enemy, for many Anglo-Americans were frustrated in not being able to confront the Axis powers personally. The Chicano was a convenient substitute. Moreover, others were just plain racist and welcomed any excuse to legally persecute Chicanos. The Chicano was thus rioted against in a tradition of violence; considering the facts, the term "*Pachuco* riots" is a misnomer and a distortion of history.

Toward the 1960s

World War II and the *Pachucos* represent a significant change in the direction of Chicano awareness. Although the war, for all practical purposes, ended the momentum that was built up in the 1930s, it also had some other effects: (1) Many Anglo-Americans and Chicanos started thinking about the hypocrisy of their own society; they were fighting against Hitler because of his superman theories, while these same ideas were strongly fostered in the United States. (2) During the war, many Chicanos, for the first time, were able to fill skilled jobs because of the Fair Employment Practice acts. The result was a widening of the Chicano middle-income population. After the war, these Chicanos were not content to return to unskilled jobs. (3) Large numbers of Chicanos had been uprooted by the war and, again, for the first time, had had continuing contact with people and institutions outside the *barrios.* (4) The war accelerated the Chicanos' shift from rural Anglo-America to the city. (5) Probably for the first time, because of the uniform, many Chicanos identified themselves as U.S. citizens. (6) The G.I. Bill of Rights' housing provision further dispersed Chicanos. Many took advantage of the loans and bought homes outside the *barrios.* (7) A number of Chicanos went into skilled trades and professions as a result of the educational stipend of the G.I. Bill of Rights.

After World War II, profound changes took place in Anglo-American society in general. Revolutions were ignited, and the period saw unprecedented technological and social changes. Most important to the Chicano was the growth of the communication media and the Black revolution that began in the 1950s.

Most Chicanos, because of their involvement in the armed forces, realized that they would never return to Mexico. Many also became superpatriots who did not want to be identified with the collective community. In the urban *barrio,* many parents, remembering their own tribulations, taught their children only English. Middle-class organizations and, for that matter, civic organizations became increasingly integrationist in the face of the Red-baiting of the 1950s. Organizational efforts in the urban *barrio* revolved around a small nucleus of activists who became active supporters of the Democratic party. Nevertheless, it must not be concluded that the latter-day activists were a failure; in fact, they did remarkably well in the hostile waters in which they sailed.

Many community organizations, which were comprised of the Chicano urban dweller and which began after World War II, were intent upon fighting for the rights for which many had died. An example of these early organizations was the Unity Leagues, which were founded in the small towns south of the big *barrio* of East Los Angeles—in the Chino, Ontario, and Pomona areas. The driving force behind these leagues was Ignacio López, the editor of *El Espectador.* During the war, he had received his training organizing European minorities in the East into Liberty Leagues. The Unity Leagues were also assisted by Fred Ross, an associate of Saul Alinsky.

The Unity Leagues differed from previous Chicano organizations in that they were not formed to meet the needs of the middle class, nor were they trade unionist in orientation. They were designed to stimulate political action among the grass-roots Chicanos. In Chino, California, for instance, the league worked to elect Andrew Morales to the city council. Intensive voter registration drives were conducted. The tactics of the leagues were similar to Alinsky's methods of waiting for the Establishment to make a mistake, allowing this mistake to precipitate a crisis, and then organizing around the issue. Following this formula, Unity Leagues were established in San Bernardino and Riverside, California, where school discrimination was a prime issue. Using the Unity Leagues as a model, the Community Service Organization (CSO) was established in 1947. At first, the CSO was organized mainly by middle-class urban Chicanos as a "conscious attempt at further 'Americanization,'" i.e., "assimilation."[60]

The currents that organized the CSO stemmed from Chicano steel workers and the volunteers in Edward Roybal's unsuccessful bid for a Los Angeles city council seat in 1947. These groups held open forums and discussed community problems, drawing many working men to their meetings. Fred Ross supplied much of the direction for the CSO, and he drew on his experience with the Unity Leagues. Although the CSO's stated purpose was not political, it registered 12,000 new voters. This increase of registered Chicano voters elected Edward Roybal to the Los Angeles City Council in 1949. He was the first person of Mexican descent to serve on the council since 1881. (At the present time, there are no Chicanos serving on the council.) After the Roybal victory, the CSO devoted itself to civic issues and did not support another candidate for office.[61] The CSO today operates mostly in rural areas. It has lost much of its crusading spirit, and its leadership has become increasingly middle class. For example, in Delano, California, the CSO chapter did not back the farm workers, but has worked in collusion with the Anglo Establishment there.

The American G.I. Forum was founded in Corpus Christi, Texas, in 1948 by World War II veterans. Discrimination against Chicanos in Texas was and is the most blatant in the United States. When they returned from the war, Chicano G.I.s from Texas found that they were still "greasers" to most of the Anglo-Americans there. Discrimination in housing, education, and employment was rampant. Many of the former servicemen were not allowed to join the Veterans of Foreign Wars or the American Legion. The incident that served as the catalyst for the Texas organization was the refusal of the white Texan Establishment to bury a Chicano war hero at Three Rivers, Texas; he had to be taken outside his home state to be buried at Arlington Cemetery. Chicano G.I.s vowed that this would never happen again, and they organized under the leadership of Dr. Hector García. By the end of 1949, over 100 American G.I. Forums had been organized. Today, forums are found in 23 states and have a total membership of over 20,000.[62] They are nonpartisan organizations that have promoted political and social reform. Their veteran composition helped them to remain a vital force, even during the 1950s, since they were less open to Red-baiting. The forums, like the LULAC, have a dedicated following. Again, the key to the forums' success has been the inclusion of the entire family, prominently featuring ladies' auxiliaries and junior forums.

The Breaking of a Movement

The 1950s presented an enigma. Many Anglo-Americans tend to associate the decade with President Dwight D. Eisenhower and, therefore, have concluded that it was a period of stability during which nothing much happened. To Chicanos, the 1950s represented a "decade of defense," a decade in which the proponents of reaction attempted to crush the rising aspirations for liberation by overtly intimidating them. Chicanos defended themselves against this onslaught. The most blatant attack upon the Chicano community came in the form of what facetiously has been called "Operation Wetback." A "wetback," supposedly, refers to an illegal Mexican immigrant who swam the Rio Grande to avoid the border patrol. Chicanos, however, take exception to this term, not only because they claim that Anglos are the illegals in the Southwest, but because it is used in a pejorative manner.

The alarm over the invasion of undocumented Mexican workers (those not having a permit to remain in the United States, i.e., "illegals") began in the late 1940s when many Anglo-Americans worried about the serious side effects that so many illegals would have on economic and social structures. Farm labor organizers and other union men complained that the undocumented workers depressed wages and impeded union organization because the growers used them for that purpose. Others considered it literally an invasion of the nation's privacy. During these years it seemed as if the undocumented worker had no friends other than the relatives or fellow *barrio* Chicanos who shielded him. He worked below the wage scale, so was exploited by the growers, who paid him less than they did legal *braceros*. In the lower Rio Grande River Valley he was paid 15 cents an hour, while *braceros* were paid 25 to 40 cents an hour. Many times he was handed over to immigration authorities by unscrupulous employers as a way to defraud him of his wages. While in the United States, he paid taxes and contributed to the economic growth of the country; however, when caught, he had no rights and was subject to immediate deportation. Most undocumented workers did not believe that they harmed anyone; their attitude can be summed up in the exchange between an undocumented Mexican and a judge. The judge asked, "Don't you respect the laws of this country?" The illegal replied, "Our necessities know no law."[63]

The actions of the U.S. government in dealing with undocumented workers have been hypocritical at best. It has assumed the facade of wanting to limit their entry, while at the same time maintaining a revolving door to allow the Mexican to enter at will when it was to the advantage of the Anglo-American grower. In other words, the United States has only wanted the Mexican in time of need and then only to exploit his labor. When there were enough *braceros* or "legal" workers to do the work, the laws were enforced; when there was a labor shortage, the doors were open, regardless of international or moral law. In chapter 7 we related what happened when negotiations between the United States and Mexico broke down over the terms of the *bracero* program in 1954. A similar incident had occurred in 1949.

In October 1948, when Mexican officials took a hard line in support of their nationals and contended that they should be paid $3 per hundred pounds for picked cotton, Anglo-American officials stated that the wage should be $2 per hundred pounds. Mexican officials were also concerned about discrimination in Texas toward its nationals. Moreover, Mexican authorities wanted the United States to recruit workers from the interior of Mexico and not at the border, as was then the case. This practice created hardships on the border towns as well as on the workers who frequently came thousands of miles, only to be disappointed when they were not selected. But it provided an advantage to the United States, for with the surge of workers to the area, the government could blackmail Mexico into signing *bracero* contracts.*

As the harvesting time approached, Anglo-American growers grew concerned and began to pressure Anglo-American officials, whereupon Grover C. Willmoth, district director at El Paso, Texas, instructed his inspectors to admit

---

*Border towns have grown over 1000 percent since 1920. Unemployment is extremely high. They serve as employment centers for Anglo-American industry.

the Mexicans. In the border town of Juárez, thousands of hungry Mexican workers awaited the outcome of the negotiations. Many were without shelter and had not eaten in days. When U.S. officials removed the physical barriers along the border and there was no one to stop their entry, the Mexicans naturally crossed over to U.S. territory. Immediately, however, they were placed under technical arrest (for illegal entry). They were then paroled to the U.S. Employment Service, which rationed them out to employers and labor agents. Willmoth defended his actions, alleging that Mexican officials had broken the *bracero* agreement with the United States by demanding a wage guarantee of "$3 a hundred." He contended that this was blackmail, because it was done before the workers were allowed to cross. Another official stated that "These Mexicans were pointing a pistol at the American farmer's head. It was an outright breach of the labor agreement."[64]

The official U.S. policy was, however, to exclude "illegals." During the 1950s, hundreds of thousands of Mexicans crossed the border in search of work. The cry went up to exclude the "wetbacks." A drive began in 1949 entailing roundups that extended into *barrios* all over the country. Carey McWilliams commented on this drive:

> The viciousness of the present roundup consists in the fact that once such a campaign has been decreed, there is only one way to carry it into effect; namely to make systematic house-to-house raids in every Mexican settlement in the state. In the course of these raids, it is inevitable that some long-time resident Mexicans will be picked up because they, too, are illegal entrants. The mere announcement that the Immigration Service is conducting a roundup of this character operates, of course, to spread fear and panic throughout the Mexican settlements. Many of the long resident entrants have married American citizens and have American-born children. . . . The hardship cases become inextricably mixed up with the others.[65]

Many Chicanos resent the hypocrisy of the Anglo-Americans who used the illegal crossing of the border as an excuse to exclude Mexicans, but at the same time, accepted the government's flagrant abuse of power to obtain Mexican labor at a cheap price.*

The Chicano's plight grew worse after the passage of the McCarran-Walter Act of 1952 (the U.S. Immigration and Nationality Act, which we shall discuss shortly). Lt. General Joseph M. Swing, who some called a "professional, long-time Mexican hater," was placed in command of deporting illegals.[66] The general had been with General Pershing when the latter led his punitive expedition against Pancho Villa into Mexico in 1916. Now he was commissioner of the United States Immigration and Naturalization Service. He conducted his operations in a soldier-like manner, and his objective was to flush out the Mexicans. Reports circulated in the Chicano *barrios* that Elysian Park Recreation Center was being prepared as a "security facility"

---

*The U.S. government, in fact, acted as an employment broker for agribusiness.

where Mexicans would be interned until they were shipped to the border for deportation. Swing set a quota of Mexicans to be deported for each target area. In the fiscal year 1953, the formal campaign got under way, with 875,000 Mexicans deported; in 1954, 1,035,282 were deported, after which the operation was considered a success; and in 1955 and 1956, respectively, 256,290 and 90,122 Mexicans were returned to Mexico.[67] It was a victory, but at an immeasurable price to the Chicano community. During the raids, U.S.-born Mexicans and legally immigrated Mexicans were searched just because they looked Mexican. Homes were illegally searched and U.S. citizens illegally detained. To this day, immigration authorities conduct similar periodic round-ups that spread terror in the *barrios.* One such raid occurred in Los Angeles when the 1970 census was being conducted, compromising the legitimacy of the statistics regarding the Chicano population.[68]

Reactions of the 1950s

Scholars researching the decade of defense have realized that Chicano activity during this decade demands a monograph in itself. Research has exploded the myth of the "Sleeping Giant" and the myth that the Chicano movement began in 1968 with the high school walkouts of that year. The Chicano movement in the 1950s was, in fact, driven underground or forced to use calmer methods in order to counteract the highly undemocratic and unconstitutional pressures that existed during that time.

Reactionary ultraconservative elements intimidated progressives during the early 1950s. The whip of Joseph McCarthy's U.S. Senate Special Investigative Committee was felt by Chicano leaders. Many leaders were ordered to testify at the committee hearings and, as a result, were blacklisted. Other Chicanos were denaturalized and deported. So strong was the pressure of the nativist forces that most Chicano organizations capitulated. Even the CSO had to prove its Americanism and resorted to Red-baiting tactics to vindicate itself.[69] For the most part, Chicano educators and professional groups abandoned the Chicano movement in the face of the accusations and threats of voices of reaction. As a consequence, the great bulk of the Chicano community was not informed about the gross violations of their rights and were abandoned by their leaders. Those who did fight back were harassed, imprisoned, and deported. A major force in breaking the Chicano movement of the 1950s was the McCarran-Walter Act.

The McCarran-Walter Act was not the first time in the history of the United States that deportation had been used to intimidate dissenters and the unwanted. Robert K. Murray wrote in his book *Red Scare* that "from the Alien and Sedition Acts of 1798 to the McCarran-Walter legislation of 1954,* we have most often assumed the existence of an innate affinity between alien

---

*In all, there were three McCarran-sponsored acts: in 1950, 1952, and 1954. This discussion focuses primarily on the 1950 and 1952 acts.

and radical. If every alien was not necessarily a radical, certainly every radical was in some way alien, that is, un-American. . . ."[70] In the same vein, U.S. authorities encouraged legal and illegal immigration from Mexico, then when the labor was not needed, they rounded up the illegal entrants, harassed the legal immigrants, and repatriated others. By the 1950s, the Chicanos had become much more visible in terms of numbers and, therefore, more threatening. Some Anglos were beginning to think of the Chicano as sinister and *Pachuco*-like. The growing strength of the Chicano in the trade unions put others on notice. Many new organizations within the *barrio* presented a clear and present danger to established interests. Moreover, the times were dominated by Joseph McCarthy, a heavy-handed U.S. Senator from Wisconsin, who abused his congressional immunity by slandering or libeling anyone who did not adhere to his model of an Anglo-American. He called those he singled out "Communists" or "Communist dupes."

Against this background, two other "defenders of America against infiltration and subversion" emerged to tighten immigration legislation against subversive elements.[71] The main characters were Francis E. Walter, chairman of the House Un-American Activities Committee, and Senator Pat McCarran from Nevada. Both had long been concerned about the subversive elements in society—mainly communism. They were especially concerned about the threat of refugees and other displaced persons after the war. There were many liberals who wanted to scrap the "national origins" system; however, Pat McCarran became the chief guardian of the nation's racial mix. "To forestall the impending breakdown in American culture, Senator McCarran had been busy since 1947 with hearings and drafting; his aim: the codification of all the scattered immigration and naturalization acts in the federal statute books."[72]

In 1951, McCarran testified: "The times, Mr. President, are too perilous for us to tinker blindly with our basic institutions," adding, "If we scrap the national origin formula we will, in the course of a generation or so, change the ethnic and cultural composition of this nation."[73] McCarran linked all opposition to communism. Chicanos, along with many other immigrants, became the victims of McCarran's crusade, which crushed the emerging organizational efforts in Mexican communities.

The substance of McCarran's crusade is too encompassing to elaborate on at this point. Instead, we shall concentrate on Titles I and II of the McCarran Internal Security Act of 1950 and the denaturalization aspect of the Immigration and Nationality Act of 1952.[74] In short, Title I established a Subversive Activities Control Board (still in existence) that would label and investigate subversion in the United States. Title II authorized the building of concentration camps in which to intern suspected subversives without a trial or hearing if either the president or Congress were to declare a national emergency. Two years later, six camps were built. Largely through the efforts of the Japanese American Citizens League, Title II has recently been abolished after over 20 years of controversy. A third part of the 1950 act was not passed until 1952. Briefly, the 1952 report provided for:

1. The codification of previous immigration acts, relating to national origins.
2. The abolishment of racial bars to entry and citizenship.
3. The establishment of a complicated procedure for admitting Asians.
4. The inclusion of a long list of grounds on which aliens could be deported or excluded; moreover, conditions were set up whereby naturalized citizens could be denaturalized.

The impact of these two laws opened a fight in the United States, with many liberals in Congress capitulating. Fortunately, many groups in the United States fought both acts. Supreme Court decisions struck down many of its provisions; subsequent acts amended it. The importance of the law was that it intimidated many activists. Many feared being placed in a concentration camp, being labeled a subversive, or being deported.* Interviews with Chicano union leaders and activists have confirmed that many Chicanos were intimidated during this period.

The act passed in 1952 over President Harry S. Truman's veto. The president stated it created a group of second-class citizens by distinguishing between native and naturalized citizens. It could allow U.S. citizenship to be taken away from naturalized citizens and could permit them to be deported for political reasons.

A President's Commission on Immigration and Naturalization, appointed by Truman in 1952, criticized the denaturalization clauses of the act. It charged that the provisions were too vague and gave the administrators too much latitude. It could be used to exclude visits to the United States for political reasons. The commission also complained that "a substantial proportion of deportations are based on technical violations of the laws. . . ."[75] Additionally, it stated that criminals were protected by a statute of limitations under federal law, but that the 1952 act eliminated the protection, "and therefore, an alien now is subject to deportation at any time for even minor technical violations."[76] In fact, the 1952 act "retroactively rescinded the limited statute of limitations fixed by previous law."[77] The commission stated that it violated the *ex post facto* provisions of the Constitution, and concluded that "the new act actually restores the threat of cruel and inhuman punishment for offenses long since forgiven."[78] The commission criticized the act's shotgun approach, because it forbade entry or could denaturalize and deport members or affiliates of "subversive organizations." The term "affiliation" was not spelled out but was left to the arbitrary determination of the U.S. attorney general.

Chicano activists were deported during the early 1950s. The list included Luisa Moreno, Frank Corona of the shoe workers, and Antonio Salgado, who

---

*The Los Angeles Committee for the Protection of the Foreign Born, an affiliate of the American Committee for the Protection of the Foreign Born, was placed on the subversive list by the Subversive Activities Control Board because it challenged the two acts. The committee, as well as many of its members, was cleared after extensive litigation.

had been instrumental in setting up ethnic or cultural units within the trade union locals. (These units gave the Chicanos more strength in the locals.) The McCarran Act of 1950 and the McCarran-Walter Act thwarted the development or effective organization both in the *barrios* and among working-class Chicanos in the United States by deporting some of its most effective leaders and intimidating others with the threat of deportation. The Los Angeles Committee for the Protection of the Foreign Born reported in 1954 that of the Chicanos being defended by the committee on deportation charges, seven had been in the country for over 7 years, three for more than 20 years, and three for over 30 years. Their report stated that 17 of the Chicanos had U.S.-born families—sons, daughters, grandchildren. Twenty-two of the defendants were trade unionists. It charged:

> The roster of Los Angeles' Mexican-born deportees is adequate proof that the Walter-McCarran Law is aimed straight at the heart of American labor. . . . With this law, under the pretext of hunting "illegals" and "subversives," immigration service officers serve as a terroristic police force in Mexican communities, as a strike-breaking, union-busting force in the fields, shops, and factories.[79] [Emphasis is that of the report.]

The pamphlet went on to document some of the deportation cases:

Justo Cruz, 66, in the United States since the age of 19, was a machinist who had joined the Workers' Alliance during the depression. In the alliance he had championed the workers' rights for relief and freedom from harassment. Later, the Workers' Alliance was placed on the attorney general's list of subversive organizations. Although there had been no restrictions on alliance membership in the 1930s, it was now punishable by deportation if one was either a noncitizen or a naturalized one. Immigration authorities attempted to have Cruz fired, but his employer refused. An order for his deportation was issued.[80]

María Cruz, 51, was the widow of Jesús Cruz, who died after deportation to Mexico. She entered the United States legally at the age of five, and was the mother of two U.S.-born children, one of whom was a war hero. When her purse was stolen, she applied for a new registration card. Immigration authorities then attempted to force her to inform on her dead husband and his associates, who were suspected of being Communists. When she refused, she was arrested and charged with illegal entry. Later the charge was altered to membership in the Communist party. She had once been a member of the CIO Cannery Workers Union.[81]

Agapito Gómez, 46, had legally lived in the United States since he was 21 and had a U.S.-born wife and two children. During the war, he joined the United Steelworkers of America (CIO). After the passage of the McCarran Act of 1950, immigration service agents called on him and demanded that he account for his past activities and give them a list of fellow workers and union members. When he refused, the agents took away his alien card. His crimes were that he had joined a depression relief organization and had been a member of the CIO.[82]

José Noriega, 67, came to the United States legally at the age of 25. He worked in the construction industry in Texas and became a longshoreman when he moved to California. Naturally, he joined the International Longshoremen's Association. He had taken part in the longshoremen's strike of 1923 and was arrested. He was blacklisted and had moved to San Bernardino. He later returned to the docks and joined the International Longshoremen's and Warehousemen's Union. He worked at the docks in Wilmington, the port section of Los Angeles, during the war years. Then, in 1952, the immigration agents called. They wanted information, names, dates, and places of organizational meetings and participants. When he refused to cooperate, deportation proceedings were initiated.[83]

These are just a few of the documented cases that undoubtedly will be augmented as the history of the decade of defense is written. A postscript to the above cases is that the Los Angeles Committee for the Protection of the Foreign Born won these cases, but only after considerable harassment and expense.

Conclusion

Summarizing the chapter, we note that Mexicans made several adjustments in their uprooting from the country to the city. The pattern of organization has gone full circle. The majority of the early organizations had Spanish names, which was significant in that it reflected the members' nationalism and continuing attachment to Mexico. Most of these associations were civic or political associations. Most of the organizations that followed had English names, underlining the attempt of the Chicano to accommodate to Anglo-American society; in fact, many social scientists have contended that these organizations were integrationist. The Spanish-named organizations continued, but they were, for the most part, social clubs that reflected regional identification; e.g., *El Club Sonorense, El Club Jalisco,* etc. The more militant political or activist groups used Spanish-based names: *La Liga Obrera de Habla Española* or *El Congreso de Pueblos de Habla Española.* (It is significant that the English name, "the Congress," was often used in the latter case.) This trend has continued to the present. The return to Spanish was and is used as a symbol of resistance.

As mentioned at the outset of the chapter, economics played a prominent role in the reactions of the Anglo-American to the Chicano. The habit of looking upon the Mexican as a temporary supplement to white labor carried over even to the second- and third-generation Chicano. In time of economic stress, the Anglo-American developed a "take-care-of-your-own" philosophy and considered the Mexican to be a burden on the community. Repatriation was a natural reaction to the depression of the 1930s. Chicanos were Mexicans, and all brown people were encouraged to go back to where they came from. During these years, repatriation, even though it had the cooperation of the Mexican government, meant the deportation of many Chicanos. Many were minors and U.S. citizens, but they had no choice. Even the adults, since they were so poor, had no choice. During this time, the border was a revolving door that was open and shut according to the industrial needs of the United States. It was never shut in the years when Mexican labor was needed. The mass roundups of undocumented workers, when they were conducted, made little distinction between Mexican and Chicano.

Deportation was also a weapon in the hands of the privileged. In the case of Jesús Pallares, we saw the deportation of an activist through the use of administrative proceedings that were set up in favor of the government. In union activities, as seen in chapter 7, strikers were deported. Moreover, in the 1950s the McCarran acts created an ambience of terror. Denaturalization proceedings were begun against many Mexicans who had been active in the movement. Some were actually deported, but others merely suffered the harassment of having to go through lengthy and costly proceedings. As mentioned, most organizations of that time resorted to Red-baiting in order to avoid being Red-baited themselves and to prove they were "American."[84]

Finally, from the 1930s through the 1950s, the Chicano was subjected to continued violence. Prejudice toward Mexicans was as overt as it was toward the Blacks. They were considered outsiders, and they did not benefit, as did Blacks, from the guilt feelings of white liberals. Moreover, the Mexican was considered an alien; the Black, although a second-class citizen, was at least a citizen. During World War II, the prejudice against the Chicano crystallized, and he was made a scapegoat for the failures of the Anglo-American society. During the *Pachuco* situation, a city rioted against the Chicano.[85]

In short, during this period the Chicano was victimized and his separateness was promoted. Through violence, economic exploitation, and political chicanery, he was controlled within "occupied America."

Notes

1. Albert Memmi, *The Colonizer and the Colonized* (Boston, Mass.: Beacon Press, 1965), p. 107.

2. See John Higham, *Strangers in the Land* (New York: Atheneum Publishers, 1971), who makes the point that when the security of the Anglo-American people is threatened they react violently against alien people and ideas.

3. This section relies heavily on the following works: Miguel Tirado, "Mexican American Political Organization: The Key to Chicano Political Power," *Aztlán,* Spring 1970, pp. 53–78; John R. Martínez, "Leadership and Politics," in *La Raza: Forgotten Americans,* ed. Julian Samora (Notre Dame, Inc.: University of Notre Dame Press, 1966), pp. 47–62; Kaye Briegel, "The Development of Mexican-American Organizations," in *The Mexican-Americans: An Awakening Minority,* ed. Manuel P. Servín (Beverly Hills, Calif.: Glencoe Press, 1970), pp. 160–178.

4. Quoted in Tirado, p. 56.

5. Quoted in Tirado, p. 57; taken from the first LULAC constitution.

6. Since material is scattered throughout the Southwest and Midwest, the available information on the repatriation of Mexicans is scarce. Two excellent works are: Ronald W. López, "Los Repatriados" (Seminar paper, University of California at Los Angeles, 1968), and Gregory Ochoa, "Some Aspects of the Repatriation of Mexican Aliens in Los Angeles County, 1931–1938" (Seminar paper, San Fernando Valley State College at Northridge, California, 1966). The López

paper relies heavily on the Clements Collection at the University of California at Los Angeles. Ochoa bases his paper largely on documents found in the office of the Los Angeles County Clerk.

7. López, p. 80.

8. Emory S. Bogardus, "Repatriation and Readjustment," in *Mexican-Americans,* ed. Servín, p. 89.

9. Ochoa, p. 22.

10. Quoted in López, p. 51.

11. López, p. 63.

12. Norman D. Humphrey, "Mexican Repatriation from Michigan: Public Assistance in Historical Perspective," *Social Service Review,* September 1941, p. 497.

13. López, p. 55.

14. López, p. 58.

15. López, p. 43.

16. Bogardus, pp. 92–93.

17. Humphrey, p. 505.

18. Bogardus, p. 93.

19. Ochoa, p. 66, states: "The average Mexican family repatriated had four children, all or most of whom were American citizens by birthright."

20. Ochoa, pp. 65–66.

21. Office of the Los Angeles County Clerk, Document no. 40, pp. 31–340, quoted in Ochoa, p. 24.

22. Carey McWilliams, *North From Mexico* (New York: Greenwood Press, Publishers, 1968), p. 193.

23. López, p. 69.

24. This section draws heavily on Philip Stevenson, "Deporting Jesus," *The Nation* 143 (18 July 1936): 67–69.

25. Taped speech in my possession by Manuel Banda, presented at University of California at Santa Barbara Extension, Oxnard, California (Spring 1965). Banda is a long-time activist and currently is at the University of California at Riverside.

26. This congress is often called the "Mexican Congress." The data were obtained by interviewing the participants. I am especially indebted to Bert Corona, with whom an interview was taped (Spring 1971).

27. Tirado, pp. 59–60.

28. Ruth Lucretia Martínez, "The Unusual Mexican: A Study in Acculturation (M.A. thesis, Claremont Colleges, 1942), pp. 36–38.

29. Martínez, pp. 38–39.

30. Raul Morín, *Among the Valiant* (Alhambra, Calif.: Borden Publishing Co., 1966), p. 16.

31. Morín, p. 16.

32. Octavio Paz, *The Labyrinth of Solitude* (New York: Grove Press, Inc., 1961), pp. 14–15.

33. Octavio I. Romano, "The Historical and Intellectual Presence of Mexican-Americans," *El Grito,* Winter 1969, pp. 39–40.

34. "Pachucos" (Press release in the Sleepy Lagoon Defense Committee File), found in the Special Collections Library at the University of California at Los Angeles.

35. McWilliams, pp. 233–235.

36. Stephanie Dias, "The Zoot Suit Riots" (Pro-seminar paper, San Fernando Valley State College at Northridge, California), pp. 12–14; McWilliams, pp. 233–234.

37. McWilliams, pp. 228–231.

38. McWilliams, pp. 232–233.

39. McWilliams, p. 231.

40. McWilliams, p. 248.

41. Quoted in Dias, p. 18.

42. Dias, pp. 18–19.

43. McWilliams, pp. 244–254.
44. Dias, pp. 22–23.
45. McWilliams, pp. 246–247.
46. *Los Angeles Times,* 7 June 1943.
47. McWilliams, pp. 248–250.
48. *Time* magazine, 21 June 1943; *PM,* 10 June 1943.
49. McWilliams, pp. 251–252.
50. McWilliams, p. 250.
51. McWilliams, p. 250.
52. Ed Robbins, *PM,* 9 June 1943.
53. McWilliams, p. 251.
54. *Los Angeles Times,* 10 June 1943.
55. *Los Angeles Times,* 10 June 1943.
56. *Los Angeles Times,* 10 July 1943.
57. *Los Angeles Times,* 4 August 1942.
58. Ed Rusco, "Community Service Organization" (Seminar paper in political science, University of California Library, Berkeley, n.d.), p. 8.
59. Rusco, p. 8.
60. Rusco, p. 13.
61. Tirado, p. 63.
62. Tirado, p. 65.
63. William Korick, "The Wetback Story," *Commonwealth,* 13 June 1951, p. 327.
64. Hart Stillwell, "The Wetback Tide," *Common Ground,* Summer 1949, pp. 3–4.
65. Carey McWilliams, "California and the Wetback," *Common Ground,* Summer 1949, p. 19.
66. Patricia Morgan, *Shame of a Nation* (Los Angeles, Calif.: Los Angeles Committee for Protection of the Foreign Born, 1954), p. 3.
67. Leo Grebler, Joan W. Moore, and Ralph Guzman, *The Mexican-American People* (New York: The Free Press, 1970), p. 521.
68. For further data on the weaknesses of the census data, see Rudy Acuña, *A Mexican American Chronicle* (New York: American Book Company, 1971), pp. 182–184.
69. Bert Corona, taped interview, April 1971.
70. Robert K. Murray, *Red Scare* (Minneapolis: University of Minnesota Press, 1955), p. 65.
71. Jethro K. Lieberman, *Are Americans Extinct?* (New York: Walter and Company, 1968), p. 106.
72. Lieberman, p. 106.
73. Lieberman, p. 109.
74. *Whom We Shall Welcome* (New York: Da Capo Press, 1971) includes an excellent analysis of the McCarran acts, published by the President's Commission on Immigration and Naturalization, 1 January 1953.
75. *Whom We Shall Welcome,* p. 196. I had extensive talks with Rosaura Revueltas in Cuernavaca, Morelos, Mexico, in May and June 1971. She starred in *Salt of the Earth,* a controversial film about Chicano miners. As a result of appearing in the film, she was deported to Mexico. Anglo-American authorities claimed that her passport was not stamped. She has not been able to visit the United States since the film was made in the early 1950s. Moreover, she was blacklisted by the Mexican film industry, over which the United States has considerable control.
76. *Whom We Shall Welcome,* p. 197.
77. *Whom We Shall Welcome,* p. 198.
78. *Whom We Shall Welcome,* p. 198.
79. Morgan, pp. 38–39.
80. Morgan, pp. 39–41.
81. Morgan, pp. 42–43.
82. Morgan, pp. 44–45.

83. Morgan, pp. 45–47.

84. The American Civil Liberties Union also handled countless cases for Chicanos who had no political involvement. Again, their only crime was that they were Mexicans. An in-depth study of these proceedings should be made, since they are at the heart of the breaking of the Chicano movement during the 1950s.

85. Richard Hofstadter and Michael Wallace, eds., *American Violence* (New York: Vintage Books, 1971), p. 33.

Chapter Nine

Goodbye America, I

If the 1950s produced a decade of defense, the 1960s represented a decade of both awareness and disillusionment. Many Chicanos actively participated in the political life of the nation, during which time they took a hard look at their assigned role in the United States, evaluated it, and then decided that they had had enough, so they bid good-bye to America. Until 1960, the Chicanos in the United States had been invisible on the national scene. They just did not count in the centers of power—Washington, D.C., and the state capitals. They were, therefore, politically and economically managed. The oligarchy of privilege looked at them as foreigners and effectively suffocated any insurgency on the part of the few Chicano radicals who remained in the community. As we have seen, deportation and denaturalization were potent weapons in subverting the efforts of Chicano organizations. However, in 1960 the Chicano could no longer be ignored or deported en masse; 85 percent of the Chicano population was native-born and thus U.S. citizens.[1]

During the 1960 presidential campaign, Democratic politicians capitalized on the Chicano vote, harnessing the voting force for John Fitzgerald Kennedy. *Viva Kennedy* clubs worked feverishly throughout the Southwest and even enjoyed direct contact with the Democratic presidential candidate. Active registration drives were conducted, producing significant results: the Kennedy-Johnson ticket barely won in Texas and surely would have lost that state without the support of the Chicano bloc. In California the Chicano vote also went to Kennedy, but Richard Nixon, a native of that state, won by a narrow margin. At that time, it was conceded by most political analysts that the Chicano vote henceforth would be very important. Both the Mexican American Political Association, which was prominent in California, and the Political Association of Spanish-Speaking Organizations, active mainly in Texas, received considerable impetus as a result of the Chicano's political potential.[2] This prestige carried over to the activity in other organizations, such as the League of United Latin American Citizens, the Community Service Organization, and the American G.I. Forum.

Washington, D.C., had begun to make gestures indicating that the Chicano did count, and promises of relief for the inequities Chicanos faced were made. This trend stimulated many Chicanos to join organizations, since they recognized the importance of acting collectively.

In 1960, the U.S. census revealed the subservient status of the Chicano in the United States. Many Chicanos still lived under the illusion that they did not have problems. Its small middle class had been almost totally socialized, and many believed that they were different from the lower-class Mexicans. After all, they rationalized, Mexicans were white and, therefore, not subject to the same problems faced by Black people. They believed that the Mexican had only to get an education and make more money, and he would then be accepted. Many even refused to recognize that discrimination, either racial or cultural, existed. The 1960 census destroyed the myth that Chicanos were succeeding in Anglo-American society; it documented, once and for all, that Chicanos collectively belonged to a subjugated caste.

The 1960 census reported that 3,464,999 Spanish-surnamed persons legally resided in the Southwest;[3] that their per capita income was $968, compared to $2047 for Anglos and $1044 for nonwhites other than Chicanos;[4] that 29.7 percent of the Spanish-surnamed population lived in deteriorated houses, while 7.5 percent of the Anglos and 27.1 percent of the other nonwhites occupied dwellings of this type.[5] The census further showed that the average size of the Spanish-surnamed family was 4.77 compared to 3.39 for Anglos and 4.54 for other nonwhites.[6] Unemployment was higher among Chicanos than among Anglos, and although Chicanos were not as strictly segregated as Blacks, the majority were segregated from the Anglo community. In addition, the Chicano was at the bottom of the scale educationally. The educational grade median for Spanish-surnamed persons over 14 years of age was 8.1, versus 12.0 for Anglos and 9.7 for other nonwhites.[7] Significantly, the grade median for the Spanish-surnamed in Texas was 4.8.[8]

What the census did not show was that the education Mexicans received in the public schools was far inferior to that received by Anglo-Americans. Their reading level was below that of Anglos; many who completed junior high school were functionally illiterate. For the most part, Mexicans were placed in nonacademic tracks from the first grade through junior high school; this left them ill-equipped to take academic courses in high school and killed learning motivation. On the basis of the census, one analyst observed: "That more education fails to improve the income position of Mexican Americans in proportion to that of the majority is a matter of considerable social significance."[9] The census showed that 60.6 percent of the Spanish-surnamed population was employed in low-skilled manual labor occupations.[10]

In short, the Chicano was at the bottom of the economic, political, and educational scales, and he did have a problem. Many Chicanos, especially educators, were forced to reevaluate their thinking. A growing number joined the movement to reform, but not to revolutionize, the system; they had been too Americanized, and they believed that equal opportunity existed. To blame the Chicano's status on a master-servant relationship or on the economic distribution would have been un-American to them.

Small civic groups emerged, most of which were concerned about the education gap. They advanced different reasons for the disparity. Many contended that Chicano students were behind Anglo students because of the language barrier; others blamed it on the lack of bilingual instruction; some said it was because of discrimination in the schools; while still others held that it was the cultural conflict, which created a negative self-image in the Chicano student. Solutions were advanced: preschool education; bilingual programs; empathetic teachers; relevant materials; and more Chicano teachers. Although the solutions and demands were reformist at best, to date they have not been achieved. The Chicano community soon became frustrated with the inaction of those in control. Chicano groups continued to work through the civil rights framework, which the Blacks had helped to popularize. They worked in the areas of housing, employment, police brutality, etc. Their methods were confined to petitions and the courts; occasionally they took part in a sit-in. During this period, the groups, comprised mostly of volunteers, were small, but enthusiastic.[11]

The Chicano community won minor victories during the first half of the 1960s. In 1963 they briefly captured the city council of Crystal City, Texas.[12] In California and the Southwest, activists were able to muster enough support to end the *bracero* program in 1964. Moreover, César Chávez's small union was growing, and activists watched it with considerable interest. The brown man in the field was romanticized by the urban activists who were searching for roots and causes. The farm workers caught an emotional nerve. Chicano activists identified with the *huelga* that began on September 16, 1965, and the later march from Delano to Sacramento, under the Mexican flag, the *huelga* flag, and *La Virgen de Guadalupe.*[13] The Chávez movement also caught the imagination of the news media, which began to report on the plight of the migrant as well as that of Chicanos. In the years that followed, leading politicians and personages made pilgrimages to Delano. Meanwhile, the Black community conducted an intense crusade to win their rights, with Martin Luther King leading the nonviolent struggle. Suddenly, however, the bubble burst, and Black urban ghettoes throughout the United States exploded. The Watts riots of the summer of 1965 sparked the activity.

These riots greatly affected the direction of the newly instituted Economic Opportunity Act of 1964 and the subsequent "War on Poverty." The act emphasized education and training programs: job corps, neighborhood youth corps, work-study and community-action programs. The spin-offs were loans to farmers and small businessmen, as well as the formation of VISTA (Volunteers in Service to America). The War on Poverty supposedly attacked the causes of poverty through community participation. To understand the program, the mentality of President Lyndon B. Johnson has to be explored. Johnson was a machine politician from Texas, with a basically conservative philosophy. He had, however, been affected greatly by Franklin D. Roosevelt and the New Deal. Fundamentally, the New Deal was aimed at preserving the capitalistic system in the United States and was designed to bring about a coalition of labor and ethnic peoples to support the Democratic party. Control of the national government was essential to perpetuating the Democratic party. Johnson also was influenced greatly by John Fitzgerald Kennedy and his "New Frontier," which in many ways was the revival of idealism at home and abroad. Young people entered into the New Frontier's coalition, since they believed they could change society. They represented a large bloc vote. Johnson, in his War on Poverty, attempted to revive the New Deal: involving the poor, setting up new agencies, creating a leadership of co-opted leaders who were committed to the system and the Democratic party. Basically, the program enlarged the role of the national government and increased its control. It bolstered the system through reformist measures.

The War on Poverty played a role similar to the one played by the Alliance for Progress in Latin America.* In spite of the alliance's declared purpose to create a "peaceful revolution," in reality it became an instrument for the infiltration and support of established governments in order to protect Anglo-American investments. The aid given to Latin America, in other words, had strings attached. Rómulo Betancourt, a friend of the United States and a former president of Venezuela, summed up its purpose: "We must help the poor in order to save the rich."[14] The alliance's purpose was to forestall revolutionary change, and in the process, Latin American nations became more dependent on the United States. The War on Poverty had a similar purpose. Fortunately, it was sabotaged by Johnson's inability to carry the program into operation because of the Vietnam War. Meanwhile, the expecta-

---

*The Alliance was a foreign aid program initiated by John F. Kennedy in 1961. It was supposed to force internal reform in 19 Latin American nations. It was a reaction to the failure of the U.S. Cuban policy.

tions of the poor were raised by a taste of power—or at least the illusion of it.

Planners and administrators of the new agencies were white liberals who were based in Washington. For the most part, they had never seen a Chicano and did not know his needs. These liberals, riddled with guilt feelings toward the Blacks and shaken by the urgency of the ghetto revolts, excluded the Chicano from the planning stages. Most of the money, jobs, and programs were directed to Blacks, even though in the Southwest the Chicano outnumbered the Black two or three to one. This made Mexicans bitter, and they began to battle for their share of the pie. This had positive side effects, since many of the new Chicano leaders were forced to mobilize the poor as a means of pressuring authorities to service them. New high-paying jobs attracted many Mexicans who previously had avoided the movement. They soon became infected by the fervor, realizing that their effectiveness depended on the people. This stimulated activity. Many Chicano bureaucrats were committed at least to eroding the "Black-white syndrome" (the habit of white politicians and liberals of looking at problems through the perspective of the Black-white experience) that operated in the United States.

On March 28, 1966, an Equal Opportunity Commission meeting was held in Albuquerque, New Mexico, to investigate the Chicanos' employment problems, and approximately 50 Chicanos walked out of the conference. They resented the fact that although the commission advocated equal employment it did not have one Mexican on its staff. This walkout was significant, since most of the delegates were established professionals and were not accustomed to such assertive action.[15] On September 4, 1966, farm workers, with 8000 supporters, marched into Austin, Texas, further increasing the public's consciousness of the Chicano. Although these actions were within the civil rights framework, they shook the stereotype of the docile Mexican. As a result of the walkout in Albuquerque and the growing ferment among Chicanos, the federal government pacified the community on June 1967, by appointing Vicente Ximenes to the Equal Employment Opportunity Commission. Shortly thereafter, he was named as head of the newly created Interagency Committee on Mexican American Affairs.[16] This office was largely symbolic, acting mainly to mollify the middle-class activists, whose primary goal was to create higher level and better paying jobs for Chicanos.

Johnson also promised that he would hold a White House Conference for Chicano leaders, but was afraid that the Chicanos would walk out of the conference and thus embarrass him politically. Therefore, he did not keep his promise; instead, in October 1967, he held Cabinet Committee Hearings at El Paso, Texas. The purpose of the conference was to educate cabinet members to the problems of the Mexican American. Johnson did not bother to invite the leading activists: César Chávez, Reies Tijerina, or Rodolfo "Corky" Gonzales. At El Paso he bussed his Mexicans to the *Chamizal* celebrations, which marked the return of the *Chamizal* to Mexico. (It was a disputed section of land that was claimed by both the United States and Mexico. It must be added that the *Chamizal* was an abandoned dump yard of little value.) Many Chicanos wondered if this had not, in fact, been the main reason for the conference, since little else was accomplished. Meanwhile, activists boycotted and picketed the cabinet conference. They called their group *La Raza Unida.* Ernesto Galarza of San Jose, Corky Gonzales, and Reies Tijerina played leading roles in this opposition. To many observers, it was clear that the lid was about to blow off in the Chicano community.[17]

The breaking point came in March 1968, when Chicano students walked out of five Los Angeles high schools. This was the first clear break with the civil rights traditions of the 1960s. The schools involved were in East Los Angeles, with populations that were overwhelmingly Mexican. The Chicanos' grievances and demands can be summarized as follows: over 50 percent of the Chicano high school community was being forced to drop out of school either through expulsion, transfers to other schools, or simply because they had not been taught to read and thus failed their courses; the Chicano schools were overcrowded and run down compared to the Anglo and Black schools of the district; many teachers openly discriminated against Chicanos and the students wanted racist teachers removed; the curriculum was designed to obscure the Chicanos' culture and condition the students to be content with low-skilled jobs; and the students demanded more Chicano teachers and administrators.[18]

When the students walked out, sheriff deputies and police reacted by treating the protest as an insurrection: breaking up the demonstrations by beating students, and arresting those who did not move fast enough. Many activists were caught by surprise; however, in general, community organizations supported the walkout and condemned police brutality. Meanwhile, Sal Castro, a teacher at Lincoln High School, emerged as the central figure of the walkouts. He stated that he could not in good conscience remain inside the school, since the demands of his students were legitimate. Moreover, he condemned the schools for crippling Chicano children. Along with others, he was indicted by the Los Angeles Grand Jury on several charges, among them conspiracy to commit misdemeanors. After two years of appeals, the courts found the charges unconstitutional. Meanwhile, Castro has been harassed by the California Department of Education, which attempted to revoke his credentials, and he has been subject to frequent and arbitrary administrative transfers.

Ironically, the tactics used by Castro and the students were in the trade union tradition—they attempted to stop production. They, however, did not receive the support of trade unions, which failed to protest the violence against the strikers. In general, teachers also condemned the walkouts. (Two years later they were also to go on strike because their demands were not met.) The Los Angeles walkouts called national attention to the Chicano's plight in education. The results were: Chicano walkouts were encouraged throughout the Southwest and the Midwest; they served notice that some Chicanos would not work within the system; they did bring about improvements, since they gave leverage to Mexicans working within the system, enabling them to get more Chicano administrators, courses, budgets, etc.; and they marked the entrance of youth into the mainstream of the Chicano movement.[19]

The change in the Chicano youth during this period had been subtle. It began before the walkouts with the founding of *barrio* groups like the Brown Berets in 1967 (to be discussed later) and student organizations in both secondary schools and institutions of higher learning. The unifying theme among students was nationalism. It was not the same as that of the first-generation Mexicans, but it was a search for roots. While their fathers had rejected their Mexicanism, the third generation did not identify with their parents' aspirations of blending into the system. They identified with their grandparents. By this time, many of them no longer spoke Spanish; nevertheless, they attempted to learn it. They also sought to revive cultural symbols. This is important for the colonized. In Africa and Asia, the conquered could be distinguished easily from the conquerors by their dress and their language, but in the United States, only color distinguished the oppressed.

In this new nationalism, youth rejected Anglo-American values. Luis Váldez, of the *Teatro Campesino,* contributed to the spread of this new philosophy. The *Teatro* used one-act plays to advertise the struggle of the farm worker and the Chicano. They played *corridos* (ballads) that popularized the Chicano's struggle for liberation in the United States. Also, in 1967, the first issue of the newspaper *La Raza* was published. It openly proclaimed itself a *barrio* newspaper that would defend the rights of its community. The first editor was Elizar Risco, a Cuban and long-time activist in the Chicano movement. When he left the paper, Joe Razo took over, and with capable assistants such as Raúl Ruiz, *La Raza* was expanded.

The importance of *La Raza* is that it has documented the major events in the Chicano *barrio* of East Los Angeles, as well as those throughout the nation. Its photos and articles are a social commentary on the struggle of the Chicano to achieve social, political, and economic self-determination. Without its reporting, much of the Chicano's history would be lost, for it has been ignored by the Establishment press. In Chicano history, the role played by Joe Razo and Raúl Ruiz in documenting the events of the Chicano moratorium and the murder of Ruben Salazar, which we shall discuss later, would have been lost. They played a similar role to that which Carey McWilliams filled with his interpretation of the so-called *Pachuco* riots. Many other Chicano newspapers have followed in the tradition of *La Raza.*

Another milestone was the publication of *El Grito: A Journal of Contemporary Mexican-American Thought* in the fall of 1967. The journal was organized by a group called *Quinto Sol* Publications, headed by Octavio Romano, a professor at the University of California at Berkeley. The first editor was Nick C. Vaca, who until recently regularly contributed to the journal. *El Grito,* an inspiration to other publications, is published quarterly and features essays on the Chicano movement, scholarly articles, poetry, and art. Although *El Grito* is more scholarly than *La Raza,* its themes are also those of national liberation.

These media contributed to the change in the attitude of many students and led to the formation of a common ideological base. Youthful victories, moreover, gave the movement a tremendous boost. The importance of the student's role cannot be overestimated, for close to 60 percent of the Chicano community is under 21. The lack of formal organizations in that community made their impact that much greater. No organization today exists of the national stature of the National Association for the Advancement of Colored People or the Urban League. At the same time, the Chicanos' middle class is small compared to that of the Blacks, and they lack a counterpart to the Black colleges, which have helped the Blacks to forge a group consciousness and commitment. Nonetheless, Chicano youth moved into the void which had been created by the dearth of Chicano organization and, with sheer numbers and zeal, affected the course of the movement.

The militancy of youth was fed by *barrio* groups such as the Brown Berets and student organizations such as the Mexican American Youth Organization (MAYO) in Texas* and various other Mexican American student associations. It is significant that since the spring of 1969 most university and college student organizations have changed their name to *El Movimiento Estudiantil Chicanos de Aztlán* (The Chicano Student Movement of Aztlán) or (MECHA).[20] The reason for this name change was to bring most student groups under one umbrella. Regional central committees were formed to coordinate the efforts of the numerous chapters. But, more important, the new name meant a change in the direction of the student movement to a commitment to confront the established order. No longer did many students want to use integrationist methods and to adapt to Anglo-Americans by using English names; the use of Spanish was a symbol of liberation. Each word in MECHA symbolizes a confrontation. *Movimiento* means that the organization is dedicated to the movement to gain self-determination for their people. *Estudiantil* identifies the organization as a student group. At the heart of the name change was the use of the word *Chicano*. Historically, Mexican students had received an education and passed into the middle sector. The Chicano to the middle-class Mexican symbolized the lower-caste Mexicans. In adopting their new identity, the students committed themselves to returning to the *barrios* and identifying with the oppressed. MECHA also rejected the identity that Anglo-Americans had forced upon them—that of being a Mexican American. Lastly, the students affirmed that they were from *Aztlán,* the legendary birthplace of the Aztecs, which reputedly was in today's Southwest. This reaffirmed their Indian heritage as well as the fact that Chicanos were indigenous to the Southwest; therefore, if the Anglo-Americans did not like it there, they could go back to from where they came. It announced to the Anglo-American the commitment of the Chicano to achieve self-determination. This change was made at a statewide conference held at the University of California at Santa Barbara and

---

*See the section on José Ángel Gutiérrez later in this chapter.

was incorporated in *El Plan de Santa Barbara,* which was a detailed plan of action.*

The ideology emanating from the student community and from militants is difficult to define. Chicano nationalism remains very strong in the giant *barrios* of Los Angeles, San Jose, and San Antonio and in the rural areas of Texas and the Southwest; in fact, it is strong wherever a large Spanish-speaking population exists. Among most radicals, the feeling of *mi raza primero* (my people first) is popular. Chicano nationalism has engendered a spirit of collectivism. A rejection of the "individual success" philosophy of the more established segments of the community is popular. The theme is not reform, but separatism, through which a bloc powerful enough to seize self-determination can be forged. The cult of Ché has also spread among the youth. To students, Ché became a hero after his death; he was one man who did not betray his ideals, but who died for them. He is especially appealing to Chicano youth, since he was a Latin American and because he was an enemy of the same forces that have oppressed them. The Chicanos' nationalism closely resembled that of other Third World people, and it distinguished them from the colonizer.

At this point, the conclusion could be reached that the 1960s were dominated by the activities of California Chicanos. This is not true; Reies Tijerina, Corky Gonzales, and José Ángel Gutíerrez and their followers (whom we shall discuss later) have had considerable impact upon the course of the movement. They are all non-Californians. In fact, in an effort to meet the demands of Chicanos, California has raided Texas as well as other states of many of their educators and activists.** The pull has been economic, but in addition the oppression in other areas has been more severe. This dominance on the part of Californians is called by many "California Chicano imperialism."***

The Catalysts

In spite of the enthusiasm of youth, they have failed to integrate collectively into the *barrio* community. Those who are attending colleges or universities necessarily are removed physically from it. The students nonetheless understand the forces that oppress them. In addition, many civic, education, political, and community groups are working day to day in the tedious task of organizing *barrio* legal defense groups, associations of ex-convicts, welfare rights organizations, etc. Most of these groups deal with the everyday crises that are attendant to the oppression. For example, Bert Corona, an old-time organizer and one of the founders of the Mexican American Political Association, is active in assisting undocumented Mexicans fill out immigration papers

---

*Historically, in Mexico a plan of action, announcing the grievances of the revolutionaries and telling the people the plan to end the injustices, is issued before every revolution.

**Pay and working conditions are better in California than in most Southwestern states.

***This section is based on my participation in the movement since 1961. I have also received considerable insight from my students and community-based friends.

and in helping to ameliorate the exploitation of these workers by unscrupulous employers in the Los Angeles area. His organization, called CASA MAPA (The House of MAPA), has over 2000 members. Meanwhile, other work is done by community volunteers at considerable personal sacrifice. The story of these *barrio* organizations is undocumented, but in reality they are the heart of the struggle toward liberation. Nevertheless, there are key catalysts that have helped to pump blood to the heart. The narrative that follows singles out as catalysts one organization and three major leaders; César Chávez has been omitted because his activities have been discussed previously at some length.

The Brown Berets

Most Chicano organizations have had defensive postures and have reacted to crisis situations. These organizations, for the most part, have worked within the system and have been reform oriented. The Brown Berets is an exception; it is one of the few Chicano organizations advocating physical measures to defend the Chicano community's rights. The Brown Berets' impact on the Chicano movement has, to date, been far greater than its influence in it, for in the last four years, it has exposed a basic weakness in the Anglo-American fabric; it has aroused a fear in Anglo-Americans that a Chicano group would counter U.S. oppression with its own violence. Whether or not the threat was real is not at issue. More important is that law enforcement authorities believed that the Brown Berets were capable of violence or arousing this kind of action in other groups. In effect, it is an affirmation of the police's increasing awareness of the resentment toward police brutality and the realization that the theme of liberation is becoming more popular among Chicanos. The Brown Berets, in effect, panicked police officials and exposed their basic undemocratic attitudes toward Mexicans or groups attempting to achieve liberation. This is especially true in Los Angeles, where the Berets were founded. The police and sheriff's departments there abandoned reason in harassing, intimidating, and persecuting the Brown Berets in a way that no other Chicano organization has experienced in recent times. Police and sheriff's deputies raided the Berets, infiltrated them, libeled and slandered them, and even encouraged countergroups to attack the members. The objective was to destroy the Berets and to invalidate the membership in the eyes of both the Anglo and the Chicano communities.

The Brown Berets were formed in 1967 in East Los Angeles. At first they were known as Young Citizens for Community Action (YCCA). The group was sponsored by an interfaith church organization, and its founding leader was David Sánchez, a teenager from an upper lower-class family. Four other Chicanos joined Sánchez as charter members. In time, the group's defensive posture crystallized, with the organization evolving from a community service club into a quasi "alert patrol." Later in the year, the YCCA opened a coffee shop called *La Piranya* to raise operating expenses. Events meanwhile forced the organization to become more militant; this is reflected in the change in the group's name to the Young Chicanos for Community Action. The members began to wear brown berets, and they took on a paramilitary stance. The YCCA became popularly known as the Brown Berets. This militant profile attracted a large number of young Chicanos and had considerable impact on the student organizations of the time. Simultaneously, the Los Angeles Sheriff's Department began a vicious "bust the Berets" operation. They raided them, picked up members, and spread rumors that they were Communists.

Beret chapters spread throughout the Southwest and Midwest.[21] In Los Angeles, sheriff's deputies harassed the Brown Berets and so disorganized them that they were forced to shut down their coffee shop in March 1968. That same month, the Berets were escalated into the national limelight by the East Los Angeles school walkouts. There is little evidence that the organization itself took a leadership role in planning the walkouts, but as one observer stated: "When the crap came down, the Berets were there, offering to serve and taking the brunt of the police brutality. They were the shock troops."[22] During the walkout, the police and sheriff's departments attempted to make the Brown Berets the scapegoats, branding them as outside agitators, while playing down the legitimate grievances of the Chicano students. A grand jury later indicted 13 Chicanos on conspiracy charges stemming from the walkout; seven were Brown Berets. This case was appealed and later declared unconstitutional, but only after three years of legal harassment. As the police and sheriff's repression increased, the popularity of the group spread. Ironically, the only offensive action during this time was on the part of law enforcement agencies. Meanwhile, obvious parallels between the Brown Berets and the Black Panthers emerged. Both organizations were paramilitary, and they had a similar organizational structure, e.g., the prime minister, the ministers of defense, education, etc. There were also very real differences: the Black Panthers evolved from a Poverty Agency, whereas the Berets were much younger and their base was the *barrio*. In addition, the Black Panthers attracted many middle-class Black intellectuals as well as white radicals (nonmembers); whereas the leadership of the Berets was primarily comprised of high school dropouts who were highly suspicious of educated Chicanos and who almost totally rejected Anglos. Moreover, the Panthers have received considerable financial support from the Anglo-American liberal community; the Berets operated with no budget. The lack of funds prevented the Berets from building a Panther-like network among its own chapters, and they were not able to attract high-powered legal assistance to advertise the police harassment of the group, or to obtain editorial help in producing sophisticated literature.

Law enforcement agencies have inundated the Berets with informers and special agents to entrap the members by encouraging acts of violence. They have purposely subverted the Berets, keeping them in a state of flux and preventing the organization from solidifying.

In spite of the police and the press, the Berets have created considerable awareness. They frightened many Anglo-Americans who considered the Chicano passive, and Anglos were forced to deal with the reality that Chicanos were capable of reacting violently. The Berets inspired a revolutionary fervor in many youth, especially those in their early teens, who not only wanted to defend themselves, but wanted to stand up and fight. _The Battle of Algiers,_ a film depicting the Algerian struggle against the French, became a model. These youth were attracted by the physical nature of the Beret-defined form of confrontation. Moreover, the Berets, unlike the Black Panthers, did not attract large numbers of middle-class activists with a revolutionary ideology. They attracted the street _batos_ (guys) who directly felt the oppression of the police and the street. At the same time, the _batos_ were alienated from the mainstream of the Chicano community, which did not understand their hybrid culture or, many times, their frustrations. Unable to articulate their feelings or their grievances, the uniform and the paramilitary nature of the group gave members and nonmembers the feeling that they could strike back in the manner that they felt and understood best—physically. The ability to serve and to protect the Chicano _barrio_ by any means necessary provided a link with the Chicano community.

The Berets evolved into a radical group. Imbued with the politics of liberation, they dealt with the immediate needs of the _barrio_—food, housing, unemployment, education, etc.. Their philosophy has been molded by the conflict and the street. This is not to say that there have been no outside influences. For example, Father John Luce, an Episcopalian minister, has worked closely with David Sánchez since the latter was 15 years old.[23] The Berets have also had close contact with college and university students. But, over all, the main thrust has been from the _barrio._

A basic weakness in the Brown Berets is that it does not have the strong family structure that has heretofore marked survival and success for most Chicano organizations. It has not been accepted as the "Army of the Brown People." Most people have been puzzled by the failure of the group to define what it considers to be its role in society. The Berets have allowed outside groups, such as the police, to direct their course of action; this interference has led members to react to crises rather than to remain in control of the situation. Many times this has caused the group to become a disorganizing influence in the movement. Its attempt to operate a free clinic in East Los Angeles, for example, has been frustrated by outside interference such as police harassment and Red-baiting. Nonetheless, despite the failures, the Brown Berets are important, because they are one of the few Chicano groups that have not attempted to work entirely within the civil rights framework of the present reform movement. They are the bridge between the groups of the past and those of liberation, which shall become more offensive.

José Ángel Gutíerrez

Chicano leaders in general have followed a different pattern from that of the Black leadership. In the Black movement there are national leaders with large organizations and efficient staffs. In the Chicano movement, César

Chávez is the only leader of national prominence who has a large organization, and it is a service or trade union that promotes the interests of a special-interest group rather than Chicanos as a whole. The entire Chicano leadership pattern, in fact, closely resembles the pattern of the Mexican Revolution, where revolutionary juntas and local leaders emerged. These leaders took care of their home bases, and, in turn, were supported by their followers. Chávez, Gutiérrez, and Corky Gonzales all adhere to this basic pattern, inspiring intense loyalty among their followers.

José Ángel Gutiérrez, who is 27 years old, has risen to national prominence in meteoric fashion. In 1967 he and a group of fellow Chicano students founded MAYO (Mexican American Youth Organization) at St. Mary's College in San Antonio, Texas. MAYO is unique in that the membership is made up of activist organizers. Gutiérrez, along with Carlos Guerra and Mario Compean, has been a leading influence in the organization. These men have given the organization an activist profile. Gutiérrez's approach was to attack the *gringo* Establishment personally in order to create awareness among Chicanos as well as to call attention to the exploitation of Chicanos in Texas. His "Kill the *gringo*" speech caused considerable reaction among Anglo-Americans, who took the speech literally.[24] Instantly, Gutiérrez became a controversial figure and was attacked by Establishment Chicano politicians such as Congressman Henry B. Gonzales from San Antonio. The speech also had the effect of creating pride among many Chicanos who had always wanted to confront the oppressor, but who had feared doing so. It was a key to liberating many from fear. When José Ángel got away with it, it was an indication that they also could speak up. Furthermore, he had specifically attacked and identified the oppressor—the *gringo.*

Gutiérrez and MAYO, however, are not sensationalist in nature. They used militant tactics to get steam blowing. Fundamentally, they are organizers who drew up projects to take control of the political, economic, and education institutions that managed the Chicanos' lives. The first target model was the Winter Garden area of Texas. MAYO planned to experiment with methods of organization in that region, develop a blueprint for action, and then export it to other parts of the Southwest. The base of operation was José Ángel's home town of Crystal City, a small hamlet of about 10,000 residents. The operation was started on June 20, 1969. Gutiérrez was accompanied by his young wife, Luz, and several young volunteers. This was an important maneuver for MAYO, since Gutiérrez wanted experienced organizers.[25] He wrote:

> We wanted to be a group of active crusaders for social justice—Chicano style. This demanded that MAYO members be well versed in one or more problem areas confronting the Mexicano; but more important it meant that the members of MAYO had to experience the frustration of defeat; the joy of victory; the grind of day-to-day work; as well as learning to be a real Mexicano. We wanted to begin Aztlan![26]

Gutiérrez and his followers had few friends in the Winter Garden area, which was dominated by the Anglo-American minority. Chicanos comprised over 85 percent of the region's population. Gutíerrez knew that they could do nothing without involvement of the people at the grass-roots level. He therefore planned a campaign to increase awareness. The conditions for change were there; the MAYO volunteers did not have to invent issues: the Anglo-Americans owned 95 percent of the land. In Zavala County, the median family income was $1754 a year; in contrast, "In 1967 the agribusiness income in Dummit, La Salle, and Zavala counties totaled about $31 million."[27] The median years of education for Chicanos was 2.3. On the school grounds, a no-Spanish rule was vigorously enforced. Over 70 percent of the Chicano students dropped out of the Crystal High School. There were few Mexican officeholders or professionals in the area. Those who received an education moved away. Discrimination was rampant, with Anglo-Americans considering themselves racially and culturally superior to Chicanos. The Texas Rangers patrolled the area, terrorizing the occupied. Adding to the plight of the Chicano was that a substantial number of them were migrants who had to follow the crops. They left the Winter Garden area in late spring and did not return until the fall. The small hamlets of the area became ghost towns. The main tasks of MAYO were to expose the *gringo* to the people and then to confront him.

The first assault was on the political privilege of the Anglo-American. The Anglos protected this privilege through the use of fraud and intimidation at the polls, especially by the Texas Rangers. Control of the political parties was at the ballot box. The Democratic party, for example, held its primary elections shortly after most of the Chicanos left on their northern migration.* At that time, the voters chose the man who would be the Democratic candidate, usually an Anglo-American who was committed to the privileged. When the Chicano returned in time for the general elections, he only had a choice between an Anglo-Republican or an Anglo-Democrat. Most Chicanos had been traditionally loyal to the Democratic party, and Gutíerrez knew that it would be difficult to get Mexicans to break with this tradition.[28]

A school crisis at Crystal City in November 1969 gave the young volunteers the issue to help organize the Chicanos to confront the *gringo.* Chicano students presented demands to the Crystal City school board. They simply wanted relevant and quality education. The students were emotionally charged and were tired of the injustices suffered at school. For example, for a girl to qualify as a candidate for homecoming queen, her parents had to be graduates of Crystal City High School. There were not many Chicanos who were eligible. The school board ignored the students' demands and refused to discuss their grievances. By December, tempers were high, and the parents and students organized a school boycott. Picket lines were formed, and after several days, 1700 Chicano students had walked out. During the walkout, meetings were

*Absentee ballots were not really an alternative for the Chicanos; political sophistication was almost nonexistent and, in addition, many could not read or write.

held and a citizens' organization was formed. The Mexican Americans decided at that time that they would take over the school board in the spring election of 1970. A spirit of solidarity developed that was exported to the surrounding areas. More important, this activity polarized the community, putting the issues and the enemy clearly into perspective.[29]

Gutierrez was a realist who knew that the people must organize themselves, so the new organizations were centered around the family. However, he also knew that these groups needed assistance. From the citizens' groups that were formed, *La Raza Unida* party (LRUP) emerged. This party was the vehicle to achieve political self-determination. Gutierrez had to get around the two-party system, which dictated the candidates. He knew that the Chicanos could not always tell the difference between a good and a bad Anglo, but that they knew the difference between a García and a Smith. Intensive organization took place during the first quarter of 1970. In April 1970, LRUP won four of the seven seats on the Crystal City Board of Education, and all of the Chicano city-council candidates were elected in Carrizo Springs, Cotulla, and Crystal City. In Cotulla, the first Chicano mayor was elected. The box score for Chicanos in the Winter Garden area ran: "15 were elected: two new mayors; two school board majorities; and two city council majorities."[30] In all, fifteen *Raza Unida* candidates and one *gringo* were elected. Nationalism, as well as the identification of the enemy, had paid off.

The Chicano-controlled school boards initiated free breakfast and lunch programs, as well as bilingual and bicultural curriculums. They hired more Chicano teachers and counselors. Special programs were initiated for the children of the migrants. Chicano students now take great pride in their school, and for the first time Chicanos are being elected as student representatives.

Chicano control of education has carried over into other fields. Citizens' groups were formed for the express purpose of taking control of Winter Garden's economic institutions. Cooperative buying groups were formed. Chicanos boycotted establishments owned by hostile *gringos,* and many joined together to establish businesses where Chicanos were encouraged to buy. In short, plans are under way to gain economic self-determination by collectively competing with the Anglo-American.*

La Raza Unida party prepared to take control of the county government in the fall of 1970. However, the Establishment did not underestimate the youthful organizers this time around. They knew that the loss of this power would greatly endanger Anglo-American control of the area. The LRUP, moreover, announced that when it took control of the county governments it

---

*It is the author's opinion that the only way the Chicanos of South Texas (or, for that matter, the United States) are going to realize self-determination is for the federal government to intervene and expropriate the land and means of production and give it to the people living in the *barrios* and *colonias.* The same principle must be applied internally that is applied when U.S. business is expropriated abroad.

would bring a suit against the oil companies for back taxes. The oil corporations followed the practice of drilling wells and then capping them. They then classified the wells as nonproductive and therefore did not pay taxes on them. The oil companies then used the capped wells as collateral for prime-interest loans and used the money for further development. The LRUP claimed that the companies were defrauding the people. In Texas, as in other states in the Southwest, oil is power, and this power was used to invalidate the LRUP from the ballot. In spite of this, the party won a few write-in victories, which is significant since a substantial number of the Mexicans in the Winter Garden cannot write.

Today, José Ángel Gutíerrez and other activists are preparing to export their successes to other areas of Texas. The target areas are San Antonio, West and Southwest Texas. Gutíerrez, meanwhile, is a strong advocate of regional development and has traveled extensively throughout the United States to help other regions develop *La Raza Unida* parties. Gutíerrez, Compean, or Guerra can be found in California, Washington, and other states assisting other Chicano groups. Gutíerrez's growing appeal is among those who want hard-core organizations that are determined to gain political and economic power for the Chicano.

Reies López Tijerina

Reies López Tijerina, or *El Tigre,* is undoubtedly the most charismatic of the Chicano leaders. Corky Gonzales once said that "Reies Tijerina put everything he had on the line. You don't get people like that anymore. Everyone wants to go home and watch TV."[31] This, however, has been typical of Tijerina's life; since birth he has been fighting. Born on September 21, 1926, in the farm fields close to Fall City, Texas, he lived a marginal existence, with the Tijerina family, six sons and two daughters, following the crops. Reies soon learned to hate his oppressors, especially the Texas Rangers.

His mother, a devout Catholic, died when Reies was seven years old. In 1942, a Baptist preacher interested him in the Bible. Subsequently, he attended a theological seminary and was ordained. His early years were controversial, and he was arrested on various charges. Eventually, he wandered into northern New Mexico with a handful of faithful disciples. In New Mexico he witnessed the poverty of the Hispanos. The more Tijerina learned about Bill Mundy, a rich agriculturalist in the area, and about the Catrons and the other Anglo-Americans who had robbed the Mexican of his land, the more interested he became in the land-grant question.[32] He studied the Treaty of Guadalupe Hidalgo and became convinced that the national forest in Tierra Amarilla belonged to the *Pueblo de San Joaquín de Chama.* This was *ejido* land (communal or village land) that, according to Hispano-Mexican law, could not be sold and was to be held in common by the people. The villagers had the right to graze their animals and cut and gather timber in these forest lands. The Treaty of Guadalupe, according to Tijerina, committed the U.S. government to protect the rights of the people, but instead it participated in frauds that deprived the people of the *ejido* lands. Tijerina, meanwhile, got involved with the *Albiquiu* Corporation, an organization committed to the return of land grants to the Hispanos.[33]

In the 1960s, Tijerina advocated the return of the land through constitutional means. Gradually, he grew more assertive and called for the return of the land by any means necessary. In 1963, Tijerina incorporated *La Alianza Federal de Mercedes* (the Federal Alliance of Land Grants), which organized to effect the return. Its program appealed to the poor Hispanos and to their lost dreams. *La Alianza* led marches on the state capital, where they petitioned state authorities. On October 15, 1966, Tijerina and *La Alianza* physically occupied the national forest campgrounds known as the Echo Amphitheatre. Three hundred and fifty *Alianza* members asserted the revival of the *ejido* rights of the *Pueblo de San Joaquín de Chama,* whose 1400 acres lay mainly within the confines of the Kit Carson National Forest. The group elected a governing board reminiscent of the *ayuntamiento* (city council) of old and elected an *alcalde* (mayor), Francisco Salazar, who was a direct descendant of the founder of the pueblo. In less than a week, state police, sheriff's deputies, and Rangers began to move in. On October 22, *La Alianza* members took two Rangers into custody and tried them for trespassing and being a public nuisance. The court fined them and handed down a sentence of 11 months and 21 days in jail, then "mercifully" suspended the sentence.[34]

Meanwhile, state authorities called Tijerina a Communist. State District Attorney Alfonso Sánchez vehemently condemned Tijerina. Sánchez intemperately attacked Tijerina to the extent that colleagues termed his remarks "unintelligent." A federal court then demanded that Tijerina hand over a list of *Alianza* members; Tijerina refused and circumvented the order by resigning as president of the association and reorganizing it as *La Confederación de Pueblos Libres.* On November 6, 1967, Tijerina stood trial for the Amphitheatre affair. The original charges included that of conspiracy, but the jury threw it out. It did, however, convict him of two counts of assault. He was sentenced to two years in a state penitentiary, with five years' probation. Tijerina protested that the court had convicted him for a political crime and that the court had no jurisdiction. He appealed the conviction and was released on bond.

Before the trial, Tijerina made national news by leading the so-called raid on the Tierra Amarilla courthouse. District Attorney Alfonso Sánchez continued to harass Tijerina's followers. He attempted to prevent public meetings and arrested several people who were merely on their way to a meeting. He explained that he feared another Amphitheatre incident. Tijerina publicly condemned Sánchez's actions as illegal and, soon afterwards, entered Tierra Amarilla with a group of his followers to make a citizen's arrest of Sánchez. They could not find the district attorney, but they met resistance. A fight broke out and several people were wounded. The Tijerina group then left the area with two lawmen as hostages. The Tierra Amarilla raid touched off a massive manhunt that involved the New Mexican National Guard, planes, helicopters, and tanks. Relatives and suspects were rounded up and kept prisoner in an open yard with a minimum of conveniences. Tijerina decided to surrender, but as soon as he was out on bail, *El Tigre* continued his activities. In October 1967, he took part in the opposition activities to the El Paso Cabinet Committee Hearings, where his followers carried signs stating: "Today We Demonstrate; Tomorrow We Revolt." Tijerina's actions alienated the Hispano Establishment under the leadership of Senator Joseph Montoya of New Mexico. Tijerina appeared on numerous college and university campuses and attended numerous rallies called by Black militants. Meanwhile, his support dwindled in New Mexico. Many of his followers were frightened by his growing militancy. The assassination of John Kennedy, as well as the Black riots, unsettled them. Some New Mexicans were afraid of being associated with Black militants. Senator Joseph Montoya, who up to this point had been silent about Tijerina, now called him "a damned liar; an enemy of the United States; an exploiter, discredited charlatan, imposter, racist, and creature of the darkness."[35] Rumors circulated that Tijerina had bilked the people. Moreover, Tijerina was a *Tejano* (Texan), not a New Mexican; therefore, many *manitos* (diminutive for *Hermanito,* meaning "little brother") resented him as an outsider. Nevertheless, Tijerina's uncompromising tactics gained him the admiration of militants and activists throughout the United States. In May and June 1968, Tijerina participated in the Poor People's Campaign. There, he proved to be an independent leader, threatening to pull the Chicano contingent out if the Black organizers did not treat them better. In the fall of 1968, he ran for governor of New Mexico on the People's Constitutional party ticket.[36]

That fall Tijerina stood trial for the Tierra Amarilla incident. A key witness for the prosecution had been murdered, and it was rumored that Tijerina was responsible. Even elected officials insinuated or accused Tijerina of complicity in the murder. Charges were not brought against him, but an onus settled over the trial. Tijerina was charged with assault on a jail, false imprisonment, and kidnapping. The state tried him separately from the rest of the defendants who were similarly charged. District Attorney Sánchez made the case a personal vendetta and hired Jack Love, who had conducted the Echo Amphitheatre case against Tijerina, as a special prosecutor. He asked for a special appropriation of $40,000 from the state legislature. The case was sensational, with Tijerina charging that the prosecution monitored telephone conversations between him and his attorneys and finally announcing that he would represent himself. Much of the trial centered around the right to make a citizen's arrest. Tijerina proved his points, and the jury ultimately entered a verdict of not guilty.[37]

Tijerina traveled extensively in the months that followed, speaking before student groups. By mid-February 1969, the Tenth Circuit Court of Appeals upheld the Amphitheatre conviction; Tijerina's lawyer immediately appealed to the Supreme Court. On June 5, 1969, *El Tigre* again attempted to occupy the Kit Carson National Forest at the Coyote Campsite. His wife, Patsy, and some of the participants burned a few signs. Two days later, the Rangers and police arrested several of the liberators. Tijerina allegedly resisted and pointed a carbine at one of the Rangers.* He was charged with aiding and abetting the destruction of U.S. Forest Service signs and assaulting and threatening a federal agent. He was sentenced to three years in the federal penitentiary. Several days later, on October 13, Chief Justice Berger refused to hear his appeal on the previous case, and Tijerina went into prison to serve the two sentences concurrently. For seven months he was isolated from the other prisoners, held in what amounted to solitary confinement. To most of the activists, Tijerina became a symbol; the feeling was that he had been convicted of political crimes, rather than of crimes against "society."[38]

Tijerina was released in the summer of 1971. His own thoughts should be analyzed at this point. Before his imprisonment, he became more and more fatalistic, saying on one occasion:

> I used to be afraid of dying. But I'm not afraid anymore. Sometimes I almost want it. Whatever happens, I'm ready now. I have been ever since I first came to New Mexico and found out what I had to do for my people. Somehow, all at once, everything was settled, and I didn't doubt anymore, so I wasn't afraid.[39]

When appearing before an audience, however, his calm evaporated. He told a middle-liberal Establishment audience at St. John College in Santa Fe: "I told Robert F. Kennedy, 'You think you have trouble with the Negroes, wait until we get started; by the year 2000 we will have 600 million people who speak Spanish down across the Rio Grande. . . .' "[40] This was one of Tijerina's constant themes—that the Chicano movement was not limited to the United States, but was inextricably linked to Latin America. Shortly after the above speech before TV cameras and the news media, he declared: "Those who say we are Communist are more Communist than we. What moves us is hunger and a thirst for justice, not desire for fame, for the cinema, for perfumed clothes. We want our land, our rights. They will not beat us with that stick, the dollar. We are 500,000 strong and getting stronger. . . ."[41]

Tijerina also talked about the crucifixion at Tierra Amarilla. He spoke about the new breed and the society that Chicanos would bring about, stating: "There won't be any Anglos of any kind. First we have to become a walking power, like a child. We are not just after land. It isn't just the land. We have to prove our identity, our strength, our knowledge. . . ."[42] He added:

> We are in a good position from the historical point of view, the global point of view. Most nations are against the United States, believing that the U.S. has made a habit to impose its views on other nations. Mankind is sick of these wars and the development of these nuclear weapons. There will be a great destructive war, and when it comes to that day, we will not be blamed.[43]

When asked who the "we" were, he answered: "The Spanish-Americans, the

---

*The deputies had threatened his wife.

Negroes, the darker-skinned people, the nonwhites." Tijerina seemed to see the vision of Armaggedon and the coalition of the Third World peoples—important and growing ideas among the militants he represented.

Corky Gonzales: Barrio Leader

The most influential Chicano leader among the youth—students and *barrio batos*—is Rodolfo "Corky" Gonzales.[44] He is the Chicano leader about whom the least has been written. Corky is in his early 40s, married, the father of eight children, and lives in Denver, Colorado. He came up the hard way —with his fists. A Golden Gloves champion who turned pro, he was a featherweight contender for the championship from 1947 to 1955. Later, he became a bailbondsman. In the 1960s, he worked within the Democratic party of Denver, Colorado, and in 1965 became a director of one of the War on Poverty's youth programs. Soon afterwards, he resigned in disgust. He had grown alienated from the War on Poverty Establishment, as well as the Democratic party. The following year he founded the Crusade for Justice, a community-based organization that emphasized total family involvement. His epic poem, "I am Joaquin," is probably the most influential piece of movement literature ever written. Its impact is immeasurable and Luis Váldez of the *Teatro Campesino* has made it into a movie. These accomplishments alone, however, do not explain Corky's appeal to youth. It is true that he is a well-built, beautifully tanned man and the epitome of the *macho* (male), but there is something more that sets Corky apart from the pack. Chávez appeals to the *campesino* (rural people); he understands them, and they follow him fanatically. The Texas Chicanos listen to José Ángel, for he articulates their frustrations. For a time, Tijerina represented a prophet who would deliver the lands back to their rightful owners; the fact that he did put everything on the line catapulted him into the national limelight. To young people he represented a mixture of Don Quixote and Ché. Corky, however, represents the frustrations of the *bato* and the *barrio* youth, who have been so mesmerized by the public schools that they suffer from a mental block in speaking Spanish. Among the *campesinos* of the Rio Grande Valley, the identity problem does not exist; the Chicanos know that they are Mexican, and they learn Spanish. It is different for the *barrio* dwellers. The schools menace them. Corky understands this, and he understands the loss of identity when the Anglo teacher changes one's name from Rodolfo to Rudolph, when one is punished for speaking Spanish, and he understands the fight against marginality. All this is expressed in his poem. Few of the national leaders really sympathize with the non-Spanish-speaking Chicano. When they go to Delano, they are reprimanded for not knowing Spanish, and the same happens when they go to Texas. However, they can go to Denver, and they are accepted. While followers of the other national leaders might snicker at a young *barrio* youth for yelling, *"Víva la relevacion!"* instead of *"Víva la revolución!"* and might even comment, *"Pendejo* (ass hole)," Corky would understand. He also understands the growing nationalism and the need of *barrio* youth to prove themselves. Such understanding is of increasing significance, since the young people of the urban *barrios* are becoming the majority population of the Chicano community; you find them in San Jose, San Francisco, Oakland, Houston, Denver, and Los Angeles.

Corky, however, is not just a pied piper of youth; he is an organizer. The Crusade for Justice is a family organization. It has a center in which there is a school, a curio shop, a book store, and a social center. The school is called *Tlatelolco, La Plaza de las Tres Culturas.* It has about 200 students, from preschool to college. In the meantime, since Corky is a realist, and since he knows that his school cannot accommodate all Chicano children, he is working for community control of the schools. He states, "We intend to nationalize every school in our community." This thought expresses his main thrust: cultural nationalism and the formation of separate Chicano communities in which Chicanos control their political, economic, social, and educational destinies. He realizes that there can be no liberation until this happens.

Corky was one of the few leaders who realized early that cultural awareness was imperative among the youth, and from the beginning he has encouraged Chicano studies programs at colleges and universities. In this, he demonstrated a patience with youth that others did not have. Expressing a deep insight into organization and an ability to appraise the present situation, he said: "We realize that we have this tremendous lack of polished leadership that can handle all facets of organizing and creating a movement and bring it to a positive solution."[45] In other words, every Chicano is a potential organizer, but he must be trained. To give the Chicano youth of the United States a feeling of movement (which is not necessarily organization—the latter must be done on the local level), he called the First Annual Chicano Youth Conference at Denver in 1969. This is now a yearly event that brings together Chicanos from all the numerous *barrios* for the purpose of exchanging ideas.

In Denver, Corky actively participates in community affairs and has demonstrated that he will not merely plan strategy, but will lead its implementation. In 1969, students walked out of the West Side High School, protesting the discrimination and lack of quality education, and demanding more Chicano teachers and administrators. Corky went with parents to support the students and to demonstrate against school authorities. They were harassed by the police, and an altercation followed in which both sides sustained injuries. In addition, several squad cars were damaged and a few policemen roughed up; the Chicanos seemed to have gotten the best of things. The police termed the incident a "riot," and Corky and a number of other Chicanos were arrested; however, at the trials, films were produced that proved that it was actually a "police riot," and the defendants were acquitted.

Gonzales also was instrumental in establishing *La Raza Unida* party in Colorado, which ran candidates for state and local offices on November 4, 1970. He organized the party in his state because he maintains that along with awareness, a political philosophy must be developed. Hopefully, *La Raza Unida* party is the vehicle of this philosophy.

In the 1970 election, *La Raza Unida* received between 2 and 5 percent of the vote. Many would be disappointed by the results—no offices were won. However, Gonzales knew that the party could not win in the conventional sense; he points out that, as a result of the party's activities, two Chicanos were elected to the Colorado House of Representatives on the Democratic ticket. Also, he knows that he hit a nerve, for police indicated how worried they were by raiding the Crusade for Justice Center at 3:00 A.M. on election day. The police said they were looking for arms, but they held volunteers incommunicado at the Center for a number of hours. They also broke down doors, destroyed equipment, and took tapes and the film *I Am Joaquin.* Moreover, $800 in cash was missing after the Denver police left.

Gonzales has stated that young people want action and that they are tired of meetings. Through his organization, youth are provided with an alternative. In his various activities, he astutely realizes that "There are different levels of revolutionary action."

Conclusion

By the 1960s, Chicanos constituted the second-largest minority in the United States. Their sheer numbers made them a threat to the status quo. The Anglo majority had the choice of absorbing them, remaking its own society to enable cultural and political pluralism to function, or protecting the master-servant relationship at any cost. Although giving lip service to the first two, Anglo-Americans actually have become more color conscious during the last decade and, at the same time, more defensive about their Anglo-American ways, especially the economy. Meanwhile, the migration of Mexicans to the city has given roots to the community, which in turn has enhanced its political potential. The urbanization of the Chicano ended the odyssey that, in some cases, has lasted for 50 years. This was important, since a society on the move has little opportunity to organize itself. The stabilization of the Chicano community solidified it and gave the members the base with which to begin to confront their oppressor.

Prior to the 1960s, most Mexican professionals had been socialized by the system, and they vigorously supported it. In turn, the privileged used them to keep the colony under control. During this time, youth sought their own identity and revolted against their parents in many cases, admonishing them for failing to teach them Spanish and for not preserving the Mexican culture. Like youth throughout the United States, the Chicano rejected the materialism of Anglo-American society. What distinguished Chicano youth from Anglo youth was that the former belonged to a community that lacked political and economic self-determination; in other words, they were members of a colonized group. Furthermore, they could be distinguished by their color. The Mexicans' background also gave them a natural community of interests with the Third World people of Latin America. Lastly, culture has played a significant role in setting the Chicano apart from the colonizer. He had a different language, attitudes, and life style.

Youth, as we have seen, added drama to the Chicano movement. Numbers could be counted upon to support an issue. Moreover, they were important because they added the possibility of violence, which has always been the stimulus to which Anglo-American society best responds. The weakness of the youth movement is that, except for a few cases, it has produced few organizers. In fact, this has been one of the weaknesses of the Chicano movement to date: too many leaders and not enough solid organizations. As we have seen, going into the 1970s, this trend is changing. More regional leaders are appearing who are directly responsible to specific bases rather than to Chicanos in general.

In conclusion, this chapter has dealt with the 1960s, which was a decade that saw the solidifying of the Chicano community and its recognition by national leaders. Attempts to gain an equity in society through the system failed, and a stalemate resulted that was broken by the entrance of youth into the movement. Extralegal methods became more usual, giving spirit to the struggle. By the end of the 1960s one thing was certain: most activists were disillusioned with the existing system, and many were calling for separatism and bidding good-bye to America. The next chapter focuses on the reasons for the disillusionment.

Notes

1. Leo Grebler, Joan W. Moore, and Ralph Guzman, *The Mexican-American People* (New York: The Free Press, 1970), p. 29.

2. Carey McWilliams, *North From Mexico* (New York: Greenwood Press, Publishers, 1968), pp. 15–16.

3. Grebler, Moore, and Guzman, p. 106. The 1970 census reported that there are over three million Spanish-surnamed residents legally in California (16.1 percent of the state's population). The white and Black communities remained constant during the 1960s. Many Chicanos project that the Spanish-surnamed population will reach 30 percent of Californians by 1980. (*Los Angeles Times,* 23 December 1971.)

4. Grebler, Moore, and Guzman, p. 185.

5. Grebler, Moore, and Guzman, p. 251.

6. Grebler, Moore, and Guzman, p. 126.

7. Grebler, Moore, and Guzman, p. 143.

8. Grebler, Moore, and Guzman, p. 150.

9. Grebler, Moore, and Guzman, p. 196.

10. Grebler, Moore, and Guzman, p. 211.

11. I have been involved in community organizations since the early 1960s and have observed much of the ferment.

12. "Revolt of the Mexicans," *Time* magazine, 12 April 1963.

13. Mark Day, *Forty Acres* (New York: Frederick A. Praeger, Publishers, 1971), pp. 41–42.

14. Jack Woddis, *Introduction to Neo-Colonialism* (New York: International Publishers, 1967), p. 105.

15. McWilliams, p. 17. I had extensive conversations with Miguel Montes and Louis Garcia, both of San Fernando, California, who participated in the conference. They felt that what they did was a radical act, and so did most of us at that time.

16. McWilliams, p. 17.

17. Richard Gardner, *Grito! Reies Tijerina and the New Mexico Land Grant War of 1967* (New York: The Bobbs-Merrill Company, Inc., 1970), pp. 231–232; Rudy Acuña, *A Mexican*

American Chronicle (New York: American Book Company, 1971), p. 131.

18.   Ironically, an M.A. thesis on the East Los Angeles walkouts has been written: Nyle C. Frank, "An Analysis of the March 1968 East Los Angeles High School Walkouts" (M.A. thesis, University of North Carolina at Chapel Hill, 1968). Professor Carlos Muñoz, of the Department of Political Science, University of California at Irvine, is doing definitive research on the topic.

19.   I attended numerous meetings during the walkout and was in close contact with many participants. Many of the former walkout students are now students in my classes.

20.   *El Plan de Santa Barbara: A Chicano Plan for Higher Education,* Chicano Coordinating Council for Higher Education (Oakland, Calif.: La Causa Publications, 1969).

21.   Our focus is on the Los Angeles chapter, since it was the first and the best-known chapter. Data on the rural chapters are almost impossible to gather. See Rona M. Fields and Charles J. Fox, "Viva La Raza: The Saga of the Brown Berets" (Manuscript). Additional information was obtained by interviewing members of the Brown Berets.

22.   John Ortiz, an associate editor of *Regeneración,* offered pertinent insights.

23.   Fields and Fox.

24.   Patty Newman, *Do It Up Brown!* (San Diego, Calif.: Viewpoint Books, 1971), p. 286. This is a right-wing work. The author totally ignored the context of the speech. The *gringo* was the symbol of colonization, and Gutíerrez's purpose was to encourage Chicanos to cast off this domination by killing the symbolic *gringo.*

25.   José Ángel Gutíerrez, "Aztlán: Chicano Revolt in the Winter Garden," *La Raza* 1, no. 4 (1971): 34–35.

26.   Gutíerrez, p. 37.

27.   Gutíerrez, p. 37.

28.   Conversations and interviews with José Ángel Gutíerrez and other well-known organizers.

29.   Gutíerrez, pp. 39–40.

30.   Gutíerrez, p. 40.

31.   Gardner, p. 208.

32.   Peter Nabokov, *Tijerina and the Courthouse Raid* (Albuquerque: University of New Mexico Press, 1969), pp. 163–164.

33.   Nabokov, pp. 19, 28, 30; Gardner, pp. 66–84.

34.   Gardner, pp. 129–130.

35.   Gardner, p. 235.

36.   Nabokov, pp. 250, 256.

37.   Nabokov, pp. 257–266; Gardner, pp. 265–279. The latter presents a gripping account of the trial.

38.   Gardner, p. 290.

39.   Gardner, p. 259.

40.   Gardner, p. 259.

41.   Gardner, pp. 210–211.

42.   Gardner, p. 213.

43.   Gardner, p. 214.

44.   Much of the material on "Corky" Gonzales has been pieced together by interviewing people in the movement. I understand that he is writing an autobiography, which will be a major contribution, since his role has been most important to the development of Chicano awareness. Stan Steiner, in *La Raza: The Mexican Americans* (New York: Harper & Row, Publishers, Inc., 1969), pp. 378–392, has included a rare chapter on Gonzales.

45.   *The Militant,* 4 December 1970.

Chapter Ten

Goodbye America, II

Awareness increased among Chicanos during the 1960s and the direction of the movement solidified. Considerable pluralism in approaches to the movement developed, and a common cultural base unified Mexicans at the different levels of involvement. Although activists realized that they did not have control of their economic destinies, it was more difficult to convince them that they lacked political self-determination; they were in the habit of voting for candidates of the Democratic party or blaming the failure of the system on the apathy of their own people. A growing number have now realized that their political captivity was closely related to their economic status. As mentioned, this chapter examines why Mexicans became disillusioned with the system. Disillusionment has been predicated by the political realities, the Catholic church, the effect of the Vietnam war and the Chicano moratoria, and the lack of justice for Chicanos in the United States.

The Political Realities

At the root of the internal problem is the lack of political control by those in the colony. Chicanos in the United States have almost no political representation at the local, state, or national level. The reason for this is that those with power never intended them to have representation. The Mexican is poor and, therefore, without a voice in the political process, which is predicated on campaign contributions and the ability to convince those in power that you deserve a share. Jess Unruh, a former Speaker of the California Assembly, graphically summed up the importance of money in politics when he stated that "Money is the mother's milk of politics." The Chicano, therefore, remains one of the few minorities in this nation that has not achieved political self-determination. As oppressed as the Black American has been, he has fared much better in politics than the Mexican, since in a few cases he has been included in the Democratic party's councils. Outside of New Mexico, the Chicano has been the victim of a conspiracy to keep him from gaining political representation and has been gerrymandered and managed for the benefit of a few politicos. The following case studies illustrate this point.

The California Story

In California, there is not one Chicano elected to state office; there has not been a Chicano in the state senate since the 1880s, and at the present time, there are only two assemblymen—Alex García and Peter Chacón. This condition is the result of a strategy of the Democratic party to exploit the community's vote without allowing them to control a representative.

In the past, Chicanos have attempted to run for state office and in two cases have won the Democratic party primary. In both cases—Ed Roybal (1954) and Hank López (1958)—the party subsequently did not support the candidates. The party leadership even refused to contribute to their campaigns. In 1970, another Chicano attempted to run for a state office. Max Rafferty, the state superintendent of schools, was bidding for a third term. Dr. Julian Nava, president of the board of education of the Los Angeles city schools, declared his intention to run for that office. He had refused gubernatorial candidate Jess Unruh's invitation to share the Democratic party ticket as the candidate for lieutenant governor, although the latter promised that political patronage intended for Chicanos would be assigned to Nava to dispense if he ran. Meanwhile, a committee of white liberals headed by Dormon Commons, vice-president of Occidental Petroleum and former member of the California Board of Education, met and decided to support Wilson Riles, a Black man, for that office. The committee had no Black or Chicano members and was, in fact, comprised of a small clique of about eight Anglos. Its main power was that it could raise money. The members were upset with Nava for wanting to run, for, after all, they had made their decision. They believed that Nava's candidacy would lessen Riles' chances in the primary. Pressure was applied on Nava to drop out of the race.* However, he refused to be dictated to by a small self-appointed group and ran for office anyway. His campaign lacked funds and was stymied from the beginning. He came in third. Ironically, he pulled enough votes away from the other two candidates to force a run-off between Riles and the incumbent. The well-known political reality is that money is necessary to conduct statewide campaigns, and Chicanos run only by the grace of the moneymen who control the party.

The Democratic party of California has practiced a domestic imperialism in its relationship with the Chicano community. It has gerrymandered and politically emasculated the *barrios.*** An example of this kind of colonialism is the large Chicano *barrio* of East Los Angeles that encompasses the east end of the city and an unincorporated portion of Los Angeles County and has a Chicano population of some 750,000. In addition, of the estimated 4.5 million to 5 million inhabitants in Los Angeles County, Chicanos number close to a million. In spite of this, there is not one county supervisor or city councilman of Mexican extraction. In fact, in the city portion of the big *barrio,* the community has been gerrymandered three ways, with the Ninth, Thirteenth, and Fourteenth council districts purposely cutting into it, picking up just enough of the Mexican population to make the district seat safe for the incumbents. The same thing happens in the East Los Angeles community as a whole. There are five assembly districts in East Los Angeles: the Fortieth, the Forty-fifth, the Forty-eighth, the Fiftieth, and the Fifty-first. Each of these districts has a heavy concentration of Chicano voters, and rarely do Mexicans constitute 30 percent of the districts' voting population. Only one of the districts, the Fortieth, has elected a Mexican American to the Assembly, and even that seat is not "safe." The same underrepresentation occurs with the state senatorial and the U.S. congressional districts. At the congressional level, there is one Chicano congressman from California, although Chicanos comprise 16 percent of the state's population. Congressman Ed Roybal represents the Thirtieth Congressional District. However, he openly admits that he is not totally representing Chicanos, since his district is not exclusively Chicano. He has to rely on Japanese, Filipino, Jewish, Black, and Anglo support. His district is under 30 percent Chicano. Privately, Roybal has lamented the situation. It is estimated that two if not three good Chicano congressional districts could be carved out of East Los Angeles. At present, it is gerrymandered to include the Nineteenth, Twenty-third, Twenty-ninth, and Thirtieth. The result is that Chicanos do not control their political destinies.

---

*I attended the meeting between the Commons group and Julian Nava.

**"Gerrymandering" is the practice of drawing up political districts by fixing the boundaries to favor one or the other political party. The districts are not drawn up to represent a community or a compact area, but are purposely drafted to take in a large percentage of the registered voters of the favored party. This has resulted in odd-shaped districts. In California, Mexicans charge that the Democratic party has remained in power and in control of the state legislature at the expense of the Chicano community. Chicanos are dispersed throughout the state, and in almost all cases, their communities have been gerrymandered to beef up safe Democratic party strongholds. In return, the party has taken the Chicano vote for granted and even discouraged Chicano candidates.

In the Los Angeles city schools, a district of almost 700,000 students, with a budget approaching $1 billion, the Chicano community has only one representative on the seven-man board of education. Representatives to the school board are elected at large; that is, they are elected by the registered voters as a whole. Chicano students comprise about 23 percent of the students in the Los Angeles School District (the percentage would be higher if parochial schools were included), and Blacks comprise another 23 percent. If other racial minorities were included in this count, the minorities would form a majority for the district, and if they voted in a bloc, they could gain more seats on the board.* But instead of controlling their schools, Chicanos have only one member on the board of education; the Blacks do not have a representative. Conservative members dominate the body. The Chicano representative is compromised, since if he wants to get reelected, he cannot become a Chicano advocate. In sum, Chicanos have no control over the education of their children.**

A further indictment of the Democratic party is the case of Richard Calderon. In 1966 he ran against Assemblyman George Danielson in the Democratic primary election for an open state senate seat. He had considerable support in the Chicano community. The United Auto Workers, the Californians for Liberal Representation, and Women For (a very powerful association of liberal women in Los Angeles) supported him. Moreover, Congressman George Brown of the Twenty-ninth District supported him. In spite of this support, however, he lost by 301 votes. Why? Chicano apathy? No; the deck was stacked. The year before, Danielson had been named vice-chairman of the Reapportionment Committee, which had redrawn the senatorial district. Everyone knew that the new district was potentially Chicano. By coincidence or design, 8000 Chicanos were lopped off the senate district by the Reapportionment Committee, making it impossible for Chicanos to consolidate behind one candidate.*** Furthermore, Danielson's forces got a number

---

*The major problems standing in the way of bloc voting are the political unawareness and a lack of effective organizing among the different minorities.

**School officials are, at the present time, going through the motions of decentralizing; they say their actions are designed to give a greater voice to the local communities. It is too early to judge the effectiveness of their moves; however, I am skeptical because the ultimate power rests, not with the board of education, but with the bureaucrats that run the gigantic district. A better move would' have been to break the system up into at least 24 autonomous districts, with a countywide tax base to support them.

***At the present time, the state legislature is again redistricting California. Presentations have been made before the appropriate committee hearings by members of the Chicano community, pointing out that, according to population ratios, the community is entitled to at least four to seven new seats. There have been a number of news editorials endorsing the need for more Chicano representation and requesting that the legislature address itself to that problem. State Senator Merv Dymally, a Black and in the past sympathetic to Chicanos, is the chairman of the Senate Committee on Reapportionment. He had promised more representation for Chicanos; however, in the last days of July 1971, Dymally stated that the Chicanos probably would get only one additional seat, since any further change would jeopardize party balance in the Senate. This is an example of how, to even the most sympathetic elected officials, party loyalty is more important than self-determination for Chicanos.

of candidates with Spanish surnames to file for the office in order to split the Chicano vote. Ten candidates, five of whom were Chicanos, ran in the election. Only two of these five Chicanos acted as though they believed they had a chance. One of the Chicanos attacked Calderon personally; another, a woman, suddenly acquired a travel agency a month after the campaign—a time when most candidates are broke from the campaign costs. The result was that they split the Chicano vote. Calderon lost by a bare 301 votes.*

The Calderon experience is typical. In November of 1971 Chicanos changed their tactics and attempted to change their dependency on the Democratic party. They exercised their power to disrupt and ran Raúl Ruiz, a professor at San Fernando Valley State College and an editor of *La Raza* magazine, as a candidate for the Forty-eighth Assembly District. The Democrats spent over $100,000 in support of their candidates for that seat. Ralph Ochoa and Richard Alatorre were handpicked by two prominent Democratic politicians in a power struggle for control of the Democratic party in California. Alatorre won the Democratic primary and seemed to be a likely winner, since the district was over 65 percent Democrat. However, when the final results came in, approximate totals were:

Republican candidate	47 percent
Democratic candidate	42 percent
La Raza Unida Candidate	7 percent**

Alatorre pointed up the difference between his viewpoint and that of LRUP when he said that he believed the Democrats had worked for the Chicano; *La Raza Unida,* on the other hand, claimed that the Democratic party had not represented their interests. To LRUP it was a question of self-determination—i.e., who pulled the strings?

The outcome was significant, since *La Raza Unida* party spent a total of only $3000 for the special primary and the run-off elections. Chicano precincts, which traditionally voted overwhelmingly for Democratic candidates, voted from 20 to 95 percent for Ruiz.[1] Moreover, the Chicano vote represented only 10 to 15 percent of the registered voters of the district. In beating the Democrats, it illustrated that Chicanos had the power to disrupt and that they would not be managed by a few powerful Democrats.

The election was also important in the context of the current California reapportionment, in which the Democrats gerrymandered the state in an obvious attempt to perpetuate their power. Although Democratic politicians

---

*This information comes from a taped interview I had with Richard Calderon in April 1971. I had been a volunteer worker for the campaign.

**The results indicate that the 65 percent Democratic population either did not vote or that there was some crossover to the Republican party. The significant point, however, is that if *La Raza Unida* had not run a candidate and if the 7 percent of the vote it received had gone to Alatorre, the Democratic candidate would have won the election.

admit that the Mexican is underrepresented, they need his bloc vote to elect incumbents. Therefore, in their original reapportionment plan, they did not create any new assembly or congressional districts that contained a Chicano majority, and only one state senate seat. This was so arbitrary that the Republicans used that fact as an excuse to condemn the reapportionment plan. The Republican governor vetoed the plan, accusing the Democrats of purposely using the Mexicans to keep Democrats in office. According to the 1970 census figures, Spanish-surnamed Californians comprise some 16 percent of the population. Their representation, however, does not reflect this figure:

Total No. of Representatives	No. of Chicano Representatives Proportional to Chicano Population*	Actual No. of Chicano Representatives
Calif. Assembly 80	12.8	2
Calif. Senate 40	6.4	0
U.S. Congress 43	6.88	1

In view of the fact that their representation is *disproportionate* to their numbers, many Chicanos favor exercising the only power they have: disruption of the Democratic party. In doing so, they are calling attention to issues that have been ignored by the Democrats and Republicans, as well as to the inequities of the political system.**

The Texas Story

O. Douglas Weeks, a professor at the University of Texas in the 1930s, described politics as a "great game." For Chicanos of South Texas, it has been a game in which the rules have been arranged so they could never win. The Anglo-Americans gained economic and political control of the Rio Grande Valley through violence, and by the same means they have perpetuated this power.

The Anglo superimposed on the state a system he knew well, but to the Chicano it was foreign. He was more familiar with localized participation where the *alcalde* was well known to the people and where corruption was obvious to him. In the Anglo system, politicians talked about democracy,

---

*I.e., if California Chicanos were represented in the state legislature and in the U.S. Congress *in proportion* to their numbers in the total state population.

**We have focused on the Democratic party, because that part traditionally has claimed to be responsive to the Chicano community. The Republicans have not geared their programs to minorities and, in turn, have not received their support. Moreover, while Governor Ronald Regan of California has spoken out for Chicano representation, his record of appointments for Chicanos to commissions and committees has been dismal. When the Ryan Commission was formed to revamp teacher training in California, the governor did not appoint a single Chicano to the 15-member commission. A few months ago, he appointed one.

about a system that the people controlled, but the reality was something different. From the start, the Anglo's approach was the "patronage reward system" used by eastern political machines.

Colonel Stephen Powers, who had been a Tammany Hall politician, established the Democratic party machine in South Texas in the 1870s. In 1882, Jim Wells, a lawyer-politician, assumed control of this machine, which dominated electoral politics in the thirteen counties of the Rio Grande Valley. Cameron County was his own bailiwick. He owned large tracts of land, which he ruled like a Southern plantation owner. He became a patriarch to the Chicanos; he attended weddings and funerals and became a godfather to many children. In time of need, he used his own money to help Chicanos. Judge Wells knew how to rule, and he once said:

> The Mexican people . . . if you understand them, are the most humble people you ever knew. . . . They are largely like Indians in that respect. Their friendship is individual. For instance, you have a great many friends among them, and they would follow your name and your fortunes, and that is the way it is . . .[2]

Wells ruled through *caciques* (local bosses) who were loyal to him, and in return, he was generous to them. By 1920, Wells's political empire was too large for one man to control. The reclamation of the area with citrus orchards and vegetable truck farms pushed the population of the valley from 100,000 in 1910 to 170,000 ten years later, and to 326,000 in 1928. After Wells left politics, the control of the area's political machinery was taken over by more ruthless men. Again, control was predicated on the Mexican vote. This electorate was kept in line through numerous methods:

1. A poll tax was instituted that discouraged Mexicans from voting, since they did not have the money. The Democratic party bosses often capitalized on this either by encouraging the Chicano vote to remain low in relation to the votes of Anglo-Americans and Mexicans who were loyal to them, or by paying the tax for selected Chicanos in return for their commitment to vote their way.

2. Growers rounded up their workers and herded them to the polls. If the vote went against the grower's man, many Chicanos lost their jobs or their homes or were otherwise intimidated.

3. The party bosses many times had workers register Mexican aliens to vote for the machine candidate.

4. The party registered or reregistered dead Chicanos and had their cronies vote for the dead voters.

5. Many false ballots were printed and the ballot boxes stuffed with these ballots which were marked with the party's selected candidates.

6. When Chicanos attempted to break this syndrome, the Texas Rangers

were called out to intimidate their rallies and even beat Chicanos, discouraging them from voting. Many times, Chicano leaders who opposed the machine were arrested by the Rangers or the local police.

7. The party controlled the Mexican community through the patronage system. Chicanos were paid off by the party to work for it and to keep the Mexicans voting Democrat. Chicanos were given nonelective jobs, such as janitor, street sweeper, sheriff, county clerk, etc. Their jobs depended on their ability to deliver the vote.

As a result, the Mexican vote was always delivered by the Democratic machine, and the Democratic party in Texas stayed in power.

To the west of the Rio Grande Valley in the Winter Garden area, politics followed a similar pattern. *La Raza Unida* party was formed there, and plans were made to take over local and county politics. The main thrust of the party's effort was to gain control of school systems. As we discussed in chapter 9, Chicanos knew that working through the Democratic party was useless, since their community would never have a voice in the nomination of candidates. It is true that open primaries were, and are, held, but the Chicanos of that area followed a pattern of migration that undermined their participation in the system. In the spring they left to follow the crops, and they did not return to Winter Garden until late summer or early fall. The Democratic party primaries were held after the Chicanos left, and the general elections were held after they returned. Therefore, they had no voice in the nomination of candidates, and their vote only counted to elect a party hack. Write-in campaigns were not a viable solution, because in many places the median educational grade level of the Chicano was below the second grade. Therefore, the solution was *La Raza Unida* party, which could run its own slate of Chicano candidates that would be controlled by Chicanos.

The party suffered a setback during the fall 1970 elections, when, on a technicality, *La Raza Unida* candidates were excluded from the ballot. As an alternative, the impossible was tried: a write-in campaign. People who had never written before were taught to write the Chicano candidate's name. In La Salle County, one *La Raza Unida* candidate was elected, another lost by only 40 votes, and still another lost by only 46 votes. In the city of Cotulla, Roel Rodríguez was elected mayor. On April 3, 1971, *La Raza Unida* candidates for the board of education of Crystal City, Texas, won—giving Chicanos a five-to-two majority on the board. Three days later, in the municipal elections, LRUP won three positions on the city council by a two-to-one majority, giving the party control of all five seats on that body. Mass rallies were held at which María Hernández, a 75-year-old Chicana whose son was killed in World War II, proclaimed, "We are going to be repaid for that sacrifice [referring to the loss of Chicano lives in the war] by rising up and demanding our rights."[3] The crux of this struggle was that 85 percent of the Winter Garden residents are Chicano. Establishment sources look upon this challenge as a threat, since if Chicanos could control the region politically, the economic privilege of the few would also be challenged.

Crystal City is an indication of what happens when Chicanos get control. There, the educational system is being revamped to *educate* Chicanos and other students, not just to train them to work on the farms of South Texas growers. Moreover, city officials are challenging deals made in the past between industrialists and their agents. For example, Chicanos ended the special status of the Del Monte Corporation's food-processing factory just outside the city limits. The company moved to the area in 1945. At that time, the Anglo-controlled city council promised the company that it would never be taxed, never be regulated, and never be incorporated into the city limits. In this way, the Del Monte Corporation circumvented the city codes and the supervision of the city police. It had only dealt with the Texas Rangers, of which it had control.

When Chicanos had captured the city council previously in 1963, the Del Monte Corporation decided to formalize the agreement before the newly elected councilmen assumed office. They signed a seven-year contract with the lame-duck Anglo-controlled council that protected these "rights." When the Chicanos won in 1970, Del Monte again attempted to enter into a collusive contract with the outgoing council. However, this time it made a mistake. The city councilman who signed the contract was a foreman at the Del Monte plant. Under Texas law, this constituted a conflict of interest, and, therefore, the contract was invalid. Chicano city councilmen took steps to incorporate the area where the Del Monte plant was located. The collusion had cost the city about $13,000 a year in taxes. José Ángel Gutíerrez, the leader of LRUP, pointed out that over the past ten years the contract represented a loss of $130,000 in tax income. Gutíerrez further stated that the amount lost is even more significant; when one considers the funds for educational and civic projects that would have been matched by federal funds, the amount runs to over $600,000. The agreement, therefore, was at the expense of the children —Chicano and Anglo alike.

Furthermore, the Del Monte Corporation signed a sweetheart contract with the Teamsters Union. The Del Monte employees, who were mostly Chicanos, asked José Ángel Gutíerrez of the LRUP to be their business agent. He accepted, but Teamster officials balked at the idea. The Teamsters had negotiated a contract with Del Monte, but the members had had to approve it. Union officials, in cooperation with the Del Monte officials, locked the employees into a large room and demanded that they vote on the contract. Those voting "yes" would put their ballots into one box; the "no" votes would go into another box. The men refused to vote. There were 257 workers in the plant; 247 quit the Teamsters and joined a new union called *Los Obreros Unidos Independientes* (The Independent United Workers). The Teamsters showed their disregard for the workers; they had four of the ten men remaining in the Teamsters sign the contract with Del Monte. Under Texas contract law, the Chicano union was prohibited from challenging the contract, because once labor and management sign a contract, it is binding until its termination date. But Chicanos challenged the contract on the grounds of fraud. Since the fall of 1970, Chicanos have refused to join the Teamsters under the right-to-work provision of the present labor laws. These laws, which generally worked to the advantage of management, in this case fortunately worked to the advantage of the Chicano workers.[4]

The Chicanos' plight is not limited to South Texas or to the Winter Garden district. Robert Coles, a medical doctor, and Harry Huge, an attorney, have researched hunger among the Mexicans in San Antonio and other parts of Texas. In an article, "Thorns on the Yellow Rose of Texas,"[5] they reported that the Mexican comprised 41.7 percent of the 700,000 people of San Antonio. After an extensive investigation, they concluded that two San Antonios existed, one that was Anglo-American and the other that was Mexican. They further reported that city officials admitted that 28 percent of the families had an income of less than $3000 per year, whereas 6 percent earned under $1000. Coles and Huge painted a dismal picture of the city's west side, which is one of the Mexican *barrios.*

> What San Antonio's officials spell out, we saw: unpaved, undrained streets; homes without water; homes with outdoor privies; homes that are nothing but rural shacks packed together in an urban ghetto that comprises 8 percent of San Antonio's land area, but whose residents must put up with a far higher percentage of suffering—32.3 percent of the city's infant deaths; 44.6 percent of its tuberculosis; and well over half its mid-wife deliveries. After we had gone from home to home on one street, we began to realize that in almost every way thousands of people are walled off—as in the ghettoes once present in Europe.[6]

The authors reported that they met few whites on the west side.

Everywhere they went, the investigators found that the picture repeated itself. They quoted Albert Peña, one of Bexar County's four commissioners, as saying of the plight of the poor Chicano:

> They've gerrymandered the city so that the Mexican Americans have one congressman and the rest of the city shares two others. They won't let our children speak Spanish in school. . . . The children are scared and confused; soon they drop out. . . . As for welfare and public assistance, it's almost unbelievable. Over 100,000 people in the county make below $2000 a year, but only 20,000 people get public assistance, and *less* than that have been allowed to take part in the Agriculture Department's food program.[7]

Coles and Huge found that:

> Fifty-two percent of all Mexican Americans in Texas over 25 finished only four years of school, and a mere 11 percent went to high school. The city manager of San Antonio admits that 44.3 percent of the Mexican Americans are "functionally illiterate." The 1960 census showed that 20 percent of adult Mexican Americans in Bexar County have not completed any years of school at all.[8]

Coles and Huge painted an equally dismal picture of the Chicanos' plight in the rest of Texas. They pointed out that Texas was a rich state:

Texaco had a net income of $754,386,000 in 1967; Gulf managed to reap $578,-287,000 that year; and Sinclair, a modest $95,322,000. At the same time, as of November 1968, Texas, whose large cities and industrial wealth make it comparable to Michigan and Pennsylvania, ranks 47th among states in welfare payments per recipient. . . .

In one congressional district, during 1966, the poor received $244,000 in food assistance from the U.S. Department of Agriculture, whereas 0.01 percent of the people, the rich farmers, got $5,318,892 in benefits from that same department.[9] In short, the political and economic realities in Texas are that Chicanos are controlled by an oligarchy of white Anglo capitalists.

The Story of the Catholic Church

As we have mentioned, the Roman Catholic church is the most important institution to the Chicano, aside from the family. However, his status within that church is even worse than in the political and economic life of the United States. Until recently, the church's authority stood unchallenged by the older generation; but again, youth led to the critical questioning as to its relevance. Groups like MAYO in Texas criticized its hypocrisy and led demonstrations against it. In November 1969, opposition crystallized with the formation of an organization called *Católicos Por La Raza* (CPLR), which was led by a young law student, Ricardo Cruz, from Loyola University Law School. The organization's members were infuriated over the closing, because of the alleged lack of funds, of Our Lady Queen of Girls' High School, which was predominately Mexican. At the same time, Cardinal James Francis McIntyre had just had a $4-million cathedral built as a memorial to himself. Moreover, the members were incensed at the church's refusal to involve itself in promoting social justice for Mexicans.

The responsibility of the church to Chicanos has already been documented, since 65 percent of the Catholics in the Southwest are Mexican. However, Mexicans have little voice in this institution; less than 180 priests are of Mexican extraction. and in 1969, there were no Chicano bishops in the United States. The power remained in the hands of a few Irishmen.

The church's power was immense. In 1970, *La Raza* magazine researched the holdings of the church in Los Angeles County and estimated that it owned about $1 billion in real property alone. Most of this property was tax free, and in other cases, the church was an absentee landlord to the poor. The cardinal, himself, lived in a palace in one of the most exclusive districts of the city, and was chauffeured about in a Cadillac. The cardinal represented everything that was material.

On Christmas Eve of 1969, members of *Católicos Por La Raza* demonstrated in front of St. Basil's Cathedral. The picketing was peaceful and orderly. When the Mass began, the demonstrators, who were for the most part

256

Catholics, attempted to enter the church to listen to the Mass. They were locked out, and when a few gained entrance, they were met by sheriff's deputies who were acting as ushers. These "ushers" were armed, and they carried clubs, which they used to expel the demonstrators. Units of the Los Angeles Police Department arrived almost immediately, and they continued the violence. They arrested 21 demonstrators, 20 of whom stood trial for disturbing the peace and for assaults on police officers. Ricardo Cruz was convicted of a misdemeanor. This was Cruz's first and last arrest; however, since then he has passed the California Bar examinations, yet that body has refused to certify him because of his involvement in the demonstrations. On May 8, 1972, he began serving a 120-day sentence for his conviction.[10]

Católicos Por La Raza brought national notoriety by their disruption. They were supported by Chicanos throughout the Southwest, but condemned by many nonactivists. Shortly afterwards, a Chicano bishop in Texas, Patrick Fernándes Flores, was elevated to the post of auxiliary bishop. Cardinal James Francis McIntyre retired, but not before, in a fit of anger, he told a group of Chicano students: "I was here before there were even Mexicans. I came to Los Angeles 21 years ago."[11] The church was also forced to play a more active role in the farm workers' struggle, and it actively mediated between the growers and Chávez. Many attribute the increased involvement of the church to the pressure of *Católicos Por La Raza*.

The church continues to treat Mexicans in a patronizing manner. Seminarians who are close to Bishop Flores claim that he is infuriated by discrimination in the Anglo-American seminaries and that he would like to found a Chicano seminary. They charge that, in 1970, 12 Chicanos from the Rio Grande Valley of Texas were sent to a seminary in the Midwest. However, after their parents had outfitted them at considerable personal sacrifice, 11 were sent back when they did not pass an aptitude test. In short, there is discrimination in the church, and most Anglo-American priests have refused to get involved in questions of social justice. Nevertheless, conditions are changing.

As we have said, most Anglo and Mexican Catholics condemned CPLR after the violence of December 24, 1969. However, opinion has changed. At a meeting at a Mexican Catholic church in Lincoln Heights in East Los Angeles on January 13, 1972, I heard devout Catholics praise the CPLR before Jesús García, the papal delegate, and Tomás Clavel, archbishop of Panama. The papal delegate is charged with reporting to the pope on conditions in Latin America and with promoting the involvement of the church in social-action programs. His authority has been extended to the Chicano in the United States, whom many churchmen now consider a colonized people. Father García encouraged those present to get involved in the economic and political liberation of their people. He condemned the church and the state as being too materialistic, telling the people that it was their duty to confront the oppressors. The papal delegate, ironically, was expressing what CPLR had said two years before.

The Vietnam war has politicized the Chicano community, clearly identifying the oppressor and crystallizing the exploitation of the poor. Statistics indicate that the rate of Chicano deaths in Vietnam is greater than that of the general population. Dr. Ralph Guzmán, political scientist from the University of California at Santa Cruz, points out that between January 1961 and February 1967, although the Chicano population was officially 10 to 12 percent of the total population of the Southwest, the Chicano comprised 19.4 percent of those from that area who were killed. From December 1967 to March 1969, Chicanos suffered 19 percent of all casualties from the Southwest. During this same period, Chicanos from Texas, where discrimination is the crudest, sustained 25.2 percent of the casualties of that state.[12] These statistics are well known among Chicano activists, who have launched protests against the war. Moreover, these activists protest the denial of self-determination for the Vietnamese people, an issue that is at the heart of the Chicano struggle.

At first the antiwar demonstrations were small, since many Mexicans believed that protests contradicted their concept of manhood. They rationalized that there had never been a Chicano draft resister or a defector; they were not like the *gringos*—cowards. Rosalio Muñoz, a former student-body president at the University of California at Los Angeles, broke this syndrome and refused induction. This step encouraged others to take similar action. Many Chicanos now realized that they did not have to prove that they were good "Americans." Instead of fighting in Vietnam, many directed their energies to changing the system that oppressed them. The moratoria that followed were protests against all injustices suffered by Chicanos. On December 20, 1969, in Los Angeles, Rosalio Muñoz, with Ramses Noriega, Roberto Elías, Ernie Vigil, and Gilbert Cano, organized the first Chicano antiwar rally in the United States. Two thousand people attended. On February 28, 1970, they staged another protest, with 6000 Chicanos marching through the pouring rain.[13]

In March 1970, Chicanos from all over the United States flocked to Denver to the Second Annual Chicano Youth Conference. There, the National Chicano Moratorium became a reality. Hundreds of local Chicano moratoria were planned, with the culmination to be a national moratorium in Los Angeles on August 29. This stimulated Chicano youth to organize demonstrations that ranged from a few hundred to several thousand participants. Without exception, the events went off without a major incident. Enthusiasm increased as August 29 neared.

On the morning of the 29th, contingents from all over the United States arrived at the staging area in East Los Angeles. By noon, the participants numbered between 20,000 and 30,000. *Conjuntos* (musical groups) blared out *corridos; Vívas* and yells filled the air. Placards read: *"Raza si, guerra no!"* *"Aztlán:* Love it or Leave it!" etc.[14]

Los Angeles County sheriff's deputies lined the parade route. They stood there, helmeted, making no attempt to establish contact with the marchers: no smiles, no small talk. The march ended peaceably as the parade turned into

Laguna Park. At the park, the marchers settled down to enjoy the program that had been planned; many had brought picnic lunches. Mexican music and Chicano children entertained those assembled.

What touched off the violence has been obscured by police and newspaper accounts. Events should, however, be put into perspective. A minor incident at a liquor store took place a block from Laguna Park (two deputies were subsequently assaulted there after the Laguna Park riot was well under way).*[15] The police, instead of isolating this incident, rushed squad cars to the park, with officers armed for action as they prepared to enter the park area. This action caused general confusion and panic. Deputies refused to talk to monitors or Chicano leaders. Their demeanor caused a reaction, with some of those present—less than 0.01 percent—angrily throwing objects at the police. The authorities could see that monitors were restraining the few protestors. The reasonable man could also deduce that the presence of such a large number of police was causing the reaction. It became evident that the police had found an excuse to break up the demonstration.

Monitors begged the police not to enter the park, explaining that there were many women and small children in the area. The deputies, in spite of this, rushed into the area, trapping men, women, and children and causing considerable panic. They wielded their clubs, trampled spectators, and clubbed those who did not move fast enough. In the main section of the park, the crowd was surprised. Many did not know what had happened, for up to that time, they had not heard a warning to disperse. The deputies fired tear-gas cannisters into the crowd. Participants admittedly hurled objects at the troops, maintaining that they did this in self-defense and others claiming that they acted simply out of hatred for what the police represented. By this time the deputies numbered over 500. They moved in military formation, sweeping the park. Wreckage could be seen everywhere: baby strollers trampled into the ground; a young man with a cane frantically looking for his 80-year-old grandmother; four deputies beating a man in his sixties, while tear gas filled the air.

Armando Morales, in his work on Mexican American–police conflict, reports that "Dr. James S. Koopman, a physician at the UCLA School of Medicine, Department of Pediatrics, was a participant in the moratorium march, along with his wife." Morales quotes the doctor:

> Everyone was assembled peacefully at Laguna Park. My wife and I sat on the grass amongst diverse people. Immediately around us were little children playing with a puppy, an older woman with a cane, a pregnant woman with a small baby and a family eating hamburgers and French fries. The program began and after two speeches a Puerto Rican rhythm group was providing entertainment. The first sign of any disturbance I saw was when some people in the distance began to stand up. The loudspeaker calmly assured us that nothing was happening and that we should sit down. Seconds later I saw a row of gold helmets marching

---

*Significantly, officers claimed that the liquor store incident brought them to the vicinity of Laguna Park. The Morales work cited in this chapter questions the police story.

across the park, forcing everyone toward the high fences. The exit was too small for everyone to leave quickly. I, along with everyone else, panicked. The terrible tragedies of human stampedes in the soccer stadiums of Peru and Argentina were uppermost in my mind.[16]

Eventually, 1200 officers occupied Laguna Park. Los Angeles police joined the Los Angeles County sheriff's deputies, as did police units from surrounding communities.[17] By this time a small minority of the participants extended the area of confrontation to Whittier Boulevard. Mass arrests followed. The prisoners were kept, chained in fours, in two buses at the East Los Angeles substation. The sheriff's deputies did not allow them to drink water or go to the bathroom for about four hours. A pregnant girl was manhandled by a deputy, and the deputies repeatedly maced the chained occupants of the bus.*

Meanwhile, deputies at Laguna Park had shot at a Chicano when he allegedly ran a blockade; his car hit a telephone pole and he was electrocuted. A tear-gas cannister exploded in a trash can, killing a 15-year-old boy. These events preceded the most controversial event of the day. Late in the afternoon, Ruben Salazar and two coworkers from KEMEX-TV had stopped at the Silver Dollar Bar for a beer. They had been covering the moratorium. Soon afterward, deputies surrounded the bar, allegedly looking for a man with a rifle. When some occupants of the Silver Dollar attempted to leave the establishment, police forced them back into the premises. Police claimed that they then broadcast warnings for all the occupants to come out; witnesses testified that no warning was heard. The suspect with the gun had been apprehended elsewhere and since released, but the officers continued their activities at the Silver Dollar. They shot a ten-inch tear-gas projectile into the bar. The missile could pierce one-inch plywood at 100 yards. It struck Salazar in the head. Another shot filled the bar with gas. The customers made their way out of the establishment.

It was about 5:30 P.M. when Salazar's two colleagues frantically informed the deputies that their friend was still in the bar. The deputies refused to listen, and not until two hours later was Salazar's body discovered.

In retrospect, the observations of Danny Villanueva, general manager of KEMEX-TV and former professional NFL football player, have a bearing on the case. Villanueva stated that Salazar had acted strangely the week before his death, putting many small details in order.[18] Salazar had commented to others that he was concerned about threats made to him by Police Chief Ed Davis. The newsman's problems had begun on July 16, 1970, when five Los Angeles detectives and two San Leandro police officers burst into the room of a hotel in downtown Los Angeles, shooting and killing two Mexican nationals, Guillermo, 22, and Beltrán, 23, now known as the Sánchez cousins. The police were hunting another man; it was a case of "mistaken identity."** No warrant had been issued for the cousins. The police allege that they shouted: "Police!

---

*I was a witness to these events; I was one of those arrested.

**The man they were looking for has since been caught and released.

Give up!" The Sánchezes spoke no English. One of the cousins was shot in the room; the other was shot to death while dangling from a window sill as he attempted to leave through a window.[19]

Ruben Salazar exposed the inconsistencies of the police reports. Law enforcement officials called on Salazar and ordered him to tone down his television coverage.* They alleged that he was inflaming the people. Salazar responded that he was merely reporting the facts. However, the police persisted that the Chicano community was not ready for this kind of analysis. The police authorities left, telling Salazar that they would get him if he continued his coverage. Salazar did not stop and at the time of his death was, in fact, working on a series of articles on the enforcement agencies in the Los Angeles area, entitled "What Progress in Thirty Years of Police Community Relations?"[20]

The federal grand jury brought in an indictment against the officers involved in the Sánchez shootings for violation of the civil rights of the two men. The city of Los Angeles paid for the defense of three of the Los Angeles police officers, which produced a storm of protest. The officers were acquitted by a federal court. An interesting sidelight is that the U.S. attorney who persisted in prosecuting the case resigned about a year later.[21] The news media have attributed this resignation to pressure and criticisms by Chief Ed Davis and Mayor Sam Yorty.**

On September 10, 1970, a coroner's inquest probed the circumstances surrounding Ruben Salazar's death. In Los Angeles, a coroner's inquest is generally informal, with seven jurors selected at random. A hearing officer without judicial standing is appointed. Because of the general interest, the local television stations cooperated in airing the entire proceedings. From the start it was obvious that the sheriff's department had unduly influenced the hearing officer. Instead of limiting the testimony to the issue—the death of Salazar— the inquest judge allowed the proceedings to begin with an edited film taken by the film crews of the sheriff's department. A cadre of officers testified as to the Chicano community's riotous nature. The hearing officer made no attempt to restrain the deputies from introducing immaterial facts. He did not question them, and did not allow numerous Chicano witnesses to testify, because, as he maintained, their testimony was redundant.

However, Chicano photographers saved the day. A series of photographs taken by La Raza reporters Raúl Ruiz and Joe Razo, who were eyewitnesses to the events at the Silver Dollar Bar, were shown. The photographs contradicted the testimony of the deputies. For example, the deputies claimed that they did not force the occupants of the bar to return to the bar. Raúl Ruiz produced a photo that showed that they did. The hearing officer repeatedly

---

*This seems to be standard procedure for Ed Davis; he called the managers of KTTV in Los Angeles after they showed the films of the moratorium and ordered the station manager not to show them again. My highly reliable source reports that although the management of Metromedia is conservative, they resented this attempted censorship by the police chief.

**Ed Davis was criticized by an officer in January 1972 for soliciting contributions from the Los Angeles Police Department for a bronze bust of Mayor Yorty.

attempted to limit Ruiz's testimony, and he questioned him at length. Shortly afterward, *La Raza* newspaper published a special issue featuring the photos taken on August 29. The *Los Angeles Times* was so impressed that it obtained permission from the *barrio* newspaper to reprint many of the photos.

Four of the inquest jurors decided that there had been "death at the hands of another"; the three remaining jurors decided on "death by accident." The *Los Angeles Times,* on October 8, 1970, interviewed the jurors. A majority juror, George W. Sherard, stated: "All seven jurors reached the rapid conclusion that the killing was unintended. Four of us felt . . . deputies expected they had a good chance of killing someone." Another juror, Betty J. Clements, added: "The main surprise to me was the deputies' lack of organization, their lack of consideration for innocent people. I like to go into cocktail lounges to have a drink. I'd certainly hate to think somebody was going to shoot tear gas or anything else in there simply because somebody reported there was a man with a gun. . . ." This juror also questioned the deputies leaving Salazar's body in the *cantina* for two hours and wondered whether they would have acted in the same manner in Beverly Hills.

Chicanos as well as many Anglos believed that Deputy Thomas Wilson would be tried. However, Los Angeles District Attorney Evelle J. Younger announced on October 14, 1970, that he would not prosecute. Many Chicanos charged that Younger did not prosecute because of political expediency. He was a candidate for California state attorney general (he was elected), and he knew that the law-and-order mentality of Californians demanded this decision. Younger also feared the baiting of Mayor Sam Yorty, a notorious "support your local police" advocate.

The *Los Angeles Times,* which usually supported Younger, criticized his actions in an editorial on October 16, 1970:

> So this is where the matter stands: an innocent man was killed by a weapon that should not have been used when it was used, but the public authorities assign no blame. One does not have to enter a legal argument over whether there was, or was not, sufficient evidence for prosecution of the deputy to observe that the decision not to prosecute leaves the public in the dark as to the facts it should know.

Among these facts are the following questions:

1. What were the standing orders of Deputy Thomas Wilson, who shot the grenade that killed Ruben Salazar? Why had he shot such a dangerous and lethal missile contrary to the training manual's instructions? Exactly what was the department's policy concerning the use of the projectile?

2. Had the warning, in fact, been given?

3. Why did the deputies not enter the premises of the Silver Dollar Bar after thoroughly neutralizing the establishment with gas? Why didn't

they look for Salazar's body when told by his companions that he was still in the bar?

4. Did the officers, in fact, know that Salazar was in the bar before shooting the projectile?

Until these questions are answered, many citizens in the Los Angeles area and throughout the United States will continue to believe that Salazar was intentionally murdered.*

September 16, 1970

September 16 is Mexico's Independence Day. Traditionally, on that day the Mexican community of Los Angeles celebrates, and civic groups sponsor a parade. Many believed that the 1970 parade would be cancelled because of the violence of August 29. However, even many moderates and nonactivists had been enraged by the slaying of Ruben Salazar, so they invited the moratorium people to join the parade. They wanted to show the public that Chicanos could march peaceably. Moreover, they were determined not to be intimidated. The organizers arranged for heavy monitoring of the parade. They also planned for the marchers to file into the East Los Angeles College football stadium for festivities after the parade. At the last minute, the Los Angeles Community College Board of Trustees refused to issue a permit for the use of the stadium. The festivities had to be cancelled, thus undermining the planners' security measures.

The parade began in the late afternoon. In prior years the turnout had been moderate. To the surprise of the marchers, between 200,000 and 300,000 Mexicans lined the streets, cheering, especially, the moratorium contingent. As it passed, they yelled: *"Víva la raza!"* "Chicano power!" "Remember Ruben Salazar!" etc. People displayed placards lettered with similar messages and several that asked: "Who killed Ruben Salazar?"

The parade went off without major incident. As the last of the marchers reached the end of the parade route, night approached. Thousands of marchers congregated on Brooklyn Avenue in front of East Los Angeles College; a bottleneck developed. Organizers, as mentioned before, had planned to filter the people into the football stadium, but they had not been able to get the permit at the eleventh hour.

An incident broke out when teenagers threw rocks at the police. The Monterey City policemen and the Los Angeles County sheriff's deputies moved in and ordered the crowd to disperse. Both sides soon polarized: the Chicanos hating the police and wanting them to leave their land, and the police hating the demonstrators as Mexicans. Soon the confrontation escalated, and foot units moved in from all sides, with a fire engine speeding east up Brooklyn

---

*A number of *corridos* have been written about Ruben Salazar. They portray him as a martyr who was assassinated.

Avenue with sirens blaring, and accompanied by squad cars. They trapped the marchers. The crowd panicked, not knowing which way to go. People ran in every direction in an effort to leave the area, only to be met by squads of club-swinging officers. Many escaped into the low-cost housing projects, where residents offered them sanctuary. Officers broke into the apartments, destroying furniture and beating up the occupants. Hector Verdugo and William Bojorano, two of my students, and the girls they were dating were badly beaten, suffering scalp wounds. They were kept in jail for 48 hours and charged with assaulting officers. While in jail, they did not receive medical treatment, and Bojorano was taken to a doctor and his wounds sewed up after he was released. (They were both tried and acquitted.) Immediately, the press condemned the marchers. In fact, TV newscasters Baxter Ward and George Putnam were inflammatory. Both relied on police information; they had not been there.[22]

January 9, 1971

Unlike the previous two demonstrations, the march of January 9 was held in the city of Los Angeles instead of the county. The city police, led by Chief Edward Davis, have dubbed themselves as "Los Angeles's finest." Davis, following the incidents of August 29 and September 16, had made inflammatory statements on how he thought the militants should be handled. On January 9 he had his chance to show the public just how tough Los Angeles's finest were.

The demonstration began at the Hollenbeck Police Station; leaders planned to picket the station as a protest against police brutality. The march had been organized by the Chicano Moratorium Committee, and the Brown Berets acted as monitors. About 1000 participated. No major incident occurred at Hollenbeck, but from the beginning the police intimidated the marchers. At the First Street Bridge, some of the marchers spilled into the street; police pushed them back onto the sidewalks. Monitors cooled tempers. The main body reached Parker Center—the Los Angeles Police Department headquarters—and began to picket it.

The demonstration was peaceable, but across the street some teenagers climbed onto some construction project structures that overlooked the street. A loudspeaker ordered the crowd to disperse, and Chicanos were ordered off the structures. They did not move fast enough to suit the police, who mobilized to clear the area. As in the case of August 29 and September 16, the actions of the police escalated the affair, with many people rioting and committing acts of vandalism. Three hours later, when the melee was finally quelled, the police had arrested 32 people. Again the news media condemned the Chicanos, with few questioning the methods of the police or asking if they would have used similar vindictiveness in the west side of the city. Chief Edward Davis blamed "swimming pool Communists" and the Brown Berets for the riot.[23] To many of us, the actions of the police were natural to an army of occupation: control through violence.

A three-day march from the four largest *barrios* in the vicinity of Los Angeles ended at Belvedere Park in East Los Angeles on January 31. The marchers from those *barrios* were joined by Chicanos from all over California. The rally was to protest the war as well as police brutality. The scheduled rally began about noon; it was peaceable. Before the event, both Sheriff Peter Pitchess and Chief Ed Davis had thrown down the gauntlet and played up the role of law and order in the news media of Los Angeles. Therefore, most participants fully expected the police to incite a riot. They were therefore surprised not to find an army of sheriff's deputies awaiting them at Belvedere Park. They could only hear the "audible sound . . . of a helicopter buzzing overhead."[24] The speakers emphasized that this was a nonviolent demonstration; however, they did not shy away from condemning the oppression and the violence of the past five months. At about 2:30 P.M., the rally officially ended, and Rosalio Muñoz, cochairman of the moratorium committee, told the crowd of 5000 to "disperse peaceably."

The majority did disperse; however, a small group began a march on the sheriff's substation on Third Street. When they reached the station, antipolice chants went up. It was clear that the members of the crowd had no respect for the police, whom they viewed as their oppressor. The police was the enemy. Monitors, meanwhile, attempted to disperse the mob. They could not control it, and the frustrations of a generation erupted. The crowd rioted—burning and looting—and when the police arrived, the rioters hurled stones and other objects at them.

The protesters walked up Whittier Boulevard: "A few windows were broken along the way and street signs were torn down."[25] At about 3:45 P.M., gunshots were heard at Whittier Boulevard, and the police moved in, shooting tear gas at the demonstrators. They fired shotguns into the crowd, and the protesters, in turn, hurled objects at the police. The confrontation left one man dead, nineteen wounded by buckshot, two with stab wounds, and numerous with broken bones. The property damage was over $200,000. Almost immediately, Sheriff Pitchess stated: "This time they can't blame the disturbance on the department . . . because deputies were not in the area until after the burning and looting had started."[26] Chicano leaders saw the problem in a different light. They stated that the trouble, in reality, had begun many months, if not years, before. At the crux of the problem was what Ruben Salazar had been attempting to answer: What progress in thirty years of police community relations?

Subversion and the Provocateurs

At this point it would be premature to conclude that the Los Angeles riots were revolutionary rebellions. They were, in fact, more defensive than offensive: on each occasion Mexicans defended themselves, after conducting a nonviolent demonstration, against police provocations. Evidence indicates that the reaction of the demonstrators was spontaneous and in response to specific police aggressions. The subsequent actions of the police escalated the initial confrontation into a riot. The violence of the mob had deep-rooted causes; it was, in essence, a reaction to years of police oppression. Meanwhile, in recent years, increased awareness has polarized many Chicanos, and their relationship with the police clearly has become that of the occupiers and the occupied. The police, on the other hand, also have become polarized, and to them the Chicano is the enemy. It is their duty to protect property against the rebellious natives. The police solution to the growing unrest has been a military one.

Attendant to most military solutions is subversion and provocateuring. Occupying forces extensively use secret police and spies. In the United States, most people find it difficult to believe that this type of activity takes place in their "free society." However, recent exposés leave doubts. For example, the involvement of the Central Intelligence Agency (CIA) in other parts of the world is now well documented; in 1954 it played a key role in the overthrow of the Arbenz government in Guatemala; it planned the abortive Bay of Pigs invasion in the early 1960s; and it planned the assassination of Diem in South Vietnam in 1963. Among most Latin American scholars, it is generally conceded that the CIA finances and manages most of the Anglo-American scholarship and research grants in Latin America. At home, Anglo-Americans realize that the Federal Bureau of Investigation has become an independent agency that operates with few restraints. To criticize the FBI is a subversive act, although FBI agents invade the privacy of public figures, as well as civil rights leaders, by wire tappings and uncalled-for investigations. The Armed Forces independently make investigations and keep files on those they consider to be suspect or subversive. These actions have extended to the local authorities, who work in collusion with federal agencies to protect "America."

In the Los Angeles area, the police agencies have become sacred cows that are beyond public control. While other segments of the city and county civil-servant Establishment go without pay raises, most law enforcement budget requests are approved, and police and sheriff's deputies receive their raises as a matter of course. Any charge of police brutality or criticism of police transgressions is branded as subversive, with Mayor Sam Yorty publicly denouncing the claims as Communist-inspired. Furthermore, the only check on the Los Angeles Police Department is a Police Commission, which is appointed by Yorty.

It is true that the Los Angeles Police Department is one of the most professional police departments in the United States. Therein is the problem. It has become an elite guard that is dedicated to maintaining the status quo and protecting the privileged of the city. The only serious challenge to the power of those self-legitimizing agencies has come from the Black and Chicano communities. The response of the police has been to brand protests as Communist-inspired and to react to crush the revolutionaries. In the process, a secret police, along with a network of spies, has been developed. This story has only recently emerged. Much of the story began to unfold with the defection of Louis Tackwood, a spy for the Los Angeles Police Department.

In October 1971, Louis Tackwood, a Black informer, stunned the Los Angeles public by testifying that he was paid by the Criminal Conspiracy Section (CCS) of the Los Angeles Police Department. He was assigned to a group of officers who, in cooperation with the FBI, planned to instigate a disruption by militants of the 1972 Republican convention in San Diego; minor officials were to be killed to force President Richard Nixon to use his powers to break the militant movement. Tackwood named Dan Mahoney (CCS) and Ed Birch (FBI) as those in charge of the operation.[27] In private conversations he has also described the police use of drug pushers who are used as informers in return for protection from prosecution.*

There is also the case of Officer Fernando Sumaya, who worked as an undercover agent for the Los Angeles Police Department. In the fall semester of 1967, he attempted to infiltrate the United Mexican American Student Chapter at San Fernando Valley State College during campus protests there. He was ousted from the group because he was unknown, and because he came on too strong. Sumaya then moved to East Los Angeles where he infiltrated the Brown Berets. In the spring of 1969 he was involved in the Biltmore Hotel affair where Chicanos were accused of disrupting a speech by Governor Ronald Reagan at a Nuevas Vistas Education Conference, sponsored by the California Department of Education. Thirteen Chicanos were arrested and seven were charged on numerous counts of conspiracy and arson. After two years of appeals, they were finally tried. The key witness was Sumaya. The key to the defense was the contention that Sumaya had provoked one of the original defendants into setting the fires. (That defendant fled, and his whereabouts is unknown.) The jury evidently believed this contention, since all but two of the defendants were acquitted; it could not reach a verdict on the remaining two. In other words, Sumaya had planned and provoked the burnings.[28]

Justicia O, a Chicano law student newspaper, also reported that Bob Navarro was a police undercover agent. He had infiltrated a community group in the Venice area and participated in numerous protests.[29]

Most astounding, however, was the testimony of Eustacio (Frank) Martínez, 23, in a press conference on January 31, 1972. He revealed that since July 1969 he had infiltrated Chicano groups. He was recruited by a federal agent for the Alcohol, Tobacco, and Firearms Division (ATF) of the Internal Revenue Service.[30] In return for not being prosecuted for a federal firearms violation, he had agreed to work as an informant and agent provocateur. During his service, he infiltrated the Mexican American Youth Organization and the Brown Berets in Houston and Kingsville, Texas. Through his own admission, he committed acts of violence in an effort to provoke others. From September 1969 to October 1970, he participated in a protest march in Alice, Texas, and attempted to provoke a disruption "by jumping on a car and trying to cave its top in."[31] He also attempted to get militants to buy guns and to get police

---

*A tape is in the possession of a colleague who remains nameless for obvious reasons.

to cause violence. He was admonished by the MAYO members.

In October 1970, ATF agents sent him to Los Angeles where he worked for agents Fernando Ramos and Jim Riggs. "Once in Los Angeles, Martínez began spreading rumors against Rosalio Muñoz, the chairman of the Chicano Moratorium Committee. He accused Muñoz of being too soft."[32] In November 1970, Martínez ousted Muñoz and became chairman of the Moratorium Committee. He continued in this capacity until March 1971, when he returned to Texas. During this period, Martínez was a member of the Brown Berets and went around, according to informants, waving a carbine and advocating violent tactics. During his testimony, Martínez identified Officers Valencia, Armas, Savillos, and Dominguez of the CCS as contacts. In other words, when Martínez took part in the Los Angeles riots on January 9 and 31, 1972, the Los Angeles police knew of his involvement. Upon his return from Texas, he was instructed by Ramos and Riggs to infiltrate *La Casa de Carnalismo* to establish links between *La Casa* and the Chicano Liberation Front (CLF), which had been involved in numerous bombings. Martínez reported that the main functions of the group were to eliminate narcotics, to sponsor English classes, and to dispense food to the needy. He could find no links with CLF. The officers told him that his "information was a bunch of bullshit."[33] He was to find evidence by any means necessary. They then instructed him to use his influence to get a heroin addict by the name of "Nacho" to infiltrate *Carnalismo.* Martínez refused to become a part of the frameup. He finally became disillusioned when, on the first anniversary of the Chicano National Moratorium, agents told him to plead guilty to charges of inciting a riot. He had been promised protection from prosecution.

Although newsmen have not questioned the validity of the Martínez disclosures, they have not called for a congressional investigation into the provocateur activities of federal and local agencies. Louis Tackwood and Frank Martínez are admitted provocateurs. The latter's role casts a shadow on the actions of the police in the Los Angeles Chicano riots. The local police authorities knew of Martínez's involvement with the moratorium. It is reasonable to speculate that they had other informants and provocateurs involved in the confrontations of 1970 and 1971. What their role was is buried in the files of the secret police of the different branches of the federal and local police agencies. These are the aspects of history that remain closed to the historian.

Justice in the Southwest

We now come to the last important question: Is there civil or criminal justice for the Chicano in "occupied America"? According to *A Report of the United States Commission on Civil Rights: Mexican-Americans and the Administration of Justice in the Southwest,* published in March 1970, the answer is no. The official government report documents the Chicanos' inequality before the law. It underscores that conditions have not changed since the "bloody Christmas beatings" of 1951, when eight Los Angeles police officers beat four Mexicans—Eddie Nora, Manuel Hernández, Elías Rondela, and Raymond Márquez—while they were being held at the city jail. Márquez suffered internal injuries; contusions of the nose, knees, and arms; and lacerated ears. The others suffered similar injuries.[34] The report indicts Los Angeles police authorities, as well as the FBI, reinforcing a case of collusion between federal and local authorities in the repression of the Mexican community. Specific examples follow:

November 9, 1968. Salvador Barba, 13, was beaten by Los Angeles policemen, needing 40 stitches in the head. An FBI investigation found that the facts of the case did not warrant the arrest of the officers involved. The findings of agents were based largely on Los Angeles Police Department reports.[35]

September 1, 1968. Jess Domínguez, 41, of Los Angeles, was looking for his teenage children in the early morning. He approached a police car and asked the officers for assistance. They answered: "We don't have any time for you Mexicans." Domínguez became indignant, whereupon the officers got out of their car and beat him. At least 15 officers joined in the brutal beating of Domínguez. He was arrested and charged with assaulting an officer. Domínguez was badly bruised, could not move his jaw, and constantly vomited; subsequently, he had to undergo surgery. The FBI investigated and again, based on police reports, claimed that no investigation or prosecution of officers was warranted.[36]

May 5, 1969. Frank Gonzales, 14, Los Angeles, was skipping school when an officer called to him, and the boy ran away. Officer Thomas Parkham, who had been suspended twice before—once for pointing a cocked pistol at a juvenile and another time for being drunk and disorderly while off duty—drew his gun. He claimed that he fired a warning shot before he fired at the boy. He was allowed to resign in lieu of disciplinary action. District Attorney Evelle Younger decided not to prosecute Parkham.[37]

Attitude of Law Enforcement Agents

The report bluntly states that police generally have no respect for Mexicans. Ray Anaya, sheriff of Carlsbad, New Mexico, is quoted as saying, "For instance, an officer goes [to] a house of a man who has a long police record, knocks on the door, the wife opens the door, and [the officer] goes into the house. If that were in another place in town, Riverside Drive, I am sure it would not happen. . . ."[38] In San Antonio, Texas, police officers address Chicanos as, "Hey, punk, come here."[39]

We must remember that the report is selective, and that there are many other cases not documented in that study. For example, in Lamesa, Texas, when dog catchers were rounding up stray dogs in the Chicano community, they shot indiscriminately at the dogs on the street. A housewife stated that she realized that the dogs should have been licensed, but that did not warrant the shooting; bullets might ricochet and hit a child. She also maintained that it was not right for small children to see their pets killed. She added that she had never heard of this occurring in the Anglo part of town.[40]

There is also the case of a Chicano student who had been studentbody president in both high school and junior college. He broke up with his Anglo girl friend when her father objected to his being Mexican. The student had collected .22 caliber rifles as a hobby. Someone shot holes in the windows of his former girl friend's house as well as those of several other houses in the neighborhood. Police picked him up, and when he arrived at the station, the desk sergeant asked him: "Hey, brown boy, what were you doing going around with a white girl?"[41]

The Civil Rights Commission report points out that it is difficult to get federal agencies to act against local authorities, and it cites numerous examples. For example, on January 7, 1968, Natividad Fuentes, of Uvalde, Texas, was driving home when his car spun and ended up on the other side of the road. When the deputy sheriff of Uvalde arrived, Fuentes attempted to explain to him what had happened. The deputy accused him of being drunk, dragged him from the car, and hit him with a blackjack. He was jailed and the next morning he was charged with drunk driving. The judge released him on his own recognizance. After his release, Fuentes went to a medical doctor, who ordered him to bed. As Fuentes was returning home, the arresting deputy and his assistant saw him and attempted to arrest him again, but they let him go when he convinced them that the judge had released him. He made a complaint to the FBI, who called to interview him over the phone. When Fuentes insisted on a personal interview, an agent came out for five minutes. The FBI did not recommend any action.[42]

Another book that underscores the mistreatment of Chicanos is Armando Morales's *¡Ando Sangrando! i am bleeding: A Study of Mexican American–Police Conflict.* He condenses well-known cases in the Chicano community, which clearly demonstrate the Hitler-like attitude of many judges:

> In 1964 Miguel Vega Andrade pleaded guilty to nonsupport of four children by a common-law wife. Pasadena [California] Municipal Court Judge Joseph Sprankle stated: "If you do not marry and be sterilized, I will put you in jail." The defendant was denied a hearing in the California and U.S. Supreme Court.
>
> In May 1966, Nancy Hernández, 21, convicted on a misdemeanor, refused to submit to sterilization as part of her probation. Judge Frank P. sentenced her to six months in jail because of her refusal.[43]

The most infamous case took place on September 2, 1969, when Judge Gerald S. Chargin of Santa Clara County (California) Juvenile Court passed sentence on a 17-year-old Chicano, allegedly convicted of incest. Chargin stated:

> Mexican people, after 13 years of age, think it is perfectly all right to go out and act like an animal. We ought to send you out of the country—send you back to Mexico. You belong in prison for the rest of your life for doing things of this kind.

You ought to commit suicide. That's what I think of people of this kind. You are lower than animals and haven't the right to live in organized society—just miserable, lousy, rotten people. Maybe Hitler was right. The animals in our society probably ought to be destroyed because they have no right to live among human beings.[44]

The defense attorney attempted to restrain Chargin's intemperate attack on the entire Chicano community, but the judge would not be silenced.

Congressman Ed Roybal and U.S. Senator Joseph Montoya (New Mexico) called for an investigation, as well as for the dismissal of Chargin. Widespread demonstrations took place. But despite this, Chargin was merely transferred to the civil division of the Superior Court. The Chargin incident is another example of the powerlessness of Chicanos. One can only speculate on the reaction to the judge's remarks had they been made in the Jewish community, especially considering their similarity to statements made by Hitler.

Trial By One's Peers

Throughout the Southwest, Chicanos are excluded from trial juries and grand juries. As in the case of the Blacks, Chicanos have been kept off trial juries by being excluded from the roll of prospective jurors. This exclusion, as we shall see, is more prevalent in the "redneck" areas of the Southwest. Grand juries are selected by county judges, who submit names that are, in turn, drawn out of the proverbial hat. Judges in Los Angeles readily admit that they submit, primarily, names of prominent people. Judge Leopoldo Sánchez told me, "they are the only ones who can afford it [the time from their occupations]."[45] As a consequence, the Chicano often is judged by anti-Mexican Anglo-Americans who are convinced the defendant is guilty before he stands trial. Even well-meaning Anglo-Americans are ill equipped to judge Chicanos, who live under different social, economic, and cultural conditions from their own.

The findings of the report of the Civil Rights Commission document the assertion that Chicanos are seriously underrepresented and, in fact, excluded from juries. Mike Gonzáles, an attorney in South Texas, says that in ten years of courtroom activity he has never seen a Chicano on a jury, even though the population in some areas is 85 percent Chicano. R. P. Sánchez, a lawyer from McAllen, Texas, said that although Hidalgo County has a Mexican population of about 75 percent, only one or two Chicanos had served on juries.[46] Similar data were collected in Phoenix and Tucson, Arizona. In Fort Sumner, New Mexico, an area more than 60 percent Mexican American, local Mexican Americans stated that their peers just did not serve on juries. Public Defender Richard S. Buckley of Los Angeles claims: "I recall very few Mexican Americans on any juries I have tried in a period of 15 years."[47] Pete Tijerina, attorney from San Antonio, Texas, tells of a case he attempted to try in Jourdantown, Texas, in March 1966. Tijerina stated that the town was 65 percent Mexican.

Only one juror out of 48 listed was Mexican. The case was postponed until July when two Mexican Americans were on the jury list, but it was found that one of these was dead. The case was again postponed until December. Five Chicanos were now on the list, but all five were peremptorily challenged by the insurance company. Tijerina's client was a Chicano.[48]

The same pattern is repeated on the grand juries. In the county of Los Angeles, where the Chicano population is about one million, the Civil Rights Commission report stated that only four Mexicans have served on the grand jury in 12 years. In adjacent Orange County, which has over 44,000 Mexicans, only one has served in 12 years. Further investigation by the commission revealed that the grand juror who did serve was Spanish, and that no Chicano had served on the grand jury of Monterey County from 1938 through 1968.[49]

An analysis of the Civil Rights Commission report leads the reader to one conclusion: as far as Chicanos and other poor people are concerned, justice in the Southwest is actually injustice. How can the law be relevant to a people who cannot afford bail or the high costs of adequate representation? If the case must be appealed, costs are so prohibitive that justice through the judicial system is an impossibility. The problem is further complicated by most district attorney's offices having available to them the services of police department investigators, as well as their own detectives. In contrast, the public defender usually is overburdened with cases, and even the best attorneys available to Chicanos (and other poor people) do not have investigative units. It all costs money. In the late 1960s, through federal grants, the California Rural Legal Assistance (CRLA) unit was organized. CRLA has a distinguished record in defending the rights of the poor. Although it does not handle criminal cases, it represents the poor in various other matters. In King County, California, for example, where growers received $10,179,917 *not* to produce crops, and where the board of supervisors raised their annual salaries from $2400 to $12,000, less than $6000 was spent on food for the poor.[50] The CRLA sued the county on behalf of the poor, charging that it was violating federal statutes. The poor could not have afforded to pay an attorney for such an action. Nevertheless, as complaints mounted against the CRLA by reactionary elements such as the California growers, Governor Ronald Reagan became more incensed about the federal government's support of an agency that brought suits against private enterprise. In December 1970, Reagan vetoed the federal appropriation to CRLA. The matter was taken to Washington, and the CRLA was put on a year's probation, during which time their actions would be reviewed. An investigation, however, showed that the CRLA had done nothing improper. To date, they continue to champion the underdog.[51]

There is also the case of the Mexican American Legal Defense Fund (MALDF), which was established by a $2-million grant from the Ford Foundation. MALDF supposedly furnished legal services to Chicanos throughout the United States. Since it was not financed through federal funds, it was hoped that it would be more independent. But from the first, MALDF was handicapped by too much work. Civil rights test cases received first attention.

MALDF was also the victim of political pressure. In Los Angeles the board of MALDF dismissed militant lawyer Oscar Acosta; his defense of clients was too aggressive. Congressman Henry B. Gonzales was upset because money had been given to MAYO in Texas. Gonzales applied pressure on the Ford Foundation to curtail grants to the Southwest Council of *La Raza* which was the funding agent through which the Ford Foundation went. Gonzales charged that they were funding subversive organizations.* Pressure was also applied to limit the scope of MALDF's cases. As a consequence, the headquarters of MALDF was moved out of San Antonio. This seriously compromised the organization's effectiveness, since San Antonio is to Chicanos what Selma is to Blacks.

The plight of the Chicano is accentuated in rural areas such as West Texas, where conditions are, perhaps, the most aggravated in the United States. Redneck farmers control the economy of the region. Cities such as Abilene, Texas, the City of the Churches, are fundamentalists and notoriously anti-Catholic. In Abilene and Lubbock, about 160 miles apart, there were only a few Chicano school teachers and ministers as of the summer of 1970, and no Chicano medical doctors or attorneys. The only attorney who took "Meskin" civil rights cases was Mark Smith of Lubbock. As a consequence of his activities, Mark Smith, an exceedingly bright and articulate attorney, has lost a considerable portion of his Anglo practice. Many businessmen simply do not approve of his defense of the rights of "Meskin" and "niggers." The name of Mark Smith especially terrorizes school board members in small towns in West Texas. They consider him an agent of Peking, since he has been the only attorney who has regularly filed suits against them. Ironically, Mark Smith is not a radical, but an old-time liberal who believes that all citizens of the United States are entitled to equal protection under the law.

During October 1969, Mark Smith defended the rights of Chicano students in Abilene, Texas, when they walked out of school because of long-standing discrimination.

Smith has filed countless desegregation suits against school districts that are circumventing the order of the Department of Health, Education, and Welfare to integrate. In Lamesa, Texas, a town of about 6000 where over 40 percent of the school children are Mexican, the school board in 1969 believed that it had complied with desegregation orders by integrating Blacks with Chicanos, leaving the whites segregated. Smith took the matter to court. He also has defended the rights of students to wear brown armbands to school as symbols of their protest against the discrimination of administrators and teachers.[52]

Smith himself readily admits the inadequate legal representation available

*Henry B. Gonzales is a prime example of the socialized Mexican. To protect his political bailiwick, he has resorted to Red-baiting his critics. His actions have alienated even many prominent Chicanos; they refer to him as Henry "Baines" Gonzales.

to Chicanos in the West Texas area. He states that usually Mexicans do not have enough money to pay a lawyer; even if they can pay the fees, they have difficulty finding a lawyer who will take the case. Even with a lawyer, the chances of a Chicano winning a civil or criminal case are very slim. The Chicano's lawyer usually has to rely on the possibility of a reversible error whereby he can appeal the case to the federal courts; but then, the costs of appealing the case are prohibitive.

As in King County, California, the counties of West Texas have considerable agribusiness. Growers in the area receive generous federal farm subsidies. Many receive hundreds of thousands of dollars from the federal government, but they, in turn, are vehemently opposed to any form of federal aid to education or welfare for the poor. The Chicanos in many of the small hamlets of West Texas often have less than a third-grade education. From birth they are conditioned to go into farm labor. There are innumerable instances where teachers literally have pushed Chicanos into the fields. The growers control the school boards; they also employ a substantial number of the townspeople. Leaders and participants of protest movements are dismissed from their jobs. The Chicanos of West Texas are valiant. A poor *campesino* who earns $60 to $80 a week and must support five children is limited in his alternatives. To be blacklisted is a major threat to the Chicano. Because of this repression, Chicanos are organizing in towns such as Tahoka, Lamesa, and Rotan, and they are demanding their rights. In Lamesa, they organized *Los Ciudadanos Para La Justicia* and led a peaceful march on the board of education. The leader of the march was employed by a member of the board. The protester was firm in his demands and was later edged out of his job.* In Rotan, school administrator Marshall Hill allegedly beat several Chicano students, one of whom was a 90-pound girl who missed two weeks of school because of her injuries. The school board refused to meet with the Chicano representatives to discuss this and other cases of discrimination and brutality. On the average, out of fifty Chicanos beginning the first grade in Rotan, two to five will graduate from high school.

Conclusion

The theme of "Good-bye America" represents the increased awareness of a considerable number of Chicanos that they are living in captivity, and a growing commitment by many to do something about it. "America" has, from the start, been a European term that symbolized the colonization of the so-called New World. The United States appropriated the name for its thirteen small colonies; and as the country grew, the name became, in effect, a declaration of the United States' intention to dominate, control, occupy, and own all of the New World's land and people. In the process, the nation took land from the Indians and moved west to conquer the Mexican nation, robbing it of its

---

*Name withheld. I interviewed the subject and spent considerable time in the locale.

northwest territory. This land, as we have seen, became "occupied America." The Mexicans in what became the Anglo-American Southwest were, in turn, robbed of both their land and heritage and, through the use of violence, were relegated to a colonized caste. Further territorial expansion at the expense of Mexico was thwarted by internal difficulties in the United States; nevertheless, Mexico did come under the sway of the economic imperialism of the United States. This imperialism brought more Mexicans into the Southwest so that they could be exploited for their labor.

In time, the Mexican in the United States became a citizen. He joined the "nation within a nation" to which Chicanos were relegated. As a result of racism, nativism, violence, and the schools, the Chicano was conditioned to accept his caste and to believe that it was his fault, not America's, if he did not make it. After all, America was the symbol of opportunity, democracy, and equality. The bidding of "good-bye to America" symbolizes the nonacceptance of this myth and the rejection of racism, nativism, and exploitation of the many by the few.

In the bidding of "good-bye to America" the Chicano has become exceedingly nationalistic. His transformation is similar to that described by Frantz Fanon in the conclusion to his book *A Dying Colonialism:*

> The thesis that the launching of a new society is possible only within the framework of national independence here finds its corollary. The same time that the colonized man braces himself to reject oppression, a radical transformation takes place within him which makes any attempt to maintain the colonial system impossible and shocking. It is this transformation that we have studied here.[53]

What national independence means to the Chicano is control of his political, economic, and social institutions. No longer does he accept the Anglo-American system that has controlled him.

An exploration of the 1960s is vital to understanding how this transformation came about. These years were important, since the oppression was lifted long enough to make the Chicano liberation movement possible. In the past, violence quickly suffocated any challenges to the established order. In the 1960s it became popular to expose exploitation, and minorities lost their fear of violence. Public opinion would not support the blatant oppression of the past. Communication among Chicano groups increased during the 1960s and a general spirit of *La Raza* developed. The awareness of being oppressed and being a Chicano was more widespread among the youth. This is important because youth comprises the majority of the Chicano community, and it forecasts the future. Moreover, the crisis in education became visible, and mothers began to question whether the failures of their children were not, in reality, the failures of the educational system. In other words, the critical ambience fostered in the 1960s was carried over to Chicanos. An awareness of discrimination increased among Chicanos, and many, for the first time, recognized it. This awareness was reinforced and spread through Chicano-controlled media and arts. The inability of the privileged to deal effectively with Chicano demands and the efforts to subvert the Chicano movement caused polarization, which further stiffened Chicano resistance to "occupied America."

Walkouts in the 1960s were important, because Chicanos learned that they had the power to disrupt. For the first time in their lives, the system adjusted to them. They walked out of meetings sponsored by the federal government, they walked out of school, and recently, many began to walk out of the Democratic party. (This is a revolutionary act in itself; most Chicanos have been nurtured to believe in the *Virgen de Guadalupe,* the Sacred Heart, and the party of Franklin D. Roosevelt.)* Disruption is the Chicanos' only power in the political arena, since they are so badly gerrymandered that political self-determination is impossible. Only in selected districts can the Chicano upset the Establishment. The Chicanos' powerlessness was the constant theme of the 1960s, whether in Los Angeles or San Antonio. For the first time, however, there is hope of ending this powerlessness through legal or illegal processes.

How Anglo-Americans have kept their power is also important. This has been exposed in the breaking of strikes, as well as in the movement in the cities. An effective colonial organization suppresses the colonized through co-optation, efficient superimposition of its administrative rules, and covert control. When mass violence erupts, this is an indication of the weakness of the colonial structure; it also indicates a primitive revolt of people. Violence is only effective in localized situations and only possible in isolated regions where it can be contained. However, in the case of the moratorium, the police provoked the riot. The overreaction of the police showed how they feared the currents of liberation, and how, in fact, they were the occupiers. The Vietnam war exposed how the poor, most visibly the Chicano and the Black, were being used as cannon fodder. The shooting of the Sánchezes and the indifference of the judicial system to the wrongful death of Ruben Salazar made it clear to many Chicanos that a double standard of justice operated for Anglo-Americans and Chicanos. There is also the question of police provocation. One might question these conclusions if the above were isolated cases, but the history of the Chicano and Anglo-American justice documents that Chicanos are colonized —in other words, that Chicanos are controlled, that they are not able to obtain justice, and that they are not even allowed to be judged by their peers in "America."

The voice of liberation in the Chicano movement, while similar to that in the Third World, at the same time is different. The colonization is different. The conquest is over 124 years in the past, and the colonized are no longer in the majority. Americanization and the enticement of middle-class standards have taken their toll, and Chicanos are far from being united in their awareness of the causes of their oppressed status. Moreover, the internal colonization has

---

*My parents hung a picture of each on the walls of our home, each with a candle below it.

taken place inside the most developed and powerful nation in the world. Today, the movement is toward separatism, with the goal of increasing awareness in a small but unified Chicano community that is inner-directed instead of being directed from without. Defense of this community is through the retention of culture: collective liberation instead of individual co-optation. This is the message of the Gutíerrezes, the Gonzales, and the Tijerinas as they bid good-bye to the forces that have controlled them in the past. The Chicano people seek self-determination in what were formerly and rightfully their lands, not those of "Anglo-America."

Notes

1.   *Los Angeles Times,* 13 December 1971.
2.   O. Douglas Weeks, "The Texan-Mexican and the Politics of South Texas," *American Political and Social Science Review,* August 1930, p. 613. Much of the data on Texas, up to this point, has been based on this article.
3.   María Hernández, as quoted in *The Militant,* 23 April 1971.
4.   Interview with José Ángel Gutíerrez, May 1971.
5.   Robert Coles and Harry Huge, "Thorns on the Yellow Rose of Texas," *New Republic,* 19 April 1969, pp. 13–17.
6.   *New Republic,* p. 14.
7.   *New Republic,* p. 14.
8.   *New Republic,* p. 15.
9.   *New Republic,* p. 17.
10.   Conversations and interviews with Ricardo Cruz.   In addition, I was an eyewitness to many of the events surrounding the CPLR (Católicos Por La Raza).
11.   Tapes in the possession of the staff of *La Raza.*
12.   Ralph Guzman, "Mexican American Casualties in Vietnam," *La Raza* 1, no. 1 (n.d.): 12.
13.   Interviews with Rosalio Muñoz and Gilbert Cano, both of whom were prominent organizers.
14.   I was a witness.
15.   Armando Morales, *¡Ando Sangrando! i am bleeding* (Los Angeles, Calif.: The Congress of Mexican American Unity, 1971), p. 106.
16.   Morales, p. 105.
17.   The units used by the Los Angeles County Sheriff's Department were special riot-control contingents. These units were also used at Isla Vista, California, in the spring of 1970. Officers were charged with using unwarranted force against the rioters, which included students of the University of California at Santa Barbara. A grand jury investigation substantiated the charges.
18.   The remarks were made by Villanueva at a panel discussion on the Mexican American, sponsored by the West Valley Public Library, in December 1970. I was a member of the panel.
19.   *Los Angeles Times,* 17 July 1970; Gene Blake and Howard Hertel, "Court Won't Drop Cast Against Officers in 'Mistake' Slayings," *Los Angeles Times,* 27 April 1971.
20.   Letter from Manuel Ruiz, Commissioner of the U.S. Commission on Civil Rights, to Herman Sillas, Chairman of the California State Advisory Committee to the Commission, 14 September 1970, in "A Report of the California State Advisory Committee to the United States Commission on Civil Rights: Police-Community Relations in East Los Angeles, California" (October 1970).
21.   *New York Times,* 18 December 1971, and *Los Angeles Times,* 18 December 1971.
22.   I was a witness to the events of September 16 and have Putnam's transcript on file.

23. Morales, p. 117.
24. *Eastside Sun,* 4 February 1971.
25. *Eastside Sun,* 4 February 1971.
26. *Eastside Sun,* 4 February 1971.
27. *New York Times,* 25 October 1971.
28. *Los Angeles Times,* 27 July and 18 August 1971.
29. *Justicia O,* vol. 1, no. 9 (n.d.), Los Angeles.
30. Frank Del Olmo, "Provoked Trouble for Lawmen, Chicano Informer Claims," *Los Angeles Times,* 1 February 1972.
31. *Los Angeles Free Press,* 4–10 February 1972.
32. *Los Angeles Free Press,* 4–10 February 1972.
33. *Los Angeles Free Press,* 4–10 February 1972.
34. Morales, p. 21.
35. U.S. Commission on Civil Rights, *Mexican Americans and Administration of Justice in the Southwest* (Washington, D.C.: U.S. Government Printing Office, 1970), p. 5.
36. *Mexican Americans and Administration of Justice,* pp. 4–5.
37. *La Raza* 1, no. 2 (1970), 18–19.
38. *Mexican Americans and Administration of Justice,* p. 9.
39. *Mexican Americans and Administration of Justice,* p. 9.
40. Interview at La Mesa, Texas, with community leader in the presence of Fr. Pat Hoffman (Summer 1970).
41. Student (who wishes to be anonymous) at California State College, Dominguez Hills.
42. *Mexican Americans and Administration of Justice,* pp. 29–31.
43. Morales, p. 43.
44. Quoted in Morales, p. 43.
45. Conversation with Judge Leopoldo Sánchez at a farewell party in honor of Dr. Ralph Guzman in May 1969.
46. *Mexican Americans and Administration of Justice,* p. 37.
47. *Mexican Americans and Administration of Justice,* pp. 37–38.
48. *Mexican Americans and Administration of Justice,* p. 38. It is interesting that the insurance companies for Los Angeles County are so powerful that they have succeeded in getting more Anglos on juries in civil cases in south-central Los Angeles. Since the population in this section of the county is predominantly Chicano and Black, so were the juries. The insurance companies, as well as business firms, believed that they were not getting fair hearings, so in civil cases, middle-class Anglo jurors from other sections of the county were brought in. Unfortunately, it has not worked the other way; authorities have not applied the same standard to the grand jury nor to Chicanos and Blacks who are on trial in areas where they cannot be tried by their peers. Los Angeles Councilman Billy Mills led the fight against bringing Anglo jurors into minority areas since the practice is one-sided. Further information can be obtained from his office.
49. *Mexican Americans and Administration of Justice,* p. 40.
50. *Ideal,* 15–28 February 1970.
51. *Los Angeles Times,* 7 February 1972; *Justicia O* 1, no. 3 (January 1971).
52. I was an eyewitness to these events and have had numerous conversations with Counselor Smith, dating back to October 1969.
53. Frantz Fanon, *A Dying Colonialism* (New York: Grove Press, Inc., 1965), p. 179.

Index

Adams, John Quincy, 11, 15
Agricultural Workers Industrial League, *see* Cannery and Agricultural Workers Industrial Union
Agricultural Workers Organizing Committee (AWOC), 176, 179, 181
Agriculture, 121–122, 124, 130, 141–142, 148
  in Arizona, 89
  in California, 101
  and immigration, 130, 131, 132, 134, 135, 137, 138, 140, 141
  and irrigation, 127–128, 252
  of Mexican settlers, 42, 60–61
  in Mexico, 125–127
  in New Mexico, 61–62, 69, 73, 77
  and unions, 145, 153–167, 172–184
  and War on Poverty, 225
  See also Bracero program, Contract labor
AFL, 97, 154, 164, 172, 173
Alamo, 10, 16–18
Alianza Federal de Mercedes, La, 238
Alianza Hispano Americana, 188–189
American Federation of Labor (AFL), 97, 154, 164, 172, 173
Annexation, 20, 24, 83–85, 114
Arizona, 8, 28, 30, 47, 97, 131
  See also Southwest, and individual cities
Arizona Rangers, 95, 96, 156
Army of the West, 58, 104
Arvin (Calif.), 172–175
Atchison, Topeka & Santa Fe Railroad, 132
Austin, Stephen, 11, 13–16
AWOC, 176, 179, 181
Aztlán, 229, 234, 258

Bancroft, Hubert Howe, 57–58, 90, 91
Bear Flaggers, 103, 110, 117
Black movement, 179, 209, 224–226, 229, 233, 239, 240, 247, 266
Black Panthers, 232–233
Blacks, 24, 52, 108, 110, 139, 142, 143, 145, 172, 202, 205, 207, 223, 227, 248, 249, 271
Boundary question, 20, 22, 28, 35, 57
Bowie, James, 17, 19
Box, John, 136–138, 140
Bracero program, 168–172, 176, 199, 224
  See also Contract labor
Brown Berets, 228, 229, 231–233, 264, 267–268
Brown, Edmund G., 180
Brownsville (Tex.), 39, 43, 45–49
Buchanan, James, 28, 84–85

Cahuenga, Treaty of, 104
Calderon, Richard, 248–250
California, 8, 47, 58, 98, 148, 230
  and Arizona, 88, 89, 92
  and civil rights, 268–272

constitution of, 104–105
  and Mexican War, 21, 23, 24, 28
  See also individual cities
California Battalion of Volunteers, 103
California Rural Legal Assistance (CRLA), 272
Calles, Plutarco Elias, 145, 162
Cananea (Mex.), 81, 96, 128, 155
Cannery and Agricultural Workers Industrual Union (CAWIU), 160, 161–163
Carson, Kit, 66, 103, 104
Catholicism, 8, 29, 122, 144, 147–149, 196, 256–257
  and Chávez, 177, 178
  and Mexican-American War, 25–27
  in Mexico, 125, 126
  in New Mexico, 65–66
  in Texas, 11, 166
Católicos Por La Raza (CPLR), 256–257
Catron, Thomas B., 67, 71, 72, 77
CAWIU, 160, 161–163
Central Intelligence Agency (CIA), 266
Chávez, César, 38, 41, 176–183, 224–225, 226, 231, 233–234, 257
Chicano Liberation Front (CLF), 268
Chicano Youth Conference, 242, 258
Chihuahua (Mex.), 50, 58, 85
Chinese, 92–93, 118, 125, 127, 155
Chisum, John H., 70–72
CIA, 266
CIO, *see* Congress of Industrial Organizations
Civil Rights Commission, 268–270, 271, 272
Civil rights movement, 178, 179, 224, 226
Civil War, 45, 61, 73, 124
Clamor Público, El, 111–114
Cleveland, Grover, 67
CLF, 268
Clifton (Ariz.), 89, 96–97
Communalism, 42, 60–62, 73–74, 125–126, 237–238
Communist party, 160–164, 166–167, 181, 195, 196, 207, 216, 232, 238
Community Service Organization (CSO), 177, 209–210, 213, 223
Confederación de Pueblos Libres, La, 238
Confederación de Uniones de Campesinos y Obreras Mexicanos del Estado de California, La (CUCOM), 162
Confederación de Uniones Obreras Mexicanos, La (CUOM), 159
Confederación Regional Obrera Mexicana (CROM), 162
Congreso de Pueblos de Habla Española, El, 196–197, 217
Congress, Mexican, 28, 30
Congress, U.S., 11, 20, 21, 28, 45, 67, 73, 85, 121, 133, 137–144, 169

Congress of Industrial Organizations
  (CIO), 145, 154, 164–167, 196, 216
Constitution, U.S., 87, 112, 159, 215, 227
Contract labor, 94, 129, 133–134, 137,
  143, 157–158, 164
  See also Bracero program
Cortina, Juan N., 38, 40, 45, 46–50, 52,
  114
CPLR, 256–257
Crabb, Henry, 84, 90
CRLA, 272
Crockett, Davey, 17, 18, 19
CROM, 162
Crusade for Justice, 241–243
Crystal City (Tex.), 53, 224, 234–246,
  253–254
CSO, *see* Community Service
  Organization
CUCOM, 162
CUOM, 159

Daniel, Pancho, 113–114
Davis, Edward, 260–261, 264, 265
Defense, Department of, 182
Delano (Calif.), 155, 176–182, 210,
  224–225, 241
Democratic party, 209, 223, 225
  in California, 106, 113, 247–251
  in Colorado, 241, 243
  in New Mexico, 56, 67, 69, 70, 76
  in Texas, 235, 252–253
Denver (Colo.), 241–243
Díaz, Porfirio, 50, 94, 96, 125–126, 128,
  156
Di Giorgio Fruit Corporation, 172,
  173–176, 180–181
Dolan, James, 71–72, 77

East Los Angeles, 199, 203–204, 206,
  227, 228, 231, 233, 248, 257, 260,
  263, 265
  See also Los Angeles
El Paso (Tex.), 46, 50–52, 94, 226–227,
  239
Elkins, Stephen B., 67, 69, 71, 72

Fanon, Frantz, 92, 275
Federal Bureau of Investigation (FBI),
  197, 266, 267, 269
Fehrenbach, T. R., 12–14, 35, 36, 38,
  45–46
Filipinos, 141, 161, 172, 176, 178, 183,
  205, 248
Flores, Juan, 110–111, 113–114
Foreign Miner's Tax, 106–107, 109, 118
France, 35, 49, 81–82, 125, 129, 130
Frémont, John C., 102–104

Gadsden Treaty, 81–82, 83
Galarza, Ernesto, 167–168, 171, 172, 175,
  176, 227
Gold, 102, 104, 107, 117
Gonzales, Rodolfo "Corky", 226–227,
  230, 234, 237, 241–243
Gorras Blancas, Las, 73–77
Grant, Ulysses S., 21, 25
Grito, El, 201, 228
Guadalupe Hidalgo, Treaty of, 28–29, 43,
  47, 48, 89, 104, 105, 188, 237
Guaymas (Mex.), 81, 82, 85

Guerrilla warfare, 46–49, 58, 103
Guevara, Ché, 230
Gutiérrez, José Ángel, 230, 234–237, 254

Harris Bill, 140–142
Harrison, Benjamin, 67
Hayes, Rutherford B., 72
Hererra, Juan José, 75–77
Hoffa, Jimmy, 179n, 181
Hoover, Herbert, 191
Houston, Sam, 12–14, 18, 19, 49, 84, 85n

Immigration, 88, 93, 121–123, 125,
  127–144, 190, 212–214
  Anglo-American, to Texas, 11–14, 35
Immigration Acts, 93, 94, 127, 133–135,
  139, 191
Imperial Valley (Calif.), 157–160, 163,
  171, 176
Indians, 7, 19, 27, 29, 30, 139, 143
  of Arizona, 81, 83–84, 86, 90
  of California, 103, 109
  of Mexico, 87, 125
  of New Mexico, 56, 59, 60, 68n, 69
  of Texas, 35, 38, 164
Internal Revenue Service, 267–268
Industrial Workers of the World
  (IWW), 41, 97, 154, 155

Jackson, Andrew, 12, 102
Japanese, 41, 125, 155, 161, 168,
  201–202, 208, 214, 248
Johnson, Lyndon B., 225, 226
Juárez, Benito, 125

Kearny, Stephen Watts, 57, 58, 104
Kenedy, Mifflin, 37, 43, 45, 46, 49n
Kennedy, John Fitzgerald, 223, 225, 239
Kennedy, Robert, 181, 240
King, Martin Luther, 225
King, Richard, 37, 38, 40, 43, 44–46, 49n
Knights of Labor, 75–76

Labor, Department of, 138–139, 176
Land Act of 1851, 105, 108, 118
Land-grabbing, 14, 24, 60–63, 73–75,
  105–106
Land grants, 28–30, 43–45, 47, 60–63, 65,
  67–69, 73, 91–92, 154, 237
  See also Guadalupe Hidalgo, Treaty
  of, and Statement of Protocol
League of United Latin American
  Citizens (LULAC), 189–190, 210, 223
League of Workers and Peasants of
  Mexico, 192
Lee, Robert E., 49
Leo XIII, 177
Lewis, John L., 164
Liga Obrera de Habla Española, La, 195,
  217
Liga Protectiva Mexicana, La, 189
Lincoln County War, 68, 69–73
López, Ignacio, 197–198, 209
Los Angeles (Calif.), 103, 113, 115, 156,
  159, 162, 191–193, 199–200,
  203–207, 231–232, 257–269
  See also East Los Angeles
LRUP, *see Raza Unida* party, *La*
LULAC, 189–190, 210, 223

Magón, Ricardo Flores, 155–157
MALDF, 272–273
Manifest Destiny, 20, 21, 23
MAPA, 196, 197, 223, 230–231
Martínez, Antonio Jose, 59, 65–66, 68
Martínez, Eustacio (Frank), 267–268
MAYO, 229, 234–235, 256, 267–268, 273
McCarran-Walter Act, 212, 213–216
McCarthy, Joseph, 213–214
McDonnell, Donald, 148, 177
McNeely, L. H., 37, 40, 45
McWilliams, Carey, 56, 66–67, 127–128, 155, 183, 193, 201, 203, 205, 212
MECHA, 229
Mexican American Legal Defense Fund (MALDF), 272–273
Mexican American Movement (MAM), *see* Mexican Youth Conference
Mexican American Political Association (MAPA), 196, 197, 223, 230–231
Mexican-American War, 7, 9, 19–30, 45, 49–50
Mexican American Youth Organization (MAYO), 229, 234–235, 256, 267–268, 273
Mexican Mutual Aid Society, 158–159, 160
    See also Unión de Trabajadores del Valle Imperial
Mexican Revolution of 1910, 126, 128, 130, 132, 155, 192
Mexico, 9–31, 35, 47–50, 58, 147, 155–157, 226
    and Arizona, 81–85, 91, 96
    and *bracero* program, 168–171, 211–212
    and California, 102–104, 108, 112–113, 206
    and repatriation, 190, 192, 212–213
    See also Immigration; Mexican-American War, and individual cities and provinces
Mexico City, 13, 21, 27, 28, 37, 50
Mining, 121, 124, 125, 131, 144, 154
    in Arizona, 81–84, 86, 87–89, 95–97
    in Mexico, 127–128, 130, 155
    in New Mexico, 76–77
Monroe Doctrine, 22
Monterey (Calif.), 102–105, 115
Moratoria, 258–259, 264, 265, 268, 276
Morena, Luisa, 196–197, 215
Morton, Thruston B., 173, 174, 176
Movimiento Estudiantil Chicanos de Aztlán, El, (MECHA), 229
Muñoz, Rosalio, 258, 265, 268
Murietta, Joaquín, 111, 116–117
Murphy, Laurence Gustave, 70, 71
Mutualistas, 53, 96, 158, 177, 183, 188

National Farm Labor Union (NFLU), 172, 173, 175–177
National Farm Workers Association (NFWA), 176, 178–181, 183
National forests, 62–63, 237–240
National Industrial Relations Act (NIRA), 194–195
National Labor Relations Board, 167, 181, 197
Nativism, 43, 89, 92, 112, 118, 125, 127, 132, 135–136, 138, 141–142, 148

New Mexico, 8, 30, 35, 47, 50, 55–77, 86, 93, 94, 98, 104, 131
    in Mexican-American War, 21, 23, 28
Nixon, Richard M., 173–176, 223, 267

Obreros Unidos Independientes, Los, 254
Orden de Hijos de America, La, 189

Pachucos, 188, 199–208
Pallares, Jésus, 194–195, 218
Partido Liberal Mexicano, El (PLM), 155–156
Patrón, Juan, 70–73, 77.
Pecan Shelling Workers'Union, 165
Peonage, 86–88
Pesquiera, Ignacio, 85, 91
Pico, Andres, 104, 113–114
PLM, 155–156
Polk, James K., 20–21, 22, 24, 102–103
Poor People's Campaign, 239
Poverty in the Land of Plenty, 173–175
Public education, 142, 144, 146–147, 149, 223–224
    in California, 247, 249
    and high school walkouts, 227–228, 235–236, 242
    in New Mexico, 62
    in Texas, 235–236, 253–255, 273

Railroads, 116, 121, 124–125, 154
    in Arizona, 81, 82, 92–93, 97
    in Mexico, 126–127, 129
    in New Mexico, 62, 73, 75
Ramírez, Francisco, 111–114
Ranching, 39–40, 45, 52, 69–71, 73, 83, 86, 95, 105–106
    See also King, Richard; Land grants
Raza, La, 228, 250, 256, 261–262
Raza Unida party, *La,* 53, 227, 236–237 242–243, 250, 253, 254
Razo, Joe, 228, 261
Reagan, Ronald, 267, 272
Reclamation Act, 127–128
Reconstruction Finance Corporation (RFC), 193
Regeneración, 155–156
Republican party, 56, 67, 69, 70, 72, 76, 171, 251, 267
Rio Grande river, 20, 25, 28, 35, 45, 50, 57, 61
Rio Grande valley, 37, 39, 42, 43, 45, 251–253
Romano, Octavio, 183, 201, 228
Roosevelt, Eleanor, 206–207
Roosevelt, Franklin D., 225, 276
Roybal, Edward, 209–210, 247, 248, 271
Ruiz, Raúl, 228, 250, 261–262

Salazar, Ruben, 38, 228, 260–263, 265, 276
Salt War (El Paso), 50–52
San Antonio (Tex.), 13, 16, 18, 46, 50, 52, 155, 164, 189, 234, 237, 255, 271, 273
San Diego (Calif.), 21, 104, 171, 203–204, 267
San Joaquin Valley, 163, 173–176, 178, 182
San Patricio Corps, 25–26,

San Quentin prison, 110, 113, 115, 118
Santa Anna, Antonio López de, 14, 16, 18, 19, 27, 35, 81
Santa Fe expedition, 35, 57–58
Santa Fe Ring, 63, 66–69, 70–72
Scott, Winfield, 27, 28
Slavery, 11–13, 15, 24n, 35, 106, 108, 139
Sleepy Lagoon case, 202–203
Slidell, John, 20
Smith, Mark, 273–274
Sonora (Mex.), 81, 82–86, 91, 112
Southern Pacific Railroad, 92–93, 116, 132
Spain, 10, 129, 147
Statehood, 13, 77, 94, 98, 104
Statement of Protocol, 29–30, 43, 105
Stillman, Charles, 43–45
Stockton, Robert F., 23–24, 85, 103
Subversive Activities Control Board, 214

Tackwood, Louis, 266–268
Tamaulipas (Mex.), 46–47, 49–50
Taos (New Mex.), 57, 59, 65
Taylor Grazing Act, 63
Taylor, Zachary, 20, 25, 27, 35, 58
Teamsters Union, 179–182, 254–255
Teatro Campesino, 179, 228, 241
Texas, 7–8, 10–21, 24, 30, 85, 86, 98, 131, 210, 230, 272–273
    and *bracero* program, 169–170
    and California, 102, 107, 110, 113–114
    colonialism in, 34–46
    and Cortina uprising, 47–50
    Cursillo movement in, 177
    and Kennedy election, 223
    and LRUP, 234–237
    law enforcement in, 269–270
    and New Mexico, 56–58, 70–72
    pecan strike in, 164–167
    politics in, 251–256
    and Vietnam war, 258
Texas Rangers, 26–27, 36–41, 42, 45, 48, 49, 51–52, 113, 235, 237, 239, 252–253, 254, 269–270
Texas War, 9, 10, 16–19, 30
Tierra Amarilla, 237–240
Tijerina, Reies López, 38, 55–56, 64, 77, 226–227, 230, 237–241
Tombstone (Ariz.), 80, 91, 156

Trade Union Unity League, 160
Transcontinental Treaty, 10
Travis, William Barret, 14, 17, 19
Truman, Harry S., 215
Tucson (Ariz.), 81, 94, 98, 188, 271
Tunstall, John H., 71–72
Tyler, James, 20

Unión de Trabajadores del Valle Imperial, 157–159
Unión Liberal Humanidad, 155
Unions, 41, 53, 122, 144–146, 211
    in Arizona, 95–98
    and *bracero* program, 170, 172
    in California, 153–164, 172–184, 196
    and deportation, 215–217
    and high school walkouts, 227
    in New Mexico, 75–76, 194–195
    in Texas, 164–167, 254–255
United Auto Workers (UAW), 179, 249
United Cannery, Agricultural, Packing and Allied Workers of America (UCAPAWA), 164, 166, 197, 216
United Farm Workers Organizing Committee (UFWOC), 181, 182
United People's party, 76
Unity Leagues, 197, 209

Valdez, Luis, 179, 228, 241
Vásquez, Tiburcio, 46, 111, 114–117
Vietnam war, 225, 258, 276

War of 1812, 22
War on Poverty, 225, 241
War of the Reform, 125
Warren, Earl, 207
Water rights, 30, 60–61, 74, 97, 101
Webb, Walter Prescott, 30–31, 36–41, 52, 69
Werdel Report, 174–176
Western Federation of Miners (WFM), 95–97
White Caps, *see Gorras Blancas, Las*
Winter Garden area, 234–236, 253–255
World War I, 16, 133, 189
World War II, 21, 24, 143, 167, 168, 188, 196, 198–199, 253

Yorty, Sam, 261–262, 265